NetSuite OneWorld Implementation 2011 R2

A step-by-step guide to implementing NetSuite OneWorld 2011 R2

Thomas Foydel

BIRMINGHAM - MUMBAI

NetSuite OneWorld Implementation 2011 R2

Copyright © 2011 Packt Publishing

First published: November 2011

Production Reference: 1171111

Published by Packt Publishing Ltd.
Livery Place
35 Livery Street
Birmingham B3 2PB, UK.

ISBN 978-1-84968-132-2

www.packtpub.com

Cover Image by Artie Ng (artherng@yahoo.com.au)

Credits

Author
Thomas Foydel

Reviewers
Jason Smith
David Rowley

Acquisition Editor
Kerry George

Development Editor
Meeta Rajani

Technical Editor
Lubna Shaikh

Copy Editor
Leonard D'Silva

Project Coordinator
Vishal Bodwani

Proofreader
Sandra Hopper

Indexer
Monica Ajmera

Graphics
Valentina D'Silva

Production Coordinator
Prachali Bhiwandkar

Cover Work
Prachali Bhiwandkar

About the Author

Thomas Foydel is a veteran of the software and software consulting industries. Tom's work history covers mainframes to Software as a Service. Since 2004, he has been president of SightLines Consulting, focusing on the implementation of NetSuite for organizations in e-commerce, wholesales distribution, software, and professional services. His previous stints with ADP, Oracle, and Ciber Enterprise Solutions laid the groundwork for his strong enthusiasm for Software as a Service and Agile software implementation. Tom
has published articles on CRM and ERP in a number of widely read trade journals, and blogs regularly at http://sightlog.sightlinesconsulting.com and http://enterpriseirregulars.com.

This book required about eight months of late nights and weekends. Hopefully, I have not been too remiss in my home responsibilities, especially to my wife, Mary, and daughter, Haley. I feel like this book was a family effort in many ways, so a heartfelt "thank you" to you both, for all your love and support.

I would also like to thank the many NetSuite clients who, over the last seven years, have allowed SightLines the opportunity to understand their unique business models and implement creative solutions with them. Your entrepreneurial spirit is unforgettable.

About the Reviewer

Jason Smith is the Co-Founder and CTO of Veridian Ventures, LLC, a NetSuite Solution Provider Partner, and a full-service web development and consulting company that provides comprehensive business solutions to small and medium-sized businesses. Jason has been working in web-development since 2001, and specifically with the NetSuite platform since 2007. He has extensive experience in developing NetSuite e-Commerce stores as well as customizing NetSuite, using all aspects of SuiteFlex. Besides his extensive experience, Jason holds a Bachelor's degree in Integrated Strategic Communication, from the University of Kentucky. Jason currently resides in Jacksonville, Florida. In his spare time, he enjoys spending time with his wife, Ashley Smith, and dog, Callie.

 # www.PacktPub.com

This book is published by Packt Publishing. You might want to visit Packt's website at `www.PacktPub.com` and take advantage of the following features and offers:

Discounts

Have you bought the print copy or Kindle version of this book? If so, you can get a massive 85% off the price of the eBook version, available in PDF, ePub, and MOBI.

Simply go to `http://www.packtpub.com/netsuite-oneworld-implementation-2011-r1/book`, add it to your cart, and enter the following discount code:

nowimebk

Free eBooks

If you sign up to an account on `www.PacktPub.com`, you will have access to nine free eBooks.

Newsletters

Sign up for Packt's newsletters at `www.PacktPub.com/newsletters`, which will keep you up to date with offers, discounts, books, and downloads.

Code Downloads, Errata and Support

Packt supports all of its books with errata. While we work hard to eradicate errors from our books, some do creep in. Meanwhile, many Packt books have accompanying snippets of code to download.

You can find errata and code downloads at `www.PacktPub.com/support`

Instant Updates on New Packt Books

Get notified! Find out when new books are published by following @PacktEnterprise on Twitter, or the *Packt Enterprise* Facebook page.

 **PACKTLiB**

PacktLib.PacktPub.com

PacktLib offers instant solutions to your IT questions. It is Packt's fully searchable online digital book library, accessible from any device with a web browser.

- Contains every Packt book ever published. That's over 100,000 pages of content
- Fully searchable. Find an immediate solution to your problem
- Copy, paste, print, and bookmark content
- Available on demand via your web browser

If you have a Packt account, you might want to have a look at the nine free books which you can access now on PacktLib. Head to `PacktLib.PacktPub.com` and log in or register.

Table of Contents

Preface

When I first heard of NetLedger in an internal Oracle e-mail around the turn of the century, it was one of those 'aha' moments that we all have in life. There was, at this time, a fledgling industry of **Application Service Providers (ASPs)**, who offered to host enterprise software at a data center. But I was skeptical, since I could not see an economy of scale in the ASP model, and no economy of scale meant no competitive advantage. NetLedger, I believed, had the right technical and business model: Run multiple customer accounts or tenants on a single instance of the software. The model, now known as **Software as a Service (SaaS)**, was scalable, reliable, and most importantly, competitively disruptive. Over the years, while NetLedger thrived, the ASP model all but disappeared.

NetLedger evolved into NetSuite, and at about the same time, I was ready to make a move out of Oracle Consulting, too. This was 2005, and the past six years have been challenging, successful, and a lot of fun. NetSuite not only continues to update its NetCRM+ and NetSuite offerings, but has added OneWorld to its stable of business management software, allowing it to serve organizations with multiple legal entities.

When the opportunity arose to write a book on OneWorld implementation, I jumped at the chance. I consider it an honor to have a title in the Packt Publishing house, and authorship seems a natural progression for me. I probably have two books this length in my blog articles over the years.

What I hope to accomplish in *NetSuite OneWorld Implementation R2* is to provide the business and IT managers at small and medium enterprises with the answers to critical questions about OneWorld: What it is, how it works, and how to implement it from a new account through configuration, testing, customization, data migration, and go-live.

You may be looking at alternative business systems for your organization, or you may be on a OneWorld implementation team or seeking to join one; in any of these cases, this book has useful information that ought to help you participate thoroughly in your role.

To move from a blank screen to a completed book also means that I must take a realistic approach to the project. I cannot possibly answer every question about how the system works. OneWorld is a comprehensive system that covers a wide area of modern business system functionality. Hopefully, if I get you started down a well-travelled implementation path, you will have enough information and momentum to carry forward and establish your business model in your OneWorld account.

One idea that I have juggled with while writing is whether the book suggests that self-implementation is a good idea. Obviously, some organization do opt to implement OneWorld themselves, while others look to NetSuite partners. How you decide this question is your call, but again, I think this book helps you to formulate a strategy for implementation, regardless of the direction you decide to take. In either case, you must eventually have OneWorld system knowledge in house to succeed long term, and I hope this book provides the base understanding of OneWorld for new and experienced users alike.

Finally, while I believe this book will prove very helpful to those who are either in the process of looking at OneWorld for their organizations, or who have already decided on OneWorld, it is not the only resource at your disposal. If you have already purchased OneWorld there is a user forum where you can network with other users to learn more about the system. If you do not yet have access to an account, or you would simply like to pose your question to me, then you can always visit this book's site at `http://owimplementation.com` and post your question, concern, or issue in the comments section. I would be happy to answer any query or clarify any statement.

System selection and implementation are important challenges for any organization, and perhaps, even more important for small and medium enterprises who have less room for error. I take your challenge seriously and I sincerely hope that *NetSuite OneWorld Implementation R2* proves a useful tool for your organization. Nothing would please me more than finding a torn, creased, underlined, notated, dog-eared copy of this book lying on a conference room table of a OneWorld customer.

What this book covers

Chapter 1, What is NetSuite OneWorld, introduces the reader to OneWorld in the context of business management software. Meant primarily for those who are in the process of assessing OneWorld for their organization, we explain the main functions of the system and how they are used by various business models.

Chapter 2, OneWorld's Foundation, begins our discussion of OneWorld by focusing on the basics, such as navigation and security, and enabling the base functions and preferences of CRM and ERP. We also discuss much of the OneWorld foundation, including departments, classes, locations, and, most importantly, subsidiaries.

Chapter 3, OneWorld Implementation, discusses the implementation process for OneWorld from resources — who needs to be involved — to the actual project tasks that must be completed. We also focus on various implementation challenges and different approaches to implementation. Finally, we spend some effort on explaining agile implementation and why it fits the OneWorld implementation so well.

Chapter 4, Nailing OneWorld Basics, gets us started on the configuration of OneWorld with the view to the first prototype. In this chapter, we start to set up much of the system foundation including the chart of accounts, taxation, and the item catalog. Also, we discuss how to use location, department, and class across the system.

Chapter 5, Nuts and Bolts of OneWorld CRM, covers the configuration of the CRM modules, including sales, marketing, and customer service. We not only discuss the functions of these modules, but also how they are used by various business models and how the modules integrate with the rest of the OneWorld Suite. The reader will gain an excellent idea of how to use the CRM modules to the advantage of the business.

Chapter 6, Nuts and Bolts of OneWorld ERP, discusses the configuration of the operations modules of ERP, including purchasing, order management, inventory and warehouse management, selling and billing services, and e-commerce basics.

Chapter 7, Nuts and Bolts of OneWorld ERP — Financial Management, takes the configurations of the preceding chapter to the next step and covers the financial modules and functions from accounts payable to accounts receivable, from cash management to month-end close. This chapter concludes the work for the first prototype.

Chapter 8, OneWorld Customization and Advanced Configuration, starts the customization of the system with the view to the second prototype. Here we cover the customization of forms and roles, and the addition of fields, records, and workflows. The end result should be a prototype of the system that begins to look like your organization's business model in both concept and detail.

Chapter 9, OneWorld Data Migration, focuses on data migration and how and when to use the various data import tools to migrate data, including both entity and transaction data.

Chapter 10, Data Analysis, looks at data analysis in-depth with a review of search, the report writer, the financial report writer, and data presentation on dashboards.

Appendix, provides additional coverage of the key aspects of OneWorld implementation that we have not discussed so far. In this appendix, we provide some of our experience with the basic blocking and tackling of the implementation, in the hope of giving you a head start to complete your project successfully.

What you need for this book

Since OneWorld is business management software, a basic understanding of business and its processes is helpful. If you have access to a OneWorld account (even a test account), it would be helpful, but it is by no means required.

Who this book is for

If you are an application administrator, business analyst, project team member, or business process owner who wants to implement NetSuite OneWorld into your organization, then this book is for you. This book might also be useful if you are a business manager considering a new system for your organization, by providing a real assessment of the current system landscape in relation to NetSuite OneWorld.

You should have a basic understanding of business management systems and their implementation. You should also have basic knowledge of NetSuite as an integrated business system and NetSuite OneWorld specifically.

Conventions

In this book, you will find a number of styles of text that distinguish between different kinds of information. Here are some examples of these styles, and an explanation of their meaning."

Code words in text are shown as follows: " Select a year end and load the balances as a journal entry on 12/31/xxxx.

A block of code is set as follows:

```
<iframe src ="
  https://forms.netsuite.com/app/site/crm/externalleadpage.nl?
  compid=12345678&formid=2&h=123456789" width="100%" height="300">

</iframe>

<a href="
  https://forms.netsuite.com/app/site/crm/externalleadpage.nl?
  compid=12345678&formid=2&h=123456789">
  Please Click here to download our whitepaper.
</a>
```

New terms and **important words** are shown in bold. Words that you see on the screen, in menus or dialog boxes for example, appear in the text like this: "and then click on the **Enable Features** option."

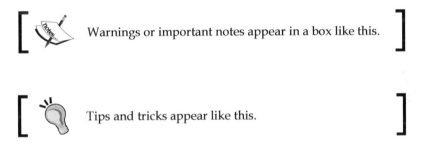

Warnings or important notes appear in a box like this.

Tips and tricks appear like this.

Reader feedback

Feedback from our readers is always welcome. Let us know what you think about this book—what you liked or may have disliked. Reader feedback is important for us to develop titles that you really get the most out of.

To send us general feedback, simply send an e-mail to feedback@packtpub.com, and mention the book title via the subject of your message.

If there is a book that you need and would like to see us publish, please send us a note in the **SUGGEST A TITLE** form on www.packtpub.com or e-mail suggest@packtpub.com.

If there is a topic that you have expertise in and you are interested in either writing or contributing to a book, see our author guide on www.packtpub.com/authors.

Customer support

Now that you are the proud owner of a Packt book, we have a number of things to help you to get the most from your purchase.

Downloading the example code

You can download the example code files for all Packt books you have purchased from your account at http://www.PacktPub.com. If you purchased this book elsewhere, you can visit http://www.PacktPub.com/support and register to have the files e-mailed directly to you.

Errata

Although we have taken every care to ensure the accuracy of our content, mistakes do happen. If you find a mistake in one of our books—maybe a mistake in the text or the code—we would be grateful if you would report this to us. By doing so, you can save other readers from frustration and help us improve subsequent versions of this book. If you find any errata, please report them by visiting http://www.packtpub.com/support, selecting your book, clicking on the **errata submission form** link, and entering the details of your errata. Once your errata are verified, your submission will be accepted and the errata will be uploaded on our website, or added to any list of existing errata, under the Errata section of that title. Any existing errata can be viewed by selecting your title from http://www.packtpub.com/support.

Piracy

Piracy of copyright material on the Internet is an ongoing problem across all media. At Packt, we take the protection of our copyright and licenses very seriously. If you come across any illegal copies of our works, in any form, on the Internet, please provide us with the location address or website name immediately so that we can pursue a remedy.

Please contact us at copyright@packtpub.com with a link to the suspected pirated material.

We appreciate your help in protecting our authors, and our ability to bring you valuable content.

Questions

You can contact us at questions@packtpub.com if you are having a problem with any aspect of the book, and we will do our best to address it.

1
What is NetSuite OneWorld?

ERP, CRM, Web Presence/E-Commerce, On-demand, Cloud Computing, SaaS, ASP, and Oracle products – these are just a few of the common words and phrases used to describe NetSuite and its OneWorld software suite. Confusion abounds, as it often does in the world of information technology. The goal of this chapter is to lay out the basics of what NetSuite OneWorld is for people who do not spend late nights reading the technology blogosphere.

We want to give you an understanding of how OneWorld evolved within the context of information technology for business enterprises. We believe that an understanding of OneWorld's competitive landscape helps to define OneWorld, as well as its competitors.

We also want to help you understand OneWorld's primary target markets and what it offers to each. We assume that some of the readers have not yet made the decision to purchase OneWorld, so we hope this will help you answer some of your basic questions.

Finally, we want to give you a 10,000-foot view of what OneWorld is, what the components are, how they work together to manage an entire business, and the organizations for whom OneWorld offers great value.

In this chapter, we will specifically discuss the following:

- An overview of OneWorld
- OneWorld business model examples
- OneWorld is **Software as a Service (SaaS)**
- Customizing, integrating, configuring, and extending OneWorld
- Due diligence for SaaS
- OneWorld Suite or best of breeds
- Total cost of ownership
- Three different scenarios for OneWorld

An overview of OneWorld

NetSuite originally began as NetLedger in the late 1990s. Since its founding, the company and its software have undergone a number of changes. Today, NetSuite offers essentially three software services: **NetSuite CRM+**, **NetSuite**, and **OneWorld**.

The NetSuite product includes much of the functionality offered in OneWorld, but is meant for organizations with only a single legal entity. Clearly, the NetSuite product targets the upper end of the small business market. It's specially suited to small businesses that forecast rapid near and long-term growth.

Among the early adopters of NetSuite were companies in wholesale distribution, e-commerce, software, and software services. Also, companies with hybrid or non-mainstream business models often found NetSuite's highly configurable software very attractive. Geographically dispersed organizations also found NetSuite to be an excellent solution, as it allowed access to remote users while avoiding costly infrastructure. Vendors, customers, partners, and especially employees could log in from anywhere at any time to do business in the same NetSuite account. NetSuite's cost-effective and accessible software effectively leverages the Internet, which is now the most dominant feature of our business landscape.

The theme of offering an integrated end-to-end solution to modern business challenges continued with NetSuite OneWorld. With OneWorld, rolled out in late 2007, you could operate not only from any location in the world, but also through multiple legal subsidiaries, in multiple currencies and languages. OneWorld is therefore, in the simplest terms, a business management software solution for small and medium enterprises operating in a global economy that the Internet has changed forever.

Answering new challenges

Think about what **small business** meant just 20 years ago: a restaurant, a tool and die maker, and the mechanics shop. Of course, these all still exist, but to their number, we now have small businesses with under a hundred employees that operate world wide, with offices and employees in three or four different countries moving goods and services in a myriad of ways. There was a time when only the largest businesses operated globally.

Twenty years ago, managing a dispersed global business was incredibly difficult. First, if you wanted to connect your dispersed organization electronically, you had to establish a wide area network solution through frame relay, or just rely on dial-up modem connectivity. Secondly, you had to find a software package that mostly met your needs and install it in each of your organization's locations and on your own hardware infrastructure. Finally, you had to collect the business results from each subsidiary and consolidate them manually with significant effort, each month.

The **global solution** was expensive, time consuming, and fraught with error. We have witnessed large companies attempt this solution and it was painful for everyone. But there really were no other options.

Today, you can operate a multi-national business with the OneWorld software suite, from anywhere in the world, without having to worry about technology infrastructure. All you need is a computer and the ubiquitous pipe from your physical location to the Internet. One system managing multiple subsidiaries, buying and selling in multiple languages and currencies across the world is now a reality. Not only does OneWorld automatically consolidate your financial statements across subsidiaries and base currencies, but it also provides the same consolidated business views across operational and sales data. When you stop and think about it, it's obvious that this is no small achievement.

OneWorld and NetSuite

We often field questions about the difference between NetSuite's main software suites, so it probably makes sense to look at them in a little more detail and make sure the differences and similarities are well understood.

NetSuite now has three main products:

- NetSuite
- NetSuite CRM+
- NetSuite OneWorld

NetSuite CRM+ is simply the CRM modules of NetSuite, including sales, marketing, and support. We will cover all of the CRM modules in our discussion of OneWorld, but we will not spend any time talking about NetSuite CRM+ as a separate product offering. Let's also note here that a NetSuite CRM+ account may be upgraded to NetSuite or to OneWorld. We'll cover the upgrade process in more detail in later chapters.

NetSuite is the full suite, including CRM, ERP, and Web Presence/E-commerce, which allows a single company or legal entity to operate its whole business on one system. If you have just one legal entity, then you can use NetSuite to run the business. Later, should you want to add another legal entity, you can upgrade your NetSuite account to OneWorld. All of the base OneWorld functionality described in this book also covers NetSuite, minus the ability to consolidate multiple legal entities every month, and a few functions that would only be useful to organizations with multiple legal entities. Again, it is possible to upgrade NetSuite to OneWorld, and we cover this in a later chapter.

The key difference between NetSuite and OneWorld is the addition of multiple subsidiary functionality in OneWorld. Of course, running several legal entities in a single OneWorld account raises some challenges: inter-company journal entries, intercompany sale and purchase transactions, inter-company time and expenses, inter-company commissions, inter-company inventory transfers, and inter-company accounting allocations.

While you can operate a single world wide company in NetSuite, you can operate multiple companies in your OneWorld account, with the functionality you need to do it all very efficiently.

OneWorld business model examples

Let's take a quick overview of some of the common business models that use OneWorld. This will help you to place your organization on the OneWorld map and see where you fit in the following descriptions. These descriptions help to answer the question of whether OneWorld generally supports your organization's business model.

OneWorld's best fit is the organization that has several legal entities, all engaged in the same business, using the same business model. For example, a company operating several wholesale distribution subsidiaries would be an excellent fit, but an organization with a wholesale distribution subsidiary and a software services subsidiary is less ideal. This is because we set many of the operational preferences across all subsidiaries. When an organization has subsidiaries engaged in highly diverse businesses, separate NetSuite or OneWorld accounts may be the most appropriate solution.

Assume that for all of these business models, we have an organization with multiple subsidiaries operating with one or more of the following:

- Where they have foreign subsidiaries, each subsidiary keeps its own customer list and sells in its own currency.

- Subsidiaries might also sell in other currencies.

- Where they do not have a subsidiary, the organization sells from the parent to partners/distributors, and also maintains a list of the end-user customers in OneWorld. These sales can be in the parent's or in the partner's currency.

- The organization maintains employees, customers, and vendors in each subsidiary and runs their financials by subsidiary, and consolidates at necessary levels within the organization's legal entity hierarchy, in real time.

- Each subsidiary uses OneWorld in its own language, including English, Japanese, Chinese, and the major languages of Europe, such as French, German, Spanish, and Italian.

Business models

- **Selling software**: The software sales business model, when combined with software support and services, requires special accounting, including revenue recognition and **Vendor Specific Objective Evidence (VSOE)**. In this business model, revenue must be spread out over the period of support services, and any discounting of the software or the support must be taken into account. Sale items are one-time downloads or hard media. OneWorld covers these requirements and also enables organizations in this business model to operate globally.

- **Selling subscriptions to content or services**: OneWorld enables the sale of subscription services through direct rep, partners, or by e-commerce, from one or more websites. You sell the service for the year and bill monthly, or sell a contract for the year and bill annually, again recognizing revenue monthly over the life of the contract. Customers might also require a professional services implementation project, billed by milestones, and ongoing support, billed per use. Each year, the contract renews automatically.

- **Manufacturing products**: For this business model, OneWorld enables the sourcing and purchase of raw materials from any country and in any currency; the receipt of goods to multiple locations; the assembly of finished goods based on work orders; the transfer of goods between locations and subsidiaries; the sale and fulfillment of goods from multiple locations; and the sale or management of inventory, by location or by subsidiary.

- **Selling professional services**: For this project-based business model, OneWorld provides its own project management and accounting modules, or integration with NetSuite's subsidiary OpenAir. In either case, OneWorld supports multiple project types and their billing methods; time and expense entry, including inter-company **Time and Expenses (T&E)**; project resourcing; and profitability reporting.

- **Wholesale/distribution**: OneWorld supports **Business to Business (B2B)** sales for large-item catalogs, in multiple currencies, and through multiple sales channels, by direct rep, partners/distributors, and e-commerce websites. OneWorld also supports multiple inventory locations for product receipt, kitting, and order fulfillment, or you can link it to third-party logistics providers. OneWorld supports EDI and integrations with common shipping providers (UPS, FedEx, USPS), drop ship, specific-vendor item sourcing and contract pricing, multiple customer-pricing scenarios, and multiple units of measure for buying and selling.

- **E-tailing products**: With both multiple subsidiaries and multiple e-commerce sites functionality, OneWorld supports the consolidated e-tailer's business model. OneWorld enables multiple sites, each of which can run in multiple languages and charge in the appropriate currency. There is also functionality for sales through brick and mortar locations using the same item catalog and inventory, and e-tailers may also integrate with multiple sales channels through pre-developed integrations with Amazon, eBay, and so on.

- **Division of a Fortune 500 company**: This is a newer beachhead for OneWorld: managing the operations of business units or divisions of very large companies. As we mentioned previously, running multiple small international divisions can be a technical challenge for any organization, but with OneWorld, your international business units and HQ can access an online system where results are viewed in real-time and without the need for infrastructure maintenance. At the end of each accounting period, results are uploaded to HQ's system of records. All of the benefits of the large, well-funded multi-national with the agility of OneWorld; it's a nice combination.

This is just a quick overview of the types of business models that use NetSuite OneWorld. They sell a wide variety of products and services in a wide variety of sales channels, including the Web, a direct sales force, partner channels, and in many cases, a combination of these. They also operate warehouses or work through 3PLs; they manufacture or purchase manufactured goods; they drop ship or ship direct; they bill in monthly increments or annually and then recognize revenue monthly; they are project based or order based; and many of them have hybrid business models, featuring unique combinations of the business processes mentioned previously.

NetSuite customers may have as many as a thousand users, or as few as five. What most companies who use NetSuite have in common is that they are enterprises, in the sense that they are entrepreneurial. They may have a simple business model or a complex business model, but they are doing something different. For example, a small tool and die maker would not be a good NetSuite candidate. But a tool and die maker with a line of performance-enhancing parts for mountain bikes, selling to the aftermarket in an online store and actively engaged in worldwide OEM contracts, and distributing products through multiple retail store locations or other sales channels, with other partners, would indeed be a good candidate. This is more than just a business; this is an enterprise organized around growth through new products and services. We call this business a **Small Medium Enterprise(SME)**. This is NetSuite's sweet spot. When the small manufacturer rolls out worldwide operations, sales, and distribution, they graduate to OneWorld.

OneWorld is Software as a Service (SaaS)

SaaS is software with a multi-tenant architecture that runs in the cloud and is accessed through the Internet. However, this simple definition has huge ramifications, so let's start at the beginning and lay it out.

To put OneWorld into a larger information technology context, remember that there was a time when only the largest organizations could afford data processing. All others used technology services offered by local and regional data processors. ADP, the large payroll service bureau, is an excellent example of this model. You send them your new hires, pay rates, hours, and so on, and they deliver a payroll to your door, complete with checks, vouchers, and reports.

As technology became more affordable and more necessary, organizations made significant capital investments in technology. Soon the average organization was running multiple servers and multiple desktop or laptop computers, all linked to their own local area network.

This infrastructure has come down in price, but we need more of it, and the one thing which has not come down in price is the people we need to run it all. This is a problem. Competing in a global market requires sophisticated systems, and running sophisticated systems requires high-end skill sets. Organizations soon had IT departments, and IT departments soon amassed more than their share of power and influence. Large organizations on average spend about 8 percent of their revenue on technology, including software, hardware devices, maintenance and support, human resources and training, and so on.

With the advent of the Internet, new models for consuming software came to the market. Although there have been some ups and downs, the Internet has grown in use and usability. By offering a public data highway, the Internet enabled new businesses and organizational models to flourish. SaaS is one of these new models. It is interesting that we have now come full circle, back to the original model where organizations run their business and IT experts run the systems in a remote data processing center. Is this a step forward? Many believe it is, because at the end of the day, running your own servers not only wastes a lot of electricity, but also leaves you highly exposed to a lot of issues, some of which follow:

- **Theft**: We actually know of several businesses that lost their server in a smash and grab.
- **Accident**: Do you have the systems necessary to put out a fire, before it destroys your systems? How prone is your business to a natural disaster?
- **Employees**: An employee with a special skill set can hold you hostage. They have all of the systems knowledge, and without them you are exposed.

- **Backup and restore**: When was the last time you did a test system restore of your financial system? Do you have the funds, discipline, and knowledge to do a proper restore of your data systems? See *The Total Cost of Ownership* section later for more details..

- **Ongoing system maintenance**: This takes employees and today's complex IT environment, a myriad of technical skills. As you grow, so grows your IT head count. See the bullet *Employees* previously.

- **Relevance**: Are your systems taking advantage of the most current changes in technology? Can you access your business applications through an iPhone, for example? Can you link your business applications with social networking sites such as Yammer?

- **Security holes**: With NetSuite, you have a system that undergoes a rigorous annual security audit by an independent auditor, an exercise few organizations are set up to do for themselves.

For these reasons and many others, the new SaaS model for business applications makes incredibly good sense. However, the competition is not going to stand by idly and not fire up **Fear**, **Uncertainty**, and **Doubt** (**FUD**). Following are a few examples:

- Your data will be exposed to anyone and everyone. This is nonsense, of course. Any company or individual who has received the payroll from a service bureau knows that systems are extremely capable of separating one company's data from another, just as they keep one employees record separate from the other. Systems that are built to handle multiple tenants strictly enforce separation of data. This is simply how computers work and there is no reason why your organization's records are more vulnerable than any other record. They are not. As a SaaS provider, NetSuite also undergoes the SAS70 audit which goes far past the scrutiny most organizations put on their data security and IT management processes.

- You can't integrate a SaaS application with other applications. In fact, SaaS offerings, including OneWorld, all have the ability to integrate through a web services API. This is part of what they call **Service Oriented Architecture** (**SOA**). The Web service's API enables integration with both on-premise systems and other SaaS offerings. Web services are also agnostic, meaning it is an open architecture that makes it easy for other systems, regardless of operating system or programming language, to communicate back and forth with NetSuite. For light-weight integration with other web-based applications, such as google mail or applications, or phone applications, NetSuite also offers RESTlets, enabling access to a REST-based web services API.

- You can't customize SaaS. Again, this is not true. We know of at least one large on-premise vendor who would not, under any circumstances, allow customers to add new tables, new fields, custom scripts, and custom forms to their system. NetSuite's level of **customizability** is beyond anything we have seen in any other applications. In truth, what would be customizations in on-premise systems are configurations in NetSuite, and many can be done without writing a line of code. We go into a lot more detail next and in the last two chapters, but it is sufficient to say that you can really customize NetSuite in amazing ways, and most customizations require only minimal attention during upgrades.

Multi-tenancy

The idea is to create software that can be used by many customers simultaneously, not unlike the example of ADP, mentioned previously. When we deploy on-premise software, we do it for one or a few related organizations. It's like a home with a single tenant. When we create a SaaS offering, we start with the premise that it can house as many users, tenants, as we want. In a nutshell, this is the concept of **multi-tenancy**: one software code base, one database, one application server serving many customer tenants.

The upshot is that the SaaS vendor can now offer sophisticated software at a fraction of the price that any individual customer can run a single tenant, on-premise system. But, saving customers the capital cost of infrastructure is just the beginning. There are also savings on the infrastructure maintenance, the database and system administrator human resource costs.

There are also savings on maintaining the software code. The customer no longer has to worry about upgrades and patch fixes. This is the vendor's concern in the SaaS model. The vendor, likewise, does not have to maintain multiple versions of the software for multiple hardware stacks, and can thus afford to concentrate his/ her efforts on a single system's upgrade and maintenance.

For any business or IT manager who has spent a day off trying to upgrade the server before your vendor pulls support, this is no longer your responsibility. NetSuite, for all of its services including OneWorld, manages all upgrades and code base fixes. This is what SaaS means to you. We have all used the services of a payroll service bureau at some point in our careers because we view them as a secure, hassle-free way of doing a task, which must be nearly perfect. We can find the same hassle-free security with OneWorld.

What SaaS means to you

OneWorld has a very different approach. You simply pay for the service annually, in most cases, based on the current number of users. NetSuite handles running, balancing, backing up, restoring, patching, and generally maintaining the entire system. As a result, the entire customer base runs off of the same code base. This is a big plus for the customer. They never hope to have functionality that was already delivered, but of which they are unaware. And with a single code base, they know that the software is being constantly used, tested, fixed, and enhanced, by a large number of companies, leading to improved code quality.

To really understand the value of SaaS, compare it to the **Application Service Provider (ASP)** model. ASPs attempted to add value by running on-premise software in their data center, which the customer accessed through an internet or **Virtual Private Network (VPN)** connection. In the end, they really added no value for the customer, and the ASP business model is now defunct. You can, of course, find companies that will host your applications, but they are just providing servers. Managing a separate application stack for each customer turned out to be expensive for the customer and a very costly service to provide. The ASPs simply mirrored what was happening in corporate data centers without ever finding new efficiencies that could add value and generate profit. The speed at which the ASP model went bankrupt should be a clear indication that corporate data centers are more costly to operate than is often recognized.

When we implemented on-premise software, the first third of the implementation was a costly one-time, custom infrastructure implementation. Understanding data volumes, then matching those to machines and other infrastructure necessities, getting all these equipments ordered, installed, and loaded with the software and then patching for days or weeks until the applications started to work normally, was the work of several human resources. This is no longer necessary. When you purchase a OneWorld account, NetSuite provisions the account the next business day and you are ready to work. We'll get into the implementation process more in *Chapter 3, OneWorld Implementation*, but understand that a OneWorld business implementation literally starts the day after you sign your contract with NetSuite.

Finally, we say that one of the most important elements of SaaS is only now becoming understood, that is, the fact that SaaS runs in the connected Internet world, where your customers, your partners, your vendors, and your employees now spend most of their professional time, pays huge dividends going forward. SaaS applications have only started to tap the potential here.

Consider one example of a company that sells to engineers. When your CRM software talks to LinkedIn, you have the ability to know when engineers move from company-to-company, or even from position-to-position in the same company. That's invaluable information. These linkages are only now starting to come online, but they will flourish in the future as our business applications begin to connect in the same ways that we connect to each other in our social networks.

SaaS and Cloud Computing

Within the last couple of years, the SaaS vendors, including NetSuite, have morphed their marketing from SaaS to Cloud Computing. Is there an advantage to calling it Cloud Computing instead of on-demand or SaaS?

Cloud Computing elevates the idea of utility computing, and surely OneWorld possesses some of the virtues of utility computing, by letting users buy the computing power they need and only what they need. Putting software into the cloud also reinforces the idea that it's capable of integration, because cloud software is really built with integration as forethought, and not an afterthought.

If you would like to learn more about Cloud Computing in general, we advise you to try this excellent write-up at Wikipedia: `http://en.wikipedia.org/wiki/Cloud_computing`

Customize, integrate, configure, and extend OneWorld

NetSuite's OneWorld enables the following:

- **Customization**: Add new tables and manage business processes with server-side or client-side code.
- **Integration**: There is a Web services API allowing you to write from or to the database. There are also SaaS services such as Boomi, or appliances such as CloudConnect and Pervasive for running your integration. For lightweight integration, there are RESTlets, a type of SuiteScript that enables access to a REST API for integration with other web-based applications, or for development of phone applications.
- **Configuration**: Add fields and code to reshape forms to your specific business model.
- **Extension**: Using the previous options plus the ability to design custom workflows yourself, you can create solution bundles for your organization, or a specific market vertical. Alternatively, you can purchase third-party extension bundles already built.

We will cover all of these in detail in the final couple of chapters. But here we will introduce you to some terms that might be helpful as you focus on OneWorld's capabilities.

SuiteCloud platform

To prevent confusion, we start at the lowest level of the NetSuite pyramid. The SuiteCloud platform is NetSuite's term for all of the major parts of their system:

- **The SaaS Infrastructure and the Physical Data Center**: As you would expect, these are the foundation of all things in NetSuite.
- The next level is the Software Suites, in our case, OneWorld. These provide the base functionality for all other development.
- The third level is NS-BOS. This is the development platform that we dive into a bit more later on.
- **SuiteCloud Developer Network (SDN)** is the group to which outside developers belong, providing them with support for the NetSuite extensions they build.
- Finally, there is the SuiteApp marketplace, a collection of all of the third-party developments that you can add to your OneWorld deployment.

NetSuite Business Operating System (NS BOS)

NS BOS refers specifically to a set of functions, which enable developers to build applications on top of NetSuite's OneWorld, or their other suites, adding important functionality. Sometimes, this functionality is broad, like a *Fixed Assets* module that generates depreciation journals. Sometimes the functionality creates a new vertical-like manufacturing. In either case, what is happening is that developers are using a set of NetSuite tools to develop a new module or group of modules that's completely integrated with OneWorld. This is an important point to understand. These applications run in the same physical and logical environment as OneWorld itself. In fact, at the recent SuiteWorld 2011 conference, NetSuite announced that their own developers were going to add extensions to NetSuite using the NS BOS tools.

The ability to develop within OneWorld is in marked contrast to many on-premise systems where one develops on a separate system and then links the two systems together. The integration was never as tight as it should be, and every change to one system or the other has the potential to bring both systems down. NS BOS not only enables development within the same system as OneWorld, but it also provides all of the tools to generate new applications and modules, and then replicate them:

SuiteFlex is the name given to the tools, listed as follows, that enable development within the NetSuite system:

- **SuiteBuilder**: The basics of development, enables new records, new fields, and new forms.
- **SuiteScript**: When you need to manipulate data, update, or delete, write your JavaScript on either the client or the server.
- **SuiteTalk**: When you have to communicate with another SaaS application or an on-premise application, this is the Web services API (application programming interface that exposes NetSuite records to read and write processes). NetSuite already offers SuiteTalk integrations with salesforce.com, SAP, and Oracle. When you need a lightweight integration with a phone application or with another web-based application, such as Google mail, you can use a RESTlet to gain access to a REST-based web services API.
- **SuiteScript d-bug**: This recent addition enables developers to debug their work as they go, making them more agile and saving precious development time.
- **Single Sign on**: Enables users who sign onto NetSuite to navigate to other web-based applications.
- **SuiteBundler**: Allows developers to bundle all of their development efforts and then inject the bundle into a NetSuite account with a couple of clicks. This saves an enormous amount of time when re-creating applications and modules, or when enhancing an upgrade.

Okay, that's the full picture of the SuiteCloud platform. Hopefully, our explanations have not confused you. It's pretty simple when you think about it this way: NetSuite gives you the ability to develop add-on applications and modules, increasing the functionality of OneWorld, or integrate OneWorld with already-existing applications that you may be using. If you would like to get a better handle on what's available, we suggest that you visit the SuiteApp marketplace here: `http://www.netsuite.com/portal/suiteapp/main.shtml`

Due diligence for SaaS

Before taking mission-critical data to a SaaS vendor such as NetSuite, senior managers ought to look for answers to commonsense questions about the vendor's operations; in other words, due diligence.

In general, due diligence focuses on the vendor's security controls and standards for maintaining data integrity and application up-time under all possible conditions, and their ability to scale the system without loss of service quality. In short, security, redundancy, and scalability are key questions for potential service users of not only NetSuite OneWorld, but any SaaS offering.

Let's get the basic stuff out of the way first. NetSuite has a publicly accessible web page that reports system availability, or the lack thereof, at `https://status.netsuite.com/status_en_US.html`. The page will look like the following screenshot, and it reports the current status of the NetSuite system:

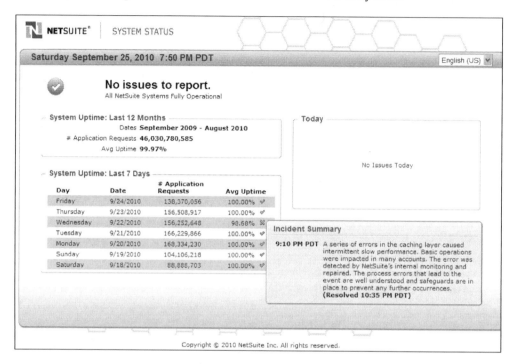

The page is updated, at least daily.

NetSuite also offers several other pages on their site devoted to due diligence. Start at the NetSuite Infrastructure page: `http://www.netsuite.com/portal/infrastructure/main.shtml`.

There are several pages that contain useful information and also a video prepared by the VP of Engineering Operations that touches on several key points.

The SAS 70 Audit

The SAS 70 Audit was created to attest to the effectiveness of the control environment for service providers who, in turn, provide services deemed critical to the control environment of their customers; and to provide a document to organizations that use outside services, which affect their own financial results, describing the controls in place, by the service provider, to ensure correct results for user organizations.

The audit is done by highly specialized professionals, and if you are a firm that also does an annual financial audit done by your accounting firm, then you will need to take a look at the SaaS vendor's SAS 70 Audit.

When it comes to due diligence, the most oft-quoted terms in the SaaS world is the SAS 70 Audit. In general, the SAS 70 is an audit of the service provider's, NetSuite's, internal controls with respect to information technology. The purpose of the SAS 70 Audit is to provide user organizations and you with reasonable assurance that the necessary controls are in place, by the service organization, to satisfy the user organization's internal financial reporting controls. By performing the audit and distributing a SAS 70 Audit's results, the service provider must undergo only a single audit, instead many audits, by every user organization.

There are two types of SAS 70 Audits, namely, **Type I** and **Type II**. The Type I audit states that the service provider has the necessary internal controls relative to the user organization's financial reporting at a single point in time. The Type II audit includes the testing of these controls over a six-month period. The Type II audit includes a description of the tests and the test results of the controls stated in Type I. A service organization who has undergone a SAS 70 Audit can state that they have the systems and controls in place to provide reasonable assurance to user organizations that the controls meet their objectives during the testing period. It's also important to understand that the vendor selects the controls and objectives that they believe are pertinent to their business.

It's important to note that the SAS 70 is not a checklist audit. There is, in other words, no set or standard list of objectives to measure a service organization. Therefore, each service organization may have a different set of control objectives. To see a description of the SAS 70 Audit, you can visit this site: `http://umiss.lib.` `olemiss.edu:82/articles/1038093.6671/1.PDF`. If you want to see an actual SAS 70 Audit, however, you will search high and low for one. These are not handed out to just anyone, but are very guarded by both the auditors who perform the audit and the organizations that are audited. If you require one of NetSuite, you may ask your sales person or partner to provide it.

Sarbanes-Oxley, often referred to as Sarbox, is legislation that was passed in the US, after the Enron scandal of 2002. Among the many provisions of the law, is the necessity for user organizations to have a service organization's SAS 70 Audit for their own auditors. So, if you are a company which operates under Sarbox, then you must obtain a SAS 70 Audit from NetSuite. Happily they have one to give you. However, even if you do not operate under Sarbox, you can still obtain the SAS 70 Audit.

The SAS 70 Audit continues to evolve. In the US, SAS 70 will be usurped by SSAE 16, which, fortunately, aligns closely with IASB 3402, the international standard for auditing service firms. So, in the near future, we can look forward to more extensive audit reports from service providers.

More common security questions

While there is no question that the SAS 70 Audit, or the SSAE 16 Audit, is a key piece of information for any company that regularly undergoes an audit by its accounting firm, there are also more mundane questions around security that require answers.

These are very common questions when corporate officers consider any SaaS offering, including OneWorld. Let's note the following: Connecting to NetSuite is done through a **Secure Sockets Layer** (**SSL**) connection, which provides data encryption; the software you connect to runs on servers at a professionally managed data center, meaning that there are multiple levels of physical security. The application stack is a Linux operating system, Oracle database, and Apache application server, each of which together offer several additional layers of logical security.

There are also security questions, which are part of the sign-in process, and you can further lock down access for some of your employees by enabling IP rules.

NetSuite answers several other security, business continuity, and system availability questions on their website. Following are a couple of quick points:

- The system has multiple levels of backup. All production data is stored immediately to redundant locations. That's the first one, and is followed by hot daily backups and backups to hard media, also.

- The system is scalable, meaning that NetSuite was built from the ground up to manage spikes in usage. NetSuite's customer roll includes a large number of e-commerce firms who successfully experience a huge surge in business every Christmas season.

- NetSuite's Infrastructure is extremely efficient. The savings in electricity alone amounts to thousands of dollars per customer.

Service Level Agreement (SLA)

All SaaS companies offer an SLA. The SLA states the level of performance that the user or customer can expect. In this instance, we'll let NetSuite speak for itself, from `http://www.netsuite.com/portal/infrastructure/availability.shtml`:

We know that downtime is not an option in your business. This is one reason that our service agreement guarantees 99.5 percent uptime outside the scheduled service windows. We guarantee 99.5 percent uptime across the entire NetSuite family of production applications for all of our customers. A credit is available, if NetSuite does not deliver its application services with 99.5 percent uptime.

OneWorld Suite or best of breeds

A **Suite** is software written to run most or all of a business's processes. It covers front office, operations, accounting, and so on. Best of breeds focus on a part of the business, such as sales and marketing in the case of CRM. Vertical suites manage most or all of a particular business type, such as steel service centers, for example. In this section, we want to lay out the good, the bad, and the ugly of all three modes of software use.

The Suite

The debate between best of breed and Suites has been going on since the suite was introduced in the late 1980s. When packaged business software, as opposed to custom developed software, first appeared on the scene, it was developed for a specific business process, such as general ledger or accounts payable. Over time, the idea caught on that a package ought to cover all of an organization's business processes. The evolution of the Suite began, and it's been going strong ever since. (Recently, however, many CIO's have returned to the best of breed model because of consolidation among on-premise software vendors that has reduced their negotiating power and left them exposed to the arbitrary business practices of one vendor.)

In its essence, the OneWorld suite is a number of business processes that share a single database. The marketing group attracts new leads, the sales person works with leads to identify an opportunity and potentially create a quote, the customer service person opens a customer ticket, the operations person fulfills an order, the accounting person invoices the order, and all of them use the same **Customer** table. It makes a lot of sense, so much sense that the best of breed vendors could only compete on the depth of functionality.

Best of breed

In the best-of-breed model, each vendor focuses on a narrow set of business processes, such as paying bills, invoicing customers, or paying sales commissions. They often offer very deep functionality in their niche, a practice that appeals to some IT and business managers who frankly have a lot of complexity to manage. But the problem with the best-of-breed approach is that you must figure out how to pass the data along from breed to breed, as you complete a transaction. The quotes must become an order, the order must be fulfilled, and the customer must be invoiced and then serviced.

When packaged applications replaced custom development, this integration of various packages kept IT departments busy. What sounds like a fairly simple integration process actually becomes a huge programming challenge for software developers. It turns out that each application has its own idea of what a customer is, how a customer behaves, what a customer expects, and how an organization wants to work with its customers. Integrations are developed and then maintained over their lifetime by programmers who must become intimate with the code. There are, as you can imagine, serious costs associated with best-of-breed integrations.

The Suite goes in the opposite direction. It requires no integrations for the business processes it covers. The upside is less resources required to maintain the system and, more importantly, a single, complete view of the main objects of your business, such as customers, vendors, and employees. However, let us be honest, the best of breeds can offer a serious depth of functionality. If you have to compensate a sales force of 800 who sell multiple product lines in multiple overlapping territories under multiple series of complex rules, then OneWorld's commission module is probably not going to work for you.

On the other hand, if you like to keep it simple and straightforward, like a lot of SMEs, concentrating your focus on delivering the right products and services to customers, then the commission module in OneWorld works well. It covers a lot of different scenarios and every company that uses it has a different take on commissions. What they all have in common, however, is an understanding that commission plans, which sales people and managers understand, create the best incentives for increased sales.

The Vertical Suite

Finally, there are Vertical Suites written for a specific business type. These proliferate in the SME space, because there are a lot of unique businesses in the SME space, and the normal SME does not have the time, the skills, or the cash to write its own custom software product, such as a Fortune 500 might.

Vertical Suites cover all or most of the business processes and functions, and from a purely business function perspective, they can be quite good. There are, however, two Achilles' heels, both stemming from the fact that they are so narrow in their focus.

Written for a specific business type, Vertical Suites often hit a sales wall very quickly. When you are selling to steel service centers and there are only 1200 of them in your market, and you have three competitors, that's going to present a problem. You very quickly reach the peak of sales and profit, and without growth in the future, you must cut back. At some point, you eventually sell off the code and customer base to a company that harvests the software for maintenance fees. They keep one or a few support people around to handle customer questions.

As the Vertical Suite vendor hits the sales wall, they have to minimize development efforts. Further, product development is simply not going to increase sales, so the product comes to a technical standstill, and while the world your business operates in changes, the product does not.

The alternative to narrow Vertical Suite software is to build vertical solutions within a robust suite. This creates the best of all possible worlds: strong vertical functionality backed with a strong business model for the software developer. Buying software from a company with deep roots and flourishing branches is always a good strategy. They don't have to be one of the mega software companies, but a sound company. After all, you are going to be partners for a long time! OneWorld has several of these vertical offerings already.

The Open Source Suite

Some open source software makes sense. A lot of companies run their websites on an open source platform that includes several different open source software offerings. So open source has its place, however, the open source business suite is a difficult egg to crack. At the end of the day, how does a vendor support multiple installations of highly customized open source software, or maintain them in a multi-tenant system? They really need to become NetSuite with all the development and support staff required to give your customers the service you require, but after exposing the base code to customization, that's not an option. Even if you were to purchase, install, customize, and maintain the open source base code yourself, over time, as you move through personnel changes, the challenge of maintaining and adding new functionality becomes a huge burden. If you are interested in reducing the size and responsibilities of your IT department, or in not having one at all, then the open source suite is not a good option.

Suite summary

At the end of the day, business managers contemplating a business software solution from a best-of-breed or suite angle have to ask themselves the question *What does the system cost in total?* Not just the software, not just the infrastructure, but the personnel to install, manage, update, fix, and document – these are often the uncounted costs of system ownership. On-premise or SaaS? Best of breed or the Suite? Understanding the costs associated with these alternatives, including the opportunity costs, can prevent a lot of buyer's remorse.

Sometimes the difference is also just a matter of degree. Even some OneWorld customers require a certain amount of integration. There are no perfect answers. We have put together the following table to help you sort out some of the questions around the best approach to business software solutions:

Requirements by system type	Best of breed	OneWorld Integrated Suite	Vertical Suite	Open source Suite
System integration required	Certainty. Possibly two integrations per breed: one to bring the data in and one to move it to its next destination.	Low probability. Depends on business model. If you need some special function not covered, you'll have to extend or integrate.	Low probability. Vertical Suite should have exactly what you require for business operations, though it may not have modules like CRM.	Low probability. You should be able to build whatever you need by extending the suite, unless it's cost prohibitive.
Training requirements	Training needed for each system, plus understanding of integrations.	One system; keeps training to a minimum.	One system; keeps training to a minimum.	One system; keeps training to a minimum.
Short-term support provided	High probability. Vendors in this sector have long lives.	High probability. Vendors in this sector have long lives.	High probability.	High probability.
Long-term support provided	High probability.	High probability.	Low probability – technology purchased by third party, minimal support.	Low probability – system maintained by consulting company and not a software company.

Requirements by system type	Best of breed	OneWorld Integrated Suite	Vertical Suite	Open source Suite
Depth of functionality	Very deep; should cover all possible requirements in its specific niche.	Medium depth of functionality. Suites require business flexibility or customization. See next line.	Very deep or really is not worth the trouble. Do not hope for continued enhancements, though.	Low depth of functionality - open source expects clients to add what they need.
System customizability	Very little customization required, and product may be difficult to customize.	Yes, very customizable. You build it; NetSuite supports it through upgrade process.	Not required – Vertical Suite should already have all required processes.	Yes, very customizable. You build it; you support it.
System configurability	Ought to have high degree of configurability to cover all possible scenarios in its niche.	Yes, very configurable	Not required; functions and processes complete for its vertical.	Yes, very configurable.

Total cost of ownership

Several years ago, Yankee Group Research published a study that compared Software as a Service NetSuite against two on-premise applications that together offered the same functionality. You can still download the complete paper from the NetSuite site here: `http://www.netsuite.com/portal/resource/collateral.shtml`.

 The paper is under the title *TCO of On-Demand Applications Is Significantly Better for SMBs and Mid-Market Enterprises.*

Let us challenge you before you read the paper to fill out the short form next and see how close you come to the scenarios raised in Yankee's paper. We have simplified the table that Yankee Group used, to try to spur your thinking around where system costs are both obvious and hidden in your organization.

Current Application Mix	Year 1	Year 2	Year 3	Year 4	Year 5	Total
Number of Apps/Subscription or License Costs of Each						
System Integration Costs						
Manual Integration Cost (Spreadsheets)						
Application Vendor's Maintenance						
Database Vendor's Maintenance						
Hardware Operating System Vendor's Maintenance						
Other IT Infrastructure (Network, Internet Access)						
Implementation and Ongoing Management						
Software Testing and Patching						
System Admin and User Support						
User Training						
TOTAL						

The first line of the table, **Number of Apps/Subscription or License Costs of Each**, is hopefully fairly easy to find. Start with a list of the main applications that you use to run the business. These include accounting, sales, service or support, e-commerce, inventory, purchasing, order fulfillment, and marketing applications. Now, your organization may not need or use some of these; we are simply trying to spur your thinking. Once you have your list, it's quick to sum up the licensing costs for each. Likewise, you can also get the fourth line, **Application Vendor's Maintenance**, at this time.

The second line, **System Integration Costs**, may or may not be more subjective, depending on your systems. Integration through system interfaces is, for example, when your inventory system updates your accounting system. These interfaces must be written, and then they also consume a fair amount of time and energy in the IT group every month, to maintain them through upgrades to either application.

First, start again with a list of these interfaces and then try to ballpark what interfaces people are spending time on every month. There may be some interfaces that are fairly benign and others that are time black holes. Once you have a good ballpark, the rest is simple math to figure out the human resource costs.

The same process can then be used for **Manual Integration Cost (Spreadsheets)** of data between systems, which is line three in the tables. Depending on the organization, you may have one or more people who spend an inordinate amount of time doing things such as maintaining spreadsheets on revenue recognition, and then uploading the results into a month-end journal entry. These activities can add up for the organization as a whole, very quickly.

Your best bet here is to do a walk around to all your departments and ask them about the largest spreadsheets that they maintain, and where the data ultimately ends up at the end of the period. A rough guess from experience: An organization of 100 employees will have about 25 spreadsheets that are used at month end. Each of them has a human resource cost, and by the end of your system selection, you will have a good idea of which ones will remain and which will not survive (hopefully zero). One fairly common spreadsheet in many organizations is the accounting consolidation for multiple legal entities or subsidiaries.

The next three rows are maintenance fees that should be hard numbers right off of the respective software license agreement. Database software, application software, and operating system software all have annual fees that you can plug in here. Note that we are also assuming in the table that the average system will last five years, so we are not factoring in the replacement of hardware and all attendant costs, such as new software versions, and so on.

Other IT Infrastructure (Network, Internet Access) seeks to establish a cost for running a networked application, whether that Network is your own or the Internet. If you have a fair number of tele-commuters or others who work outside your physical business location, then it might be worthwhile to calculate the cost of their access to the system. Some on-premise systems may only be accessible, for example, through a VPN connection. Likewise, if you have multiple physical locations, there is a cost associated with communicating with HQ. Tally all of these here.

The last four lines are all really human resource costs. (Are you starting to see a pattern here?) On implementation costs, you will learn more about these in the next chapter, but it will suffice to say that the average on-premise system implementation is at least one-third hardware and software installation. OneWorld brings these costs to zero. Also, all of your minor customizations of most on-premise systems require a technical skill set that is expensive. With OneWorld, there is a lot of advanced configuration and customization that only requires a strong business user who has a technical bent. They do not need to be coders.

It's also worth noting here that software testing and patching really come to an end with OneWorld. Whereas on-premise systems require that you test a new patch on a test system prior to installing it on your production system, with NetSuite, you really do not have to do either. First, when a major release is imminent, you are notified and provided access to a beta account, a replica of your production account. You can run through test transactions to see if there are any issues, but you are especially encouraged to make sure that any custom scripts that you have are still working correctly. If you do not have a lot of custom scripts, then you can use the beta account to play with new functionality, and see how your organization can benefit. In all cases, you are not required to install the patch to the system yourself.

Other costs and values

As you can see, there are several categories of costs to consider when thinking about NetSuite OneWorld, or any software solution, for your organization. But just comparing costs may not give an accurate picture of what you are purchasing. There are several other key values to think about when it comes to system selection, which are not always obvious. Also, because there seems to be quite a few older legacy systems still breathing in the SME space, it is worthwhile to go through the following list to get a sense of what you are purchasing. Here are some key points to consider:

- Is this a real-time system? Meaning, do transactions immediately impact the general ledger, or is there an upload process that must be run (sometimes called a job)?

- Is it possible to drill back from any report to the base transactions?

- Does the application play nice with tools your organization uses such as e-mail clients and spreadsheets?

- Are your CRM and ERP solutions integrated? Do they require extra software or additional hardware to communicate?

- Can you write reports without technical skills?

- Does the product have a real-time dashboard that displays key metrics to each user, based on their role?

Some of these might sound like nice-to-have capabilities, but not hard business requirements. What they provide, however, is a simple, quick way to make sure that you are purchasing a modern system, one which exhibits that the development team has learned the best lessons from their predecessors.

Backup and restore

We thought it was advisable to offer a note on system backup and restore. We often hear that a company has their system backup covered. Of course, they always have the backup part covered. They do actually run the backup utility and put it on some media that they take home at night, for example. The other half of the process, the restore, is assumed to work. In most cases, it has never been tried.

Here is what you have to do to properly run the backup utility and then restore. You have to take a backup and then on another machine, you have to restore from the backup media. What this means is that you have to have a duplicate system onto which you can restore the production data. Otherwise, you simply have the backup media and no way of knowing whether you can restore it. A database administrator will tell you that restoring the data is the challenge. Until you have successfully restored a backup, you do not have a *business continuation in case of emergency* strategy.

How NetSuite is sold

NetSuite now has three main products: NetSuite, NetSuite CRM, and NetSuite OneWorld. We are concerned with NetSuite OneWorld, and we only mention the others to prevent, not create, confusion. When you purchase OneWorld, you are purchasing the full Suite, CRM, ERP, e-commerce/web presence, and the additional functionality to run multiple subsidiaries, as described previously.

Purchasing OneWorld means purchasing a NetSuite account, the multiple subsidiary functionality of OneWorld, and any additional module that you might need. There are now fourteen additional modules that you may require, based on your business model, which are listed as follows:

1. **Advanced Inventory**: This module allows you to add units of measurement, matrix items, Lot and Serialized inventory, and a number of other inventory functions. Any business model where you are purchasing, receiving, and fulfilling orders probably requires Advanced Inventory.

2. **Advanced Project Management**: Required module for any company using OpenAir. APM can also be used standalone. It provides the ability to manage and resource projects, and bill for project time and materials. Used in conjunction with Advanced Billing, you can bill projects based on completed milestones.

3. **Advanced Billing**: Companies that bill customers on a monthly or quarterly basis require this module. It lets you create billing schedules for multiple billing scenarios, including milestone completion.

4. **Revenue Recognition**: With Advanced Billing, you can sell a year and bill monthly; with Rev Rec, you can sell the whole year, invoice the year, and recognize revenue monthly. Includes VSOE for managing support or license discounts. Enables the creation of Rev Rec schedules for multiple scenarios.

5. **Incentive Management (Employee and Partner Commissions)**: This module enables the use of commission schedules to automatically calculate commissions on sale orders or invoices.

6. **Issue Management**: This is an add-on for the customer service module, enabling the tracking of issues from the point where the customer notifies you, until you fix and release a solution.

7. **Light Manufacturing**: This module enables the use of work orders to manage the manufacturing process.

8. **Site Analytics**: For e-commerce companies, this module enables the tracking of customers on your NetSuite website(s).

9. **Site Builder**: This module enables the greatest flexibility in the look and feel of your NetSuite website. It's really a must have for any company using NetSuite for the primary website. However, if you are only running a very simple store, you can use the base e-commerce functionality.

10. **Electronic File/Software Distribution**: For those companies selling electronic file downloads.

11. **ODBC**: For those who need to have a more robust reporting solution, this module offers a connection directly to the database.

12. **Contract Renewals**: This module adds automatic contract renewal functionality for primarily software companies.

13. **Advanced Manufacturing**: This module adds discrete manufacturing capability with shop floor, production, cost, and project controls.

14. **Materials Management**: This module adds comprehensive BOM and Item Master management, as well as engineering controls.

15. **Demand Planning**: For product-based organizations, this module allows you to calculate future demand for your products, and then use this demand plan to set up an associated supply plan for purchasing and assembly, if required.

16. **Fixed Assets**: An additional module for the calculation of depreciation for your organization's fixed assets, plus advanced features, such as asset revaluation and retirement.

These are the major add-on modules. These modules, like OneWorld itself, are sold for a single monthly/annual fee, regardless of the number of users. You can think of these as blocks of additional functionality.

There are also a number of other options that are sold based on quantity. For example, the Advanced Partner Center, in which partners manage their customers and transactions, is sold per partner user. The following is a list of options that are sold by quantity:

- Additional OneWorld users
- Additional employee center users (for entering time and expenses)
- Offline sales users (enables updating records offline)
- **Additional webstore items**: Over and above the OneWorld base amount
- **Webstore bandwidth**: Over and above the OneWorld base amount
- **Data storage**: Over and above the OneWorld base amount
- **Mail merge e-mail communications**: Over and above the OneWorld base amount
- **E-mail marketing campaigns**: Over and above the OneWorld base amount
- EBay Integration
- **Payroll services**: Standard or premium base rate, plus per payroll check per period.
- **Support**: Purchased as a percent of your license cost.

There are also options for a sandbox account and for a Web services integration license.

We will cover OneWorld functions in great detail in *Chapter 2, OneWorld's Foundation*. For our purposes here, we thought it would be a good idea to just detail how NetSuite is sold.

The key point is that you do not need to purchase every option of the suite, but you will own the base CRM and ERP modules. If your organization does not require Advanced Inventory, then do not purchase it, likewise Advanced Project Management. NetSuite has seen fit to remove some of the advanced functions from the base application and we think this is a win-win for them and you. Buy what you require.

It's also worth noting here that NetSuite supports the notion of *pay as you go*, a concept that is sometimes thought to be a requirement of SaaS. You pay annually for the users and modules you need. Once you lock in, that's it for the year. There are no refunds if you decide to sell a business unit, for example, and no longer need the licenses. However, it is not a situation where you purchase a lot of seats and modules, some of which you never use or implement, yet have to keep paying for year after year, as in some on-premise deals. Each year you have the opportunity to renew the licenses or modules or drop them, as business dictates. Of course, you can also add licenses and modules throughout the year, pro-rated for the duration of the contract.

Three different scenarios for OneWorld

There are three different business scenarios that lend themselves to NetSuite OneWorld. They have nothing to do with business models, processes, or geography. These are some prerequisites that ought to be taken care of prior to making the NetSuite purchase that we want to touch on here.

OneWorld's main target customer obviously is a little bit larger than the average organization that uses NetSuite. As a result, OneWorld prospects are probably not looking at a green field implementation, although this does sometimes happen when you bring OneWorld into a rapidly growing start-up. Let's go over and compare some of the challenges that happen in both scenarios – the start-up green field and the established company with legacy spaghetti, to get an idea of the implementation costs and benefits for both.

The start-up green field

For the rapidly growing start-up with a relatively open IT landscape, OneWorld is an excellent choice. You can manage multiple subsidiaries as a matter of course, meaning you don't have to consolidate multiple sets of books into a single view of the company's results every month. Additionally, using OneWorld at the beginning of your organization's ramp up prevents the adoption of numerous point solutions by each department.

All start-ups face the same constraint of tight budgets and OneWorld provides the opportunity to keep the accounting department small and focused, while you add to sales and engineering.

It also goes without saying that the OneWorld suite gives you the clearest view of your spend and revenue. From purchase to pay, and from lead to cash, you will have a clear picture of what to expect in and out of the bank every day, week, and month. Managing cash is enormously important for start-ups.

Of course, if you are not ready for OneWorld yet, then you can bring your single subsidiary into the flagship NetSuite product, and as you add those other subsidiaries, you can upgrade to OneWorld.

With either NetSuite or OneWorld, you drive your business with end-to-end processes that give you a clear picture of growth at every stage, and provide your managers with the performance metrics they need. You no longer have to wait until month-end close is wrapped up, before all of you can see the results. Your dashboard will show results as they happen. With an integrated system, departments start to work together, pulling their oars in the same direction as the old metaphor goes. Achieving a working, collaborative team that produces results is not possible with spreadsheets.

The established company on the growth curve

The more established company has a different set of opportunities and challenges. They suffer not from a deficit of systems, but a surplus. It is likely that they have five or six main systems and several lesser ones, and they have not lost any ground to the start-up in their use of spreadsheets as well. Bringing most, if not all, of their systems into an integrated suite is huge step forward.

This situation is often referred to as the legacy spaghetti. We have personally seen some legacy spaghetti visual diagrams from large companies that bordered on hilarious. We are still not sure if anyone understood exactly what was happening with the data. By adopting OneWorld, they get rid of the legacy spaghetti, or the hairball, as NetSuite's marketing group calls it, and they have real-time business visibility. That's a big deal if you want growth and efficiency.

Now, most SMEs do not have as much spaghetti as their larger competitors, but for small and medium organizations, they often have a fair share. Job one then is to get a good picture of what you have and where you have it. Job two is to understand what you do with it and who is responsible. There will be some surprises. You will find that many of the connections between your application silos are not integrations in any known sense of the word. They may be called integrations, and I may be called Brad Pitt, but calling it thus does not make it so. They may be spreadsheet exports from one system, manipulated and manually imported into another.

The question throughout this exercise is *Does this system plumbing curtail or prevent our growth?* It's a worthwhile question and there is not a perfect answer. But if you discover that people have added on to their sales, engineering, or accounting positions a number of hours for system/data manipulation over and above simple transactions, then you have discovered a blockage that needs to be removed. If you also find yourself asking for real-time reports or wishing that you had better data to make decisions with, then you have identified another symptom of multiple-system disease. Take action!

New ownership

New ownership may have never seen more than recent financial reports. In other cases, the new owners are employees of the company and they know firsthand the state of the business systems. In either case, new ownership is an opportunity to launch the company on a new course.

Over time, the systems installed in a business become calcified, as does the business thinking. Systems become turf, and turf requires protection. If you want your new business to move in a new and better direction, then you need to break down some of the walls, get your people a little off balance, ask tough questions, demand answers, and open the teams' eyes to new opportunities. A OneWorld implementation can help you 'out with the old' and 'in with the new,' replacing your confusing systems and turf battles with a system that can accommodate growth.

Whether it's for new ownership, a start-up that wants to get on the right track, or for an ongoing concern that simply wants to reinvent itself and ramp up growth again, OneWorld is an excellent tool.

Summary

In this chapter, we thought it was a good idea to discuss all of the terms, ideas, and contexts operating in and around NetSuite OneWorld. Obviously, before you implement the product, you have to choose to buy it, and before you extend it, you must implement it.

We would like to make one further point that we have not yet touched on, but feel is very important. Senior management of SMEs often lament the fact that they do not have the IT or financial resources of their larger brethren. But we would suggest that your larger competitors are mostly the prisoners of their own IT extravagance.

Together those large companies spent many billions on software, hardware, and services in the 1990s and since, are now tied into contracts with just a few vendors in a rapidly consolidating market, a change is now nearly impossible. Their sunk costs are so high that they just continue to spend without any alternatives. Their vendors have also stopped innovating. Their software is now aging rapidly, and finding resources to maintain their current systems is nearly as difficult as finding COBOL programmers for their oldest systems.

The SME is still in charge of its destiny. It has the ability to change systems to something that works better than the current roster of software silos and costs considerably less. And these new systems will not tie you down. Your sunk costs are an annual operating expense and the services to implement. You will be able to move at a fraction of the price of the Fortune 500. You will not be tied to IT resources, human or machine. It's an advantageous destiny. SaaS is a phenomenon that, unlike so many business IT innovation that started among small companies, it's a competitive advantage, that is, if you take it.

In the next chapter, we start to take a closer look at OneWorld, module-by-module, function-by-function, and process-by-process. The goal is to start the process of setting up OneWorld and help you to see how the integrated pieces work together. You may not be used to working in an integrated suite such as OneWorld. Hopefully, the next chapter will prepare you for implementing and managing the OneWorld Suite.

2

OneWorld's Foundation

This chapter devotes itself to an outline of the main functions and business processes of OneWorld and the base setups that you need to perform in order to use them. The main thrust is to get you started with your OneWorld account in an orderly, organized step-wise approach.

The purpose here is to start to introduce you to OneWorld at the infamous 10,000-foot level. It is our experience that if you dive into the details too quickly, you often lose sight of the big picture. So we think it's worthwhile to use this chapter to establish the big picture first, and then we continue to use it as the basis for more detailed discussions in later chapters.

We also think it's a good idea to organize this book much like a OneWorld implementation. Setting up NetSuite OneWorld as your business management system is a multi-step process. First, we enable the main modules and processes of the system, then we perform administrative setups for each module, and finally we get down to the setup of individual processes, forms, roles, workflows, and reports. We will follow the same regimen in this book.

There is one other thing to mention here, and that is the idea of **Iteration**. Iteration simply means that sometimes we have to start, go as far as we can, and then leave and take care of something else. Later, we circle back to finish or clean up what we started. Iteration seems messy to business people who do not do software implementation on a regular basis. In your business, you are probably much more likely to have clean linear processes, much like the ones we are going to work on in OneWorld. But implementation is rarely a linear process, yet we manage to finish our projects on time. So please bear with us when we mention the need to return to a task later. We do so with good reason.

Let's get started with some of the basics, and then take a closer look at CRM, ERP, and a few of the most important configurations of OneWorld, understanding the big picture through the primary modules, and enabling the ones we need. The main focus of this chapter is:

- OneWorld navigation primer
- OneWorld centers and roles
- General setup
- Customer relationship management
- Enterprise resource planning
- The Item catalog
- Accounting preferences
- Accounting, CRM, and employee lists

Since we begin in this chapter to navigate OneWorld, we start with a short navigation primer.

OneWorld navigation primer

OneWorld navigation can be a challenge for some users, because they may be used to systems that have a single navigation path for every task, process, and function. NetSuite is not nearly as constrained when it comes to navigation. There are sometimes so many choices that users can be confused. In this chapter, we are assuming that you have the ability to log in as the administrator, since we are doing a few base setups that only the administrator has access to.

Let us note here that we very often see the situation where a company has five to ten administrators of the system. This is not a good idea. The **administrator** has the ability to do a couple of things that can really cause problems, such as delete the account, for example. So it is best to have a single administrator and should you need to give out broad access to a few others, we suggest you use the **full access** role. It has nearly the same rights as the administrator, but without the ability to delete the account.

Any user, of course, may have more than one role in the system. We would also suggest that anyone who has access in the administrator or full access role also try to use the system with a functional role, such as **sales administrator** or **accountant**. It will be a lot easier for you in the long run, if you have a good idea of what your other users see and how they work within the system.

Speaking of which, let's take a look at the center tabs. In the following screenshot, you can see the center tabs of the administrator's role:

Here are the center tabs for the accountant's role:

As you can see, the accountant's role has a different set of center tabs, and within those tabs, a completely different set of menus. In this book, when we spell out the navigation path, we expect you to be in the administrator's role, unless we explicitly state the role we want you to be in (otherwise you will be confused).

Also, when we ask you to navigate, we expect you to always start at the center tabs. We will explain more about centers in later chapters, but for now, when we say navigate to **Setup | Company | Enable Features**, we want you to roll your mouse over the word **Setup**, then roll over the word **Company** in the drop-down menu, and then click on the **Enable Features** option.

The primary mode of navigation in OneWorld is through the center tabs, but there are other ways to navigate, and you will discover most of these on your own over time. The main point is that when you land on the **Customer** form, whether through the **Center** tabs navigation, which is a shortcut link, or a report drilldown, you are looking at the same record. The navigation does not change the underlying data.

OneWorld centers and roles

In the navigation discussion above, we introduced the concept of the center. The administrator role differs from the accountant role mainly because the administrator uses the classic center and the accountant uses the accounting center. This is why the primary navigation is called the center tabs—each center has its own set of center tabs, and the center tabs contain the menus of what you can view and do in the system.

In the following screenshot, you can see the accounting role and how it is linked to the **Accounting Center**:

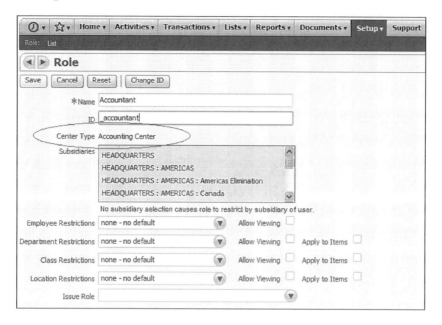

We will cover administration in depth in *Chapter 8, OneWorld Customization and Advanced Configuration*, but between now and then, you will need a working understanding of some of the basics, in order to keep abreast of the discussion.

Each role has one and only one center, and each center has a delivered menu. You can create new centers, and you can add to delivered centers, but you cannot edit or delete the delivered centers. Each role links to a center, and the options in the center tab menus are controlled by role permissions.

In the following discussions, we also make mention of the employee center, the vendor center, the partner center, and the customer center. These are delivered roles/centers, but they have taken the name **Center**. For example, if you want Mike Jones to enter time and expenses, you give him access through the **Employee Center** role.

Unlike other roles in the system, you cannot add more permissions to these centers/roles, though you may remove permissions. We mention this now, because there is often some confusion about the centers to new users. When we talk about the employee, vendor, customer, and partner center, we are really talking about access roles, which are limited to the base permissions of their particular center.

OneWorld roles and licensing

One last note on roles in OneWorld: When you have a full user license, as an accountant or sales administrator, for example, you automatically have access to any other role in the system without further cost. The question that often comes up is *Do we need to purchase employee center access for our sales people who have a full license?* No, you do not.

General setup

There are a few steps that we need to take before we start the in-depth discussion of CRM and ERP. These are straightforward and important to understand at this point. However, you do not have to make a lot of decisions right now, nor do you have to do a lot of setup. For now, as you move through the rest of this chapter, you should have some of this on your mind. If you have the information required at your fingertips, then go ahead and take some of these setup steps. Otherwise, you can circle back later and complete these steps.

General setup navigation

In order to take a look at the following four setup steps, log in as the administrator and navigate to **Setup | Company**. You now see the four options, listed next, which appear as the top four **Company** setup options.

Company information setup

Enter the address and some other basic information about the company, including the main logos that you would like to put on the GUI and on printed documents.

The most important field on the company information page is the **First Fiscal Month**. This determines your accounting period's setup. This should be the first fiscal month for the legal entity that you have designated for the top-level parent entity, the one to which all other subsidiaries roll up.

Enable features

As we go through this chapter and successive chapters, we'll provide instructions on enabling features. This is a basic task, which allows modules and functions to appear in the system, giving you the opportunity for setup and use. For example, if you do not enable marketing here, you will not see the setups for marketing, nor will you be able to use it, of course. At this time, take a close look at the **Enable Features** option and familiarize yourself with all of the tabs on this form.

Rename records/transactions

Again, rename records/transactions is another base setup, but this does not need to be done immediately. Just take a look, familiarize yourself with the ability to customize the system at this level, and then plan a strategy session to go over how you want to approach these options. Essentially, you can rename Partners to Distributors, Manufacturing Representatives, or whatever works for your organization. Likewise, Customers may become Clients, Class may become Product Line, Case may become Ticket, and so on. Keep in mind that these changes affect all records across all subsidiaries in your organization.

You can also rename transaction records and alter the abbreviations for transactions. For example, you may want to change Estimate to Proposal. You can also change the abbreviation for transactions; so, for example, EST becomes PROP. Abbreviations often show up in lists and reports.

States/Provinces/Counties

The US States, Canadian Provinces, and British Counties are delivered in the standard OneWorld edition, sold in these countries (USA, Canada, and United Kingdom). If the countries where your subsidiaries are located are not included in this short list, then you will want to add both the country and its next subdivision, be that states, provinces, or counties. When you go to add subsidiaries, you will need to locate each one in a state/country. The subsidiary's country determines its edition. Subsidiaries located in the USA use the US edition, while a Canadian subsidiary uses the CA edition. NetSuite delivers editions for the US, Canada, Australia, United Kingdom, Japan, and an international edition that covers all other countries. For the international edition, the user must set up the correct taxation.

Again, it's not important to make decisions at this point. Just be aware of these options, as you move through the rest of this chapter.

Countries

OneWorld comes with most countries already defined. Each country definition includes their address template setup, and a snippet of JavaScript that integrates mapping functionality into OneWorld. Both of these allow customer edits.

General preferences

There are some basic account preferences that need to be set for your OneWorld account to operate as you require. Most of these are not difficult to understand, so here, we only cover the ones that we think you should spend some time thinking about.

Setting the general preferences

Log in as the administrator and navigate to **Setup | Company | General Preferences**.

- **Add Primary Contact to Bill to Address**: Very useful for business-to-business sales where you want to make sure that your primary contact receives the invoice. You can always add a different **Attention To** on any address.

- **Show Display Name with Item Codes**: If you are using SKUs to name items, then **Show Display Name with Item Codes** adds a lot of value for new sales and service reps who don't know the catalog by heart.

- **Auto Name Customers**: This option, by itself, simply means that your customer's ID will automatically be their company's name or their first and last name. When combined with the **Auto-numbering** of the customer record, this option means that the customer will have a numeric ID, in addition to their company's name or their first and last name. With **Auto-numbering** turned on, the customer will display as **12345 Thomas Foydel** or **12345 SightLines Consulting**.

After setting up the **General Preferences**, you can also take a look at the tabs on the bottom-half of the form. Here, you can decide whether or not to allow your users to override the **General Preferences** on their **Personal Preferences**, on the **Overriding Preferences** tab, or which languages to translate your web properties into, on the **Languages** tab or **Sign-out landing** page for online center/users.

Now it's time to take a short look at the personal preferences that we just mentioned. They are very similar to the **General Preferences**, with a few additions.

Personal preferences

The personal preferences are useful for making the system more comfortable to work with, but they are not required at this point in the implementation. We suggest that you get the system pretty close to completion, and then during training, you introduce your users to the personal preferences. At this point, it might be worthwhile to take a look at some of these and just familiarize yourself with the preferences.

There are some important setups that happen on the personal preferences such as checking printing offsets and setting your default bank account. It's worth your time to take a look at these now, though, again, you do not need to make all of these decisions now.

Setting preferences

Log in with any role and roll over your **Home** tab; you will see the **Set Preferences** option at the bottom of the menu. Alternatively, you can click the **Home** tab and find the **Set Preferences** option at the bottom of the left-hand panel on the **Home** dashboard.

Printing, fax, and e-mail preferences

There are some important preferences to set up here, regarding both transactions and e-mail. We won't get into every one as many are self-explanatory, but let's cover the most important ones that can affect how the core system works for you.

Setting printing, fax, and e-mail preferences

Log in as the administrator and navigate to **Setup | Company | Printing, Fax & Email Preferences**.

- **Check Printing - Default Type**: There are two options here, namely, **Voucher** and **Standard**. The **Voucher** check prints the check on top and two vouchers below. The **Standard** check simply prints the check.

- **PDF - Add Extra Space Between Lines**: This option adds a line between the line items on printed sales and purchase documents, making them much easier to read.

- **Messages**: The message disclaimers are meant for standard HTML documents. These messages do not apply to custom forms, unless you specifically add it to custom forms. Most OneWorld customers customize their forms, so these options probably do not apply to you.

- **Transactions – Use Popup for Main Transaction Email Button**: If you select this option, then when a user clicks the **Email** button on a **Sales** form, the **New Email** message form opens, allowing them to select a template, enter a message, add the transaction as a PDF attachment, and so on. If you do not select this option, then when you click the **Email** button on a sales form, an HTML e-mail is sent with the sales order embedded in the mail.

Customer relationship management

There are three modules in the CRM system: **marketing**, **sales**, and **service**. Let's go through each one and discuss some of the main functions, and then we'll look at the processes that link them together. Our purpose here is to introduce the modules in your OneWorld account. We dive into the details as we move through the chapters.

Marketing functions

The main functions in OneWorld Marketing are **marketing campaigns**, **marketing templates**, and **groups**. Marketing also includes the **upsell manager** and **promotion codes**, which we will cover in depth in *Chapter 5, Nuts and Bolts of OneWorld CRM*.

Marketing templates

Marketing templates can be used for online lead capture forms and e-mail blasts. In the case of the online lead form, you have brought a new lead to your website through organic or paid search, or through a referral, perhaps by an affiliate. Once on your site's landing page, they are led though a series of pages and made an offer of some collateral, whitepaper, case study, and so on. In return, they provide some of their information, normally company name, their e-mail, their first and last name, and so on. Lead capture is normally done for B2B businesses, but there is nothing that prevents you from using it for B2C marketing in some instances.

After the lead is in the system, you can do follow-up e-mail marketing, again using templates of your invention. Templates for e-mail marketing are simpler than templates for online lead forms, because e-mail templates are only concerned with presentation of information. E-mail templates can capture opens and clicks, but they do not capture new lead records like the online form. (You could, however, direct an e-mail recipient to an online form and capture their clicks and form submits on their record.)

Templates can be built in OneWorld or they can be built outside the system, in an HTML editor, for example, and then imported. The online lead form template, once built, is placed on your website in an `iframe`, as follows:

```
<iframe src ="
   https://forms.netsuite.com/app/site/crm/externalleadpage.nl?
   compid=12345678&formid=2&h=123456789" width="100%" height="300">
</iframe>
```

Downloading the example code

You can download the example code files for all Packt books you have purchased from your account at `http://www.PacktPub.com`. If you purchased this book elsewhere, you can visit `http://www.PacktPub.com/support` and register to have the files e-mailed directly to you.

It can also be placed as a simple link, as follows:

```
<a href="
   https://forms.netsuite.com/app/site/crm/externalleadpage.nl?
   compid=12345678&formid=2&h=123456789">
   Please Click here to download our whitepaper.
</a>
```

When you save the online template, the system generates the publishable URL to use in either the `iframe` or the `link`, as shown previously.

You set up the e-mail template in the system and then you use it in a marketing campaign. In fact, you can set up a single HTML template in the system and then add the verbiage and links specific to each campaign, performing a **Save As** with each copy.

Marketing campaigns

The marketing campaign is the record in which we organize our marketing events, including everything from pay-per-click and trade shows, to banner ads and e-mail blasts. This record tells us what we did, when we did it, and what the response was, when measureable. For example, when we do an e-mail campaign, we can look up the number of e-mails that we sent, the number that were opened, the number that were clicked through, and so on. There are marketing reports that give us these measurements also.

Advanced site analytics

If you need to know more details about the activity on your website, above and beyond the online lead capture form, take a look at our discussion on advanced site analytics, which is an add-on module that captures all of the activity on your site and marries this activity with the lead/prospect and customer records in your account.

Marketing campaigns also hold information about the cost of marketing. Cost can be obvious in some campaigns, like the cost of a trade show, for example, and not so obvious in others, like the cost of an e-mail campaign. To the degree possible, it's useful to track costs at the campaign level, simply to keep track of their value. There are marketing reports that tell us the number of sales resulting from a campaign as well. Comparing revenues to costs is useful for determining the marketing budget in the future. We cover some of the ways to measure marketing in later chapters.

Groups

A group is a set of people or companies from the system. Groups can be used for several different functions, but here, we want to target the group in an e-mail marketing campaign. The group could include any entity from the system: contacts, vendors, leads, prospects, customers, employees, or partners. The group members constitute the recipients of an e-mail campaign. We generate the group either by selecting the members one-by-one or by using a search. OneWorld also supports dynamic search for groups, meaning that records are added to the group dynamically as they self-select, based on the search's criteria. Each time we use the search for a campaign, we have a fresh list of group members.

For an e-mail campaign, we bring the template and the group together on the campaign record, and tell the system when we want to execute the campaign. Later, we can go back and find out how well our campaign succeeded, by looking at the bounces, the opens, and the clicks.

Another example of a marketing campaign is the **trade show**. Again, we generate the marketing campaign, hopefully before we attend the trade show, with all the information about the show. Then, all of the leads that we gather at the show are linked to the trade show when we create their records in OneWorld. When we use the marketing function in OneWorld, the field **lead source** contains the initial marketing campaign, which brought the lead to us.

To set up the marketing function for e-mail and online lead forms

As an administrator, navigate to **Setup | Company | Enable Features**, and from the **CRM** tab, click on **Marketing Automation** under **Basic Features**. Under **Marketing**, click on **Online Forms**, **Mail Merge**, **Capture Email Replies**, **Subscription Categories**, and **Sales Campaigns**. By accepting these base functions, you will be able to set up marketing (details in *Chapter 4, Nailing OneWorld Basics* and *Chapter 5, Nuts and Bolts of OneWorld CRM*).

This brief discussion of the main marketing functions should start to make some ideas click in your own mind. How are you developing your new business? How do you engage new leads? Once engaged, how do you create the trust and confidence to pursue a sale?

With the new workflow manager, you may also enhance the marketing functions to perform fairly sophisticated drip marketing campaigns. These are campaigns where a lead/prospect/customer receives an e-mail campaign, and based on their response, further campaigns are sent. Workflows like this are also now called **lead nurturing**.

Sales functions

The sales functions you use are largely dependent on your business model. If your business model includes a long sales cycle, over a month, for example, then you probably need opportunity management. If you have a direct sales model, then you will use lead routing, sales territories, and so on.

There are several main sales functions that we want to cover in this section. They include the following:

- Sales territories
- Customer statuses

- Opportunity management
- Sales force automation
- Sales quotas
- Selling through the partner channel
- Sales commissions

The purpose of covering the main sales functions of OneWorld is to provide you with a big picture of how your marketing efforts eventually move leads into the sales cycle and how the sales cycle moves forward to revenue.

To enable the sales functions of OneWorld

Log into OneWorld as an administrator and navigate to **Setup | Company | Enable Features**. Under the **Transactions** tab, select **Estimates** and **Sales Orders**. Under the **CRM** tab, in the **Basic Features** section, select **Customer Relationship Management** and **Sales Force Automation**. In the **Sales** section, select **Opportunities**. There are several other options that affect sales functions in OneWorld, and we will cover these in *Chapter 4, Nailing OneWorld Basics* and *Chapter 5, Nuts and Bolts of OneWorld CRM.*

Sales territories

Territories have a single role in NetSuite, which is to route leads to sales reps. A territory can be set up with one or more sales rules, and each sales rule is set up based on a system record and field. For example, it is quite common to set up sales territories based on states, but in some of the larger states, such as California and Texas, it's necessary to split-up the state by zip codes. A territory for this example could contain a rule for Oklahoma and another rule for some Texas zip codes. When new leads with address come into OneWorld, the system automatically assigns them a sales rep, based on their address.

We also build sales territories, based on customer type. For example, you may have two versions of the same product: one version for the retail market and another version for the commercial market. Likewise, you match your territories to customer type, by setting up territory rules, based on whether the lead is an individual or a company. Two sales people work on the same geographic area, the Great Lakes, for example, but we route individual retail leads to Jason and company commercial leads to Lisa.

Customer statuses

Customer statuses are essentially the steps of the sales process, as your company understands them. Let's start our discussion by breaking it down, just as OneWorld does, into stages and statuses.

Lead, prospect, and customer are simply the three stages of the customer record in OneWorld. Each of these stages also may have one or more statuses. The lead stage may include both unqualified and qualified leads; the prospect may be 'In Discussion' or 'In Negotiation'. There is a single customer record in OneWorld that moves through the lead, prospect, and customer stages, and all of their attendant statuses.

Stages and statuses can be set manually, by the user working with the record, or they can be set automatically, by the **Sales Force Automation (SFA)** setup. We cover SFA below.

The important thing to remember is that statuses carry a percentage that provides a weighted amount, per opportunity or estimate. So a 1,000 dollar opportunity 'In Discussion' at 20 percent probability is a 200 dollar line on the pipeline report.

Opportunity management

Once a sales person or partner identifies a new lead, possibly from a trade show, an online registration or even a cold call, they start the sales cycle. Where should the sales cycle begin in any company? This is always an interesting question. To answer this question for OneWorld users, let's understand what an **opportunity** is first.

In some CRM systems, an opportunity is a stage in the customer cycle. A new lead arrives in the system, they become an opportunity, and then, finally, an account. You can think of it as a noun—an opportunity is what the relationship is at that moment in time.

In OneWorld, the opportunity is a step in the sales cycle. You can think of it as a verb—an opportunity is the first clear action of the sales process. A new lead arrives in the system. We work it until we come to the point where it looks like we have a chance to do business, and we start to focus resources as a result. To affirm our commitment, we generate the opportunity.

This action does a couple of important things for us:

1. It changes the record from stage lead to stage prospect.
2. It adds the opportunity and its value to our pipeline and forecast reports.

The sales person or partner uses the opportunity to tell sales management *This is where I am spending my time, and these are the odds of closing this business, and if we do close this business, then this is the present value we will add to revenue.*

Obviously, given this example, the opportunity has great weight with OneWorld users who have longer sales cycles, higher sales revenue per transaction, and either a direct sales team or a partner channel.

The most important point, and one that we always spend a fair amount of time on with clients, is that opportunities are a transaction in OneWorld, not a stage in the lifecycle of a customer as in other CRM systems. Think about it like this: You are working on a dual track. On one track there is the lead record. On the other track there are the transactions that are part of the sales cycle. In the section on SFA next, we will go into more detail on these two tracks and how they work together to manage sales in the system. It should suffice to say, at this point, that opportunities are an important addition to the sales process, when you are tracking a long sales cycle.

We should also note here that opportunity management is up to you; you can use it or choose not to. If you do not have a long sales cycle, or if you sell primarily over the Internet, then you can probably skip opportunity management. If you are sending estimates after a long sales process, opportunities provide an excellent way to keep track of the sales process as it moves forward.

Sales force automation

Setting up the customer statuses also gives the OneWorld user the ability to set up SFA. We can tell the system, for example, that when we open an opportunity on a lead, to change their stage to prospect and change their status to 'In Discussion', at 25 percent. Likewise, when we generate an estimate from the opportunity, we tell the system to change the status to the estimate provided, which increases the probability to 50 percent. Finally, when the estimate becomes a sales order, the prospect advances to a 'Customer - Closed Won' at 100 percent. This is the functionality of SFA. The benefit clearly is that it helps us to manage records with as few clicks as possible; it keeps the customer cycle and the sales cycle synchronized. Consider the following diagram:

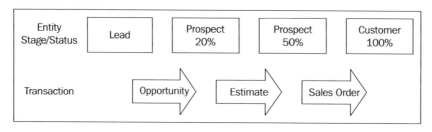

This diagram depicts the changes in **Entity Stage/Status** as the sales person performs actions in the system. Opening an **Opportunity** on a **Lead**, for example, changes the entity from a **Lead** to a **Prospect 20%**. Likewise, the **Estimate** and **Sales Order** also make changes in the **Entity Stage/Status**.

With SFA, your company adopts a process that sales reps, partners, accounting, and operations, and most importantly management, can use to their advantage. Instead of a lot of idiosyncratic sales prognostications, you view and respond to a true business forecast.

Sales quotas and forecasts

Now that you have a sales process running, it's time to measure your progress. There are as many ways of measuring sales proficiency as there are sales teams, but the key point, before we get to the OneWorld functions, is that your sales process, sales metrics, and your sales compensation have to be a whole, each part supporting and enhancing the other pieces. When you have a clear sales program, you have a clear understanding and clear chance at success. When the pieces are not in sync, it gives rise to confusion.

A sales quota is a management's sales job. You sell your reps on your numbers. You sell them on the fact that your numbers have a foundation in the real world, and as a result, your numbers are a motivation.

OneWorld enables quotas setup on various combinations of the components of your business model. If you have three major product lines, then you establish a quota for each line and for the periods of the year. For longer sales cycles, you may have a quarterly quota, while for shorter sales cycles, you may have a monthly quota. Each OneWorld account owner selects monthly or quarterly as the quota/forecast period.

You establish quotas for each of your sales people, and also team quotas for your sales managers. Then, you also establish a forecast for each rep. Of course, you can always look at pipeline and forecast reports to see the big picture, but if you want to look at each sales rep individually, then you can view all of their activity on the sales forecast. The tabs of the forecast break out opportunities, estimates, sales orders, and actual invoices. Each OneWorld account owner decides if they want to allow edits to forecasts on the forecast form.

We also establish forecasts for sales managers. These forecasts roll up the efforts of the manager's sales team by individual team members.

Selling through the partner channel

Many business models include a partner channel; some even include a multi-layer partner channel, in addition to (or in place of) a direct sales team. Partners are called many different things, depending on the industry, and the OneWorld name can be changed to reflect this reality.

When using OneWorld to manage your partner channel, it's important to realize that there are two levels: The **delivered partner center**, which does not require licensing, and the **Advanced Partner Center (APC)**, which is licensed just like regular users of the system, but at a reduced rate.

In either case, the partner only has access to their own records, meaning the records where they are identified as the partner. For the Partner Center, the partner can only see the lead, prospect, customer records, and a few sales reports. They may add a new record, but they have no access to read or write individual transactions, such as opportunities, estimates, and sales orders.

In the APC, the partner can not only view, add, and edit customer records, but they can also view, add, and edit sales transactions records, if you enable this level of access. All partners, of course, follow the same security requirements and setup as any other user. They view and do what you allow through their security setup.

If you are using NetSuite for e-commerce, each partner includes a referring URL that can be placed on the partner's website. Any visitor to your partner's website who clicks on the link will be directed to your website, and if they register, they are automatically associated with the partner. This can be a very powerful way for partners to generate leads for your company.

Some of the functionality available to direct sales reps is not available to partners. For example, partners do not have quotas or forecasts and they cannot be routed to leads through the use of territories, such as direct reps.

You can, however, automatically calculate a partner's commission, as you can for direct sales people.

Sales commissions

As we noted above, sales commissions should be one piece, a very important piece, of a total sales program, built with the goal of motivating sales in your business model. OneWorld gives you the opportunity to create an integrated sales program, because it provides the functionality to link the pieces together. You can, for example, base your forecasts and your commissions on quotas. If you do not use quotas, and it is your choice of course, then you can still create commissions based on any number of components of your business model, such as product lines, sales dollars, or quantities.

Commissions are built in two parts, namely, schedules and plans. Schedules are where we identify what we are commissioning and how; plans are how we group schedules and assign them to our reps and partners.

Commission schedules allow us to designate what commissions are based on, when we calculate commissions (by period or quarterly), and when they become eligible for calculation, based on sales, invoices, or collections. Schedules also allow us to use multiple tiers, as a rep's sales climb, they reap higher commissions.

We will examine the commissions functionality in detail in *Chapter 5, Nuts and Bolts of OneWorld CRM*.

Customer service functions

OneWorld customer service functions enable you to generate, route, and escalate service cases and, over time, build knowledge bases of solutions.

Service cases

Let's start by explaining that a service case is the record that links the customer's question/problem/issue/requirement, with the customer's record, and then saves the history of all communications on the case as you work toward resolution. The service case also serves as the place where we assign and escalate cases to specific service reps and managers.

Service cases can be used to resolve problems or to schedule service calls. Service might be included in your product or service, or you might want to charge for each service case.

There are three ways to generate a service case: **manually**, by **e-mail**, or by **online case form**. A customer service rep can create a case manually while speaking to the customer, of course. A customer in the customer center can also create a case manually. The customer can also generate a case by using an online case form or by sending an e-mail to the support e-mail address, called **E-mail Case Capture**. Any of these three methods—manual, online case form, and e-mail, perform the same function of generating a service case for a specific customer.

The online case form is very similar in functionality to the online lead capture form. There are some required fields, and you can add or remove others. You can also design the form's behavior. Once you save the form, the system generates a URL that you place on your website. Most companies that use online case forms will place them in an `iframe`, so that they appear on a regular page of the system.

If you offer e-mail case capture to your customers, you need to identify a specific e-mail address for case capture; be aware that placing your service e-mail address on your website can cause you some grief with the spammers. We suggest that you let customers know about e-mail case capture through your monthly marketing newsletter.

Service case assignment

Once we generate a case, we must assign it to a service rep who can work towards resolution. Assignment can be manual, by having a supervisor assign cases, or by allowing service reps to grab unassigned cases from a case queue.

Alternatively, we assign cases automatically, by using service territories. Territories are set up with rules, based on some criteria such as the case issue, the case type, or the location of the customer. Once we have one or a set of rules, we create a territory and assign it to a rep. Service territories operate in much the same way as sales territories, with the addition of service-oriented criteria.

Case escalation

Escalation rules are similar to the case assignment rules, with the addition of criteria measuring the length of time since a case was opened or last modified, and so on. You set up one or more of the escalation rules and then assign them to a territory. You assign the territory to a senior person in your company. You can also build the escalation function to have a hierarchy of escalation, from the service rep to the service manager, to the operations VP. The goal is to prevent a service case from falling through the cracks, if a service rep is out sick or leaves for vacation.

Help desk

You can also use the support system as an internal help desk for all technical matters. Help desk cases have a few special points to remember: they can be initiated, viewed, and edited from the employee center, whereas the normal cases cannot (they also do not show up on the case reports). Help desk cases are meant for internal tickets, opened by internal employees, and worked and closed by internal employees. Once enabled, the help desk function places a help desk case form on the employee center. With this form, employees can generate new cases for any issue that they might have.

Knowledge base

The knowledge base is a set of functions that together enable you to generate an organizational memory. You can create solutions to a service case or to general business questions, and then categorize these solutions under topics. Topics are then linked to one or more knowledge bases. The knowledge base can be published to a tab, available to internal users of the system, as in the following screenshot:

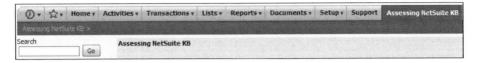

Knowledge bases may also be published to other centers, such as the employee center or vendor centers. We will describe the setup and use of knowledge bases further in *Chapter 5, Nuts and Bolts of OneWorld CRM*. At this time, it is important to understand that when you start the implementation process, it's a good idea to keep a log of the processes that are key to your business model, so that you can eventually write a solution for each of them and keep them in one of your knowledge bases.

You can also publish important documents to a knowledge base tab, such as generic sales contracts, or employee handbooks. This makes it easy to find documents that are used often.

Enabling customer service in your OneWorld account

Log in with the administrator's role and navigate to **Setup | Company | Enable Features**. On the **CRM** tab, under **Support**, select the following: **Email Case Capture**, **Automated Case Escalation**, **Knowledge Base**, and **Help Desk**.

Enterprise resource planning

We often call CRM the customer-facing frontend of the system, and we call ERP the backend of OneWorld, obviously with the meaning of the back office, the operations, accounting, and people of the organization. In this section, we take a look at the primary back office functions—accounting, operations, and human resources.

We are going to take a slightly different approach with ERP than CRM, because there are several prerequisites that have to be understood before we can discuss the main ERP functions and processes.

In later chapters, we break down the ERP modules further to the more common accounts payable, account receivable, and so on. Again, the main point here is to explain the foundation of OneWorld and enable the most basic functions, so that we can jump in with both feet, as we get started on more specific areas later.

Currencies

Currencies are one of the base setups required by OneWorld. Before you set up subsidiaries, you must set up currencies and tax nexuses. Each subsidiary requires a base currency. If you have three subsidiaries in the United States, then you only need USD setup as a base currency. If you have subsidiaries in Canada, the United States, and Mexico, then you must have Canadian Dollar, USD, and Mexican Peso all set up as base currencies.

Currency setup is simple, actually. NetSuite delivers OneWorld with four base currencies already set up: US Dollars, Canadian Dollars, Euros, and British Pounds. You may add any other base currency you require. If any of your subsidiaries sell or purchase using other currencies, then you must also set these currencies up. You can set up non-base currencies at any time. For now, make sure that you have all of the base currencies that you need in order to set up the subsidiaries.

For base currencies setup

Log in as an administrator and navigate to **Setup | Company | Enable Features**. On the **Company** tab, under **International**, enable **Multiple Currencies**. If you want to update exchange rates daily, you may also enable the **Currency Exchange Rate Integration** at this time.

Adding additional currencies

Log in as the administrator and from **Lists | Accounting | Currencies | New**, you can add additional currencies to the system.

Now you are ready to use any of the base currencies required by your subsidiaries. Keep in mind that the consolidated few of your organization, meaning the roll-up of all of your subsidiaries, will use the currency of the parent or root subsidiary.

Subsidiaries

OneWorld identifies every legal entity in your organization as a subsidiary. When you first open your OneWorld account, you will find that there is already a single subsidiary in the system. You use this as the parent organization and then fill in the rest of the organization pyramid, by adding new subsidiaries and rolling them up to their parents.

So each subsidiary represents a legal entity, normally. Then there are also subsidiaries for elimination entries. In order to use the InterCompany Auto Elimination, you need elimination subsidiaries on every level of your hierarchy.

It's also worth pointing out at this time that OneWorld assumes that all subsidiaries are wholly owned by their parent.

A typical subsidiary hierarchy might look like the following:

Subsidiaries		
Edit | View	Name ▲	Elimination
Edit | View	HEADQUARTERS	No
Edit | View	AMERICAS	No
Edit | View	Americas Elimination	Yes
Edit | View	Canada	No
Edit | View	US - East	No
Edit | View	US - West	No
Edit | View	APAC	No
Edit | View	Australia	No
Edit | View	Japan	No
Edit | View	EMEA	No
Edit | View	Denmark	No
Edit | View	Germany	No
Edit | View	United Kingdom	No

The indentation reflects the hierarchy roll-up.

Setting up subsidiaries requires first that you understand your subsidiary hierarchy completely. We suggest that you start on whiteboard and sketch the subsidiaries in a fashion similar to the following diagram:

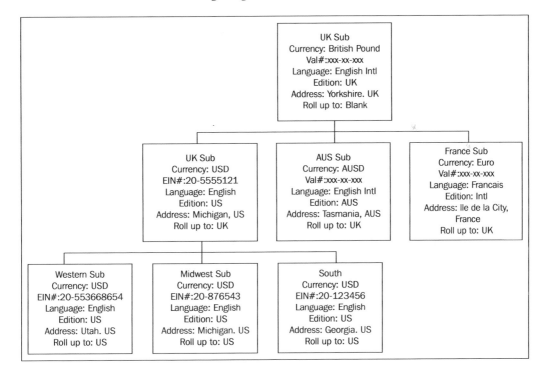

This is a simple hierarchy and we have not yet identified elimination subsidiaries. But, hopefully, the diagram serves to help you start to organize the task of understanding your subsidiaries.

In any event, it's a very good idea to organize your subsidiaries first before starting the process of setting them up in OneWorld. The setup is straightforward and should not take any time at all. The organization task itself may take several days, depending on your record keeping.

Top-level subsidiary

The question always arises: *Do we need to implement a top level entity only for the purpose of consolidation?* The answer is no. OneWorld automatically consolidates to a complete view of the organization, rolling up to the actual parent subsidiary; so you do not need to add a subsidiary in order to gain the benefit of consolidation.

Locations, classes, and departments

We will discuss the set up of departments, classes, and locations in *Chapter 4, Nailing OneWorld Basics,* but here we want to help you understand how to use these fields to deliver important processes and metrics to your business. They are important to know, because they also impact the setup of the chart of accounts, and they have links to subsidiaries as well.

Locations

This is the most important of the three classifications for any business with inventory. (There is no reason that you cannot use locations in a business that has no inventory, but just beware that if you should add inventory to your business model later, it may require changes to your location definition.)

Locations are places where you have inventory. When you receive a purchase order, you receive it into a location. When you fulfill an order you, you fulfill it from a location. You may choose to make a location's inventory available or not, also. So if you receive returns, you receive them into a location from which they are not again available for sale. These are a few of the most normal uses of locations.

Locations are key for reporting the count and value of inventory. This is always done by location. As a result, transactions that impact the cost of goods sold account, such as PO receipts and SO fulfillments, are always tagged with a location. Locations are necessarily used on both expense and revenue transactions for organizations with inventory.

You may also designate a location's transactions with a location-specific logo and transaction prefix, allowing your organization to segregate transactions, by location both internally, to you and other employees, and externally to your customers and vendors.

 Last key point: Each location belongs to one and only one subsidiary.

Classes

A class is simply another way of tagging transactions, so that you can measure later what was sold or purchased. Classes are most often used on revenue transactions, but there is no reason why you can't use a class with expense transactions.

 Classes may belong to one or more subsidiaries.

Departments

Departments are where your employees and contractors work and it's also a way of tagging transactions. Normally, we use departments for expense-side transactions, such as department costs, but they can also be used for revenue-side transactions, as in the example of multiple sales offices.

 Departments may belong to one or more subsidiaries.

Accounting functions and processes

Setting up OneWorld accounting is always an exciting time. Since it is often step one of the actual system implementation, the beginning of the journey generates an air of expectation and anticipation. So get a hold of yourself, because the real work begins here.

Of course, a lot of your focus in this section depends on your business model. If you buy and sell inventory, you have a completely different set of needs from a company selling consulting hours or software. We try to keep the discussion at a level where it has meaning and value for any organization. Here we explain what OneWorld offers, not dwelling on the actual setup.

Advanced taxes

As a OneWorld customer, you probably operate in multiple locations. As a result, you have multiple tax nexuses. A tax nexus is a term for the connection your company has to a taxing authority or jurisdiction. This might include a physical location within a tax jurisdiction, employees within a tax jurisdiction, or sales people who solicit business within the jurisdiction. For any of these situations, you may require a tax nexus. You will have to set up each of these nexuses in OneWorld. First, you must enable the advanced taxes feature.

Enabling advanced taxes

Log in as the administrator and navigate to **Setup | Company | Enable Features**, and on the **Accounting** tab, under **Advanced Features**, enable **Advanced Taxes**.

OneWorld assumes correctly that you have a tax nexus for each subsidiary address. To clarify, if you have three subsidiaries, all incorporated in Ontario, Canada, then you will have a single tax nexus, as a result of your subsidiary setup. All three are linked to the same nexus. On the other hand, if you have three subsidiaries, each in their own US State, then you will have three tax nexuses as a result of your subsidiary setup. Each subsidiary is linked to a state tax nexus.

Once you have successfully set up your subsidiaries, you may continue to set up any other tax nexuses that you have. We will cover setting up taxation in detail later on in the book.

The Chart of Accounts (COA)

At the heart of every ERP is the chart of accounts. OneWorld is much easier to understand than some we have seen. Each account has a type, a name, and in most cases, a number. It may or may not roll up to another account. There are a few other details about accounts, and we cover these later.

Sounds simple, we know. The difficulty is in adjusting your COA from your current system to OneWorld's functionality. We suggest that you keep the following in mind:

- You may need a simpler COA. There are older systems still in use, in which management, in order to see key performance indicators (KPIs) clearly, put as much detail as possible into the general ledger. For many, the G/L became the source for all reporting. As a result, their COA reflected a ton of details about the business. We've seen COAs with revenue and cost of goods sold accounts for every product, and expense reimbursement accounts, by employee. OneWorld offers you a sub ledger for each functional area of the organization that precludes the need for so much detail in the general ledger.

- Unlike some of the shelf accounting packages, OneWorld has extensive functionality to create an item catalog for inventory, non-inventory, service, and other types of items that you purchase and sell. The item catalog in combination with the sub ledgers provides a lot of visibility into what you sell and what you purchase. Keep this in mind, because it means that you do not have to have accounts for individual products. You can look into the inventory, sales, or purchasing sub ledgers for the information that you need about specific item transactions.

- OneWorld enables you to tag your transactions with other data, so that you can slice-and-dice your report later. If you have an inventory, you will receive it to a location and sell if from a location. As a result, you can look at your financial report, by location. Likewise, you can sell a class of items and report sales by class. We discuss locations, classes, and departments in great detail in *Chapter 04, Nailing OneWorld Basics*.

For now, it's important to understand that your COA might change in OneWorld. Also, a new system implementation might be a good opportunity to take a look at the COA and get rid of some of the weird things that seem to accumulate there over the years. Normally, we see several accounts in any COA that have no known meaning, at least that anyone can remember. A new system is a good time to clean some of this up and also try to make the COA more logical.

Best practice for an SME COA is a four- or five-digit field for number, where we associate the starting number with an account type:

- 1 covers assets, such as inventory, cash, AR, and fixed assets
- 2 covers liabilities, such as wages payable, AP, and loans payable
- 3 covers equity, such as common shares and owner's draw
- 4 covers income, such as product or service revenue and shipping charges to customers
- 5 covers cost of goods or services sold, such as the cost of a product
- 6 and 7 cover expenses, such as SGA expenses
- 8 covers other expenses, such as interest expenses on your loan
- 9 covers other income, such as interest income, for example

This is not etched in stone, of course, but seems to be fairly well understood in the accounting community. Keep in mind that you do not have to use account numbers. But once you turn account numbers on, every account you set up must have one. If you want to use a mix of numbered and unnumbered accounts, set up the unnumbered first and then turn on the account numbers.

You should start looking at your COA during the system selection process and address any issues that you can in the legacy system. One thing that will always hurt a little during implementation is the balance transfers that you use to synchronize the legacy system and OneWorld. After you make changes to your COA, you must also change mapping for your balances to reflect these account changes. Keep a list of all your changes handy.

Also, OneWorld automatically rolls up accounts by type. For example, on your P/L report, it rolls up all of your income accounts to income. You may still wish to have a separate roll-up account, but it is not necessary. However, if you want to create custom financial reporting, it's a good idea to have your own roll-up accounts.

When you first open your OneWorld account, you'll notice that you have a number of accounts already in the system. We suggest that you keep these base accounts and simply edit their name and number as required. Importing the COA is popular, so just keep in mind that after you manually change the delivered OneWorld accounts, some of your lines on the import will fail due to duplication. Not a huge problem, all of the other accounts will still import okay.

To view the delivered accounts

Log in to the system as an administrator, navigate to **Lists | Accounting | Accounts**, and click on the word **Accounts**. This brings up a list of all the delivered accounts. In the footer of the list, you will see a checkbox for **Report Style**. Having this checked is useful, if you want to run a report. But if you uncheck it, you will see the **Edit** column on the left-hand side of the list. You can now click **Edit** on any account and see the account setup in detail.

To enable the main accounting features

Log in as an administrator and navigate to **Setup | Company | Enable Features**. On the first tab, **Company**, enable **Departments**, **Classes**, and **Locations**. On the **Accounting** tab, make sure that you have **Accounting, A/R, A/P**, and **Accounting Periods** enabled.

Enable the ERP functions and processes

We have enabled the main accounting features, as described previously. Now we want to walk through the rest of the accounting features. Once enabled, we will be ready to talk in detail about each of these features. For now, we want to give you a good understanding of what they mean, how they work, and how they work together.

We go into the details of using all of these features in later chapters.

To enable ERP features

Log in as the administrator and navigate to **Setup | Company | Enable Features**. We will spend the rest of this section here. You will likely not find every feature that we describe here in your account. This is because many of the features need to be purchased before they can be enabled. If you did not purchase revenue recognition, you will not see this feature on the **Accounting** tab.

The Company tab

We have already discussed several of the features on the **Company** tab, including the **Classification** and **International** features. The other features on this tab are the following:

- **Multi-Currency Customers**: Enable this feature to sell to a single customer in more than one currency. Each customer has a primary currency and as many secondary currencies as they need.

- **Projects**: This feature is useful for organizations that have jobs or projects as sub-records of the customer record. The functionality of this feature is limited, however, and most project-based organizations will also require **Advanced Projects** (see next). If you are a product-based company that does some project work and you wish to capture information on the project such as activities, communications, and documents, then the base **Projects** by itself might work for you.

- **Advanced Projects** (additional module): This takes the basic **Projects** and enhances it with the ability to resource a project and its tasks, measure progress and bill based on process, process time and materials to the project, and track the progress of your projects from its sale to completion. If you enable **Advanced Projects**, also enable **Projects**.

- **KPI Scorecards**: This is for reporting metrics on the dashboard. A KPI scorecard compares one **Key Performance Indicator** (**KPI**) to another. Definitely enable this option, even if you cannot get to it right away. You'll want to use these eventually.

- **Pivot Reports Beta**: This option installs a development bundle into your account that allows you to format OneWorld searches, giving them the more refined appearance of standard reports.

- **Direct List Editing**: Enable this, as it will save you a lot of time. **Direct List Editing** allows you to generate a list of data records through a search, and then edit the fields in the list, directly from the list. It's pretty powerful stuff. There are some caveats, but it's still very powerful.

- **File Cabinet**: Allows you to store documents in OneWorld and then attach them to records as you need – a definite plus.

- **Duplicate Detection & Merge**: Some organizations, such as e-tailers, need this feature more than others, but we have never met an organization that never needed it. It helps to keep you data records clean.

- **ODBC Connections for Advanced Reporting** (additional module): Allows you to connect to your data set with a reporting tool such as Crystal Reports or Business Objects. When you have exhausted OneWorld-delivered reporting tools and metrics, this is your next option.

- **IP Address Rules**: If you do not want your office staff to access OneWorld from a cafe, you can limit access to specific IP addresses. Of course, you will need specific IP addresses in this case. Talk to your telecom provider.

The Accounting tab

We have already enabled the basic most common features on the **Accounting** tab. Now let's look at the rest:

- **Expense Allocation** (additional module – Advanced Financials): Allows you to allocate an expense to other departments, classes, locations, accounts, and subsidiaries. You can allocate the marketing expenses from HQ to all of your divisions, for example.

- **Revenue Recognition** (additional module – Revenue Recognition): With this module, you can establish multiple templates that enable the recognition of revenue over time.

- **Revenue Commitments** (additional module – Revenue Recognition): This option enables you to recognize revenue, before you issue an invoice. For example, if you have a project based on milestone billing, but you have monthly expenses, you can start to recognize revenue before achieving your milestone.

- **VSOE** (additional module – Revenue Recognition): **Vendor Specific Objective Evidence (VSOE)** is the functionality that enables a company to sell both a product, such as a software and a support service, and correctly recognize revenue from both, especially if one or more of the items is discounted. In practice, VSOE prevents the discounting of support contracts with less or no discount of the software or other service sold with the support.

- **Sales Order Revenue Forecasting** (additional module – Revenue Recognition): Allows users to forecast deferred revenue as well as earned revenue.

- **Amortization**: (additional module – Advanced Financials): Allows users to set up templates for recognizing prepaid expenses over several periods. For example, if you pay an insurance bill at the beginning of the year, a twelve-month Amortization template schedules a journal entry to recognize an equal expense for the twelve months following. It may also be used for fixed asset depreciation, if you have a few assets to manage.

- **Multiple Budgets**: Allows you to break down your organization into multiple sub units and generate different budgets for each, or generate multiple budgets for the same entity within your organization, such as flat, +10 percent, or +20 percent, for example.

- **Advanced Taxes**: Enables the use of multiple tax nexuses. A nexus is a tax jurisdiction in which you are obligated to collect and pay sales taxes. Also, with **Advanced Taxes**, you create tax schedules that allow you to change the tax treatment of an individual item by nexus; for example, a widget might be taxable in New Jersey but non-taxable in Idaho.

- **Intercompany Time and Expense**: Allows employees who work for one subsidiary to log time and expenses to the customer of another subsidiary.

- **Intercompany Auto Elimination**: Allows you to automatically generate a list of intercompany transactions at period end, drill down to verify each entry, and then post journals that eliminate any artificial profits or losses from intercompany transactions.

- **Consolidated Payments**: If you have parent and child customers, such as a customer headquarters and its multiple divisions, or a leasing company and multiple lessors, then invoicing the children and receiving payments from the parent is an important feature, as is being able to see a consolidated view of all payments.

The Transactions tab

Every organization has different needs when it comes to transactions. Not every organization will want to handle **Purchase Orders (POs)**, and e-commerce organizations probably (but not always) don't want to handle estimates. On the **Transactions** tab, you can decide which of these transactions you want to use.

Of course, use your basic business sense to make your selections. If you do not want to use POs in OneWorld, then you probably also do not want to use vendor returns. Next, we start to give you a better idea of what each of these features brings to the OneWorld table, and how they work together:

- **Estimates**: **Estimates** are often called quotes or proposals, depending on your industry. In many cases, **Estimates** constitute the signed contract with your customer. They are best suited to organizations with direct sales reps or a partner channel, and are not normally required in retail or e-tail.

- **Sales Order (SO)**: A **Sales Order** is the transaction document between an **Estimate** and an invoice. In this respect, the SO serves many purposes. For example, it is the document we use for **Advanced Shipping**, **Advanced Billing**, and **Revenue Recognition**. You can, however, turn the SO off and simply move from the **Estimate** to the invoice.

- **Return Authorizations (RA)**: If you ship products to customers, then using the RA feature is required, so that customers can return goods. However, you may also use the RA feature to allow customers to return other item types.

- **Purchase Orders (PO)**: The **Purchase Order** feature allows you to do both, purchase requisitions from employees that are approved to POs, or straight POs including drop ship and special orders. The main value of POs is that you can receive against a PO, if you turn on **Advanced Receiving**, meaning that you can register the receipt of goods into your organization.

- **Vendor Return Authorizations**: If you purchase goods from a vendor, then you probably may need to return them at some point. This is how **Vendor Return** works.

- **Multiple Prices**: Allows items that you sell to have more than one price, such as a base price, platinum price, and online price. It is used in conjunction with **Price Levels** (see **Accounting Lists** later). **Multiple Prices** and **Quantity Pricing** also works in combination.

- **Gross Profit**: This feature enables the system to calculate an estimated gross profit on sales forms from the setup of your items.

- **Quantity Pricing**: Allows your **Multiple Prices** to also have volume breaks, for example, you can charge ten dollars for one to five, and nine dollars for six to ten. The system will pick up the right price on all sales documents, based on quantity. It can also be used in combination with **Multiple Prices**.

- **Alternate Sales Amount (ASA)**: This feature adds a new column to all sales documents where you can calculate a sales amount that is more, equal, or less than the actual sales amount. The most common use of the ASA is for incentive compensation plans, based on bookings (**Sales Order**). You can also create sales quotas based on ASA.

- **Promotion Codes**: **Promotion Codes** are the most popular way of passing affiliate codes into NetSuite e-commerce. **Promotion Codes** can be linked to affiliate partners, and they can also carry discounts or markups, as the case may be.

- **Advanced Shipping**: This feature gives you a three-step process for the fulfillment of an order. Sales staff or e-commerce customers generate sales orders, operations fulfill the orders, and accounting completes the sales through a cash sale or through an invoice.

- **Pick, Pack and Ship**: This makes the fulfillment a three-step process: picking the stock from the shelves or bins, packing it into a package, and then generating the shipping labels.

- **Shipping Label Integration**: This feature allows integration with one of several shipping companies, and the generation of shipping labels.

- **Advanced Receiving**: Allows the warehouse staff to receive POs in the plant. Accounting can then compare receipts to POs and invoices received from the vendor.

- **Multiple Shipping Routes**: If you have a sales transaction where you are sending products to more than one customer location, then you can use this feature.

- **Bill Costs to Customers**: This feature allows time, material, and expenses entered on a PO to be billed through to a customer invoice.

- **Advanced Billing**: Allows an annual contract to be billed monthly, quarterly, or semi-annually, for example.

- **Credit Card Payments (CC)**: Normally used for e-commerce companies, but any organization that takes CC payments can use this feature. You may use CC payments both through your e-commerce site, or simply manually through the OneWorld order management functions.

- **Credit Card Soft Descriptors**: Simply the option of giving any item a short name or descriptor that your customer sees on the CC bill.

- **Paypal Integration**: Allows the processing of payments through Paypal.

- **Electronic Funds Transfer (EFT)**: This feature allows you to deduct payments from your customer's bank account through NetSuite's integration with the third party, Coastal Bank. Coastal charges for this service apply.

- **Online Bill Pay**: This feature allows you to cut a check through the third party, Metavante, to any entity in OneWorld, such as vendor, customer, employee, and so on. When you are paying bills, it's quite easy to click **Online Bill Pay** and all the checks are printed and mailed for you by Metavante, with your organization's name on the check.

- **ACH Vendor Payments**: Much like EFT transfers, but in this case, the cash flows from your bank account to your vendors, employees, and so on. This is very useful if you have a large number like 1099 contractors and employees needing expense reimbursements or payment for billable time. Most companies paying vendors normally print their own checks or use **Online Bill Pay**.

That's a long list of features and a lot to juggle all at once. But remember, at this point, you only need to start the set up of the features and options in OneWorld. As we implement functions and processes in later chapters, you will return to the base setups required for each OneWorld process.

The Item catalog

This topic deserves its own section, because it is so important to the value you will derive from OneWorld. Before we start discussing the setup of the Item catalog, we must understand, like we did for CRM and ERP, the base setups that are going to impact what we see in OneWorld and how OneWorld responds to our commands.

So let's get started by simply taking a look at the **Items** and **Inventory** tab of the **Enable Features** form. Even if you do not have an actual inventory, it's important to understand all of the options available when setting up your items.

First, under the **Items** section:

- **Drop Shipments & Special Orders**: If you want to generate a PO directly from a **Sales Order**, then you need this feature. A drop ship sends the item directly to the customer from the vendor, and a special order sends the item to you first, perhaps for some tweaking or rebranding, before it moves on to the customer. The key point is that you can generate an automatic PO for the vendor, and the transactions do not impact inventory or cost of goods sold.

- **Multiple Units of Measure**: For a single item, you need to purchase by the pallet, stock by the box, and sell by the carton. Then you need multiple units of measure. Another such example is that you need to purchase by the rolls, stock by the yard, and use by the foot.

- **Matrix Items**: Multiple colors and sizes for one item. Matrix items allow you to generate multiple child items from one parent, and then sell and manage the inventory of the children. It is very common in apparel, but is used in other industries as well.

- **Multiple Vendors**: This feature enables an item to have several vendors linked, providing the ability to purchase the item from any of them, with their SKUs and prices. It can also be used with drop ship and special order items.

- **Gift Certificates**: This feature enables the sale, tracking, and use of **Gift Certificates**. Your customers can purchase a certificate as a gift and the receiver can then use the certificate to purchase items from you. The system tracks the use and the balance of the certificate. This is popular, obviously, in e-commerce.

- **Sell Downloadable files**: For organizations that sell electronic files over their website, this feature enables you to process a checkout and then provide the download capability.

- **Bar Coding and Item Labels**: If you have a lot of products in a warehouse, you may want to use bar codes to identify them on item labels. OneWorld also supports UPC for bar-coded labels. Bar codes can also be used to identify transactions.

Now under the **Inventory** section:

- **Inventory**: Enable this feature if you have products that you want to track in OneWorld, meaning how much you have, how much is available for sale, how much you have on purchase orders, and so on. Obviously, this feature is for organizations that have some products in the mix.

- **Multi-Location Inventory**: If you have products, you probably have multiple locations for these products, even if some of these locations are more virtual than real. For example, you may have one warehouse location, but you probably have a place for broken items, returns, or items you no longer sell. Once you turn on **Multi-Locations Inventory** and distribute products, you cannot turn it off by contacting OneWorld Support. Also, **Multi-Location Inventory** lets you track inventory count and value by location.

- **Assembly Items**: If you take raw materials and assemble them into new items with new SKUs, you will have an assembly. When you assemble, you move the value of the parts, or members, out of Raw Material Inventory and into Finished Goods Inventory. When you ship an assembly, you credit Finished Goods Inventory and debit the **Cost of Goods Sold** for the sum of the members. We only mention this now, because this is what makes assemblies different from, say, Item Group or Kits that we will discuss later. If your COA has Raw Material and Finished Goods Inventory, then you need **Assembly Items**.

- **Work Orders (Additional Module Light Manufacturing required)**: If you want to assemble items based on **Work Orders**, then enable this feature. **Work Orders (WO)** can be generated manually to assemble to stock, or directly from a sales order, if you build to order. **Work Orders** also tell you how much 'member' inventory you need, in order to complete a WO.

- **Serialized Inventory (Additional Module Advanced Inventory required for this option and the next five options)**: This feature enables you to identify each instance of an item with a unique serial number when you purchase or sell it. Serialized inventory can also be used in combination with **Assembly Items** and **Work Orders**. **Serialized Inventory** always has a specific cost.

- **Lot Tracking**: Enable this feature if you want to track 'lots' of inventory. OneWorld tracks each 'lot' with a lot number and an expiration date. Each lot has a lot-specific cost. You can also use Units of Measure with lots, so you could purchase a lot and sell by the bushel, for example.

- **Bin Management**: If you have a large warehouse and need to divide it into more useful and definable areas, then you can enable the **Bin Management** feature. This feature allows you to receive or place finished goods into bins within a location and then fulfill from a bin. If you have multiple buildings, you can name each one a bin and still perform a single fulfillment from one location.

- **Advanced Inventory Management (AIM)**: This feature enables you to predict the demand for your items based on historical sales and purchases. The alternative is to enter reorder points and preferred stock levels for each item. However, these are static and when demand grows, you will have to manually change them. AIM uses an algorithm to calculate your demand forecast and suggest purchase amounts.

- **Advanced Bin/Numbered Inventory Management**: More advanced bin management allows Lot and Serialized items in bins and also allows the placement of inventory into any bin, whether recognized on the item setup or not.

- **Landed Cost**: Enable this feature if you want to add the costs of moving inventory from your vendor to your warehouse into the cost of the item. The alternative is that you simply pay the insurance, duties, shipping fees, and the inventory value equals the amount you paid for it. Landed Cost lets you put the costs of your inventory purchase into the inventory account, and then relieve that cost through Cost of Goods Sold when you sell the item.

- **Standard Costing**: For wholesale distributors and manufacturers, this feature enables the set up of a standard cost on inventory item records and the examination of variances between standard and actual costs.

That takes care of enabling the items and inventory features that you require in order to get started setting up your Item catalog. Next, we look at how some of the features that you enabled can be handled in OneWorld, based on their preferences.

Accounting preferences

Okay, we have come a long way so far in this chapter, but we still have two important steps to take before we jump into OneWorld transactions. First, we have to set up your preferences. The accounting preferences tell the system how you are going to use some of the features that we just enabled. They are actually just a set of flags or simple lists of values that tell OneWorld how you would like to see the system function.

It's important to understand that the preferences will change how OneWorld functions for your organization. Go through these carefully. If you are not sure, you can come back later and choose different options. As we work through OneWorld transactions, we will come back to these preferences, so that you can see how different decisions affect the system.

Many of the preferences are self-explanatory, so we have left our comments as simple as possible, devoting most of our efforts to the preferences that we think are the most important. Remember that if you don't understand a preference, you can always click on the label or click **Help** to read more in-depth explanations. Our job here is to give you some recommendations, based on business models or good business practice.

Setting the accounting preferences

Log in as the administrator and navigate to **Setup | Accounting | Accounting Preferences**. You should see four tabs on this form: **General, Items/Transactions/Order Management/Time and Expenses**.

The General tab

First under the **General Ledger** section, there are several flags we have to set:

- **Use Account Numbers**: Self-explanatory. If you turn this on, every account you create requires a number. It is normally checked.

- **Expand Account Lists**: Set to **Yes**. It means that you will see a complete list of your accounts in many cases. For example, you could set the default expense account of a vendor to a liability account. It is normally checked.

- **Cash Basis Reporting**: If you need to see a report on a cash basis, you can always customize it and set your version to cash basis. It is normally unchecked.

- **Aging Reports Use**: Due date or transaction date, your choice, really. If you use many different terms, then you might want to start aging from the due date, since terms change by customer. If you have a set term for customer invoices, such as Net 15, then you can use the transaction date just the same.

- **Void Transactions Using Reversing Journals**: This preference places a **Void** button on your transactions, which when clicked, generates a journal entry to void the transaction, possibly on a day or period other than the original transaction date or period. The only alternative is to manually make changes to transactions after the fact. It is normally checked.

- **Require Approvals on Journal Entries**: Your supervisor who has approval permission must approve your journals before they post.

- **Enable Accounting Period Window**: Keep open a minimum number of accounting periods (current + future) for transactions.

- **Minimum Period Window Size**: The number of accounting periods to keep open.

- **Allow Transaction Date Outside of Posting Period**: List of values is **Disallow**, **Warn**, and **Allow**. This gives you the option of setting the transaction date on October 15, while booking the transaction in September. It's useful when you want to give the customer the correct date for their terms, while getting your invoices into the correct period.

Next, there are a few preferences for **Accounts Receivable**:

- **Accept Payments Through Top Level Customers Only**: If you sell to a multi-level company, for example, a **headquarters (HQ)** and three divisions, you normally invoice the divisions, and receive payment from the HQ, in most cases. If this is your case, check this preference. Also, this can be used when a lot of companies are using a leasing company.

- **Show Only Open Transactions on Statements**: Your choice, but it's normally checked. However, you can also leave it unchecked, and when you run statements, you can decide at that time to include only open transactions.

- **Customer Credit Limit Handling**: Ignore, Warn, or Enforce Holds. There are some caveats. It does not work with Cash Sales. So if you have a sales counter at your warehouse, a customer could still make purchases. See the next preferences.

- **Customer Credit Limit Includes Orders**: If you check **Yes** to include Sales Orders, not just billed orders, that is, invoices, then you will have better control over late-paying customers. This then also covers e-commerce purchases. These two just depend on the nature of what you sell and to whom.

- **Days Overdue for Warning/Hold**: If you want to show warnings or place holds in the previous two preferences, then tell the system here the number of days overdue to use as a basis for warnings or holds, in an integer number.

- **Include Tax for Term Discounts**: If your organization has term discounts, you can choose to include taxes and shipping in the discount, or not. Since these discounts occur after you generate the invoice, you can choose to apply them against the items only, or the items, taxes, and shipping (see next).

- **Include Shipping for Term Discounts**: Refer to the previous bullet for an explanation.

Then, there are three preferences for **Accounts Payable (A/P)**:

- **Default Vendor Payments To Be Printed**: If you do a check run weekly for vendor payments, then this is a good default to have checked.

- **Vendor Credit Limit Warnings**: If you have a lot of A/P and need to juggle payments, then this is probably a good idea. See *associate preference* later.

- **Vendor Credit Limit Includes Orders**: Choose to include POs or not in the credit-limit calculation. If you think you might not be able to purchase stock when in arrears, then check this preference.

There are several preferences for Departments, Classes, and Locations for the **Classification** section, and their classifications are as follows:

- **Make Departments Mandatory**: See *Make Locations Mandatory*.

- **Make Classes Mandatory**: See *Make Locations Mandatory*.

- **Make Locations Mandatory**: At this time, we would caution you in making Departments, Classes, and Locations mandatory for two reasons:
    - ° First, you will be doing a lot of test transactions and it's a nuisance.
    - ° Second, you will learn a lot doing test transactions, and you'll have a better idea which classifications you want to use and how.

  So, after you have finished testing, come back and make your final configurations for production.

  Last note: By making any of these mandatory here, they will be mandatory on all forms in which they appear. A less constrained approach would be to not select mandatory here, and then make these fields mandatory on only the forms where you want them to be mandatory.

- **Allow Per-Line Departments**: We suggest you check this. During your testing, it is useful to see the classifications in both the header and the lines of transactions.

- **Allow Per-Line Classes**: See *Allow Per-Line Departments*.

- **Always Allow Per-Line Classifications on Journals**: We suggest you check **Yes** here. There may be journals that require you to tag lines, by one classification or another.

- **Allow Non-balancing Classifications on Journals**: If you check this preference, you can enter journals, which do not balance by classification, and we recommend this. You can still make them balance if you wish, but you have the choice.

- **Allow Empty Classifications on Journals**: If you make any of the classifications mandatory, then we suggest that you check this preference, which would allow you to have empty classifications on journals, which is sometimes necessary.

If you have purchased **Revenue Recognition**, there are several preferences to consider, which are given as follows:

- **Allow Users to Modify Revenue Recognition Schedule**: Rev Rec templates generate schedules when they are attached to a transaction, such as sales order or invoice, and sometimes these schedules need editing, for any number of reasons. Check this box to allow your users to edit the schedules. You can still control which users can change schedules when you set up permissions.

- **Prorate Revenue Recognition Dates for Partially Billed Orders**: When one sales order generates more than one invoice, this preference allows each rev rec schedule to have different start and end dates. This is useful for service companies that invoice a project at regular intervals.

- **Default Revenue Recognition Journal Date to**: Either the current date or the last day of the period. Your selection probably depends on how often you are running rev rec journals and how your rev rec templates are set up. If you are running once a month, then the last day of the period makes sense.

- **Allow Users to Modify VSOE Values on Transactions**: This preference allows users to modify the system-generated VSOE values per transaction. Even if you do not enable this preference, the user can still alter the delivery status.

- **Use System Percentage of Completion for Schedules**: If you have projects, you can let the system automatically recognize the revenue, based on a percentage of completion.

- **Adv. Billing: Use Sales Order Amount**: If you have projects billed on a percent complete, then enabling this preference means that the system will recognize revenue based on the amount of the sales order; if not enabled, then the system will recognize revenue based on the amount of the invoice.

- **Allow Revenue Commitments in Advance of Fulfillment**: This preference enables the recognition of sales order revenue before fulfillment of items.

- **Allow Revenue Commitment Reversals in Advance of Item Receipt**: This preference enables you to reverse a revenue commitment prior to an item's return through a return authorization.

If you are using advanced financials with **Amortization**:

- **Allow Users to Modify Amortization Schedule**: OneWorld generates the amortization schedules automatically, based on your template. If you also want to be able to manually adjust the schedule, then enable this preference.

- **Default Amortization Journal Date to**: Just like with Rev Rec journals, you can choose the date you want as default when you go to create amortization journals, the current date, or last date of the period.

For **OneWorld** accounts using Intercompany time and expense: (T&E):

- **Intercompany Time**: For human resources who book time or expenses for a subsidiary other than the one they work for, you have to use **Intercompany time** and **expense**. Be aware that the intercompany T&E automatically creates intercompany journals.
- **Intercompany Expenses**: See *Intercompany Time*.

The Items/Transaction tab

Many of the preferences on this tab have a definite impact on the operation of your system. The first group is the default accounts. There is not a lot to say here, except that after you have set up the COA, come back and enter the defaults. They do make life a little easier when you set up your item catalog. On the **Sale & Pricing** section:

- **Consolidate Projects on Sales Transactions**: If you have advanced projects, you can set up service items that allow you to generate a project directly from the **Sales Order (SO)**. This preference enables multiple service items on one SO to generate a single project.
- **Default Quote Expiration (in days)**: Self-explanatory.
- **Maximum # of Quantity-based Price Levels**: See the **Pricing** tab on one of the **Item Setup** forms. If you add **QBPL**, you will have multiple columns, and any product or service that you sell can have multiple prices based on the quantity purchased.
- **Allow Quantity Discounts per Price Level on Schedules**: It is possible to create schedules for both the purchase and the sale of items based on quantity, meaning that different items may have different quantity-based pricing. This preference asks if you want to use the price levels in your OneWorld account to assign quantity-based discounts; in effect, this creates a matrix for pricing. If you use quantity-based pricing, check this preference and you will be able to see how it works in a future chapter. You can come back later and turn it off, if it means nothing to you.
- **Include Reimbursements in Sales and Forecast Reports**: If you have billable expenses on expense reports or vendor bills, and you want to see them in your sales reports, then check this preference. It is useful for organizations that want to measure project profitability.
- **Include Shipping in Sales and Forecast Reports**: If you charge customers for shipping and want to include these amounts in your sales reports, check this preference. There are cases where shipping can be a profitable part of the business, especially where you are doing your own deliveries, or you are delivering high-value goods through a third-party long-haul trucking firm. If your shipping charges are roughly equal to your shipping bills, then you probably don't include these in your reports.

- **Transaction Types to Exclude from Sales Reports**: See *Transaction Types to Exclude from Forecast Reports*.

- **Transaction Types to Exclude from Forecast Reports**: You decide which transactions to exclude in your sales and forecasts reports. The defaults are already chosen; you may add others.

Under the **Inventory** section (for product-based companies):

- **Inventory Costing Method**: Select the default for inventory costing. **Average** means the system will take the average price that you pay for an item and use that in the Cost of Goods Sold and inventory charges when you fulfill a sale of the item. The other options are **First In First Out (FIFO)** and **Last In First Out (LIFO)**, and **Standard**. Many organizations select **FIFO**, because, normally, prices are increasing, and therefore **FIFO** gives a more accurate representation of actual profit, which can also increase an organization's taxes. **LIFO** does the opposite. The **Average** costing method offers neither the accuracy of **FIFO** nor the tax advantages of **LIFO**. Serialized and lot-based inventory use specific costing (each unit or lot has its own cost) If you enabled the **Standard Costing** feature, then select Standard as your default inventory cost method. **Standard** allows you to investigate variances between actual costs and your expected costs..

- **Scan Individual Items**: Using barcode readers and your printed labels, possibly UPC labels, you can scan your items during fulfillment. This preference asks if you want to scan the same item thrice to set the fulfillment quantity to three, or scan it once and manually set the quantity to three.

- **Allow Purchase of Assembly Items**: If your organization does assemblies, check this preference to also allow the purchases of the same items that you assemble in-house. It gives you the option of deciding when to assemble and when to purchase, based on volume and price, for example.

- **Centralize Purchasing in a Single Location**: If you have multiple locations with inventory, you can enforce a single location as the one where you receive all inventory, before transferring it out to other locations.

- **Days Before Lot Expiration Warning**: Self-explanatory, this is especially useful for organizations with inventory spoilage problems.

- **Require Bins on All Transactions Except Item Receipts**: Check this preference to enforce the use of bins when you are fulfilling orders. Also see Help for more details.

- **Use Preferred Bin on Item Receipts**: When you receive items into the warehouse, this preference allows you to place the item in the preferred bin, by default.

Under **Payment Processing**:

- **Customers Can Pay Online**: This preference allows a customer to log into the customer center and pay their invoice with a CC; you must have a merchant account setup to use this option.

- **Use Credit Card Security Code for Credit Card Transactions**: Requires the use of the three-digit security code for CC transactions.

- **Get Authorization on Customer Center Sales Orders**: This option makes the system authorize a customer's credit card when they make purchases in the customer center.

Other Transaction Preferences:

- **Duplicate Number Warnings**: The system will let you know if you submit two of the same transaction, invoices, for example, with the same number.

- **Sort Reconcile by**: You can set a default here, and then change it on individual reconciliations.

- **Recalculate Estimated Costs on the Creation of Linked Transactions**: The values listed are **Always, Through Sales Order**, and **Never**. This preference controls how OneWorld handles the calculation of estimated gross profit as you move through the sales cycle over time, like when you generate an invoice from a sales order, for example. If your organization used estimated gross profit as an important metric or as a basis for other functions, such as commission calculations, then how you recognize changes in product costs from the date of the estimate to the data of the invoice is an important question.

And finally, the **Other Item Preferences**:

- **Matrix Item Name/Number Separator**: Only for those organizations using matrix items, such as Large and Blue, this preference allows you to select a separator between the words in the item name, for example, Large-Blue or Large|Blue.

- **Gift Certificate Auth Code Generation**: For merchants selling and taking payment through a gift certificate, you can select your method of coding them. If you sell over a OneWorld web store, then use the system generated, but if you have actual plastic gift cards, then you'll have to enter the number yourself.

That's a lot of preferences! We know this, and we are not even done yet. We will hold the remaining two tabs, for order management and time and expenses, for later chapters when we can investigate how these preferences work in the context of actual transactions. It can, sometimes, be overwhelming for customers to have to go through the list and make all of these decisions. But OneWorld operates based on these base setups, so you would do well to understand them.

Remember – implementation is iterative

We will remind you more than once throughout this book that OneWorld implementation works best when it is iterative, not linear. You do not need to make every decision now. At this point, the objective is to learn the foundation of the system and how to navigate. Some of the most basic setups are easy to do at this time, while for others, we suggest you wait until your understanding increases.

Next, we have to introduce one more important setup step, namely, the **lists**. Again, you don't have to complete this task before you move on, but if you move on without knowing about the lists, then you will probably get stuck. So take a moment to understand where all the values you see in OneWorld come from.

Accounting, CRM, and employee lists

There are many fields in OneWorld that have a delivered **List Of Values** (LOV). For most of these, you can add, change, and delete the values. Let's go through them quickly, so that you can be familiar with them as we start to work through specific OneWorld functions and processes. Eventually, you will make informed decisions on what values you need and why for each list.

Accounting Lists

The **Accounting Lists** is the name given for a group of fields and their LOVs that are used in transaction processing, in most cases. The following screenshot shows several of these lists:

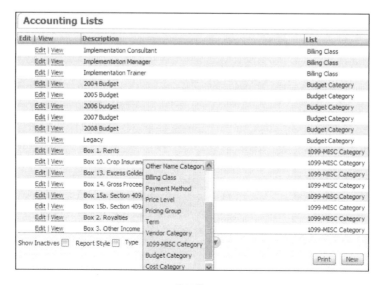

Accounting Lists
Log in as the administrator and navigate to **Setup | Accounting | Accounting Lists**.

This form shows the values in each list. Go to the footer of the form and in the **Type** field select the specific list that you want to see. The values for that list will appear in the top of the form, and then you can edit, view, or add new values. The **New** button is on the bottom-left.

Some of the lists are fairly simple and have little functionality outside of reporting. Some, however, such as **Payment Methods**, are more complex and require more understanding and effort.

- **Customer Message**: These appear under the columns on your sales documents. You can edit the delivered messages or add new ones.

- **Customer Category**: This list appears on the customer record. Its primary use is reporting results, for example, sales by category.

- **Project Type**: For example, **Fixed Price** and **Time and Materials**. This does not impact how the project bills, but it simply notifies users as to how the project ought to bill. You must enable **Projects** or **Advanced Projects**.

- **Project Status**: **Pending, Awarded**, and so on, are again for reporting purposes only. You must enable **Projects** or **Advanced Projects**.

- **Other Name Category**: There are vendors, customer, and partners in OneWorld, but if you have another entity that figures prominently in your business, then you can use the **Other Name Category**. This field allows you to categorize the **Other Entity**, just like **Customer Category** categorizes the **Customer**.

- **Billing Class**: These can be used on service items when you sell consulting hours, for example. You can have multiple billing classes, each one with a different rate, on a single service item. These also work in conjunction with the **Price Levels**, meaning you could have multiple levels for a single billing class for a single item.

- **Payment Method**: Customer payments come in many different methods. Some of them require more setup, such as the CC payments. Also, you can choose which account to deposit them to here. You probably do not have your CC processing setup yet, if you are using CC processing, nor do you have your COA setup. So mark this as a step to come back to, after you complete your COA.

- **Price Level**: These are used on item setups and customer records. When you have tiered pricing, you set different price levels on the item, then you assign the same price levels to customers. When you sell an item to a customer, the system knows its price level and assigns the correct price. Price levels are also used by quantity pricing schedules.

- **Pricing Group**: These take pricing to another level and allow you to group items into price groups, and then assign price groups to a customer with a price level by group. For example, you may have hardware and software items, and two pricing groups. Customer X receives platinum price level for the hardware group, and bronze price level for the software group.

- **Term**: OneWorld uses your **Terms** on both the vendor and customer records. So when you log payable bills, OneWorld knows that this vendor has 1 percent 10 Net 30. Likewise, when you invoice a customer, the system knows that you offered the customer Net 45.

- **Vendor Category**: Same functionality as **Customer Category**.

- **1099-MISC Category**: For US firms who have to cut 1099s to contractors, you may need certain 1099 categories, which are then linked to specific accounts on your G/L COA. We'll cover this in more detail in future chapters.

- **Budget Category**: If you have purchased advanced financials and enabled multiple budgets, then you can categorize your budgets with this list.

- **Cost Category**: For product-based companies that purchase products and want to 'land' the cost of freight, duties, insurance, and so on, incurred during shipping to the warehouse door, add these values to your **Cost Category**. Each category links to an expense account. We have examples of landed costs in later chapters. At this time, understand that for each expense type, you might add to a PO setup a landed cost category.

- Cost Categories are also used for standard costing. In this case, select the **Cost Type** of **Material** or **Service**. This enables finer variance reporting.

CRM Lists

Similar to the **Accounting Lists** mentioned previously, the **CRM Lists** add values to many fields used in the sales and marketing modules.

CRM Lists
Log in as the administrator and navigate to **Setup | Sales | CRM Lists**.

The **CRM Lists** are very straightforward and they follow much the same logic as the **Accounting list**. The only one which might throw a curve is the **Contact Roles**. You cannot edit or delete the four delivered **Contact Roles**. However, you can add your own.

These roles are used in several ways throughout the system, which will be obvious as we move forward.

Other than **Contact Roles**, we think you won't have any issues setting up the rest of the lists.

Employee Related Lists

If you are using NetSuite payroll, then you may want to take a few minutes to look at the **Employee Related Lists**. If you are not using payroll, then you might still want to know what these are and take a look at the delivered values.

Employee Related Lists
Log in as the administrator and navigate to **Setup | Accounting | Employee Related Lists**.

The **Employee Related Lists** are just like the **CRM List** and **Accounting List**, and most are straightforward. The only one I will mention is the **Employee type**, which includes checkboxes for **Statutory** and **Exempt**. Take a careful look at these, if you are using payroll.

The other lists are quite simple. We do not go into great detail about them here.

Summary

We suspect that you might be a bit overwhelmed at this point, but we ask you to be patient, both with us and with yourselves. You won't understand every aspect of this chapter, until you get further on in the book, but it is important to at least know what the underpinnings of OneWorld are at this point. You will return to these pages, and to accounting preferences and lists, later to complete your setups. By then, we hope your confidence would have increased and you are ready to make all of these decisions knowing completely well how they will affect your use of OneWorld.

You should also note that we decided to talk about a lot of these base setups now, because we have learned from experience that there is often a small lag between purchasing OneWorld and getting the implementation underway. This is the perfect opportunity to start to understand some of the OneWorld basics. Then, when you actually get underway with your implementation, you are moving forward. As we learned in physics class, a body in motion tends to stay in motion.

In the meantime, it's now the perfect time to spend a few pages on the implementation. We believe that there are a few important things to understand about the OneWorld implementation, which makes it different from the typical on-premise software implementation, so we have included a chapter on OneWorld implementation practices and tools. The idea is to help those on the implementation team to understand where the challenges lie and how to overcome them. With this in mind, we discuss the basics of OneWorld implementation and some useful tools for the project.

3
OneWorld Implementation

Software as a Service (SaaS), a concept we discussed in *Chapter 1, What is NetSuite OneWorld?*, is a horse of a different hue from on-premise software. Obviously, the way you access, use, and exploit OneWorld is very different from an on-premise software package. It would follow then that implementing a SaaS system like OneWorld is also different from implementing on-premise software, and in our experience, this is exactly the case.

One of the main differences in a OneWorld implementation is that you do not have any infrastructure issues or challenges. Your new account is ready literally the day after you sign your contract. Sourcing, purchasing, configuring, and patching machines is not the first step in the implementation, nor do these tasks ever come up later.

In a conventional on-premise package implementation, the first several weeks, or even months, are often spent with hardware and infrastructure questions. This work gives your business functions time to plan, organize, and sort out a lot of basic business issues, before they jump into the implementation.

With OneWorld, the account is ready the day after you sign the contract, and the business functions are often caught by surprise. To avoid this problem, we recommend that before you sign your contract, you have a clear **Statement Of Work (SOW)**, agreed upon by management and understood by department heads, a project plan that provides a timeline and prioritization for the work described in the SOW, and the start of an Implementation Master, a spreadsheet that holds the details of the project, from beginning to end. You should also start to schedule your meetings for the first couple of weeks, using your project plan as a guide.

In the next chapter, we move directly into OneWorld configuration, but we think it's a good idea in this chapter to take a small step back and review some of the important tools that will help you to manage your OneWorld project to a successful conclusion.

While on-premise package implementations are often document heavy and plodding, OneWorld implementations start quickly and move forward rapidly in most cases. What you need are the tools that help you to keep pace with the project and preserve a semblance of order and continuity.

In this chapter, we want to help you understand the logistics of OneWorld implementation, the how, what, when, where, and who of implementing OneWorld. Our discussion focuses on the following areas:

- Preparing for the OneWorld implementation
- The agile OneWorld implementation
- Implementation basics
- Documentation tools
- Planning your OneWorld implementation

Preparing for the OneWorld implementation

There are some basic considerations before starting your OneWorld implementation that we want to bring to your attention. First, do you have enough broadband access to the Internet and do you have a reliable internal network, so that everyone can access the Internet from their work areas? If you are using wireless access, make sure that it can handle a busy training room. It's frustrating to try to train a group in a room where access is limited and very slow, or simply goes down regularly. There is little infrastructure to worry about with OneWorld, but you do need reliable access to the Internet to work.

It's also helpful if you have a projector setup in a conference room, where several people can meet and view a single screen of the system. It's likely that a fair portion of the implementation will be done remotely and it's very helpful if small groups of users can meet and work together with a single view of the system.

These basic physical needs are fairly easy to meet, but human resources are another story. The OneWorld implementation does require time and effort from all of your users, and management team, some more than others. From our experience, you should plan the following amount of time by functional role and by project phase, assuming you are implementing CRM and ERP.

Project resources by role (in hours)

This table details what members of your organization should expect in terms of effort for a basic vanilla OneWorld implementation. Obviously, not all of these roles are available for each OneWorld customer, so this is a very general estimate.

Role	Project management	Requirements, configuration, and testing	Decision making	Training
CFO	20			4
CEO				4
CIO	20			8
Project Manager	80	40	80	
Administrator		16		16
Sales VP	10	16	8	16
Sales Admin		16	8	16
Operations VP	10	32	16	32
Controller	10	32	16	32
Bookkeepers		32	8	32
Sales Reps				16
Service Manager	10	16	8	16
Service Rep				16
Marketing Manager	10	16	8	16
Marketing Admin		16	8	16
IT Super User		Variable		Variable

This table is based on a typical ten-week OneWorld implementation plan. It also assumes that there is a good deal of buy-in from the management group and that there is a project manager devoted to the project.

At the C level, that is the top three rows in this table, the executives spend a couple of hours a week monitoring the progress of the project. They will also require a few hours of training to understand dashboards and reports in most cases. What the table does not show is that the executives are responsible for the SOW, which lays out the broad outlines of the project and the goals that must be achieved for success. Once the SOW is complete, it is up to the project manager to construct a project plan and get the buy-in from the department heads.

The project manager spends about eight hours a week managing the project and at least another eight hours facilitating decision making within and among departments. The task of decision making cannot be over emphasized in the project. If there is one thing that derails a project's timeline, it is decisions that are not made promptly. It is the project manager's responsibility to understand and lay out the options for decisions to department heads and then document the decisions.

Department heads are responsible for making decisions on how to configure and use OneWorld to achieve their business results. The formula in the table is simply that for every two hours that a department head spends in requirements, configuration, and testing, they have about an hour of decisions to make. This might mean that they spend this time working through options in the system or they might spend time with their supervisors or other managers to come to a satisfactory decision. Again, the important thing is that you set aside time for decision-making activity, as it is key to a successful implementation.

As OneWorld is a Suite, it is also important to understand that managers on the implementation team should spend at least an hour together a week going through project management and discussing decisions that cross department boundaries.

Finally, for every hour spent in requirements, configuration, and testing, expect to spend an hour in training. Training may take many forms outside of formal training classes, but overall it's our experience that after you go through the requirements, configuration, and testing, and then sort out the resulting decisions, it's a really good idea to bring the team back together, with other users if you wish, and go over the steps in the business process again. We advocate at least two prototypes, and scheduling a short training session after each would make sense, followed by a more formal training session towards the end of the project.

There are usually two prototypes built during an implementation—a first rough draft and then a more refined version. Training normally happens once the prototype has been refined. We explain this more next.

There is always more project management work on software projects than we would like, but keeping the various gears turning together and managing organizational change are very important tasks for a OneWorld project manager. Getting your department heads to work together on an integrated software suite will take some effort, because, in many cases, people who have worked in their own siloed systems will not initially enjoy having an integrated system. Accounting, for example, we will have issues with sales, because they keep finding errors in sales orders that they want to bill. In the past, sales orders might have been keyed into the accounting software manually and errors were caught and removed during this step. But in the integrated OneWorld, where sales takes responsibility for entering sales orders, accounting does not see the order until it becomes an invoice, and will be at the mercy of sales to some degree, so be prepared to manage the tension.

While it is not necessary to have the usual hardware and database administrators on staff at a OneWorld site, it does make sense to have and develop at least one super user. It's important to understand that your users have varied levels of understanding of data and data processing. You don't have time to educate everyone on relational data schemas and similar subjects, we assume. This means that you must have at least one super user who understands your business model very well, continues to train users after the implementation is over, creates custom reports and searches, and knows how to handle system security. He/she must obviously be a person that you trust explicitly. We included an *IT Super User* in the previous table for this reason, but in reality, you can give this role to one or more of the implementation team. Every organization is different in this respect, but the key point is to make sure that you have resources on the implementation team who are willing and able to help manage, not simply use, the live system going forward.

Super users

The payback on a super user is immediate and visible. Having a person your team knows and trusts to help them through all of the little 'gotchas' of a new system and also provide some technical know-how for managing the system long term, increases the value of your system and helps to pay back on your investment in OneWorld. A super user makes a lot of sense. Make the investment.

While all project resources should spend significant time during the implementation, unraveling their business processes and laying out the future in OneWorld, it's also useful if they do some system configuration. It is likely that a technical resource uploads the chart of accounts, but it also makes sense if your accountant sets up some of the accounts manually. Performing simple tasks like this in the system helps project resources gain confidence and take a fresh look at how the system works. Sometimes great ideas are born out of these simple tasks. Working in the system pays dividends by helping to uncover unusual business practices, and it gives people a better idea of how to use OneWorld to manage the irregular off-process occurrences that happen every day. Also, while we often focus on business processes, there is also the matter of policy, such as who has the ability to set up a new account or post a transaction in a past period. Policy questions often come up during system interaction.

Prototyping and sandbox accounts

Speaking of prototyping, we should mention that you have two choices in regards to prototyping. NetSuite sells a sandbox account, which you can purchase with the system. It includes regular copies of your production account to the sandbox account. You do the prototyping of the system in the sandbox and then, when you have a clear understanding of what you want, you build it in production. NetSuite then copies production to your sandbox, keeping the systems in sync and allowing you to continue prototyping and testing in the sandbox with the refined production setups.

The value of the sandbox is that you can set up your prototype in the production account as you refine it, and at regular intervals, copy that prototype into the sandbox. We advise OneWorld customers to prototype early and often, and the sandbox dovetails nicely with this idea.

The sandbox is also useful for integration and scripting development. Of course, both of these activities require a lot of testing, so the sandbox starts to really gain value as you move past basic business processes and start to develop custom solutions.

The alternative to the sandbox is to use your production account to prototype and test. This sounds odd to many people who have done system implementations in the past, but it actually works out fine in many cases.

After you have prototyped your business process, you can always remove the transactions. It takes a little time, but is certainly not an insurmountable task. Then you can either remove the test entity data also, such as test customers and vendors, or you can simply deactivate it, and thereby remove it from searches and reports. Setups, such as the *Accounting Lists* that we discussed in *Chapter 2, OneWorld's Foundation*, can also be altered as you refine your prototype. In some cases, you might want to delete values in these lists, or simply change them. It's not a problem.

You can also change item setups in some cases, though you cannot change the item's type, or delete items that you no longer need, as long as they are not used on a transaction still in the system. Keep in mind that you have to unwind your test data, both transactions and entities, by starting at the end and moving backwards. For example, delete the payment, then the invoice, then the fulfillment, then the sales order, and then the quote. When the transactions are all deleted, you can then remove the item and the customer.

Plenty of OneWorld implementations succeed without a sandbox. However, if you have a lot of business process variation and you need to run several hundred transactions to test them all, or if you have a lot of custom development, then by all means, purchase the sandbox. You don't have to own it forever, but it will make implementation easier for larger and more complex organizations.

We have seen customers who use a sandbox during implementation and then keep it indefinitely. These are companies that expand quickly, and therefore the sandbox becomes the platform to test new acquisition companies, before moving them into production.

The agile OneWorld implementation

Agile software development has been around for quite a while and has a lot of converts in the software business. Like everything else, there are people who now make their living teaching agile development or are otherwise involved in the agile bandwagon. Honestly though, this is not a hard idea and it does not require advanced theories, classes, or certifications.

First, let's state what agile is not, or what agile is in response to. In the past, it was common for software development to happen behind closed doors in many respects. A team of analysts would take a look at a business problem and interview people knowledgeable about the business functions and processes. This was called **Requirements Gathering**.

Then the analysts wrote up their findings into process descriptions and visual maps, had the customer sign off on them, and then handed them over to developers. The developers disappeared for several weeks or months and then came back with a developed software product. It contained the requirements, as interpreted by the analysts and understood by the software developers.

This regimented, sequential model is called the **Waterfall Model**. It's heavy on documentation and sign-offs. Software developers and system users, however, were not happy with this method, because it always created black and white software for a world of high definition color. You can find an interesting discussion of the waterfall method here at `http://en.wikipedia.org/wiki/Waterfall_model`.

People started to see the issues with the waterfall model long ago, but it takes time for things to change. Recently, more developers use one of the many agile methods. In agile, the idea is to do incremental software development while in constant communication with the software owners, the organization's managers, and users. Agile relies on communication and collaboration more than documentation. It also believes that flexibility is a better use of time than constant contract negotiation. You can find a good agile discussion here: `http://en.wikipedia.org/wiki/Agile_software_development`.

Now, if you are actually developing software from scratch, then there is a lot more about agile that you might like to know. But for software implementation, we are happy simply to pilfer their best ideas and apply them to our project. So how does agile work for a OneWorld implementation?

There are several ideas that we believe are really worthwhile for a OneWorld implementation, a few of which are as follows:

- **By module, by function**: Map out the main departments of the organization, work to prototype, and test the modules required by each department. For example, it is useful to prototype customer service with the customer service manager. Start with a list of common functions, such as receive a service request, assign a case, escalate a case, and then build from this basic list of functions until you cover the department's work in detail.

- **In collaboration**: Prototyping should always be done in collaboration with the user, or manager, of the department. Do the configuration with them, in front of the system, and test together. Let them enter setup values, click the buttons, and see how the system uses various inputs to process service cases, in our example. During this work session, new requirements arise and more testing takes place. Tweak and change, if you need to. Move on to the next area and the next module. This is how we develop the first prototype, and how we refine the second prototype.

- **Wash, rinse, and repeat**: Don't be afraid to prototype a department more than once, and if necessary, break down the departments into smaller units such as A/P and A/R, or, if you have multiple sales channels, into partners, e-commerce, and direct reps.

- **Remember, it's a Suite**: After you complete the prototype, by department, start the process again. This time, prototype the department and the next step in the process. For example, use the prototype to walk through the process from marketing to sales, delivery or fulfillment, accounting, ongoing service, and additional marketing and sales. At this time, you'll want to have the manager of each affected department in the room, not just users. This is the second prototype.

- **Be cross-functional**: The trickiest setup in the system is the *Item Catalog*. Depending on your business, it may be extensive and, regardless of how large it is, it requires input from almost every department—sales, of course, operations and accounting, and even service. Prototyping the behavior of your items is a good example of where a cross-functional team makes a lot of sense.

Why is agile difficult?

Often when we explain agile to our customers, they respond *"Well, of course."* Agile makes perfect sense when you think about it by itself, outside of the context of the typical organization.

Organizations have hierarchies, and if there is one thing that the hierarchy believes in, it is the hierarchy. To understand our meaning here, imagine running a prototyping session in front of the senior manager who is responsible for your department. Are they going to be patient with the idea that this is a prototype and therefore has some rough edges? Or do they expect to see a finished product? And how do they see their role in the project? Have they delegated some responsibility to the implementation team or do they feel it necessary to take an active role in the set up of the system?

It is useful to think about these questions, before you start the prototyping sessions. You might also want to meet with management and prepare them for the steps in the agile project process. If they come to a prototyping session looking for a finished product, then they are not going to be pleased. They may see some confusion as business people struggle with the system (or system people struggle with the business). It's at this point that some managers feel the need to start to manage the project, because they feel it is out of control. Agile is open, collaborative, and at times, a little messy.

If your management team is not okay with this, then the waterfall project is a better idea. Have a few key people work behind the scenes to set up everything, bring it to the point of 99 percent completed, and then show the rest of the organization. This also works, and some organizations find it a lot easier.

You also need to establish some rules with users of the system who participate in the prototyping. Though it is an open process, it's not a free for all. Take a moment before beginning to explain the need for some discipline. When you are working on product pricing, don't go off in ten different directions. Lots of things pop into our heads all day long, but stick to the topic, as much as possible. Keep notes of other ideas, but try to focus on one solution at a time.

Again, if your team lacks discipline and cannot make headway, then you might have to turn back to the waterfall method. Agile does not work everywhere. In some organizations, managers and users might be more comfortable if the implementation team assumes responsibility for building the final product. System implementations only expose organization culture, they cannot redeem it. The implementation team and the organization's project sponsor should take stock of the situation after a few preliminary meetings and make the call for the right project approach.

Why agile is best

Obviously, we have a higher regard for agile than we do for the waterfall method. We like collaboration with users; it gets them excited, and we like to hear about their challenges and what they need to be successful in their work. It gets us half the way through training. Users are the ones who are going to create value in the system, or not, so having them fully on board always means a win for us as implementation consultants.

Agile also has the affect of dividing the project responsibility evenly between the implementation group, which could be an internal group or an external third party, and the main organization stakeholders. Without an even division, both sides feel vulnerable, though for different reasons. The implementation team feels like the responsibility for project success is theirs solely, while other organization stakeholders are left wondering what's happening on the project. The result is suspicion and a lot of risk avoidance behavior that takes time and energy away from the project.

Agile asks if this chasm can be bridged, by bringing the two groups together on a regular basis to work on the system. For this reason, the agile method says prototype early and often. Don't wait for a finished product to lay out your setup decisions. Prototype the setup decisions for your organization's key decision makers, let them help to make decisions, and keep them in the loop.

Interestingly, a lot of implementation consultants abhor the agile method:

- They prefer to work in solitude, because configuration in front of the customer exposes the so-called "Guru" as a normal human being challenged by the system.

- They harbor disdain for end users and prefer as little engagement with them as possible.

- They listen to interview answers and then use their own judgment to decide the best way to set up the system.

- They prefer to play a key role in the project and not act as a consultant, facilitator, and trainer.

Because we believe that the agile method has the best chance of helping customers manage OneWorld projects to a successful conclusion, and because it lets the implementation team and other organization stakeholders act collaboratively in each other's best interest, we prefer agile implementations. However, we again caution you that agile does not work everywhere. While we find it valuable, there are organizations that prefer to hand implementation over to a team of gurus and let them set it all up. Again, we suggest that you take a close look at the available resources and the organization's expectations, and make your choice carefully between agile and waterfall.

Implementation basics

Regardless of the method you use, the organization implementing OneWorld, or the systems you replace, there are some implementation basics that you ought to follow. Questions about how to handle some aspects of the implementation are so common that it's obvious there is some need for clarification. Next, we will go through the most common areas of confusion.

Historical data

If you ask an enterprise executive if they would like to keep their organization's historical transaction data, the answer is always "Yes!" This is why you avoid asking the question. The better approach to this subject is to state the plan that you have for historical data and ask if there are any objections. This might sound sneaky or underhanded, but it is not. A sound plan for managing historical data just makes sense, and there is no useful reason to ask questions that take you down paths to the data wilderness. There is simply no known way to transfer transactional data from one system to another, without inordinate investments in time, energy, and cash, with very little return.

The challenge of transferring your historical entity data, such as your customers, vendors, items, and so on, keeps you busy and also takes a toll on the implementation team in time and energy. The data requires cleanup, sometimes called data scrubbing, and interpretation. The import process itself takes several hours to perfect for each entity. But it can be done.

Transactional data, however, is another order of magnitude more difficult. It requires not only the scrubbing of the data, but also the synching of entity and transactional data to a very high degree. For example, you have items that you sold in the past, such as products or services that were discontinued or were recreated under different names, and now you must add them to OneWorld in order to transact them. You start to see the mountain of small challenges you face. Then you have all of the other transactions, such as returns, and so on that are not easy to transact, much less to import as transactions.

A more manageable approach to historical data is the following, starting with entity data:

- Import your scrubbed chart of accounts.
- Import customers, leads, and prospects after intensive data scrubbing. If you need to massage the data into the shape you want it in OneWorld, then do it before import; it's a lot easier. (Massaging refers to shaping the data, so you might be adding or changing fields.)

- Import vendors, again after scrubbing and massaging.

- Import employees. (If you have direct sales reps, and you want them linked to leads, prospects, and customers, you may want to import employees right after the chart of accounts.)

- Import the current Item catalog.

You now have the basic entity data in the system and can turn your attention to the transactional data. Pick a month end, based on your project plan as you approach the project's go-live, and then bring over the following. We'll go into greater detail on these in *Chapter 9, OneWorld Data Migration*, but for now, it's important to understand the basic idea:

- All of the open A/R transactions

- All of the open A/P transactions

- Any bills with amortization – just the balance to be amortized

- Any fixed assets – just the balance to be depreciated

- Any invoices with revenue recognition – just the balance to be recognized

- Load your current inventory

- Any checks or other un-reconciled bank items

Now that you have all open transactions and items in the system, run a monthly trial balance for each month, go back as far as you need to, and then do a journal entry to reverse each month's charges. The net result should be a trial balance of 0.00 for every month.

Finally, you now have your open transactions in OneWorld, so you can take payments or make them, and you have a clean slate on the general ledger. Select a year end and load the balances as a journal entry on 12/31/xxxx. Then, for each month to the present, load a journal for net activity. At the end of the process, your balances from your legacy system and OneWorld ought to be equal. If they are not, then check your balance loads.

Keep in mind that if you changed your G/L chart of accounts a lot in the past, you will need to map balances to the new accounts, or a combination of accounts. This can add a lot of work and time. So make the decision on where to begin the balance loads carefully. It might be the beginning of the current year, or possibly two years ago, but the farther out you get, the more difficult the task.

Getting started on your implementation

There is no perfect answer about where to begin the implementation. Do you start by setting up the accounting preferences, then the chart of accounts, and then the Item catalog? This seems logical, but there are always going to be things that cause you to retrace your steps. If you start by understanding that the implementation is not linear, but iterative, you save yourself and your team a lot of misery and feelings of failure. This again is why we appreciate the agile method, because it emphasizes multiple prototypes and frees the implementation team from the absurd task of getting it all correct on the first pass.

We become so used to linear processes in business that the iterative process always seems messy and inconclusive. It does not need to be this way. It takes time and effort to perform useful prototyping, and time and effort to learn from each prototype and improve the next one. If you manage this process with a semblance of good sense, you master the implementation much quicker than you would were you to try to get all the 'ducks in a row' before beginning. And you save yourself a lot of wasted energy, thinking that you have mucked things up.

As we stated above, the statement of work and the project plan should really be complete, before you sign your contract, if possible. The final tool, the **Implementation Master (IM)** spreadsheet, should be drafted before NetSuite provisions your new account. The IM forms the basis of the work sessions that result in the OneWorld prototypes. (We give concrete example of all three tools in the *Appendix*.)

The day after you sign your contract, you should have the IM in hand and you should be ready to sit down and start working on your first prototype. In the next chapter, we walk you through most of the foundation setups, to get you started. Without the IM with you, you can very quickly get lost and have little to show after several days or weeks on OneWorld. It's important to have all three tools in hand before starting your project.

Changing the business or changing the software

We would be remiss if we did not also discuss the common question of whether the business conforms to the software or the software conforms to your business. During every implementation, you find gaps between your desired business processes and the system's assumed business processes. After all, OneWorld implementation is not custom development, though there is much room for customization. Gaps are normal, but they create headaches for management, because they have authored the current processes in many cases, and have disciplined the organization to use these processes. Changing the processes to work in the software often means abandoning highly-regarded ideas, and it can be hard to do.

To avoid this conundrum, we suggest that the implementation team plan for the eventuality of business process gaps and have a process in place to ease the pain of change. For example, keeping a log of gaps is a good idea, and using the log to describe how far the given process was accommodated in the software until the gap could not be bridged is a better idea.

The best idea is to then use the gap log as the start of the customization list. This provides the benefit of giving every remaining gap a price for remediation. The process of logging gaps and customizations gives management a way of making changes that makes sense, saves the best ideas, and gives management a cost/benefit tool for custom work.

Documentation tools

Documentation runs the gamut. For smaller companies, many implementations end with little, if any, documentation completed. Larger companies generate a lot of written words, most with little effect. While we don't think that a lot of documentation is necessary, we do believe that it makes sense to document the following important aspects of the implementation, which we covered previously as well:

- A completed SOW and a completed project plan that outline and prioritize the implementation work
- An IM spreadsheet that includes the following:
  - Your main business departments/modules and the functions required for each
  - A log of gaps and issues
  - Unusual processes and practices that are material to your business
  - Decisions you make during the implementation

If you document these, you create an organizational memory of the implementation, and going forward, you can adjust whenever necessary, without constantly revisiting every aspect of the system.

In the case of no documentation, it is easy to fall into the problem of not remembering why you decided to do X and not Y; pursuing the same decision many times does not make for a better implementation. It's simply a waste of time. We advise that you document as follows:

1. Create informal business process diagrams well before you start implementing OneWorld, and even before you have purchased it. Talk about your business processes as if you do not currently have systems at all—this is a good way to prevent current solutions from becoming business requirements. We read a lot of requests for proposal that are really a laundry list of the current business processes.

2. Once you begin the implementation, document your important decisions carefully: "In response to our business requirement for XYZ, we decided to do ABC because…". This is the most important documentation that you generate during the implementation. It's so easy to think that your decisions are clear and easy to remember, but your head will be bursting with 'stuff' during the implementation, and if you have to keep remembering why you made a decision, you'll drive yourself crazy. Also, it helps to prevent others in the organization from overturning carefully thought-out decisions.

3. When you have unusual processes to manage in OneWorld, for whatever reason, take some time to document them. It might change a bit over time and it's useful to know where you started and where you are currently.

Implementation documentation helps avoid solution shopping. This is one of the reasons why we advise that you document your decisions. All too often, we see implementation teams that are being harangued by someone on the business side who does not like the new reality, and therefore doggedly pursues some answer other than the one you have already given them. Having the decision documented avoids the situation where they manage to confuse someone and force the issue to resurface. If you can simply point them to the decision document, you waste neither your time nor theirs.

OneWorld knowledge base

And if you want to point users to process descriptions and decision maps, then why not use OneWorld? After all, OneWorld includes functionality in the customer service module for managing a knowledge base of topics and solutions. You can easily generate another tab on your system and keep all of the pertinent information just a click away (see *Chapter 4, Nailing OneWorld Basics*).

Business process example

When creating process maps of any kind, we prefer the least formal tools possible. If you have your implementation team in one place, then a whiteboard is a great idea. It lets you create, edit, and adjust on the fly as a team. This is the best of all possible scenarios in our view. The only downside to the whiteboard is that you cannot print it and keep a copy.

For a printable copy, or for when you have a dispersed group working on a process, we suggest that you try one of the online whiteboards. There are several, and we have tried many of them. `http://www.twiddla.com/` is one example. It's very simple, quick to learn, and gives you the ability to print the result when you're done with the editing.

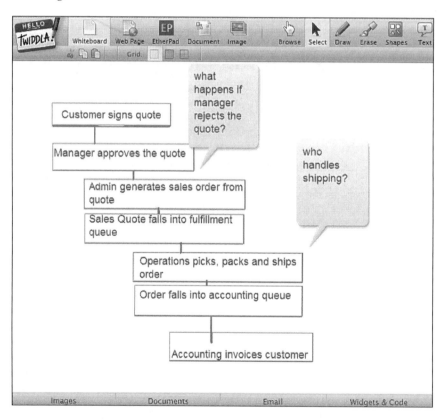

You can use this same tool, or a similar one, to map your finished business process or even to create decision maps that detail how you came to important decisions during the implementation. Also, with a paid subscription, you can keep copies of all your work with the host vendor.

Planning your OneWorld implementation

To be honest, effective business analysis is effective, regardless of the software system that it ultimately assists. But we thought that we might advise some of you who are perhaps taking on a OneWorld implementation and are looking for some help.

First, it's probably a good idea to understand the implementation in broad strokes. We assume that you can put together your own project plan, but some of the main points that you need to consider as headings are as follows:

- **Requirements, configuration, and testing**: For each department/module, you need to go through a process of understanding how they do business, set it up in OneWorld, and test it. It's also useful to anticipate the module preferences in your work sessions, so that you can come out of prototyping with these configured. For example, there is an accounting preference that asks the default status of a sales order: pending approval, or pending fulfillment. Discuss approvals in the sales process during prototyping, so that you know if the delivered process works or needs a custom workflow.

- While the prototyping with business users is ongoing, you can start several other tasks simultaneously, much of which is homework. Hand these out to users as you move forward. For example:

  - Accounting needs to complete any work they have to do on the chart of accounts

  - They can also start to pull together the balances they are going to load for the most recent year end and any months to present

  - There are several lists of values that need to be completed in the system, by accounting, sales, service, and so on

- The Item catalog requires the most work. Pricing, item accounting, inventory, and bill rates are just a few of the discussions that happen in this area. Take your time before importing a lot of items. It's probably best to start with a prototype of different item types, before importing the whole list in OneWorld. In the meantime, try to answer as many questions as possible about the items, and work on putting together an accurate list. Like the COA, there are going to be a number of changes and variations in OneWorld.

- While you are working through the complexities of what you sell and how you sell it, a lot of other system configuration can take place. For example, you are going to have to customize your organization's main business forms and roles, so get started now. Neither of these tasks can be concluded at this point, but getting an early start keeps them front of mind and adds color to the prototype.

- Prototype testing gives you the confidence that your configuration is on track. You will have at least two of these sessions, possibly more. The first ones will not be formal tests, but users of various departments taking a first crack at the system together. Hopefully, you'll have time to have a conference room pilot test, before rolling out the final system and going live.

- Loading entity data. Start with small groups of customers, vendors, employees, and so on, until you are sure that you have the import correct. You then load the large files.

- Loading current open transactions into the system. The transactions that are currently open and against which you will have further future activity include:
  ° Open AP
  ° Open AR
  ° Amortizations
  ° Deferred revenue
  ° Depreciation
  ° Inventory adjustments

  All of these need to be loaded into the system before you create journal entries to bring your G/L back to 0.00, and move to the next step.

- Loading balances into the system.

- Reports, dashboards, lists, mass updates, duplicate detection, and so on, are all tasks that require data and time at the end of the project.

- User training and system cutover.

These are the main headers of the project plan from our point of view. Within system configuration and prototyping, there are several tasks that we discuss in the next chapter. For now, we just want to give you the main signposts for the implementation.

Summary

This chapter attempts to put the OneWorld implementation into a useable framework for both IT professionals and, more importantly, the system's business users. Certainly, it's one thing to select the right software and buy the right modules, but without a successful implementation, you have a lot of cracked eggs and still no omelets.

Because OneWorld is accessible everywhere and at any time, there is often the temptation of jumping right into the implementation, without really thinking about laying out the groundwork. This is a big mistake, in our opinion, and will create a lot of downstream issues, not least of which is the need to rework your processes once the system is live. Take your time to do some planning up front. Think about it like this: Without the need for infrastructure planning, installation, and fine tuning, you have more time for prototyping and really understanding how you would like to use OneWorld for your business.

Now that we have some understanding of the implementation process, we can turn our attention to OneWorld and start to look at, understand, and configure the system's foundation. So, in the next chapter, we will jump in and start making decisions, set up the system, and understand our business processes.

4
Nailing OneWorld Basics

In the first three chapters, we laid the groundwork of the OneWorld system and its implementation. Now we will start to dive into the details and start the actual OneWorld configuration. Again, we will proceed with the configuration, just as we would in a real implementation. The first step is to take care of several of the basics and configure the legal entities with their currencies, languages, countries, and states.

There are also practical reasons to start here. The setup of the **Chart of Accounts (COA)** requires the subsidiaries to be set up, and the Item catalog depends on the COA, as does the import of the vendor file. There are many dependencies like this in OneWorld. We will point them out as we go along, but please understand that it is not a good idea to jump back and forth through the next few chapters, as we have been careful to take as many dependencies as possible into account. So these chapters contain logic, which is not always apparent to a person new to OneWorld.

After we get through some of the basics, we turn our attention to more significant matters. Since the heart and soul of business is the **Profit and Loss (P&L)**, the **Balance Sheet**, and the **Cash Flow Statement**, the next step is setting up the COA.

The COA is just the first step in the configuration of the OneWorld financials. There are also the locations, departments, and classes. We started discussing these in *Chapter 2, OneWorld's Foundation*, and now we will complete a thorough examination of how these 'tags' are used in OneWorld transactions to provide you with finer financial, sales, and operation reporting, and metrics.

In this chapter, we also begin to provide our judgment, based on experience, on topics such as when to use auto-numbering in OneWorld and when to avoid it. Of course, it is your account and you must make the final decisions about how best to use OneWorld. Keep in mind though that just because you are offered functionality, it does not mean that you need to use it. Be judicious in your approach to deciding what to implement and what simply makes no sense in your business. A OneWorld implementation always goes smoothly when you have just what you need, neither more nor less.

The major headings of this chapter are:

- Setting up the basics
- The chart of accounts
- Departments, classes, and locations
- Naming and numbering in OneWorld
- Advanced taxes
- Setting up the Item catalog
- Completing the accounting preferences

After completing this chapter, we'll be ready to start looking at actual transactions in OneWorld, and how to process the most important transactions for your organization.

Setting up the basics

As we have mentioned at several points earlier in the book, configuring OneWorld requires a ground-up approach. It is much like building a house. First we need a few basics, such as a foundation with access for water, electricity, and gas. Our foundation is the legal entities and the utilities are the currencies, languages, subsidiaries, and states.

Setting up currencies and currency exchange rates

If your organization does business in multiple currencies, you need to set them up in a two-step process. First, make sure that you have enabled multiple currencies, by navigating to **Setup | Company | Enable Features**, and on the **Company** tab's **International** section, click on **Multiple Currencies**. You may also want to click **Currency Exchange Rate Integration**, which allows a nightly update of the currency exchange rate table. The alternative is to use the **Default Exchange Rate (to root subsidiary currency)** on the **Currency** setup, as seen in the next screenshot. In most cases, you will want to use the auto update.

Once you have enabled the features, you can navigate to **Lists | Currencies | New** to set up a new currency, as we have done in the following screenshot. Select the **Format** of the **New Currency** first, as this fills in the **Symbol** and **Format Sample** fields automatically. Then you can enter the **Name** and the **Default Exchange Rate**. Note that the form requires a **Default Exchange Rate**, even if you plan to use the **Automatic Update**. If you have enabled the **Currency Exchange Rate Integration**, the **Automatic Update** box will have already been checked for you.

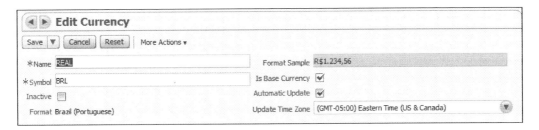

This discussion of currencies probably raises questions for you about how you sell your products abroad. If, for example, you are a US-based company reporting in USD, then you can set up your items with a USD price and then use the currency exchange rate table to calculate the sale price per customer, per sales order, based on the customer's currency.

Alternatively, you can set up prices on your items to sell each item for a set amount in each currency in which you want to transact business. In this scenario, you do not use the currency exchange rate table.

The following screenshot depicts the **Pricing** tab of the **Item setup** form; item XYZ has a price in USD, because that is the currency of the root subsidiary and it also has a price in Brazilian REAL, and several other currencies. When sold to a Brazilian customer, the system uses the price setup for the REAL on the item pricing. If there is no REAL price, then the system uses the exchange rate table.

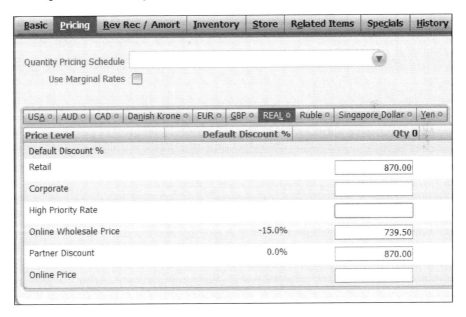

Using the currency exchange rate table or setting up prices for each currency on each item is a decision dependent upon your business model. Retail businesses, or wholesale businesses with repeat business to the same customers, might want to set prices. However, if you sell on a one-time basis to other businesses or retail customers, you might want to use the currency exchange rate table. Many service-based organizations may wish to sell with the benefit of currency exchange rates. It's a decision you need to make.

Setting up states/provinces/counties

If you have a subsidiary in Brazil, then you must set up the Brazilian states in the system prior to setting up the subsidiary. Navigate to **Setup | Company | States/Provinces/Counties** and click **New**. Then you fill out the form, as shown in the following screenshot:

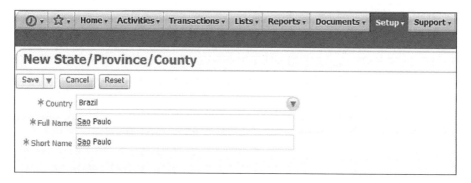

You can use a different short name if you wish, but it is not required. Now that we have our states and our currencies, we can get started with setting up the subsidiaries.

Setting up your organization's structure

In *Chapter 1, What is NetSuite OneWorld?*, we introduced the idea of the organization's structure and suggested that you start putting this together in working format, so that when the time came to begin the OneWorld configuration, you had the structure handy.

We should note here that OneWorld comes with a root subsidiary in your country, currency, and language (unless you specify otherwise to your sales person). If your organization is headquartered in Canada, then your root subsidiary will be based in Canada with the Canadian Dollar as its currency, and English or French as its language.

We should also note here that subsidiary is the term used in OneWorld to describe every legal entity that is part of your organization, even the top-level holding company.

The first thing to do is to open up your root subsidiary and then verify and complete the information. Navigate to **Setup | Company | Subsidiaries** and click on **Subsidiaries**. A form, like the one in the following screenshot, opens up:

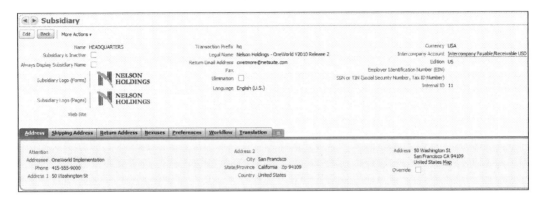

This is known as the root subsidiary. Every OneWorld account comes with a root subsidiary. You can edit some of the information on this form and add information where needed. Notice that there is no field for **Subsidiary of**, as there will be when we start to set up the rest of the subsidiaries.

Also note that this subsidiary has an intercompany account. OneWorld generates this account automatically for organizations that use the **Intercompany Time and Expense** option. These are normally service companies that have consultants who are employed by one subsidiary, but who may also work on projects in another subsidiary. If you do not have this option turned on, then you will not see this field after saving the record. If you do have this option turned on, then you will see an intercompany account generated for each subsidiary you save. In the next section of this chapter, on the chart of accounts, you will learn how to complete the setup of this account for your books.

Once your root subsidiary is correct, turn your attention to the other subsidiaries in the organization. Continue working from top to down, so that you can set up the hierarchy with the **Subsidiary of** field, as depicted in the following image:

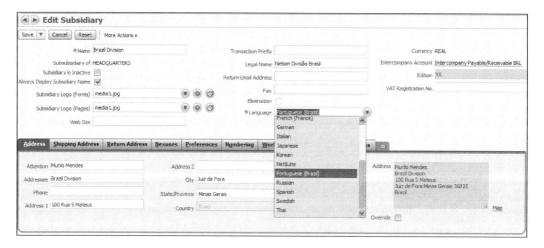

Notice that in the **Subsidiary of** field, we chose **HEADQUARTERS** as the root subsidiary. This makes our **Brazil Division** a child of the root, thus establishing the hierarchy. Each additional subsidiary added to the system generates a subsidiary record at the a subsidiary record at the same level as or at a lower level than the **Brazil Division**.

> **Editing subsidiaries**
>
> Make sure your data is correct before saving your subsidiaries; there are some fields such as **Currency** and **Country** that are not editable after you save. As you might have learned in your youth, measure twice and cut once. It's still good advice.

In the previous screenshot, note the list of languages in the pull-down menu. This is the current list of languages supported by OneWorld.

Also in the previous screenshot, there is a checkbox for **Elimination**. Depending on how your organization operates, you may need to add elimination subsidiaries to your hierarchy, in order to eliminate the value of transactions that take place between subsidiaries. As OneWorld rolls out automatic intercompany processes such as Intercompany Time and Expense or Intercompany Inventory Transfer Orders, there is less need for elimination journals, but one-off intercompany transactions are not unusual. If you want to use the Intercompany auto elimination feature, a best practice, you must setup an elimination subsidiary at every level of your hierarchy.

So how do subsidiaries work?

Before we go any further with the setup of the organization's subsidiaries, we would do well to stop and understand the complexity of the subsidiary functionality. We have created the following table to organize these ideas in a way that you can easily understand and refer to, as you move forward with the implementation:

Element	Subsidiary treatment
Customers	A customer belongs to one and only one subsidiary. If you have multiple subsidiaries doing business with the same customer, then you must set up a customer record for each subsidiary.
Projects	Projects follow the subsidiary of the parent customer.
Subcustomer	Child customers must belong to the same subsidiary as the parent.
Vendors	A vendor belongs to one and only one subsidiary. If multiple subsidiaries are doing business with one vendor, then you must set up a vendor record for each subsidiary
Employees	Each employee belongs to one and only one subsidiary. If an employee belongs to one subsidiary and works on a project belonging to another subsidiary, then their time and expenses generate an intercompany transaction.
Contacts	Contacts belong to one and only one subsidiary. However, it is possible to link a contact from subsidiary A to a customer in subsidiary B. If you must set up the same customer for two subsidiaries, then they can share a single contact.
Partners	A partner belongs to one and only one subsidiary. Each customer that the partner sets up in the system belongs to the same subsidiary as the partner.
Accounts	An account may belong to one or more subsidiaries. You can restrict the subsidiaries, if needed. Major exception: Bank and credit card accounts belong to one and only one subsidiary. Also, your elimination receivable and payable accounts should be linked to just one subsidiary.
Items	An item may belong to one or more subsidiaries. You can restrict the subsidiaries, if needed.
Sales order	A sales transaction belongs to the same subsidiary as the customer; this includes all upstream transactions such as opportunities and quotes, and downstream transactions such as fulfillments, invoices, billings, and payments.
Purchase order	A purchase order belongs to the same subsidiary as the vendor; this includes all upstream and downstream transactions, such as requisitions, receipts, and bills.

Element	Subsidiary treatment
Roles	The delivered standard roles restrict records by the subsidiary of the user, from the user's employee record. For example, the accountant role restricts access to records, by the subsidiary of the employee using the accountant role. If the accountant belongs to the Australian subsidiary, then he/she sees only the customers and vendors that also belong to the Australian subsidiary, and by the same token, he/she sees only the transactions of those customers and vendors. Custom roles may have custom subsidiary restrictions. Giving the custom accountant role access to all of the APAC subsidiaries allows the accountant to see not only Australia, but also all of the records in New Zealand, Malaysia, and Japan, for example, and all of the transactions, too.
Locations	Locations belong to one and only one subsidiary. This means that inventory belongs to a subsidiary and you receive inventory into a location of the subsidiary and release it from a location of a subsidiary. If need be, you can transfer inventory from one subsidiary to another (See *Intercompany Inventory Transfers*).
Departments and classes	Departments and classes may be used by one or many subsidiaries, depending on what you select in their setup. There are no restrictions, except the ones you require.
Commission schedules	Each commission schedule belongs to one and only one subsidiary. The employee must have access to the subsidiary of the customer through their role, and the customer must share the same subsidiary as the schedule, in order to calculate commissions.

Finally, we should note that OneWorld provides several functions for managing intercompany transactions. There are intercompany inventory transfers and intercompany time and expense. For other transactions there is also an intercompany journal which you can auto eliminate. We will discuss this more in *Chapter 6, Nuts and Bolts of OneWorld ERP*.

We have now completed the first few steps in the OneWorld configuration. Establishing your organization's hierarchical subsidiary setup is the first major step toward eventually transacting business in the system. The previous table should serve the purpose of helping you to understand how OneWorld treats various elements in the context of subsidiaries, and it should also restrain any inclination to build a hierarchy substantially different from your actual legal subsidiaries.

The chart of accounts

When you first open up your new OneWorld account and navigate, as the administrator, to **List | Accounting | Accounts** and click **Accounts**, you will see the delivered accounts. OneWorld comes with a basic list of accounts that any organization using OneWorld should probably have. These include a bank account, accounts payable, accounts receivable, income, cost of goods sold, and an expense account. There are also some accounts that OneWorld uses to manage certain transactions, such as the Inventory received not billed account, which is used to post the value of inventory until you bill the purchase order.

In the next screenshot, we want to point out that there are different ways of looking at the list of accounts. Notice in the image that we turned off **Report Style** in the footer, which adds the **Edit** column, and we selected the **All** option in **View**, adding the **Type** column.

Of course, when you first open up this view in OneWorld, you have just a few accounts and they all have a zero balance.

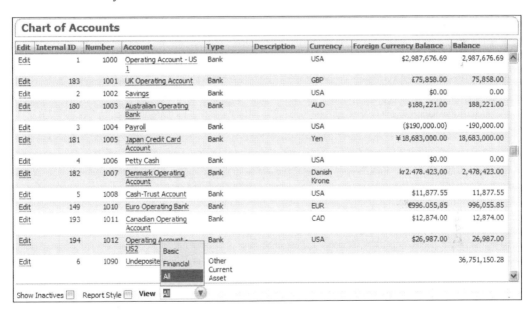

We make it a practice to use all of the delivered accounts that the business model requires. This means that we open them up one at a time and make the changes to them that our COA requires. In the following screenshot, we have opened up the delivered bank account. We changed the name, number, and some of the other information.

Some fields of note on the **Chart of Accounts** form, in the order of importance, are as follows:

1. **Type**: Each account must have a type. This is a OneWorld list that cannot be edited. You cannot change the **Type** after saving the record. If you make an error, you must ask the administrator to delete the account and then start over. Alternatively, you can make the account inactive.

2. **Currency**: The delivered accounts come in the currency of the account owner and cannot be changed. Also, after saving a new account, you cannot change the **Currency**.

3. **Subsidiaries**: The delivered accounts come in the subsidiary of the account owner, the root subsidiary as it is called. If the account works for all subsidiaries, you can click the **Include Children** box. This has the advantage of allowing all subsidiaries to use the account and also any future subsidiaries that you might add over time. Alternatively, you could select one or more subsidiaries from the multiple select list. Be aware that the subsidiary may not change after you use the account in a transaction.

4. **Restrict to (Department, Class, Location)**: These options are for security. To prevent some users from using an account, you can lock it down to users of a specific department, class, or location. This restriction must also be set on the user's role.

5. **Subacccount of**: This field provides the functionality for account rollups. Remember that OneWorld rolls up accounts, by type, in the delivered financial reports.

6. **1099-MISC Category**: If you are paying 1099 vendors, this field is one of the required setups. Select a category from the drop-down list. In order to pay a vendor as a 1099 Contractor, you must associate an account with a 1099 category, make the vendor a 1099 contractor, and then add expenses lines to the vendor bill that charges a 1099 account.

There are several other fields on the form, and you'll notice that the fields change with different account types. If you have further questions, click on the label for the field, or click on **Help** for instructions on the form and all of its fields.

In most cases, the implementation team adjusts the delivered accounts, adding the correct numbers, for example, and then imports the rest of the accounts through the Import function. We cover data migration and the import tool in detail in *Chapter 9, OneWorld Data Migration*.

Managing accounting periods

At **Setup | Accounting | Manage Accounting Periods**, you will find the current year opened with its fiscal quarters and periods. OneWorld comes with the first year setup. As we are going to start testing transactions shortly, we suggest that you click the **Set Up Year** button and add a new year, especially if you are using billing schedules, revenue recognition, or amortization, since these transactions require the periods over which the schedules stretch to be open.

Departments, classes, and locations

One of the most important questions in the early stages of the implementation is how the organization would like to see operational and financial results. Of course, you can see the general ledger impact through the COA and the financial reports, but often a high-level view does not have the detail necessary for decision making, and the G/L is not the place for every detail of the business, nor does it provide the trending data you might require.

The alternative to a granular G/L is the use of departments, classes, and locations. These fields can be used to tag your transactions and add further information that can be very useful when trying to understand business results and plan strategy. Instead of having income accounts for each major project line, you may, for example, opt to have multiple product lines expressed in the **Class** field, giving yourself the option of looking at sales results across many product lines, while preserving the G/L's focus on the whole organization.

Departments, classes, and locations not only tag your transactions, but also your employees and partners. For both partners and employees, the department, class, and location fields serve a security function, permitting or preventing them from seeing entity and transaction records in the system. For employees, the department, class, and location fields may also tag their time and expense transactions. We discuss security in detail in *Chapter 8, Advanced Configuration*. For the current discussion, let's focus on how to tag our transactions.

It's also important to recognize that the behavior of the department, class, and location fields depends significantly on where they are used on your transaction forms. A transaction form has two parts: the main line or header part where all of the data resides relating to the entity—a customer, a vendor, or an employee, or to this particular transaction such as tax rate, discount, and so on; and the line item columns, where all of the items or expenses related to the transaction are listed. We cover both business cases next. To set up departments, classes, and locations, navigate to **Setup | Company | Classifications**.

Apart from tagging transactions and providing additional security to the system, the department, class, and location fields are also used in commission schedules and other areas. If you have additional modules in your OneWorld account, take a look at how they use these fields before making your final decisions.

Lastly, we should mention that before you make all of your **Department**, **Class**, and **Location** field decisions, there are also some other ways to use OneWorld for reporting business results that are sometimes overlooked. One important method is the item hierarchy. When reporting sales by item, the system follows your hierarchy. If a group of items is the 'Child of' another item, the system reports sales results by parent and by child. This method often answers some important questions about what you are selling by looking at a multi-level item hierarchy.

Also, it is possible to tag customer records with a category, so that you can categorize sales by this field, as in what industries you sell to, such as healthcare, education, commercial, and so on. This requires that you bring the category forward from the customer record to the transaction records, but this can be done with a little advanced configuration.

Locations

Let's look at locations first, since these are probably the easiest category to understand for the simple reason that locations are where you keep inventory. If your organization buys, sells, assembles, kits, or otherwise manages, inventory, then you have one or more locations where this activity takes place.

When you enable the features of your OneWorld account, there is an option for **Multiple Locations**. Navigate to **Setup | Company | Enable Features**, and open the **Items and Inventory** tab. Our recommendation is that you enable **Multiple Locations**, even if you have only one actual physical inventory location. Eventually, you will need to add another location, even if only for returns, and it's much easier to start with multiple locations than to change later. Also understand that once you turn on **Multiple Locations** and begin using the system, you cannot turn it off.

The idea is simply to purchase inventory into a location and sell it from a location. In between the purchase and the sale, the inventory may be transferred or distributed from one location to another.

In the context of OneWorld, the location field has two important caveats. First, for any organization using OneWorld's Inventory feature, each location belongs to one and only one subsidiary. On the purchase side, this means that the vendor and the receiving location must both belong to the same subsidiary. Likewise, on the sale side, the customer and the location from which the order is being fulfilled must belong to the same subsidiary.

If you receive goods into a location that belongs to the Canadian subsidiary and you want to sell to a customer who belongs to the US subsidiary, then you must first perform an intercompany inventory transfer, moving the goods from the Canadian subsidiary's location to the US subsidiary's location.

Second, let's also note that locations are not linked directly to G/L accounts. The value of the inventory on the books follows the item setup; you must select an asset account when you set up the inventory item. As a result, the G/L account value is independent of the location. However, you can run reports that detail the value of inventory, by subsidiary and by location.

Any location may have one or more children. The Australian location may have child locations in Sydney and Perth. If you need to move inventory from Perth to Sydney, then you can do a simple inventory transfer, since they belong to the same subsidiary, and not the more complex intercompany inventory transfer. You may also bring inventory into the Australian location, and then distribute it to Perth and Sydney.

You decide where to use locations on the transactions. Take a purchase transaction as an example. (The PO itself is a non-posting transaction, but we'll start our process here.) Normally, you receive the whole PO into the same location, so having the **Location** field only in the main line or header of the PO record works well. The standard item receipt form places the Location field in the line item columns, using the PO's location as the default, and tags both the debit and credit line. When you Bill the PO, the resulting Bill, with the location field in the main line, also charges both credit and debit lines to the same Location. Below we organize the chain of transactions in a small table. We suggest you use a similar tool to verify the accounting results you want:

Transaction	Account	Location	Debit	Credit
PO	Purchase Order (non-posting)	West		$ 100.00
	Raw Materials Asset account	West	100.00	
Receipt	Inventory Received Not Billed	West		100.00
	Raw Material Asset	West	100.00	
Bill	Accounts Payable	West		100.00
	Inventory Received Not Billed	West	100.00	
Payment	Bank Account	West		100.00
	Accounts Payable	West	100.00	
			$400.00	$ 400.00

We should note that on the payment transaction, the only option for the location field is the main line.

Also, while the PO is non-posting, it makes sense to tag the transaction here for two reasons. Firstly, the tag follows on as you open the next subsequent transaction, a receipt in this case. Secondly, if you want to look at a Purchase Orders by Location report, you need to have the transaction tagged. Some reports use the tag in the main line of the transaction, while others, like the Inventory Valuation report, use the line item tag.

Sales-side transactions can be more complex because if you have multiple physical inventory locations, it is not unusual to sell products from multiple locations on the same sales order. Be aware though that when you fulfill, you fulfill from a single location. When you have an order shipping from two locations, you have two fulfillments. The item fulfillment form does not allow department, class, and location in the main line, only in the line item columns. The sales order, like the PO, is non-posting, but we start our transaction process here. Here's how an order shipping from two locations looks:

Transaction	Account	Location	Debit	Credit
SO	Revenue Item 1	West		$ 50.00
	Revenue Item 2	East		50.00
	Sales Order (non-posting)	West	100.00	
Fulfillment 1	Raw Material Asset	West		25.00
	Cost of Goods Sold	West	25.00	
Fulfillment 2	Raw Material Asset	East		25.00
	Cost of Goods Sold	East	25.00	
Invoice	Accounts Receivable	West	100.00	
	Revenue Item 1	West		50.00
	Revenue Item 2	East		50.00
Payment	Accounts Receivable	West		100.00
	Bank Account	West	100.00	
			$ 350.00	$ 350.00

We had the Location field set at both the main line and the line item columns in the sales order and the invoice, allowing us the output above.

Some important points to consider here: The income statement is correct as revenue and cost of goods sold each flow to the correct location; the balance sheet, however, is going to be off for both locations. Running balance sheets based on department, class, and location is difficult, unless all of your transactions have these fields in the main line only. In the example above, if both items had shipped from the West location, and we charged all revenue to the West location, the balance sheet would be fine for the West location.

This may be a moot discussion for you, since it is more common to look at income statements by department, class, and location, and rare to try to look at balance sheets by these metrics. Also, our split order above does provide correct results for the Inventory Valuation report by location, as one example, as we have correctly tagged the two fulfillments.

Lastly, when you create the location records, you determine whether or not the inventory is available for sale, and whether or not it is available in your web store, should you have a web store. These are two important distinctions deserving some thought. For example, if you have breakage that happens in the warehouse or that is returned to you, you can store it in a location, from which you do not resell it. By deselecting the **Available for Sale** option on the Location setup form, your operations team does not see this inventory when fulfilling orders, preventing accidentally sending items in need of repair to a customer, or simply having the impression that sellable inventory levels are higher than they are.

Departments and classes

Departments and classes are less easily implemented than locations, for the simple reason that they are less defined by OneWorld. In other words, while they are easy to configure, their use and function are less well defined and follow your definitions. We have seen OneWorld accounts setup with widely varying definitions of these fields. What's right for you really depends on your reporting or security requirements. It is often difficult for an implementation team member to come up with these definitions, but with a little knowledge of these fields and a strong understanding of your own business, you can usually make these decisions without issues.

First, understand that the names 'Department' and 'Class' can be changed to fit your needs. Departments are often profit or cost centers, while classes may be a line of business, product line, service line, or revenue type; these are just a few of the labels that we have seen.

Second, these fields can be used on either the main line of the transaction, or in the line items, as we saw in our location discussion above. You may decide to use the department in the main line of the sales order and use the class in the line item columns, depending on your requirements.

When using one of these fields, like Class, for example, in the line item columns, it's common to set up the field on the item record. This has the advantage of allowing you to select an item on a transaction line, and then have the class field, for example, default from the item record automatically. If you sell light fixtures and wish to report out sales figures based on the class of lights, then link a class to each item. Each time you select an item on a sales document, the class field populates automatically. However, if you have your forms set up for line item columns entry of the class fields, and you have not populated the class field on the item records, then you will have to select a value for this field for each line item, a task for which your sales people may not have the patience.

The following image details how department, class, and location follow the G/L charges of an invoice with two items:

GL Impact								
Account	Amount (Debit)	Amount (Credit)	Posting	Memo	Name	Subsidiary	Department	Class	Location
1140 Accounts Receivable	1,648.00		Yes		Acme Control	HEADQUARTERS : AMERICAS : US - West	Sales : Corporate Sales	New Business	01 US - West Coast Warehouse
4000 Revenue		649.00	Yes	The sleek black design of our modern cocktail table adds a touch of drama to your living space.	Acme Control	HEADQUARTERS : AMERICAS : US - West	Sales : Corporate Sales	New Business	01 US - West Coast Warehouse
4000 Revenue		999.00	Yes	Enjoy the characteristic modern curve of the Yao headboard.	Acme Control	HEADQUARTERS : AMERICAS : US - West	Sales : Corporate Sales	New Business	01 US - West Coast Warehouse

Hopefully, these examples help you to begin formulating some ideas about how to set up the departments, classes, and locations. Keep in mind that while sales-side transaction forms might have a location at the line item, purchase-side transactions could very well have the opposite (location at the main line). Obviously, there are several decisions to make here, and the next table might be useful. We filled it in with sample data for an organization selling software and hardware. Perhaps a table like this will help you to formulate your organization's department/class/location fields:

Element	What Dimension	Parent and Child	Sales Forms	Purchase Forms
Department	Sales: St Louis	Yes	Main Line	Main Line
	Sales: Austin			
	Operations: St Louis			
	Operations: Austin			
	Sales: Sydney			
Class	Sale Type:	Yes	Main Line	Main Line
	Channel: New Business			
	Channel: Upsell			
	Channel Renewal			
	Direct Sales: New Business			
	Direct Sales: Upsell			
	Direct Sales: Renewal			
Location	St Louis	No	Line Item	Main Line
	Austin			
	Sydney			

It is possible to make department, class, and location mandatory, either by setting the preference at **Setup | Accounting | Accounting Preferences | General**, or by making the fields mandatory per transaction form, which is more flexible.

Naming and numbering in OneWorld

We mentioned previously that NetSuite allows you to rename many of the fields in the system to suit your business model. Customers can be renamed Clients, Sales Orders can be renamed Pro Forma Invoice, and Employees can be renamed Associates. It's really up to you. To get the idea, navigate to **Setup | Company | Rename Records/Transactions**. On this form, you can rename the entities and transaction types, as shown in the following screenshot:

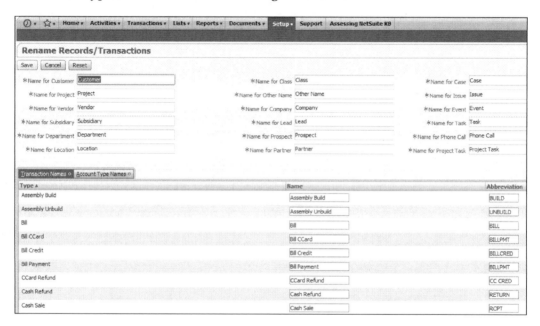

This is a fairly straightforward process. Changes that you make here will cascade to all parts of the system. Should you change Customer to Client, you will see the word Client in every area of OneWorld, for example. Also, the transaction abbreviations are used in several areas of the system; change them carefully. Normally, transaction name changes are only required in one or two instances per account. Don't feel that you have to make changes just for the sake of making changes. Estimates, for example, are known as quotes in some industries, or as proposals in others.

After deciding on your naming conventions for OneWorld, navigate to **Setup | Company | Auto-Generated Numbers**. Here, you control the auto-numbering of both entities and transactions.

Your first question should be *Do we need to number our entities?* A OneWorld account owner might number their customers if, for example, they have a business-to-consumer model with the possibility of a duplicate Mary Browns. In this case, customer numbering makes sense. There is less of a case to make for an organization that sells business-to-business, as it would be highly unlikely to have multiple business customers with the same name. If you number customers, then you also number sub-customers and projects.

It is rare to number vendors or partners, though it can happen in certain instances. Employees are again a call that only you can make, but if you have several hundred employees, then there may be decent chance that you have two Jose Gonzalezes.

Numbering transactions is a more common requirement, and one that makes perfect sense. The next question is *Do you want to use a prefix for the transaction as well?* We have seen everything from INV 999 to Inv2010 999. If you do use intelligence in your numbering, which frankly is unnecessary overkill, you may need to change it manually once a year.

There is also the possibility of using subsidiaries or locations as a prefix to transactions. For example, you could use the prefix BR for all transactions under the Brazilian subsidiary. The auto-numbering still happens, so your sales order is now SO-BR-999. You have to set this up on either the location or the subsidiary record, and also on the **Auto-Generated Numbers** form; there is a radio box you must click. In the following screenshot, we set up the sales orders to use the Prefix SO-, have four numbers, start with 0, and **Use Subsidiary** is set to yes (clicked). As a result, OneWorld added the subsidiary code "USW."

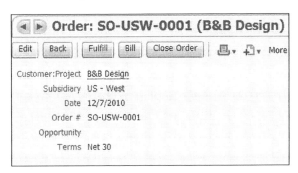

You can also number some of the CRM data, such as **Cases**; this is recommended if you have a customer service department and schedules such as **Revenue Recognition Schedules**, again recommended if your business model has a lot of deferred revenue schedules.

Keep in mind that naming and numbering OneWorld should, like all other tasks, focus on your business requirements. We have seen some customers who get carried away on these tasks and it is a real pain to change your decisions after you have a lot of data in the system. You can change your decisions, but it is not painless.

Advanced taxes

Turning on **Advanced Taxes** for calculating sales tax is nearly a universal requirement for OneWorld customers. Even a service company operating under multiple legal entities in a single country, such as the US, requires multiple nexuses. You turn on the **Advanced Taxes** option by navigating to the **Setup | Company | Enable Features | Accounting** tab, and clicking on the **Advanced Taxes** option.

The advantages of **Advanced Taxes** include the ability to have multiple nexuses, each of which might treat a sales item's taxability differently, by virtue of tax schedules, and the ability to calculate complex sales taxes, such as the VAT taxes of Europe and Canada.

Essentially, when you turn on **Advanced Taxes**, the system allows you to generate multiple nexuses. A nexus is simply a tax jurisdiction, which carries certain taxability rules. For example, in the US, every state is a nexus. When you establish your countries and states, as we did in the previous chapter, and then use them to fill out the subsidiary record, the system automatically generates a tax nexus. You then manually add the other tax nexuses that your organization requires. You may not have a legal entity in every state, but since you have a sales person living and selling there, you may have to set up a tax nexus.

After completing your subsidiary structure, navigate to **Setup | Accounting | Setup Taxes,** where you can see all of the nexuses that have been generated by country, as shown in the following screenshot:

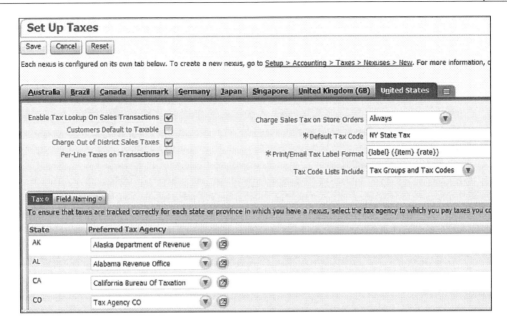

In some cases, the nexus is the country, and in others, such as the US, you must set up the states as nexuses, since each of them has their own sales tax regimen.

There are also several other decisions to make on this form. Each country tab has a different set of questions. Go to the tab and then click the **Help** link at the top of the page to learn more about each country's tax setup.

Setting up a **Nexus** at **Setup | Accounting | Nexuses | New** is straightforward, as depicted in the following screenshot:

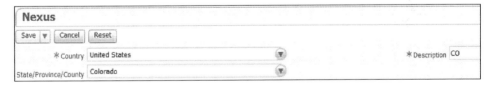

Once you set up the nexus, you can set up the following:

- Set up a vendor record for each nexus and set the vendor category to **Tax Agency**. This allows you to select the vendor record in the preferred tax agency field on the **Setup Taxes** form.
- Enter your company's tax number in the vendor record's **Account** field.

- For each nexus, the system generates a tax control account. For the **Colorado** nexus that we set up in the previous screenshot, the system generated **Sales Tax Payable CO**. This account now appears in your G/L, so navigate to your **Chart of Accounts, Setup | List | Accounting | Accounts** and provide the account with a number.

- Finally, set up your **Tax Schedules**, under **Setup | Accounting | Tax Schedules**. The **Tax Schedules** are what you use to link your nexuses to the taxability of the items you buy and sell. For example, shipping charges that appear on sales documents are taxable in some jurisdictions and not taxable in others. To solve this problem, set up a **Tax Schedule** for shipping items and specify in the setup the nexuses which tax shipping and the nexuses which do not. Then link this new schedule to all of your shipping items. Follow the same process for other items that you sell. The following screenshot shows how the tax schedules work; on the US Nexuses tab we select all the states where the Product is taxable; and on the Non Us Nexuses tab we can select a different tax code for both purchase and sale transactions:

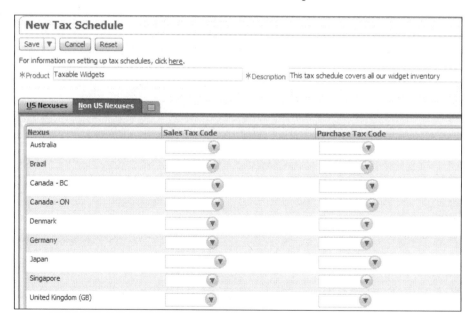

For US subsidiaries, you also need to import the sales tax tables (unless you are using a third-party tax provider). Running this process, from **Setup | Accounting | Import State Sales Tax Tables**, brings into the system all individual tax codes used in a state. If you decided to use **Tax Groups**, that is, a set of tax codes for a particular address (for example, New York State code plus New York City code is a tax group), the system imports all of the tax codes and groups them for you.

You will also notice that on the **Tax Schedule** form, the **VAT** taxes require not only a sales tax code, but also a purchase tax code also.

Advanced Taxes take a fair amount of time, and for some countries, may require extensive manual setups. For the US states, you can import tax tables into the system. If you need to add other tax codes or groups, you may have to enter them manually, so make sure that you plan this task accordingly.

Setting up the Item catalog

We are getting very close now to having a OneWorld system configured to the point where we actually run transactions. All of the work that we have done prior to the Item catalog setup was with the goal of transaction processing in mind, of course. Now with the Item catalog looming before us, let's understand what we have done so far and what's required for the next steps.

In many respects, the Item catalog is the crux of the system. The system behavior of what we buy (be it hours, widgets, or transportation services) and what we sell (again, anything under the sun that might be described as a product or service) results from how we set up the Item catalog, because many functions of the system intersect in the item setup.

For example, item behavior depends directly or indirectly on the subsidiaries, departments, classes, locations, chart of accounts, tax schedules, and units of measure configured in the system. Without these configurations, you cannot start to enter the catalog.

The Item catalog is the most important of the basic setups of OneWorld. In the following discussion, we try to lay out some of the important considerations you should keep top of mind before moving forward.

Item types

Let's start by taking a closer look at the item type. Navigate to **Lists | Accounting | Items | New**. This page displays a list of all the item types available to your account. You probably do not see all of the items in the following list, because you either have not purchased a module, such as Advanced Inventory, or you have not enabled a feature of the system. We cover the most popular item types as follows:

- **Assembly/Bill of Materials**: These items are produced from a number of member items, which are normally inventory items, but could be non-inventory or even other assemblies. An assembly tells the system which member items it requires and their quantities. The cost of the assembly is the sum of the costs of the member items. When you build an assembly, OneWorld credits the inventory of the member raw materials and decrements their counts. Likewise, the system debits the inventory of the finished assemblies and increments their count. After building an assembly, you can transfer it between locations or between subsidiaries. Assemblies can have any costing method: FIFO, LIFO, Standard, or Average.

    - **Serialized**: This is an assembly sub-type and simply means that you are going to serialize every assembly you build with a unique number. Serialized assemblies operate much the same way as assemblies, the only difference being that a serialized assembly is always the top level; a serialized assembly can never be a member of another assembly. It is, however, possible for assemblies to be members of a serialized assembly. Serialized assemblies have specific costing, meaning that each serial-numbered unit has a specific cost, or alternatively standard costing.

    - **Lot Numbered**: This is another assembly sub-type. Lots not only have a unique alpha-numeric identity in the system, but also an expiration date. Lot inventory is normally used for perishable goods. Lots use Lot Costing, meaning that every lot has its own cost or, alternatively, standard costing.

- **Inventory Item**: These are items that you have in stock, or possibly items that you drop ship, but may occasionally have in stock. Inventory items are purchased and used as members of assemblies, sold as members of kits or groups, or sold by themselves. They can use FIFO, LIFO, Standard, or Average cost methods (or Specific and Lot Costing, in the case of serialized inventory and lot inventory, respectively) and they may use a Unit of Measure. Apart from individual inventory items, there are also the following:

- ° **Lot Numbered**: Purchase a lot of inventory with Lot or Standard Costing and a lot number and Expiration Date. These can also have units of measure. Sell before the expiration date.

- ° **Serialized**: These have Specific or Standard Costing and Serial Numbers.

- All three inventory item types: **Inventory**, **Lot Numbered**, and **Serialized** may also be set up as **Matrix** inventory (Red Shirt XL is an example of a matrix item). Matrix items allow you to show one item in your Web store or catalog, but manage the inventory of all possible combinations of the matrix.

- **Item Group**: These are very simple groups of items that you sell together. An **Item Group** must have at least one member, but it has no accounting itself; it simply follows the accounting of all the member items. Item groups make sales peoples' lives easier when you sell a certain configuration of items regularly. It's an easy way to put several items on a sales document at once. It also allows you to hide the details of the group and simply display the price of the group to the customer. Also, item groups can be built on the fly.

- **Kit/Package**: Kits lie somewhere between item groups and assemblies. There is no process to put kits together; it's something you do on the fly. On the other hand, the kit has its own accounting separate from the members on the income side. The kit's cost of goods sold uses the COGS of its members. But you can enter a sales price for the kit, which may be more or less than the sum of the members' sale prices, and the system charges the revenue to whatever account you specify.

- **Non-inventory Item**: These come in three subtypes: for sale, for purchase, or for resale. We often use non-inventory items for resale, for drop ship items that we never intend to stock. A good example of a non-inventory for sale is a warranty or a support contract. A non-inventory item for purchase might be a warranty that you purchase from a vendor.

- **Service**: When you provide services to your customers, whether on a time and materials or fixed bid model, or a combination, use the **Service** item. You can enter time against a service item; link it via a sales order to a project; or link it via a project to a sales orders. They also come in three sub-types: for sale, for purchase, and for resale, with the same general functionality as the non-inventory items.

These are the most important Item types. There are a few other item types that you will see, like Discount Items, which are self-explanatory.

Setting up a well-thought-out item catalog makes the implementation move forward painlessly. Take your time and start with a couple of items for each item type your organization requires. Then, once you are comfortable with these setups, import the rest of your items through the import tool at **Setup | Import/Export | Import CSV Records**.

Item accounting

Before getting started on item setup, we suggest that you open up the item setup form for each of the item types described previously to get a better sense of the accounting that takes place for each item type when you transact it in OneWorld.

For example, when you navigate to **List | Accounting | Items | New** and select the **Inventory Item** type, on the Standard Inventory item setup form, you see fields for **Asset Account, Income Account,** and **COGS Account**. When you purchase an inventory item, you debit the asset account, and when you fulfill an order for the item, you credit the asset account and debit the cost of goods sold account. Finally, when you generate the cash sale or the invoice, you credit the income account.

The setup of the accounts on any item type tells you the story of how the system expects you to use this item in your business. Your controller should have a thorough understanding of item accounting, before you make any final decisions for the Item catalog.

Besides the accounts, there are other fields, which have a real impact on how the item transacts in the system; these are listed as follows:

- **Units of Measure**: Set up under **Lists | Accounting | Units of Measure**. UoM enables the **Purchase, Stock,** and **Sale Units** of a specific item to be different, while all relating to a base unit. For example, you might purchase an inventory item in a spool, stock in yards, and sell by the foot. The system makes the calculation for you, based on your UoM setup. UoM are used exclusively with inventory item types.

- **Costing Method**: The four options are
    - ° **FIFO**, first in first out, tracks inventory as it comes in the door; as it transacts through the system, FIFO uses the cost of the oldest inventory in stock as the cost of goods sold in order fulfillment.
    - ° **LIFO**, last in first out, tracks inventory as it comes in the door; as it transacts through the system, LIFO uses the most recent purchase cost of the inventory as the cost of goods sold in order fulfillment.

- **Average** costing averages the cost of inventory from all purchases, and uses this average for the cost of goods sold in order fulfillment.

- **Standard Costing**, by setting up your expected costs and then purchasing, assembling and selling at actual costs you can monitor costs variances.

Lot and Serialized inventory have costing specific to the lot or serial number, or standard costing.

Set the default costing method in the **Accounting Preferences | Items/ Transactions** tab. You probably need to consult your controller for advice on the best selection for your business model; manufacturing and distribution organizations have different takes on costing. Once you save an item, you cannot change the costing method.

- **Variance Accounts**: There can be variances in purchasing between the purchase price on the receipt and the bill, a variance between the quantity received on the receipt and on the bill, or between the exchange rate on the receipt and the rate on the bill. As a result, each month, as part of the accounting close, you can navigate to the **Post Vendor Bill Variances** form to post variances and clear the **Inventory received not billed** account. These three variance accounts work in conjunction with the **Match Bill to Receipt** field. There are also three variance accounts for organizations using standard costing: Production Quantity, Production Price, and Purchase Price variance accounts.

- **Match Bill to Receipt**: You can set the default for this field in your accounting preferences. This field determines the method that you use to post vendor bill variances. To post the variance based on your vendor's bill, turn it on; or to post variance based on the purchase order, turn it off.

- **Track Landed Cost**: If you want to track landed costs on an item, the costs of getting product to your warehouse door that you add to the value of inventory and COGS on a purchase, then you must have this box checked. If you are using landed costs, then you should check this box, by default, for all inventory items.

- **Tax Schedule**: This tells the system how to treat this item for sales taxes by tax nexus, as we explained previously in *Advanced Taxes*.

- **Drop Ship/Special Order**: Checking either of these options allows you to identify items on sales orders that are either drop ship, direct from vendor to customer, or special order from vendor to you to customer. By identifying a line item as either drop ship or special order, you automatically generate a PO, or purchase order. You also can change the designation of an item from drop ship to special order, or vice versa, on the sales order line item.

Groups, kits, and assemblies

A few words on groups, kits, and assemblies are in order. Groups are the least functional of the three, being simply a collection of other items that you want to sell together. The advantage of a group is you can enter it as a single item on a sales order, and then let the system expand the entry to include a line for each member of the group, which makes life easy for sales people. The other advantage is that you have the option, when printing a sales document for a customer (estimate, sales order, packing slip, or invoice), of including all the members with their quantities, prices, and so on, or just the group item quantity and price. The group's price is simply the sum of its members. In effect, you do not show the customer how you arrived at the group's price, though internally this is readily visible. The G/L impact of the item group is simply the G/L impact of each individual item, meaning that the item group itself has no accounting.

One last note on groups is that you can put them together on the fly, if need be. You may sell your products and services in multiple configurations, more than it makes sense to create them as individual group items, so create a single group with a single member and then add the rest on the sales form.

The Kit/Package is a way of selling a group of items and charging the group to the kit's income account. You might sell diving equipment and have different income accounts for bodysuits, accessories, and kits. The kit includes one or more members, such as a body suit, fins, a mask, and snorkel. The kit's income is charged to the kit's income account, and the cost of goods sold is charged to the members' COGS account. In the warehouse, you can pick a kit on the fly, but in OneWorld, you cannot change a kit on the fly, from a sales order form, for example. Whatever you defined as the kit, is what you sell as a kit.

An assembly is an item and a process. The assembly item has a number of members and a complete accounting setup. When you use the assembly process to produce an assembled unit, the system takes the value and count of the members from their 'raw materials' inventory and puts the value and count into the assembly's 'finished' goods inventory. From this point on, as you transact the assembly on a sale, the inventory count and value both transact from the assembly's accounts. The system allows you to also purchase an assembly, if you require this, but in most cases, you are doing light manufacturing when you use assemblies. Assemblies must be defined before being used; you cannot define an assembly on the fly.

Groups, kits, and assemblies are important features of the system and are used by many different business models to sell products. They can also be used together. For example, you may sell an assembly you produce as part of an item group that includes a user manual in one of several languages, for example. Not every combination is possible, however. An assembly may include another assembly, and a serialized assembly may include other assemblies, but a serialized assembly cannot include another serialized assembly.

Matrix items

A matrix item allows you to generate a single parent item with multiple child items, each of which has a different product configuration. A shirt with three colors and three sizes is a single matrix item with nine different children. We transact the children through the system: purchasing, receiving, ordering, fulfilling, and invoicing a large, red shirt. OneWorld offers you a process for generating the matrix item and all of the children, called the **Matrix Item Assistant**. This walks you through the process of generating the lists of values for the matrix and in the end, generates the parent item and its children. You must, however, edit the parent and add the rest of the data to the item, or correct the data, then save by clicking the **Update Matrix** button, which cascades all of your changes down to the child items.

Once you establish your matrix values, you can then simply use the **Create Matrix Item** process, which allows you to set up the parent item entirely, select the matrix values you want to use, and then click the **Update Matrix** button to generate the children.

Matrix items are popular for some organizations that sell online. With a matrix item, you set up and display a single item, the parent, with a box that allows the consumer to select the correct child item for them. Keep in mind that you need to add some code to the website to display only the child items that are in stock, if you sell from inventory.

Service items

There is a lot to discuss in regards to product items, but we should not lose sight of service items. It is a rare OneWorld customer who does not offer some service or another to their customers, and more recently, OneWorld has made a large push into the service industry with both its own functionality and that of NetSuite's recent acquisitions.

Service items for companies that have purchased **Advanced Project Management**, allow you to not only sell services, but also to generate projects and tasks directly from the sales order, or alternatively to link a project to a service item on a sales order. This is an important functionality for organizations that need to bill based on milestones, fixed-bid contracts with set intervals, or even time- and material-based projects.

Managing inventory

Setting up your inventory management can be as simple as telling the system for each item and each inventory location the reorder point and the preferred stock level. This setup is on the inventory item setup form, found in the **Lists | Accounting | Items | New | Inventory Items | Inventory** tab. Keep in mind that using this option means that, as an item's sales grow or slow, you may have to change these values. This can be done programmatically by exporting your item list and then importing it with new values.

Alternatively, under the **Setup | Company | Enable Features | Items/Inventory** tab, there is an option for **Advanced Inventory**. After turning this on, navigate to **Setup | Accounting | Inventory Management Preferences** and set the default preferences for your items and mass update items already in the system. Of course, you can also set these values for each item as you import or set them up in the system.

With its latest release, NetSuite now offers a **Demand Planning** module that allows you to use a number of input variables to determine required inventory levels, and then manage the supply chain for inventory also.

Item pricing

Item pricing sometimes seems like an implementation unto itself. This is obviously an area of great concern to everyone in the organization, from management to sales and accounting. The value of what you sell is usually inextricably linked to how you sell, so move carefully here.

The good news is that OneWorld provides you with a lot of options. For organizations that sell products, you can offer different prices based on the customer's price level, such as silver, gold, or platinum, for example, combined with unit quantity. For more sophisticated quantity pricing, you can set up your own **Quantity Pricing Schedules** under **Lists | Accounting**. You can also use pricing groups that allow you to put items into a special group and then give individual customers customer pricing on the group. Price levels, by the way, are set up under **Setup | Accounting | Accounting Lists**.

Of course, pricing can also be customized on sales forms, which is a common practice for service-based organizations.

Item vendors

Setting up item vendors is an important feature for products-based companies, especially if you have multiple vendors for any item. Obviously, you must first set up the vendor records, before adding a vendor to the item record. (See the *Chapter 9, Data Migration*, for more on vendor imports.) Also, if you do drop ship or special order, you must have a vendor on the item setup.

If you enable the **Drop Ship** feature, then you must set up the multiple vendor function. This adds a list of vendors to the item form, one of which must be the preferred vendor. Keep in mind that in OneWorld, the vendor and the customer must belong to the same subsidiary in order to drop ship or special order an item.

Each vendor can have their own price and volume pricing schedule as well.

Item display

How items display on your sales documents is really up to you. Every item has a **Name** field and a **Display** field. If you use a display name, OneWorld uses the display name on the sales and purchase documents. If you do not use the display name, OneWorld uses the item name. If you check the **Show Display Name with Item Codes** option at **Setup | Company | General Preferences**, then the system shows the item name and the display name together.

Vendor names/codes are also available on purchase forms and documents.

Item imports

As we mentioned previously, you can import your items at **Setup | Import/Exports | Import CSV Records**. We go into the details in *Chapter 9, OneWorld Data Migration*, but want to mention here that you can import records both to get started with the system, and to make changes, should you need to do so, such as prices, for example.

There are obviously a lot of options in the Item catalog setups and it's not always obvious which item type works best for the sales scenario that you are trying to manage in OneWorld. Our last point is to say that it makes a lot of sense to understand your organization's requirements fully, then set up a couple of items of the most appropriate type, and finally transact the item as many times as you need, for you and the end users to be comfortable that the setup is correct. Only then should you contemplate item imports.

Completing the accounting preferences

Now that we have a start on the Item catalog, we can look forward to transacting some purchases and sales in the system and sorting through the results for what we want and what we want to avoid. In *Chapter 2, OneWorld's Foundation*, we took a stab at setting up the **Accounting Preferences**, at **Setup | Accounting | Accounting Preferences**, but only worked through the first two tabs. It's now time to return to this task and understand how the following options affect transaction processing. At this point, it is only important you know that the preferences below exist. As you start to test transactions in OneWorld, you gain an understanding of how these preferences operate in the system. Some preferences might be obvious for you to answer at this point, and others less so.

The Order Management tab

These preferences are very important to how your OneWorld system operates for you.

First, for **Sales Orders**:

- **Default Order Status**: Do you want an order approval process?
- **Require Re-approval on Edit of Order**: If you selected **Pending Approval** in **Default Order Status**, then do you want the order to re-enter the approval process when edited?
- **Send Email Confirmation when Order Cancelled**: Most appropriate for a web e-tailer.
- **Default Location for Orders**: Do you want to default the fulfillment location?

Now, for **Picking/Packing**, two of the steps in product fulfillment:

- **Always Print Kit Items on Picking Tickets**: Does the warehouse picker need the member items of a kit to print on the picking ticket?
- **Show Uncommitted Items on Picking Tickets**: Do you want items that are not available to be picked, to be printed on the picking ticket?
- **Show Non-Inventory Items on Printed Forms**: Do you need to show warranty items on picking tickets?

- **Show All Ordered Items on Packing Slips**: Do you want every item on the sales order to show on the packing slip, regardless of whether it is in the package or not?

- **Show Drop Ship Items on Packing Slips**: If an item on the order is being drop shipped by a vendor, do we still show it with the items your organization picked and packed?

General Fulfillment Preferences are next:

- **Limit Status on Packing Slip Queue:** Select a filter for the the packing function, either picked or packed.

- **Fulfill Based on Commitment**: When you process a sales order, you can commit inventory to a line item, based on **Available Qty** and **Complete Qty**, or you can choose **Do Not Commit**. Your choices here include **Limit to Committed**, **Allow Uncommitted**, and **Ignore Commitment**. How you handle these two determines how you allocate inventory among many orders.

- **Default Items to Zero Received/Fulfilled**: On receipts and fulfillments, do you want the system to default a zero in, which forces the employee to enter the correct amount?

- **Allow Overage on Item Fulfillments**: Can you send more than the customer ordered? Might be useful if you have minimum order amounts, for example, which were not met on the sales order.

- **Filter Bulk Fulfillment Page by Location**: Allows you to specify the location, before you start to do bulk fulfillments on the **Transaction | Sales | Fulfill Orders** form.

- **Send Order Fulfilled Confirmation Emails**: This is especially important for web e-tailers, but can also be used by any organization delivering products through a shipper.

- **Use Website Template for Fulfillment Emails**: If you have a website, you can use the same template for a web order as other orders.

- **Build Based on Commitment**: How do you want to build assemblies, based on work orders? If your WO says 5, do you want to allow the plant to build 10?

- **Allow Overage on Assembly Builds**: If you generate a Work Order for the assembly of 10 units, do you want to allow the plant to build 12?

General Invoicing is next:

- **Show Unfulfilled Items on Invoices**: Do you want your invoices to include items that you have not yet fulfilled?

- **Invoice in Advance of Fulfillment**: Do you want to invoice the customer, before fulfilling the order?

- **Convert Absolute Discounts to Percentage**: Do you want to convert a dollar discount to a percent discount that will be spread across several invoices evenly? This applies to the sales order that has multiple invoices. Enabling this would spread the discount out evenly to each invoice, instead of taking it all on the first invoice.

- **Base Invoice Date on Billing Schedule Date**: You have the option of setting the data and period of invoices and cash sales to the date identified in the billing schedule or the date when you generate the invoice or cash sale.

For **Drop Shipment Preferences**:

- **Drop Ship P.O Form**: Select a default drop ship purchase order form.

- **Automatically Email Drop Ship P.Os**: Check this is off, if you want to send drop ship POs to vendors automatically when they are generated.

- **Queue Drop Ship P.Os for Printing**: Alternatively, you can send drop ship POs by e-mail.

- **Automatically Fax Drop Shop P.Os**: Or you can send them by fax.

- **Limit Vendor List on Items**: Limit the vendor list on the sales order line item and on the order items form to the vendors linked to the item at item setup.

- **Include Committed Quantities**: Do you want to include committed item quantities in your drop ship PO?

- **Update Drop Ship Order Quantities Automatically Prior to Shipment**: Do you want to automatically update sales and purchase order quantities to be equal, before transacting?

- **Drop Ship Fulfillment Quantity Validation**: How do you want to handle a drop ship fulfillment that has a different quantity from the PO?

- **Allow Both Marked Shipped Fulfillments and Receipts on a Drop Shipment Line**: Do you warn or prevent users from creating a receipt for a drop ship PO that already has a fulfillment line?

Purchase Order Preferences are for organizations using the PO function:

- **Allow Expenses on Purchase Orders**: Do you want to be able to add expenses to a PO? Do you need to bill expenses through to a customer?

- **Enable Custom Purchase Order Approval Process**: Do you want an approval process for purchases that are different from the delivered purchase approval process? The delivered process uses the employee's purchasing approver hierarchy. Using Suiteflow, you can generate a custom workflow for PO approvals.

- **Default Location for Purchase Orders**: Do you want to have a default location for receiving?

If your organization uses purchase orders and advanced receiving, then you must take a look at these preferences:

- **Bill in Advance of Receipt**: Do you want to bill a PO and pay a vendor prior to receiving the product?

- **Allow Overage on Item Receipts**: Do you allow receipt quantities greater than the PO?

- **Default Receiving Exchange Rate**: Should the receipt's exchange rate default from the PO, or do you want the exchange rate as of the date of receipt?

- **Use Purchase Order Rate on Bills**: Do you want to pay the rate on the PO or the rate on the receipt, by default?

For organizations that have customers' or vendors' returns of products, or software in some cases, see the following preferences:

- **Default Return Auth Status**: Your choices are **Pending Approval** or **Pending Return**.

- **Refund in Advance of Return**: Refund a customer prior to receiving their return?

- **Restock Returned Items**: Do you want to put items that are returned right back into stock to sell? This option adds a **Return to Stock** button on the **Receipts** form.

- **Write-Off Account for Returns**: If you receive but do not restock a return, then the value gets written off to the account you select here.

- **Default Vendor Return Auth Status**: Your choices are **Pending Approval** or **Pending Return**, probably depends on the value of your returns.

- **Credit in Advance of Vendor Return**: Do you want to process a credit prior to returning goods to the vendor? This might be a useful option, if you want to make sure that you process a vendor credit against a payable.

If you have inventory in multiple locations and need to ship it from one location and receive it into another location, then see the following:

- **Default Transfer Order Status**: Your choices are **Pending Approval** or **Pending Fulfillment**, and they probably depend on the layers of hierarchy in your warehouse organization.

- **Use Item Cost as Transfer Cost**: When transferring items between locations, you can decide how you want to use the item's cost. If you enable this option, OneWorld uses the item cost as the declared shipping value only; but if you do not enable this option, then the transfer price becomes the item's cost on the receipt.

And for Vendor Bills

- **Default Vendor Bill Status**:Approved or Pending Approval

And for Approval Routing:

- **Enable Custom Purchase Order Approval Routing**: Click this on if you want to customize the process with SuiteFlow

- **Enable Custom Vendor Bill Approval Routing**: Click this if you want to customize the process with SuiteFlow.

The Time and Expenses tab

If you have employees or contractors entering time for internal or customer projects, be it for payroll, billing, or both, see the **Time Tracking preferences**. If they enter expenses, then also see the **Expense preferences**. We have listed them all as follows:

- **Show Projects Only for Time and Expense Entry**: Show Projects only in the **Customer/Project** field on the **Time Entry** form, or show both customers and projects

- **Automatically Notify Supervisor**: Send e-mail notifications to supervisors when new time and expenses entries are ready for approval

- **Override Rates on Time Records**: This option locks the rates on time entries and makes sure that invoices reflect the rate shown on time entries

- **Require Approvals on Time Records**: Check this option to make sure that supervisors approve time records, before billing customers

- **Time Billable by Default**: If you enable this preference, every new time entry is 'billable' by default

- **Copy Time Memos to Invoices**: Gives customers a short description of each time entry

- **Show Planned Time in Time Entry**: When you have tasks set up on projects, OneWorld can generate planned time entries for your project resources, allowing them to simply correct the hours and enter a memo

And for **Expenses**:

- **Expenses Billable by Default**: Enable depending on whether every new expense entry is 'billable' by default

- **Items Billable by Default**: Enable depending on whether every new item entry on a PO is 'billable' by default

- **Combine Detail Items on Expense Reports**: Expenses in the same category are combined into one line, if you enable this option

- **Copy Expense Memos to Invoices**: Provides your customers with a description of each expense line

Summary

In this chapter, our goal was to get the system configured to the point where you could start running and looking at the transactions that are central to your business. Again, taking the approach that it is better to prototype early and often, we have tried to focus our efforts on setting up just enough to get our prototyping started, without tying our hands to a lot of key decisions, before we really understand them.

At this point, you should be able to start thinking about setting up a few test customers and vendors, a few items in your main item categories, and then perform some basic transactions. We walk you through this task over the next few chapters, as we look at the base setups and transactions in various, but common, business models.

5
Nuts and Bolts
of OneWorld CRM

The term 'nuts and bolts' is an old adage that means 'how it works' or 'the bottom line.' This chapter gives an in-depth review of OneWorld CRM functions and processes, aiming to provide business leaders and IT managers with a foundation of knowledge about what's possible in OneWorld. After our initial discussion of OneWorld CRM basics, we take a typical business case and focus on a real OneWorld CRM implementation and the decisions that it requires.

Why start with CRM? We might as well start where any organization starts – revenue. At some point in every organization's life, the planning and budgeting are superseded by the need to market and sell. Once sold, a customer must be cared for. This is the essence of CRM in a nutshell. We see no reason to devote tomes to explaining what it is – we all know what it is. The question is how to do it in a clearly defined, measurable, and sustainable process. That's where OneWorld starts. We'll cover the three main modules, **Marketing**, **Sales**, and **Customer Service**, in the same order that they happen in any organization.

Let us also mention that in the discussion here and in other parts of the book, we use the term 'customer record' when we are talking about the customer entity record, regardless of its **stage** – **Lead**, **Prospect**, or **Customer**, or its **status** – **Lead Unqualified 0** percent or **Customer Closed Won 100** percent, or something in between. We discuss the uses of stages and statuses later in this chapter, but to avoid any confusion on the reader's part, we always refer to the customer entity as the customer.

The major headings of this chapter are:

- Marketing
- Sales
- Customer service

Marketing

I know that half of my marketing spend is a waste; I just don't know which half, paraphrases one of the oldest conundrums of marketing. We do a whole bunch of things, sales happen, but we cannot say definitively what drove a sale. What marketing should we do more of? What marketing should we do less of? What marketing should we stop doing altogether? There are no perfect answers here, but OneWorld allows us to make some real progress towards a better understanding of what works and what does not.

Recently, NetSuite released, for all of its products, including OneWorld, a new tool called SuiteFlow that enables each account owner to create new workflows in the system. SuiteFlow adds huge new functionality to all of the modules, including marketing. We will cover the SuiteFlow functionality later in the book, but we do point out areas where it can be readily used, just to raise a flag; if you do not see functionality in the coming discussions that you need for your business, there is a strong probability that with SuiteFlow and some of the other customization capabilities of OneWorld, you can build your specific requirements into the modules of OneWorld, in some cases, without the need for custom code.

Marketing preferences

The first step to using marketing is the setup of the **Marketing Preferences**. These can be found by navigating to **Setup | Marketing | Marketing Preferences**. Most of the preferences are standard fare, but there are a few worth discussing here.

Before you set up your default e-mail address preferences, you need to set up a mail addresses here: **Setup | Marketing | Email Addresses**. This is a simple task, but seems to confuse people.

If you are going to send any e-mail campaigns to prospects or customers, you need to have these e-mail addresses registered in OneWorld. This is one of several precautions that the system takes to prevent e-mail abuse or spam.

Of course, you need to have these addresses first, so talk to your e-mail administrator. Enter the e-mail, and then go to the address's inbox and retrieve the code that OneWorld sends you. When you first set up this form, it looks like the following screenshot:

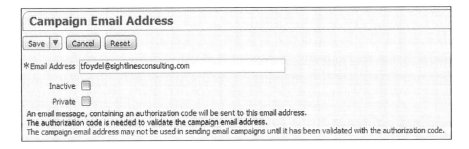

When you return to the form after saving and finding the e-mail activation code in your inbox, the form looks like the following screenshot; just cut and paste the activation code into the form:

You now have at least one e-mail address that you can use for e-mail campaigns. Of course, you can set up as many e-mail addresses as you need.

You also need to set up domains for e-mailing. Do this at **Setup | Website | Domains**, as shown in the following screenshot:

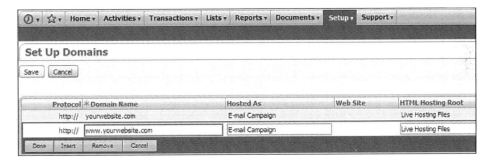

If you need to set up a domain for a Webstore, see our *E-commerce in OneWorld* section in *Chapter 6, Nuts and Bolts of OneWorld ERP*. The form in this screenshot is the same one we use for domain setups, for websites built in OneWorld.

Next, there are also a couple of preferences that require you to understand **Lead Source**. When you turn on **Marketing Automation** in **Enable Features**, you tell the system that the **Lead Source** field on the customer record is the marketing campaign to which the lead has responded, not a simple list of values (as the lead source field is otherwise). While **Lead Source** refers to the original marketing campaign the customer responded to, OneWorld does list all subsequent campaigns and how the customer responded on the **Marketing** tab of the customer record.

The first marketing campaign that a customer responds to becomes their lead source. However, subsequent campaign responses, though they do not necessarily update the **Lead Source** field on the customer record, can update the **Lead Source** field on the sales order record. This is important because it enables the analysis of marketing campaigns and the sales that they generate. While one campaign may help you to acquire a new lead, another may be very good at closing the sale. There is also similar functionality for updating sales records with promotional campaigns. The preferences for these functions are highlighted in the following screenshot:

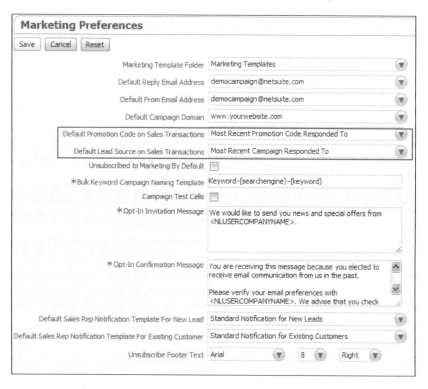

Other marketing preferences to take a look at, if you are interested in using e-mail marketing include:

- **Unsubscribed to marketing by default**: Click **Yes** if you want customers to default to soft opt-out, or **No** if you want to default to soft opt-in. Selecting **No** means that you have to ask for permission to e-mail a new customer.

- **Opt-in Invitation Message**: Write the message to invite customers to opt-in to your marketing campaign e-mails.

- **Opt-in Confirmation Message**: Write the message to ask customers to confirm their interest in your marketing campaigns.

Taken together, these three preferences help you to manage your e-mail marketing effectively. There are four statuses for e-mail marketing: Confirmed opt-in, soft opt-in, soft opt-out, and confirmed opt-out. You can use the **Mass Updates** function to send out mass e-mail invitations to the soft opt-out group, which allows them to select the categories of e-mails that they may wish to receive. Or, you could send the soft opt-in an e-mail to confirm their interest in one or more of your subscription categories. Confirmed opt-out customer records cannot be sent mass e-mails, and confirmed opt-in customer records are already set to receive the e-mails of their choice.

The subscription categories are found under **Setup | Marketing | Campaign Subscriptions**. There are several delivered categories, and you can add others or deactivate the delivered ones. The **Mass Update** functionality is under **List | Mass Update | Mass Updates**, as seen in the following screenshot:

There are several other lists of values that you might find useful under the **Marketing setups** at **Setup | Marketing | Campaign Management**. Values, such as offers and verticals, can be useful for reporting out more granular results from marketing. One list that you do need to complete if you are going to manage your keyword campaigns in OneWorld is the **Search Engine** list.

The tools

There are five main tools in OneWorld marketing: **Campaigns**, **Online Customer Forms**, **Templates**, **Upsell**, and **Promotion Codes**.

- The campaign is the data record where you organize marketing campaigns and events, whether it's a trade show, a purchased list for cold calling, a pay-per-click campaign, an e-mail blast, or a banner advertisement. All of these are campaigns in OneWorld.

- Online customer forms are forms where you capture new leads. They can also be used in other ways, but for our marketing discussion, the online customer form is on our landing page and it allows a visitor interested in our offer to sign up.

- Templates are the visual foundation for e-mail blasts and e-mail lead nurturing, and even for individual e-mails to customers, vendors, partners, and employees, as well as for online customer forms. We can generate templates and then change the content as we need to for each e-mail campaign. They are the visual representation of the e-mail campaign or online form.

- Upsell provides product-based companies, primarily e-commerce companies, with an understanding of the combinations of products that their customers purchase. If the customer purchases product A, they have a 30 percent chance of purchasing product B. If you purchase A, I will send you an e-mail reminding you about B, or even suggest product B on the e-commerce site.

- Promotion codes are a way of tracking campaigns that otherwise might not provide us with details of how well they work. A trade publication advertisement, for example, provides more value if we know that a new lead found us through the advertisement and mentioned the promotion code in our online lead capture form, or in the checkout coupon field. Promotion codes can also be used with online banner advertisements to identify the source of your web visitors.

The idea is that there are several tools in the OneWorld toolbox for marketers to use together or individually to develop new business. We sketch a new campaign below. This is how it unfolds.

Business case: Acme inc

Acme wants to increase its business development activity. It wants to do some keyword campaigns on the search engines, a banner advertisement on a trade site, add a couple of landing pages to the company's website with lead capture forms, and follow up any new leads with a drip e-mail, or lead nurture, marketing campaign. In order to achieve the goals of increasing sales and keeping the marketing budget intact, Acme needs to acquire leads, close the sale, and track the efforts that led to the improved results. They are going to use the following marketing functions.

Keyword campaign

They first set up a new keyword campaign in OneWorld by navigating to **List | Marketing | Marketing Campaign | New**. The next screenshot is this new campaign; notice that the system automatically appended the campaign ID to the company's website URL. Then they set up the same keywords as a campaign in one of the search engines, using the URL generated by OneWorld. If the visitor fills out a form or makes a purchase, this campaign becomes their lead source.

If you built your website in NetSuite, the passing of parameters from the URL to the online form and the customer's record is automatic. If you have a third-party site, then you must use some JavaScript to pass the parameters to the form.

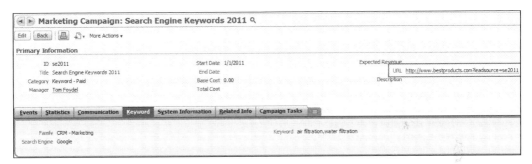

Marketing manually sets up this first keyword campaign, but there are options for setting up bulk campaigns for keywords. In this case, you navigate to **Lists | Marketing | Create Keyword Campaign**. Alternatively, you can also import keywords in bulk to generate your campaigns.

Regardless of the way you set up the campaigns, the key is to remember to use the URL on your OneWorld marketing campaign to link your clicks from the search engines to OneWorld. This link makes it possible to see the number of leads and sales generated directly by the campaign. You can also pass other parameters to a site or form through the URL, for example, partner code or name and promotion codes.

Lead capture forms

If a lead comes to your site from a paid or natural keyword search, then you will want to make sure that you can offer them a compelling reason to stay for a while and take an affirmative step toward a business relationship. The content of your site determines if the visitor finds what they are looking for, and an online lead form provides the mechanism by which you capture their information in exchange for something of value from you, for example, a whitepaper, a case study, a webinar – the list is endless. This is what we refer to as the offer.

Setting up lead capture forms in OneWorld is important for any company doing business-to-business sales, but can work equally well for a business-to-consumer site, depending on your business model. Natural or paid keyword search are two ways of pulling new potential business to your site, and paired with lead capture and e-mail lead nurture are part of a very powerful marketing strategy.

To set up a lead capture form, navigate to **Setup | Marketing | Online Lead Forms**. You can choose to use the default template form or use a custom HTML template to generate the form. Remember that the form is simply set into a page on your site, so it's up to you how much effort you want to put into the aesthetics. We very often use the default template in the same color as the page's background. Then we put it into the page in an iframe, as described in *Chapter 2, OneWorld's Foundation*.

There are a couple of things to note here. First, decide if you are going to capture individuals or companies, as this makes a difference on which fields are mandatory. Also, decide what you will do when the current customers sign up again for something new. This happens a lot in some business models. There are options for these and some other attributes on the **Setup Workflow** tab.

After you save the form, a new tab called **External** appears. This is where OneWorld stores the **Publishable Form URL** for your form.

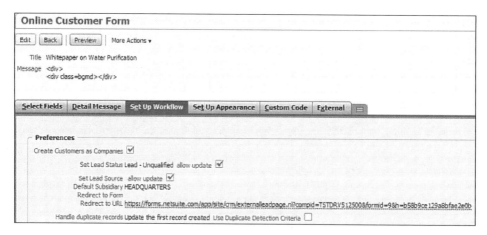

Also, if you are going to pass URL parameters into form fields, such as lead source or partner code, then add these fields to the **Select Fields** on the form, and keep them hidden.

Promotion URLs

The **Publishable Form URL** that OneWorld generated for an online form is long and difficult to read. If you need a more manageable version for public viewing, then use a **Promotional URL**, at **Setup | Marketing | Promotional URL**, to set up a more user-friendly URL.

Lead nurturing or drip marketing

With your search engine advertisements, you have pulled some new leads to your site and then also captured their information in exchange for your offer. The next step in the marketing strategy is to continue to nurture the new leads with a series of e-mails, a method known as **Drip marketing**. With OneWorld's new workflow engine, SuiteFlow, you can set up automatic drip marketing campaigns.

You set up lead nurturing by starting with a marketing campaign and then adding lead nurturing events. When you capture a new lead into OneWorld, you can use fields on their record to initiate a workflow that sends them a series of e-mails over time. The marketing campaign looks similar to the one shown in the following screenshot:

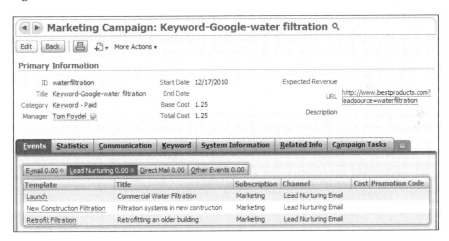

Notice that on the **Events** tab, in the **Lead Nurturing** list, we have three different e-mail templates set up and ready to go. As we capture new leads on the online form that match our criteria, we automatically start the lead nurturing campaign, based on the triggers we have set up in the workflow engine.

Templates

When we want to use OneWorld to send a single e-mail, an e-mail blast, or a single personalized lead nurture e-mail, we use templates for the format, or 'look and feel,' of the mail, and in some cases, for content also.

When we set up a template, we have the choice of using a file that we created earlier in another tool, such as an HTML editor, or, alternatively, we can use OneWorld's text editor if we want the e-mail to look less marketing oriented and more personalized, like a normal e-mail.

For an e-mail campaign template, we start by using a template file that is a rough approximation of the end result that we want, and for each instance of the template's use, we customize it for the task at hand. Consider the following rough code that was used for a newsletter template.

First, we set up the document and then we add the header:

```
<!DOCTYPE html PUBLIC "-//W3C//DTD XHTML 1.0 Transitional//EN"
   "http://www.w3.org/TR/xhtml1/DTD/xhtml1-transitional.dtd">
<html xmlns="http://www.w3.org/1999/xhtml">
  <head>
    <meta http-equiv="Content-Type" content="text/html;
      charset=iso-8859-1" />
    <title>Untitled Document</title>
    <style type="text/css">
      <!--body {background-color:#E9E2DA; margin-left:0px; margin-
        top:0px; margin-right:0px; margin-bottom:0px;}
      -->
    </style>
  </head>
  <body>
    <table width="640" border="0" align="center" cellpadding="0"
      cellspacing="0">
      <tr>
        <td height="50" align="center" style="font-family:Arial,
          Helvetica, sans-serif; font-size:11px;">
          If you can't see this email please <a href=
          "https://system.netsuite.com/core/media/media.nl?
          id=864&c=266952&h=adbaf17dbd999e051612&_xt=.htm"
          style="color:#4E9E11;">click here</a>. Add <a href=
          "mailto:info@sightlinesconsulting.com" style=
          "color:#000000; text-decoration:underline;">
          info@sightlinesconsulting.com</a> to your Address Book.
        </td>
      </tr>
      <tr>
```

```
<td height="5" bgcolor="#FFFFFF">
  <img src="https://system.netsuite.com/core/media
    /media.nl?id=837&c=266952&h=522fb0a6277a4f6db192"
    width="5" height="5" />
</td>
</tr>
<tr>
<td height="86" valign="top" bgcolor="#FFFFFF">
  <table width="100%" border="0" cellpadding="0"
    cellspacing="0">
    <tr>
      <td width="5" valign="top">
        <img src="https://system.netsuite.com/core/media
          /media.nl?id=837&c=266952&h=522fb0a6277a4f6db192"
          width="5" height="5" />
      </td>
      <td width="10" valign="top">
        <img src="https://system.netsuite.com/core/media/
          media.nl?id=830&c=266952&h=d943b1e3fd66d0bc3ece"
          width="10" height="86" />
      </td>
      <td width="172" valign="top">
        <a href="http://www.sightlinesconsulting.com">
          <img src="https://system.netsuite.com/core/media/
            media.nl?id=833&c=266952&h=c81e50519a9cc1315461
            " width="172" height="86" border="0" />
        </a>
      </td>
</td>
```

This is our logo in the header; we removed some of the other images to shorten the code sample.

Next, we add the tabs:

```
      </tr>
    </table>
  </td>
</tr>
<tr>
  <td valign="top" bgcolor="#FFFFFF">
    <table width="100%" border="0" cellspacing="0"
      cellpadding="0">
      <tr>
        <td width="5" bgcolor="#FFFFFF">
          <img src="https://system.netsuite.com/core/media/
            media.nl?id=837&c=266952&h=522fb0a6277a4f6db192"
            width="5" height="5" />
```

```
                   </td>
                   <td height="25" align="center" valign="middle"
                     bgcolor="#2C2B29" style="font-family:Arial,
                     Helvetica, sans-serif; font-size:11px; font-
                     weight:bold;">
                     <a href="http://www.sightlinesconsulting.com"
                       style="color:#FFFFFF; text-decoration:none;">HOME
                     </a>
                             
                     <a href="http://www.sightlinesconsulting.com/
                       SightLines-Implementation-Service-for-NetSuite"
                       style="color:#FFFFFF; text-decoration:none;">
                     Services</a>
   This is a sample of the header tabs
                   </td>
```

Next, we add the left panel:

```
                   <tr>
                     <td valign="top"><table width="100%" border="0"
                       cellpadding="0" cellspacing="0">
                     <tr>
                       <td width="187" valign="top" bgcolor="#FFFFFF">
                         <table width="100%" border="0"
                           cellspacing="0" cellpadding="0">
                         <tr>
                           <td valign="top">
                             <table width="100%" border="0"
                               cellpadding="0" cellspacing="0"
                               bgcolor="#FFFFFF" style="font-family:
                               Arial, Helvetica, sans-serif; font-
                               size:11px;">
                             <tr>
                               <td width="5" height="27" valign=
                                 "top">
                                 <img src="https://system.
                                   netsuite.com/core/media/media.
                                   nl?id=837&c=266952&h=
                                   522fb0a6277a4f6db192" width="5"
                                   height="5" />
                               </td>
                               <td width="17" valign="top"
                                 bgcolor="#F2EEE9"> 
                               </td>
                               <td valign="middle" bgcolor=
                                 "#F2EEE9" style="color:#4E9E11;">
                                 <strong>FEBRUARY 2008</strong>
```

```
      </td>
      <td width="17" valign="top" bgcolor
        ="#F2EEE9"> 
      </td>
      <td width="5" valign="top">
        <img src="https://system.
          netsuite.com/core/media/
          media.nl?id=837&c=266952&h=
          522fb0a6277a4f6db192" width="5"
          height="5" />
      </td>
    </tr>
    <tr>
      <td valign="top"> </td>
      <td valign="top"> </td>
      <td valign="top">
        <table width="100%" border="0"
          cellspacing="0"
          cellpadding="0">
          <tr>
            <td width="10" height="35"
              valign="top"> 
            </td>
            <td valign="middle">
              <span style="font-
                size:12px;">
                <strong>ARTICLES</strong>
              </span>
            </td>
          </tr>
          <tr>
            <tr>
              <td width="10" height="20"
                valign="top">
                <span style="color:
                  #4E9E11;">-
                </span>
              </td>
              <td valign="top">
                <a href="#whats_news"
                  style="color:#000000;">
                  What's News?
                </a>
              </td>
            </tr>
```

Following is a sample of the content:

```
<td style="font-family:Arial,
  Helvetica, sans-serif;
  font-size:12px;">
<a name="5_clues_giftcard"
</a>
<span style="color:
  #4E9E11;">
  <strong>5 Clues Giftcard
  </strong>
</span><br/>
<strong>Use these 5 clues
  to come up with an answer
  to this month's puzzler.
</strong><br/><br/>
<strong>Who was this
  person?
</strong><br/><br/>
1 - A former Mayor of
  Washington DC<br/>
  2 - A hero during WWII
  <br/>3 - A best selling
  author<br/>4 - A great
  orator<br/>5 - Friends
  never use the given first
  name<br/><br/>
<strong>Send us the right
  answer to
</strong>
<a href="mailto:5clues@
  sightlinesconsulting.com"
  style="color:#FF9900;">
  5clues@
  sightlinesconsulting.com
</a>
and we'll put your name in
  drawing for a $50
  giftcard to Amazon.com
      </td>
    </td>
  </tr>
  </table>
  </body>
</html>
```

This simple HTML code yields an e-mail that looks like the one shown in the following screenshot:

Each time we want to send the newsletter, we simply open up this file in a text or HTML editor and replace the Latin verbiage with our own and with the correct links. We rename the file to something like `newsletter_April_2011.htm` and then save it into our newsletter folder in the OneWorld file cabinet. Then when we generate our OneWorld template, we navigate to **Lists | Setup | Marketing Templates | New**; for an e-mail campaign, we select this file, as we have done in the following screenshot:

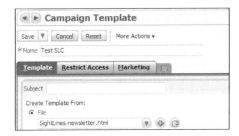

Alternatively, we can simply use the OneWorld text editor to create a personalized e-mail, without the HTML formatting, as we have done in the following screenshot:

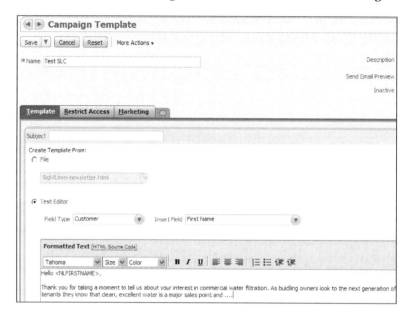

You will also notice that the template functionality for e-mails, e-mail campaigns, and online forms is very similar in OneWorld. Once you become proficient in one, you become proficient in all.

Templates can be as visually stunning or as plain as one would like, and they can hold any content you come up with. As Acme moves forward with their business development efforts, a little bit of HTML can be used over and over again, for e-mail marketing or online forms.

Marketing campaign

For our newsletter template, we set up a marketing campaign, where we tie together the template with a target group and set a time and day to execute the e-mail blast. Later, we can review the statistics for the campaign to find out how many opened the newsletter, how many clicked through it, and how many responded to it.

Promotion codes

Another tactic in online marketing strategy is the promotion code, under **Lists | Marketing Promotion Codes**. You use promotion codes with marketing campaigns and/or channel promotions when you want to identify with certainty the source of sales. For example, with an online banner advertisement, set up in OneWorld as a marketing campaign, you append the promotion code to the advertisement's click URL, for example, `www.yoursite.com?promocode=WATER2011`. When an internet visitor clicks your advertisement, they come to a specific landing page on your NetSuite site and carry with them the promotion code, which then follows them through the online sales process and provides a discount of some kind.

In an e-mail campaign, you can also append a promotion code to a link in the e-mail that works in the same way. Also enter the promotion code on the campaign itself to tie sales to this campaign. You can also simply tell customers to use a certain promotion code in online or telesales, for example.

Promotion codes operate at the intersection of campaigns, partner/affiliate channels, and sales, as they have the ability to tag transactions with a discount. In the next screenshot, we have started the promotion code setup, by defining the discount and several other rules for this promotion. We can also click the **Item** tab to link to the promotion to one or more items, or to exclude specifically one or more items from this promotion. We can also go to the **Partner** tab to include specific affiliates or partners in the promotion, and thereby exclude others. When we tie a customer to a partner, the customer becomes eligible for all of the partner's promotions.

After you save the promotion, a new tab, **Campaigns**, appears. This tells you the campaigns that have been linked to this promotion.

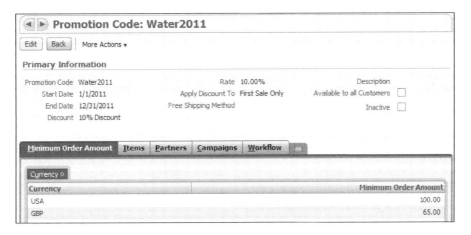

Promotion codes can be used with customers at any point in their lifecycle, from a new visitor to a current customer. Once you have sold to a customer, the next step is to ask what else they might be interested in, and your upsell metrics can help answer this question.

Upsell

The upsell function is simply a way to look at the selling relationship between various items in your catalog. You can look at this question in two ways: I want to sell item(s) XYZ, so what customers would be interested? Or, customers who purchased item(s) XYZ would be interested in purchasing what other items? The upsell manager walks you through these two scenarios and helps you to decide the best method to upsell items and customers. For each upsell scenario, you will have a group of customers that you can then use in a marketing campaign or put on a call list for direct follow up. Keep in mind that upsell takes some time to provide interesting answers, since it relies on sales history.

Before you begin using the upsell manager, you need to set up some basic upsell preferences at **Setup | Sales | Upsell Preferences**. Then, when you are ready to run an Upsell analysis, navigate to **Lists | Marketing | Upsell** to walk through the scenarios you want to look at.

OneWorld marketing functions provide the tools to market a global company to a global customer list. Keep in mind that each customer record belongs to a specific subsidiary, so you probably are going to market by subsidiary. However, the tools that you use, the templates, and so on, are available across subsidiaries and can be reused as needed.

Marketing summary

OneWorld offers the marketing functions to assist both traditional marketing, such as trade shows, cold calling campaigns, and print advertising, as well as the more recent developments, such as internet and e-mail marketing. Putting together the right functions in OneWorld to roll out a specific strategy seems to be the most challenging task for the marketing department. Here are a few marketing processes that we have seen from clients:

- Trade shows set up as campaigns, customization, and code that adds expense reports to the campaign cost total, leads from the show added manually through data entry or import of the shows lead list, and leads from the show automatically enrolled in a lead nurturing e-mail series.

- Online banner advertisement campaign with a promotion code that serves as a discount coupon for online sales.

- Upsell groups of online or offline customers, targeted through e-mail campaigns.

- Partner/affiliate promotion codes that offer specific discounts to channel partner customers, helping to track partner/affiliates on sales and calculate commissions.

- Online forms capture new leads, which are then enrolled in a lead nurturing e-mail campaign. After they return to your site and sign up for another offer, OneWorld SuiteFlow generates a task for the direct sales team to contact the customer personally.

This is just a short list, of course, and marketing departments are generally pretty creative places, so the mix and match of various marketing functions is infinite. Regardless of your tactics, OneWorld has the functions and customizability to perform a lot of sophisticated marketing.

The results of your marketing efforts are available in the customer record and on the **Marketing** tab, including how the customer responded.

Sales

In earlier chapters, we laid out some of the functionality of sales force automation in OneWorld, the process of moving from opportunity to quote to sales order and how this process determines the stage and status of the customer record.

In this section, we want to push further into the sales functionality and the tools that provide substance to both sales and company management, as they look for signs of future business results today.

Of course, much of what you set up in OneWorld depends on your business model. There are companies who do not bother with opportunities, simply because they have sales cycles that do not lend themselves to the full sweep of the OneWorld sales process. In general, longer sales cycles gain more advantage from the sales process than shorter cycles. Also, some companies are very concerned with their sales team's adoption of the software, so they try to make the system as easy as possible to understand and use, limiting any part, that requires training and explanation. In the end, there are a lot of ways to use the system that may suit your organization, a few of which are listed as follows:

- Use opportunities, quotes, sales order, and invoices – the full process is especially useful for long sales cycles, by a direct sales force or partner channel

- Use only sales orders and invoices – often used for renewals for year two of support, for example, or for online or in-person sales to regular customers with terms

- Use only quotes and invoices – signed quote is the contract and there is no fulfillment, deferred revenue, or special billing, so the quote can be immediately invoiced

- Use opportunities, quotes, and invoices – same as *Use only quotes and invoices*, with the addition of opportunities for longer sales cycles

- Use quotes, sales orders, and invoices – does not use opportunity management because sales cycle or sales team are not amenable to it

- Use sales orders and cash sales – for e-tailers or brick-and-mortar retail sales to customers without terms

These different scenarios are not mutually exclusive, so it is not unusual to see more than one of these at a single OneWorld implementation. The sales process(es) you adopt depend(s) on your requirements for sales forecasting, sales cycle management, deferred revenue recognition, advanced billing schedules, signed customer contracts, and so on.

If you are unsure of exactly how you want to use the system at the outset of the implementation, our advice, unless you are in e-commerce, is to set up the full sales process in OneWorld and then pare it back to the process that suits your business best, as you gain more understanding of the system. Until you really have the time to work with the various steps in the sales process, you cannot make an informed decision. But it will not harm anything to start with the full sales process and then pare it back.

For those OneWorld users who do e-commerce, the only caveat is to ask if you have other sales channels as well. If you are selling wholesale as well as through e-commerce, you may want to use one of the sales processes described previously. If not, then you probably only need the **Sales Order | Fulfillment | Cash Sale** process. This means that website orders generate a **Sales Order | Cash Sale**. After you fulfill the order, you then bill it to create the **Cash Sale** — a transaction that immediately recognizes either cash or credit card revenue.

Let's start by making sure that the basics are set up, and then we'll move on to the more important functions.

Sales preferences

To set up the **Sales Preferences**, navigate to **Setup | Sales | Sales Preferences**. The first five preferences are the most important, if you have a direct sales force and/or a partner channel and you want to manage their sales process. We assume here that you have already thought about the customer statuses. It is important that you have scribbled down the expected flow of sales from the value you set up in customer statuses. If not, these are the questions that you must answer first:

- When marketing brings in new leads, how will they be designated? Unqualified? Unqualified in pursuit? The verbiage is your choice. Some OneWorld users want to differentiate between a completely unqualified lead, such as a trade show participant who never visited your booth, and the inbound lead who has taken the time to introduce himself/herself to you.

- When you have made contact and discovered that the lead has real interest, what do you want the sales person or partner to do? Open an opportunity? Simply change the customer status? If you want them to open an opportunity, you will need to tell the system the status for a record with a new opportunity. It ought to be a different status than just prospect, since it makes sense to have an opportunity change the record's status automatically.

- What status does the record have when you open a quote, or when you issue a quote from the opportunity?

- Finally, when you have a sales order, what does the status become?

In the following screenshot, we have set up the customer statuses as they relate to steps in the sales process:

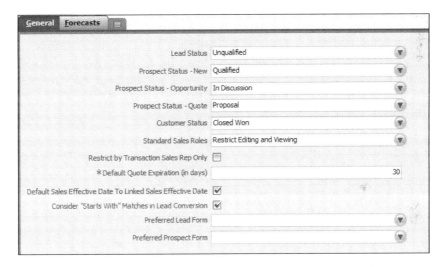

We are telling the system that when we open an opportunity, we want the stage/ status to change to Stage **Prospect Status** and Status **Opportunity – In Discussion**; likewise, when we issue an estimate, we want the stage/status to change to **Prospect** and Status **Quote – Proposal**.

The other preferences are fairly straightforward, but pay particular attention to the **Default Sales Effective Date To Linked Sales Effective Date**, if you are using OneWorld's commission module.

Also, we haven't discussed lead conversion yet, and won't spend too much time on it, but it's worth a few lines. Essentially, lead conversion is for companies who sell to individuals at other companies. It is a B2B model, but the sale is through individuals. For example, a company that sells engineering software sells to many individual engineers at big manufacturing, but ultimately invoices big manufacturing. When they send out a campaign, it's possible that several individuals at a company might respond, and they would be new leads in the system, but individual leads, not company leads. Then, as they move through the sales process, you can convert them, so that their lead record becomes a contact record linked to big manufacturing. Ultimately, you send the quote to big manufacturing in care of your individual engineer, in most cases.

Lead routing with sales territories

For companies with a direct sales force and sales territories, when your marketing VP begins to succeed in pulling visitors to your site or finding interested potential customers at trade shows or through other marketing channels, you must have a plan in place to route the new leads from all your marketing activity to the sales team. OneWorld accomplishes this through the use of **Sales Rules** and **Sales Territories**.

Base your sales rules on any of the many possibilities, by navigating to **Setup | Sales | Sales Rules | New**. Sales rules break down into geographic rules, such as states, provinces, and counties, or customer-centric rules, such as industry category. You can also create sales rules, based on custom entity fields that are linked to the customer record.

Integrated sales rules

Like many OneWorld setups, the need to manage sales territories for your direct sales staff often informs the set up of other fields and functions in the system. Customer category, for example, lends itself to sales rules when you have different sales teams selling to different market segments. Geographic sales rules often demand that your online lead capture forms have a mandatory address. Avoid the mistake of creating custom fields for every business requirement. You'll end up with a mish-mash of ill-defined fields that your employees abandon before long. Keep your configuration tightly structured.

As you move more deeply into OneWorld configuration, your ideas about how to use the system start to change. Be prepared to revisit some earlier ideas as you move forward. Be agile!

A sales territory simply gathers all of the rules pertaining to a sales person's specific defined area. A territory might be defined by one rule or tens of rules. What is most important is that you maintain the logic of your territories throughout the setup. Geographic areas cannot overlap, for example. Where the logic breaks down, OneWorld fails to route new leads correctly.

In the next screenshot, we are defining a territory, by both geography and customer category. We have the option to **Match all rules**, or **Match any rule**, giving us more flexibility in our setup. After we select our rules, we assign this territory to specific sales people. We could also include a round-robin rule, allowing us to assign leads from a single territory to multiple sales people. On the **Lead Assignment** tab, we link individual sales people to the territory.

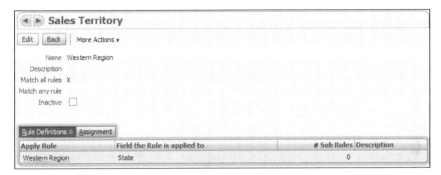

With lead assignment by territory comes the need for territory reassignment when the sales staff undergoes changes. A **Territory Reassignment** can start from **Setup | Sales | Territory Reassignment** or from **Lists | Mass Update | Sales Force Automation**. We suggest that you name the mass update for the territory that you would like to reassign, as you will probably reuse it many times until you establish completely new territories. We also suggest that you reassign one single territory at a time, since performing a wholesale reassignment has the potential to cause much disruption in the sales ranks. There are always exceptions to every rule, and sales people often swap customers as they move between territories.

Test your territories

After you set up your territories, we suggest that you test them, by manual entry of customer records first, then by entry through an online form, and finally by customer record import. It's a good practice to test your configurations robustly, and robust testing reinforces your understanding of how OneWorld works. System understanding rapidly improves with practice.

Contact management

OneWorld provides several tools for managing the contacts that you have with a lead, prospect, or customer. There are events, tasks, and phone calls, and all of these can be managed on the **Activities** dashboard.

Some important differences to note are the following:

- Events automatically go to the calendar however, tasks and phone calls can also be scheduled, landing them on the calendar as well.

- You can assign a task to another employee, or even a partner.

- All activities have a status that is easy to mark as completed from the **Activities** list, under any entity or transaction record, or from an **Activities** list on your dashboard.

- Activities entered on a transaction are also viewable from the entity record, for example, customer, vendor, and so on.

- Start an e-mail thread from OneWorld, using a personal e-mail template, and OneWorld not only saves the record of the sent e-mail, but also the return e-mail and any future e-mails that are part of the thread. It's an excellent way to save important dialog with your customer.

- You can attach documents to your e-mails, and if you want to e-mail a transaction, such as a PO, sales order, or invoice, you can have the system attach the transaction's PDF, for example.

There are times, however, when you have sales people who prefer to work in their normal e-mail system. For this situation, OneWorld offers an Outlook Integration tool that lets you synchronize contacts, events, to-do's, or tasks between the two systems, and also save e-mails in Outlook to entity records in OneWorld. There is also a synchronization tool that enables users to synchronize OneWorld with other devices. Or you can simply purchase the iPhone OneWorld application, and view your OneWorld data on your phone. In the most recent release, 2011 release 1, the iPhone application also offers data entry.

Sales forms

Let's stop and understand where we are now in the sales cycle. We succeeded in capturing a new online lead, and our lead nurturing campaign results told us that we had a very interested buyer. The lead was routed to our sales person and with the results of our marketing effort, he is now ready to start the in-person sales process.

Link marketing to sales

You can expend a good deal of time and energy, not to mention cash, bringing new leads into the system. But if the sales team does not follow up appropriately, at the appropriate time, your efforts are for nought. One way to link sales and marketing is to automatically generate a task for the sales person at a chosen point in the marketing process. You can do this with the SuiteFlow tool. Then measure sales people for their efficiency in completing the sales task that they were assigned.

We need to make sure that he has the right tools for the job. So our sales forms must be correct. There are a couple of things to know to make sure that you assign the right forms.

First, as you approach the point of configuring the sales process, take a moment and rename the forms. Navigate to **Setup | Customization | Entry Forms**, and rename the customer forms, by placing your company's name in the form name. For example, rename the **Standard Customer Form** to **Acme Customer Form**. Likewise, navigate to **Setup | Customization | Transaction Forms** and rename the standard forms you require, such as **Standard Estimate**, **Standard Sales Order**, and **Standard Product Invoice**, to **Acme Estimate**, **Acme Sales Order**, and **Acme Product Invoice**, respectively.

The reason we do this now is twofold: We know that any time you need to make a change to a form, OneWorld requires that you customize the standard form, so we must eventually customize the forms to meet the details of our business model in any event; and in the meantime, we start the customization process, and also select the right forms and make them **Preferred**. As we move through configuration and testing, the whole team uses the correct forms, and we start to make the customizations as requirements are nailed down.

Of course, it's only necessary to customize the forms that you need. Here are a few rules to keep in mind:

- You can have as many variations of a form as you need. You might require two versions of the sales order, for example, to meet the needs of two different business units, or two customer forms, one for sales and one for operations.

- You can link forms together so that Estimate XYZ always transforms into Sales Order XYZ. So if you have two sales processes, OneWorld allows you to customize both and set up the links that keep the processes correct, as they move from one step to the next.

- OneWorld also has some built-in logic in the forms. For example, the **Standard Sales Order – Invoice** always produces an invoice (even if you customize the form, the logic still stands), and **Standard Sales Order – Cash Sale** always produces a cash sale. If your business model has both invoices and cash sales, then the **Standard Sales Order** produces one or the other, based on whether the customer has **Terms**: invoice if they do, cash sale if they don't.

- You can also have different customer forms, based on the stage of the record; so you have one form for the lead stage and one form for the prospect stage, and finally one form for the customer stage. This helps to keep the forms uncluttered when you are working with an entity through the sales process.

- Forms and roles move hand in hand, as it is on the role setup that you enable or disable certain forms. This can prove helpful not only for the sales process, but also for more secured employee setup, and so on. When we get to the final stages of OneWorld configuration, we set up the custom roles and link the custom forms.

At this point, what we want is simply to start the process of customizing the entry and transaction forms necessary to your business model. Later, we will complete the form and role customizations.

Quotas and forecasts

We won't spend a lot of time on Quotas and Forecasts here. They are fairly simple and straightforward. A few moments on either form, from **Transactions | Quota/ Forecast**, is normally enough to understand how they work.

If you are using commissions based on quotas, then you obviously need to set up quotas, but we should mention that you do not have to use quota-based commission schedules to gain value from sales quotas. There are several reports and dashboard portlets devoted to quota and actual sales that many sales managers use. These help to incentivize the sales team beyond their compensation plan.

Team selling

Most of our discussion of the sales process thus far has focused on the solo sales person or partner. But it's worth mentioning that business models continue to evolve and this is nowhere truer than in an organization's sales strategies. OneWorld supports both team selling and multiple partners, meaning that you have the ability to share responsibility for sales with several direct reps or partners. You must first enable these functions under **Setup | Company | Enable Features**.

Keep in mind that when you have multiple sales reps, then you assign a contribution to each that normally adds up to 100 percent. Commission calculations, see *Commissions*, use this contribution amount to calculate the commissions for each sales team member. The same is true for multiple partners and partner commissions.

OneWorld allows you to over assign the contributions if you need to, but then you must also add an adjustment rep to make sure that the commission calculations are correct for the commissionable reps on the team.

Following is a screenshot of the **Sales Team** tab on a sales order. You can set up sales teams that often work together, or you can set them up order by order, as we have shown:

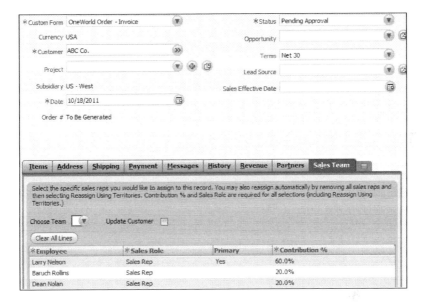

Commissions

The sales staff responds to incentives. Setting up the incentive plans in OneWorld means purchasing and configuring the Commissions module. Alternatively, you may take sales reports from OneWorld and run them through your own commission spreadsheet or third party-software, or you might integrate NetSuite with a commission system. But the value of OneWorld commissions derives not only from the fact they calculate incentive pay, but also from their ability to remind us clearly and often of how well we are meeting our incentives, both through normal reports and through dashboard portlets. For this reason, the commissions module is an important add-on for many organizations, allowing direct and partner sales staff and management to see right on their dashboard how they stack up as the commission period moves forward.

As a OneWorld customer, it is important to note that a commission schedule is always linked to a subsidiary. This means that OneWorld calculates the commissions on the schedule for sales to customers in this subsidiary and, of course, the sales people or partners who include this schedule in their commission plan must have roles that allow them access to these customers.

Configuring the commission module is a two-step process. Under **Setup | Sales | Commissions**, there are several preferences to set up, as seen in the following screenshot:

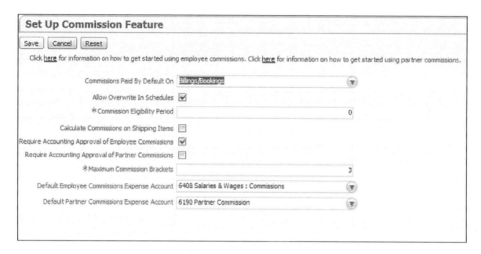

The commission preferences are fairly self-explanatory. Let's take just a moment and talk about the first one, **Commissions Paid By Default On**. Many sales teams are paid on bookings under the rationale that the booking is the sales person's responsibility, and that fulfillment, billing, and collections are the responsibility of operations and finance. If this is the case in your organization, then you will have to enable the **Alternate Sales Amount (ASA)** at **Setup | Company | Enable Features | Transactions | Alternate Sales Amount**.

ASA is a function delivered with the commission module. It adds an additional field to the line items of sales transactions, which can hold the booking amount for commission calculations. To set the **Alternate Sales Amount**, you must write a small JavaScript, and deploy it on the sales forms that you use.

Bookings mean that you have an approved sales order that is either **Pending Fulfillment** or **Pending Billing**. A billing is a billed sales order, meaning an invoice or cash sale. Collections are, of course, payments received against an invoice.

The **Commission Eligibility Period** is also important. This field tells the system the number of days that must elapse before a commissionable event, such as the creation of the invoice or the collection on an invoice, generates commissions.

To better understand the other preferences, let's take a closer look at a commission schedule. To set up commission schedules, navigate to **List | Commissions | Employee Schedule | New**. You will now see the following form:

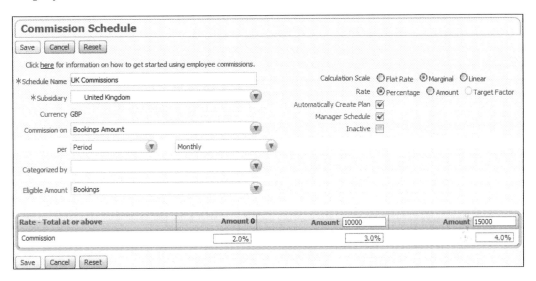

After having enabled the **Alternate Sales Amount**, we are now able to set up a schedule on **Bookings** (we have also renamed the **Alternate Sales Amount** to **Booking** on the **Sales Preference** form). This is just one way of setting the basis for the commissions. There are several other choices, which include bookings or sales against quota and profitability of sales. There are also several choices in the per field, including **Period, Transaction Total**, and **Transaction Line Item**, meaning that you can set commissions item by item; so commissions can be as granular as you require, by class, by department, by location, or even by item.

After you make your choices for the **Commission on** field, you then select the calculation options for the commissions.

The preference we set up for **Maximum Commission Brackets** enables three breaks in our commission structure when we select a **Marginal** or **Linear** option of the **Calculation Scale**. Notice that the marginal and linear options are not always available; they depend on what you select in the **Commission on** field.

A **Calculation Scale**, based on a **Flat Rate**, allows you to enter a single percentage, 10 percent, for example. Using a **Marginal** scale, only available when the basis is per period, gives you the ability to calculate commissions at a rolling scale, moving up the scale as your period sales increase past the brackets. The difference between **Marginal** and **Linear** scales is what happens in a sale that crosses two brackets: in the **Marginal** scale, both brackets are used, so part of the sale goes to the lower bracket until you meet the bracket limit and then the balance to the higher bracket; in a **Linear** scale, only the higher bracket is used.

Also notice that it is possible to use a **Commission** schedule not only for the sales staff, but also for sales management. The **Manager Schedule** checkbox tells the system that all of the sales of the manager's direct reports as well as his/her own, count towards the commission basis of this schedule.

After you complete the commission schedules, you then create the commission plans that bring one or more schedules together, and you assign the plan to a sales person or partner. These steps complete the commission setup.

Other commission requirements

If you have an issue calculating commissions in your commission testing, check to make sure you have met all requirements. Have you passed the commission eligibility date? Does the sales person or partner have the **Eligible for Commissions**, on the **Employee** form (or **Partner** form) **Custom** tab, flag set to **Yes**? On the transactions, is the **Exclude Commissions** flag set to **No**? Do the customer and commission schedule belong to the same subsidiary?

After the commission setups are complete, test some transactions. Then navigate to **Transactions | Commissions | Authorize Commissions**. This form shows all of the commissions as they happen. Very often, a sales manager or their sales administrator authorizes commissions. If you have chosen **Require Accounting Approval** for your commissions, authorized commissions fall automatically into the queue for approval, at **Transactions | Commissions | Approve Commissions**. If you do not require accounting approval, then the authorization readies the commission to be paid.

If you discover issues during your testing and actual use, then you can always make changes to the commission schedule. The system automatically starts a recalculation process for the sales under that schedule, after you save changes.

There are a huge number of possible business use cases that are covered in the commission module, more than we have the ability to cover here. If commission-based incentives are important to your sales force, either your direct or partner sales force, then you ought to take a close look at the commissions module.

Sales summary

The sales process really starts in OneWorld the day a new lead lands in the system, or when a visitor arrives on your e-commerce site, and proceeds through the actual sale and into renewals, upsells, and ongoing sales support. At what point your direct or channel sales team decides to take ownership of the sales process from marketing, is really a matter of business process/procedure. Likewise, the timing of the sales to service customer hand-off is also an executive decision.

The key takeaway from OneWorld sales is that you have a system that can help you to not only engage in the sales process, but also to incentivize your sales team and to track the results in a myriad of ways. Our recommendation is that you understand your sales process today, where the holes are, and where it makes sense to look for better ideas. Then start the sales modules implementation. As we mentioned before, it makes no sense to expect OneWorld to support a highly detailed sales process in its entirety, nor to expect it simply to guide you to a process that works well for your organization. Have a game plan and be ready to flex it when necessary.

If your organization sells around the world, then you may have customers to who you sell in more than one currency. With the recent release of Multi-Currency Customers, allowing you to set a primary currency for a customer and any number of secondary currencies, you now have the ability to manage a single customer record in multiple currencies. Test this function carefully, especially if you have customer hierarchies - a parent customer with one or more child customers - and you use consolidated payments.

As you move through the implementation, you also find points where other OneWorld configurations touch the sales process. For example, how you price products and services that you sell and how you rationalize pricing, how you discount sales, how you charge and collect taxes, and how you ship goods and deliver services once sold. There is likely no process in OneWorld that has as many interested parties in the organization as the sales process. Be prepared to spend a fair portion of the implementation here.

 All of your sales activities and transactions are viewable, by sales and, in some cases, by non-sales people, in the customer records, on the **General** and the **Activities** tab, or on the **Sales** tab. To view the transactions on the **Sales** tab, be sure that your role has the **Financial History** permission.

Customer service

Marketing brought us the lead, and together with sales or the e-commerce site, they have worked to make the lead a customer. Now that we have a customer, it's time to service their problems, issues, concerns, and questions. The first few months are always the most important for the new customer, and having a strong customer service response to any of their needs is a must.

The customer service setup in OneWorld starts as all module setups start: We first set up preferences and lists of values, and then we can move on to the service process and forms. Again, this is an iterative process, so don't try to get it all right on the first pass. Take a shot at the base setups, which should give you enough data to start some testing, perform some tests, and then when you have a good handle on the process, you can return to complete the base setups.

Keep in mind, as we discuss support options, that there are three main ways for a customer to ask for support: by e-mail, by submitting an online case form, and by calling you on the phone.

Support preferences

There are a lot of support preferences, five tabs worth to be exact. We won't go through each one here, though you need to take the time to understand them thoroughly, but a few important ones are worthy of discussion. Navigate to **Setup | Support | Support Preferences**:

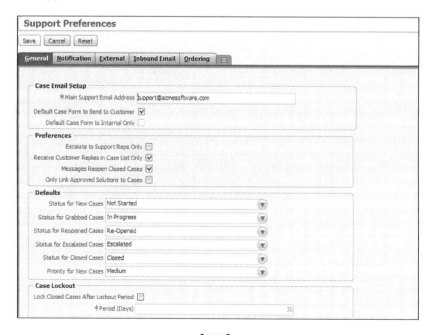

Many of your selections on the **Support Preferences** form reflect the size, scope, and processes of your customer support, so they will be idiosyncratic to your organization. There are a few that all organizations must use:

- **Main Support Email Address**: This is the 'from' e-mail address that customers see in your correspondence with them.

- **Default Case Form to Internal Only**: This controls whether you default case interactions to Internal Only, meaning how you treat the support rep's reply to the customer's case message. If you select **Default Case Form to Internal Only**, by checking this box, then the rep must affirmatively check the **Send to Customer** box on the **New Case** form (next screenshot) to have their reply sent to the customer. Otherwise, if you **Default Case Form to Send to Customer**, then all case replies are marked **Send to Customer**, and will be sent by e-mail upon save, unless the service representative remembers to change the default on the **New Case** form to **Internal Only**. (Most new OneWorld users prefer Internal Only, to avoid sending remarks to customers inadvertently. We moved the **Internal Only** and **Send to Customer** boxes on the **New Case** form to make them visible in the preceding screenshot.)

- Your support e-mail address works in tandem with the **Receive Customer Replies** in **Case List Only**. If you check it, OneWorld saves the replies on the case record only. If you leave it unchecked, OneWorld saves the reply mail in the case and the support e-mail address's inbox.

- On the **Notification** tab are several fields for e-mail notification templates. You can view/edit these at **Setup | Company | System Email Templates**. Open them up in edit mode, if you wish to modify them, and add your organization's name to the template name.

- If you want to add a case form to your website, or to the **Customer Center**, open up the **External** tab. Before you save the preferences, you must enter an **External Case Form Redirect URL**. This is the page on your site that you redirect the user to, after they submit a case form. Even if you do not use the online case form feature, you must still enter a URL here.

- If you want to use e-mail case capture, you can copy your NetSuite Address from the **Inbound Email** tab. Then, use this as a forwarding address for mail sent to support@yourcompany.com, for example. Your IT staff can help you set up the forwarding. When your customer sends an e-mail to support@ yourcompany.com, the e-mail server forwards it to the inbound e-mail address, and it generates a case in OneWorld.

- In the next step in support configuration, we set up the lists of values for specific fields. When we finish with this step, we can return to the **Ordering** tab to put the values into our preferred order.

Now that the preferences are complete, we take the next step and set up the lists of values needed for individual case generation.

Support lists of values

OneWorld delivers values for the support lists, and it makes good sense to see how they are used in a case, before spending a lot of head-scratching time trying to figure out the best way to set up these lists. So take some time now and navigate to **Lists | Support | Case | New**, and enter the data for the case, paying particular attention to the **Status, Priority, Origin, Type**, and **Issue** fields. You must come up with your own list of issues, and you can edit, add to, or delete the values in the delivered lists, as you require.

Also, take a moment and navigate to **Lists | Support | Case | Search**, and take a look at the case search form. A common question from OneWorld users is how they can search cases, since they want to know if similar cases exist and how they were resolved. The search form gives you an excellent blueprint for the fields and methods used to search cases, providing you with some important guideposts, as you set up support.

You complete the support lists of values by navigating to **Setup | Support | Setup Tasks**.

Case routing and escalation

OneWorld enables the routing of cases much like the routing of new leads. You set up rules based on some criteria, such as the subsidiary to which the customer belongs, or the case's issue. You create a rule for each specific criteria.

Once your rules are set up, you group them into territories and assign the territories to support reps. Keep in mind that you must first identify the support rep on their employee record as a support rep, before you can link them to a territory or assign them a case.

Escalation is set up similarly. You create the escalation rules and then assign them directly to support managers. In many instances, escalation rules include one of the duration rules, allowing you to escalate, based on the time elapsed since case creation or modification, enabling automatic case escalation. Alternatively, the support rep can also escalate a case manually.

Case management

It is time now to turn to the management of actual cases. Let's walk through the following screenshot, and discuss how the fields relate to an overall support strategy:

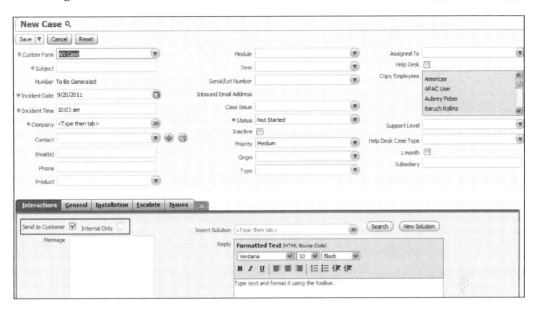

- **Custom Form**: You can customize case forms, by adding, moving, and removing fields as you need to. You can also have specific forms tied to specific support roles, if you have to support widely divergent products or customer types.

- **Subject**: This is the subject of the e-mail when the case originates through an e-mail to your support address; otherwise, it the subject your rep types into the case form while speaking to a customer, or it is the subject your customer types into the online case form. Words within the subject line are searchable, so take pains to make it clear and succinct. You can edit it.

- **Case Number**: The system generates the **Case Number**, based on your configuration of system numbering, covered in *Chapter 3, OneWorld Implementation.*

- **Incident Date and Incident Time**: These fields drive the duration escalation rules.

- **Company**: Includes customers, partners, and employees. (You can also use the support system for help desk management.)

- **Contact**: Online and e-mail case capture auto-fill this, if the contact is entered or known to the system; otherwise it is a list of the company's contacts.

- **Email**: Defaults from the contact or the individual customer; this is required if you want to get in touch about the case with the customer.

- **Product** and **Module**: These fields are for OneWorld clients who have purchased the additional Issue Management module for managing product bugs/enhancements.

- **Item** and **Serial/Lot Number**: When you set up items in your catalog, you can check **Offer Support** to add an item to this list. If you have serial or lot-based inventory, you can also enter these identifiers here.

- **Inbound email address**: Captures the 'sent from' address, when e-mail generates the case.

- **Case Issue**, **Priority**, **Type**, and **Origin**: From the support lists you configured in the *Support Preferences* section.

- **Assigned To**: List of Support Reps (they must have **Support Rep** checked on their employee record).

- **Help Desk**: Identifies this as an internal case. You must also enable this feature to have this option.

- **Copy Employees**: Updates other employees on a case. If you have another employee that you want to copy on every case interaction, then you must select them each time you update the case.

After gathering all the basic information on the top of the form, we turn to the two most important fields on the form: the **Message** and **Reply** fields.

The message is the customer's incoming message, and the reply is, of course, your support rep's reply or assessment of the problem. Both of these fields allow multiple entries, so the original message and reply move down to become lines on the **Interactions** tab when new messages or replies are added. You always have a full history of the interaction on each case.

Also notice under the **Reply** field that there are two checkboxes, namely, **Send to Customer** and **Internal only**. The default for these two fields is controlled by the support preference we discussed previously: The default **New Case** form to **Internal Only** and default **New Case** form to **Send To Customer**. Most users default to **Internal only**, at least when starting to use the system.

The last field to discuss is the **Insert Solution** field above the **Reply** text box. This deserves a section of its own on using the OneWorld Knowledge Base.

Knowledge Base

The knowledge base provides the ability to generate solutions to common problems, questions, and issues, and organizes them for search, by your employees, customers, and partners.

To get started with the knowledge base functionality, navigate to **Lists | Web Site | Tabs | New** and select **New Presentation Tab**. This is the 'physical' location of the knowledge base, the actual tab on your **Center** tabs under which the knowledge base exists.

Next, set up a couple of topics, by navigating to **Lists | Support | Topics**. Consider a topic as a category of solutions. Finally, navigate to **Lists | Support | Knowledge Base | New** and select your **Topic**, **Publish to** the tab we just set up previously, and decide whether or not you want this tab to appear on your OneWorld website (applicable only if you have a OneWorld website) through the **Display in Web Site** checkbox.

You now have a knowledge base and should be able to see the tab on your OneWorld center tabs, as shown in the following screenshot:

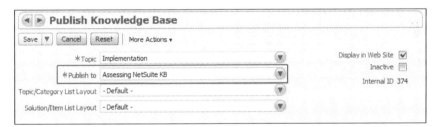

You can now create a solution and link it to a topic, either by clicking on the **New Solution** button on the case form (your role needs permission to do this) or by navigating to **List | Support | Solution | New**. Every new solution, containing a short explanation, or abstract, and long explanation of the case resolution, must be linked to at least one topic. The solution **Title** and **Abstract** should be written carefully, with the view toward finding specific solutions through keyword searches; see **Lists | Support | Solutions | Search** to find out more.

Knowledge base setup also allows you to determine which solutions you want to make available to a specific audience. If you want to limit access to a certain set of solutions, then you can publish them to topics in a Knowledge Base with limited access.

It's also a good idea to keep a Knowledge Base of the OneWorld implementation. Doesn't it make sense to maintain a base of solutions that describe how you want to transact business in OneWorld?

Customer support reps can search and add solutions as pre-defined responses to a support case. If the customer asks several questions, then the rep can build a response, by adding solutions to the response and modifying it as needed.

Support summary

OneWorld service enables support reps and operations staff to manage internal and external problems, issues, and questions, and create a base of knowledge that makes future problem solving less time consuming. Cases are viewable from the customer record, allowing users from other departments to view a customer's interaction with your organization in advance of a call or visit. Solutions to problems are not only available to employees, but to other parties including non-support employees, partners, and even customers.

There are a few other functions of the service module that we have not taken time to discuss in detail, but which we ought to note. You can track time on cases, and bill it to customers, if this is part of your business model. You can also use the Support module for an internal help desk. These features, and many of the features that we have discussed here, such as e-mail case capture and knowledge base, must first be enabled under **Setup | Company | Enable Features**.

Summary

The OneWorld CRM modules really represent a closed loop of customer interactions, from the first stirring of interest, through the sales process, and, finally, service and sales renewal and/or upsell.

We think the value here is obviously tremendous. A well-structured, efficient, and goal-meeting CRM system provides a lot of measurable value for the modern organization. We have not yet spent a lot of time on reporting and other ways of measuring your organization's success, but as we do, we think you'll start to see how using an integrated system, with both CRM and ERP, such as OneWorld, provides a level of business understanding and visibility that many business people in the small and medium enterprise never thought they could achieve.

In the next chapter, we take the sales order generated by the sales team to the next step and start the assembly, project management, fulfillment, time tracking, purchasing, expense reporting, invoicing, and financial management functions that together are called **Enterprise Resource Planning (ERP)**.

6
Nuts and Bolts of OneWorld ERP

Marketing and selling are often the first topics of discussion in a OneWorld implementation, and rightfully so. Nothing is more important to a business than revenue coming in the door. Setting up the ERP modules in OneWorld has a direct bearing on the sales, purchasing, and fulfillment processes that ultimately result in not only revenue, but net income.

In this chapter, we will tackle the configuration of OneWorld ERP modules for both product-based and service-based companies, with a view towards your organization's operations and the hand-off from sales to operations. In the next chapter, we will cover the rest of the financial management of the organization. Though we have split the ERP discussion in two, we think it wise for readers to take the time to read both *Chapter 6, Nuts and Bolts of OneWorld ERP* and *Chapter 7, Nuts and Bolts of OneWorld ERP—Financial Management*, in order to get a full appreciation of both what's possible in OneWorld and how the pieces fit together.

We start this chapter with a more in-depth discussion of the **Item catalog**. We skimmed this important implementation step earlier, but nothing impacts your organization's ability to operate effectively and profitably in OneWorld more than the item catalog. Using the catalog configuration as the focal point of our ERP discussion means that we must move back and forth between purchasing and selling, between receiving and fulfilling, and between accounts payable and accounts receivable. The main objective is to help you to see the closed-loop processes that OneWorld offers your organization, as opposed to simply understanding each module by itself. The most important attribute of OneWorld is its integration of processes from across the organization—understand this and you have the key to OneWorld success.

Most of the organizations that use OneWorld to sell product inventory purchase the **Advanced Inventory** module, enabling not only more advanced inventory setup, but also more advanced inventory processing from the purchase through to fulfillment. We base our discussion here on the assumption that you have advanced inventory. Likewise, we base our discussion of selling services on the assumption that you have the **Advanced Project Accounting** module.

The main sections of this chapter, in which we weave together sales, operations, and finance, are:

- Drop ships and special orders
- Managing inventory and warehouse processes
- Assembly, kitting, and grouping
- Selling items with deferred revenue
- Selling and managing services
- E-commerce in OneWorld

Again, the objective here is to give you enough information on the base functionality of OneWorld ERP that you can begin to set up a first draft prototype of your organization's OneWorld account. We suggest that you do not, at this time, try to complete the configuration by setting up, for example, all of your items. Rather, we recommend that you find the item types that most closely match your business model, set up a few items of those types, and then test through the whole process, from a vendor purchase to a customer sales order, to fulfillment and invoicing; or from sold project to billable time, and expenses to client invoice.

Drop ship and special order

Selling items that your organization does not inventory is not only a facet of many businesses today, but also a business model in and of itself. The idea is simply to have the vendor manage logistics, while you focus on marketing, sales, and finance.

Using drop ship and special order in OneWorld requires that you set up your items to take advantage of this tactic, as seen in the following screenshot:

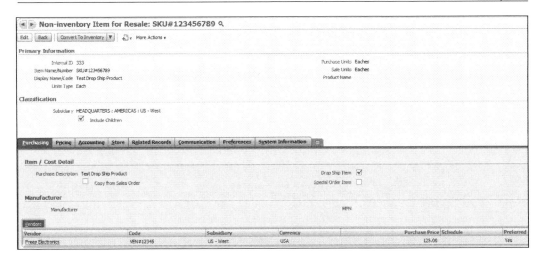

Note that we used the item type **Non-Inventory** and the sub-type **for Resale** in this example. It is also possible to use the **Inventory Item** type for drop ship/special orders. Items for resale require G/L accounts for both the purchase and sale, an Expense Account for the purchase, and an Income Account for the sale. Select your accounts on the **Accounting** tab.

Since this is a physical product, we have checked the **Can be Fulfilled/Received** checkbox, and because we have enabled **Advanced Taxes**, we must select a **Tax Schedule**.

Finally, drop ship and special order items require at least one **Vendor**, see the bottom of the form screenshot, and one **Purchase Price**. In our OneWorld account, we have **Multiple Vendors** enabled, allowing us to specify the vendor when we enter the sales order line for this item.

We also made this item available to the customers of the same subsidiary as the vendor from whom we purchase the item. This is an important point to understand: In order for drop ship/special order to work correctly, the customer and vendor must exist under the same subsidiary. If you are going to offer this product to the customers of several subsidiaries, then you must establish the vendor under each of these subsidiaries, as well.

Drop ship or special order

When setting up your items, it's useful to select either **Drop Ship** or **Special Order**, based on actual practice, but note that you can change from one to the other in the line item of the sales order. So you can drop ship a special order item and vice versa per line item.

The difference between drop ship and special order is that drop ship moves directly from the vendor to the customer, while the special order item first comes to one of your locations before moving on to the customer, perhaps for configuration, service, and so on. Whereas drop ship requires a one-step fulfillment process to move the sales order into the invoicing queue, the special order requires a receipt, into your location, and then a subsequent fulfillment to the customer.

Vendor bills and customer invoices

We note that OneWorld's terms are sometime confusing, so here's a short explanation. When we bill purchase orders, we generate vendor bills. The vendor sends their invoice to us and we match it to our bill. When we bill sales orders, we produce the customer invoices. When we have billable time and expenses, we invoice billable customers.

There are a few questions that you must answer, before heading into configuration.

Inventory or non-inventory items

Do you ever intend to inventory an item? In other words, do you sometimes keep an item in inventory, but do drop ship when it's out of inventory or being phased out? If the answer is 'yes,' then you can set up the drop ship/special order items as inventory items and decide on the sales order whether you want to drop ship or fulfill from inventory; if the answer is 'no,' then you can set up non-inventory items for drop ship or special order.

The benefits of using inventory items is, of course, the flexibility it gives you – you can decide to inventory hot items, and drop ship cold ones. Or you can decide on a sale-by-sale basis whether you want to drop ship a vanilla item configuration from the vendor, and sell a special configuration from your own inventory.

By using non-inventory items, the organization has an easy-to-use distinction, item type, between their inventory lines and the drop ship/special order lines. Also, in some cases, the business never intends to inventory an item, and therefore, they use the non-inventory item setup, which is less complex than the inventory item setup.

Each organization seems to have its own reasons to use inventory or non-inventory items as the basis of their drop ship/special order business. If you start with non-inventory items, then you do have the ability to convert them to inventory items later, should that become necessary.

For e-commerce drop ship, there is the following option, under **Setup | Web Site | Setup Web Site | Shopping**: **Drop Ship/Special Order items are always in stock**. If you turn this on, any drop ship item on your e-commerce site will always be in stock. We will cover e-commerce later in this chapter.

Using standard forms

The forms you select in OneWorld often determine not only the fields you see, but more importantly, transactional behavior. If you select the **Standard Sales Order – Invoice** form, OneWorld automatically produces an invoice, for example. We suggest that you use the standard forms until you are comfortable with their operation, taking care to select the ones that match your requirements. *Chapter 8, OneWorld Customization and Advanced Configuration*, has a section detailing the behavior of all of the standard forms.

The drop ship/special order process

The process of drop ship is fairly straightforward: Generate a sales order with at least one line for a drop ship item. If you have **Sales Order Approvals** turned on, then approve the order, and the system generates the purchase order for you. In the following screenshot, we have saved a sales order for our drop ship item:

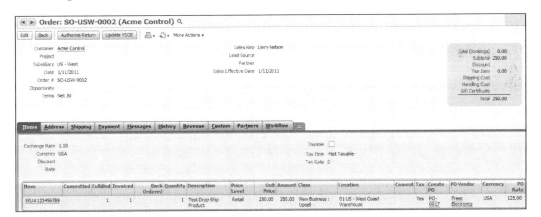

In the line, we have selected our drop ship item and also the **PO Vendor** and the **PO Rate**. The flexibility of setting vendor and rate per line is very useful if your sales or operations staff is looking for best prices regularly.

Generating sales orders

In the OneWorld account described here, we generated the sales order manually, as an internal sales person might. Sales orders also generate automatically from e-commerce sales, or they can result from an **Estimate** becoming a sales order, when a sales person or partner promotes the estimate. In any of these cases, we still have a sales order, though the sales order form does impact the next step. Notice that the sales order form in the previous screenshot has the name **OneWorld Order – Invoice**. This means that after fulfillment, this order becomes an invoice. Other sales order forms may produce a cash sale.

After saving this sales order and approving it, the system shows us the following screen, telling us that that the sales order has successfully generated a **Purchase Order, Processed Number: 17**:

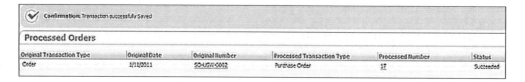

We can navigate to the PO directly from this screen by clicking the **17**, and if we ever wish to navigate to the PO from the sales order, the purchase order number is now saved in the sales order line, where we started. If desired, the drop ship POs can be automatically e-mailed to the vendor.

Use your reminders

On the home page dashboard, set up the reminders for your role. Reminders are the important link between the employees and departments in your organization. For example, when you generate a new PO from the sales order, it makes sense that your purchasing team sees this new PO as soon as possible, so that they can manage the next step. Likewise, you want operations to know a new sales order fell into the queue to be fulfilled. The best way to do this is through reminders.

After generating the drop ship PO from the sales order, the next step is fulfilling the order when the vendor ships the product. Most companies rely on their vendors to send them confirmation of shipment in order to fulfill an order. You can fulfill the order from either the PO, by clicking the **Mark Shipped** button, as seen in the next screenshot, or from the sales order, by clicking the **Fulfill** button. Either click takes you to the fulfillment form. Alternatively, you can fulfill in batch mode on the **Fulfill Orders** (sales order) form, from **Transactions | Sales | Fulfill Orders**.

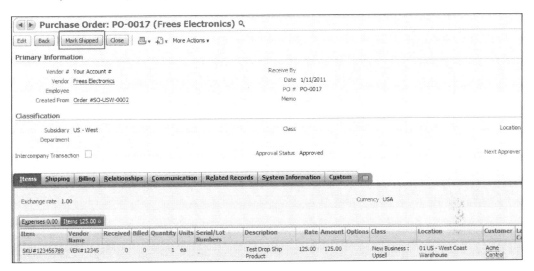

The special order process is slightly different, since the product comes to one of your locations first before moving on to the customer. As you would expect, this process requires that we **Receive By** against the PO first, then **Fulfill** the sales order when we are ready to move the product on to the customer.

Note that in both the drop ship and the special order processes, there is no general ledger impact for the receipt or the fulfillment. OneWorld does not record a change in inventory. On the purchase side, when we generate a bill from the PO, the impact is a debit to the item's expense or cost of goods sold account, and a credit to accounts payable. On the sales side, when we bill the sales order to generate the invoice, the G/L impact is a debit to accounts receivable and a credit to the item's revenue account.

Managing inventory and warehouse processes

Managing inventory, as it moves in and out of your organization, is a very important task. This section covers the most important inventory processes:

- Inventory types
- Adjusting inventory
- Selling inventory
- Inventory item pricing
- Fulfilling inventory
- Pick, pack, and ship
- Integrated shipping
- Re-ordering inventory
- Purchasing inventory
- Transferring inventory between locations
- Transferring inventory between subsidiaries
- Inventory history

Inventory types

If you are keeping inventory, then you must decide the type of inventory. OneWorld offers the following:

- **Inventory**: This is the simplest of the inventory items, just a single item that you purchase, inventory, and then sell. Inventory items might also be members of kits, groups, and assemblies.

- **Matrix Inventory**: These are items where you maintain inventory for every option combination, such as colors and sizes.

- **Lot Inventory**: This is an inventory item identified by a specific lot number, which might also have an expiration date.

- **Serialized Inventory**: This is an inventory item with a serial number that requires identification in each process, from receipt of PO to fulfillment of the sales order.

- **Lot Matrix Inventory**: Combination of Matrix and Lot inventory, such as foodstuffs that come in various flavors.

- **Serialized Matrix Inventory**: Combination of Serialized and Matrix inventory, such as serialized electronics, which come in different colors.

Setting up inventory items begins by navigating to **Lists | Accounting | Items | New** and selecting the inventory **Item type**. This brings up the following form:

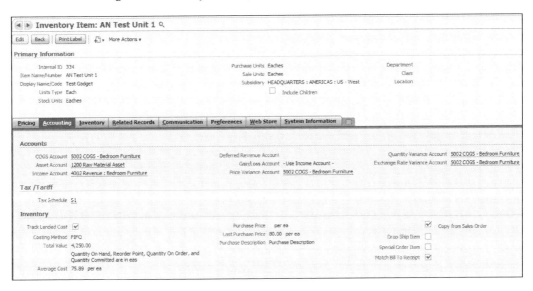

The choices that you make on the inventory item setup form affect how the item transacts in the system, so it makes sense to spend some time on each of the important fields. Note that this is a custom form that exposes only the fields that impact how the item transacts; other fields, though important, have been removed.

Inventory items have a financial impact on vendor receipts and bills, and on customer fulfillments and invoices, or cash sales, but inventory counts are only impacted on PO receipts and SO fulfillments, or inventory adjustments. Having made that bold statement, we must also note that there is an exception. When you transact an invoice, credit memo, or vendor bill, without the normal chain of transactions, for example, sales order fulfillment – invoice, OneWorld knows that the inventory count has not been decremented or incremented, depending on the case, in a prior transaction and does so on the standalone transaction.

- **Item Name/Number**: This is the SKU of the item. OneWorld also offers UPC codes for organizations that have them. This code may be used to select the item on the sales order.

- **Display Name/Code**: If you want a different name to appear to the customer, such as *Sunny Corporation Cool Gadget*, then use the display name.

- **Offer Support**: Checking this field means that you can create a service case and apply it to this item; good for reporting.

- **Subsidiary**: Each item can be sold to customers of one or more subsidiaries, or purchased from vendors of one or more subsidiaries. If you select the root or one of the parent subsidiaries, then you can also click **Include Children**. If you want to inventory this item at a specific location, then you must select the subsidiary that 'owns' the location.

- **Department, Class, and Location**: You can specify here the location at which the item is inventoried, and you can also designate the class and department, if you want these values to default on the sale or purchase line for this item.

- **COGS Account, Asset Account**, and **Income Account**: These are the accounts used in the purchase and sale transactions.

- **Tax Schedule**: The tax schedule allows you to vary taxability by tax nexus, meaning that a single item can be taxable in Texas and non-taxable in Michigan, for example.

- **Gain/Loss Account**: Holds the difference in value between the item's actual cost and its transfer cost.

- **Bill Price Variance Account, Quantity Variance Account**, and **Match Bill To Receipt**: These fields, when used together, enable you to post variances between purchase orders and bills, or between receipts and bills. You can create the variances between the PO and the bill or between the receipt and the bill. When there are differences between the value and/or quantity that you receive, and the value and/or quantity that you bill, a balance accumulates in the **Inventory Received Not Billed** account, which must then be managed.

- **Quanity, Price, and Purchase Price Variance Accounts**: These fields hold the account values where the system posts the variance between your expected costs and the actual costs. Used for organizations who implement Standard Costing.

- **Exchange Rate Variance**: Account to hold any variances that happen in exchange rates between bill and payments, or invoices and payments received.

- **Item Weight**: If you want to ship the product by carrier, such as UPS, item weights are necessary. Also used when you allocate landed costs by weight.

- **Costing Method**: Select from LIFO, FIFO, Standard, or Average, after consulting with your accountant.

- **Cost Category**: For organizations using standard costing, place each inventory item into a cost category. Cost categories help you to break down costs by different materials or labor inputs.

- **Units Type**: Units are set up under **Lists | Accounting | Units of Measure**. Units enable the purchase of a pallet, the stocking of cartons, and the sale of **Eaches**.

- **Minimum Quantity**: Smallest amount that a customer can purchase.

Setting up Lot and Serialized Inventory is very similar to a straight inventory item, though the costing method is either specific to the lot or serial number or standard.

Matrix items, on the other hand, take several additional steps to set up. There is a matrix setup wizard that you should walk through at least a few times, even if you plan on importing most of your items. Matrix items simply set up a single parent item and then a child item for each possible combination of options; so if you have three colors and three sizes, you end up with nine children. The idea is that you present a single item to the customer, but you manage inventory at the child level with unique SKUs, each SKU with its own inventory count.

Keep in mind that you do not have to set up all of your items manually. Once you have the setup process mastered, you can import the rest of your items. Getting many of your other setups done prior to item import is important though, if you want to avoid a lot of purposeless frustration. So again, we suggest that you do ample testing with a few items, before moving to complete your setups and then your imports.

If your organization wants to use standard costing, there are several additional setup steps past identifying your cost type and category on the item and selecting variance accounts. You must also set up Versions, Planned Costs, and Planned Rollups (if you do assembly). These options are all under Lists | Accounting.

Adjusting inventory

After setting up or importing a few of your inventory items, you have to adjust the inventory counts in the system, so that you have inventory to sell in your implementation testing. You could purchase inventory in order to get testing started. However, before you go live, you must take a physical inventory and adjust the system, and that's why we start by adjusting inventory here. Remember that you always purchase inventory into a specific location and you always sell inventory from a specific location, and the same goes for all inventory transactions.

There are two different forms for adjusting inventory. Navigate to **Transactions | Inventory** and you will find the **Adjust Inventory** form and the **Adjust Inventory Worksheet**. While they look fairly similar, there is a major difference between these two forms. When you use the **Adjust Inventory Worksheet**, the system sets a stake in the ground on the day specified in the worksheet. So if you say you have 10 units on Jan 1st, the system resets the count to 10 and then, regardless of what transacts in the system subsequently prior to that date (a PO receipt or a SO fulfillment prior to Jan 1st), the system maintains that you have 10 units on Jan 1.

Using the **Adjust Inventory** form tells the system to simply adjust the count, and value, by some number – simple addition. This means that if you save a receipt or fulfillment on a date prior to the adjustment, the inventory amount changes as of the adjustment date. So if you adjust the inventory of item XYZ by 10 on Jan 1, giving you a total of 20, and then you receive another 5 on Dec 26 of the prior year, OneWorld says you have a total of 25 on Jan 1. This is important to keep in mind.

In the following screenshot, we add 10 units to the **Qty On Hand**, and also increase the total dollar amount of the inventory.

In the following screenshot, we add 10 units to the **Qty On Hand**, and also increase the total dollar amount of the inventory.

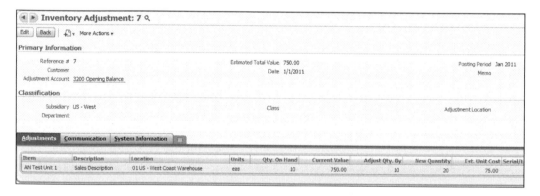

Also note that the **Adjust Inventory Worksheet** forces average costing, even for items that have FIFO or LIFO costing. After adjusting them with the worksheet, they lose their LIFO or FIFO history and are termed as Average.

When working with inventory, it's important to perform transactions that adjust inventory values and counts as they happen, when they happen, as much as possible. It is not good business practice to collect a pile of receipts and enter them into the system whenever, especially if duties at your organization are split among several employees/departments. Entering transactions into the system out of sequence can alter the results people see.

For example, your purchasing manager might look at the **Qty On Hand** on the **Adjust Inventory** form and see **25**, and then make an entry to bring the on-hand quantity in line with the actual physical inventory. If you enter receipts afterwards that he/she did not know about, the items-on-hand count is going to change again, and be incorrect. It's obviously important for everyone who works on inventory to communicate when they plan to make changes.

Test transactions

The inventory adjustment above is a test transaction. In some cases, you have purchased a sandbox account where you can run test transactions to your heart's content, but in other cases, you may be testing in the soon-to-be production account. This is not as big a deal as it might seem. You can always delete test transactions from the administrator's role. In some cases, you will have to follow the transaction chain to the end and delete backwards; for example, delete the invoice, then the fulfillment, and finally the sales order.

Selling inventory

Now that we have an inventory item setup, and we have inventory on hand, we can sell it. You can start your OneWorld ERP testing now, and set up a sales order with the item you created and sell it to a test customer.

It is normal to set up a dozen or so items manually at this stage, and a good idea to ask some of the operations staff to enter the items. Small tasks like these can really help the staff to start to understand how the system works, even if their job description does not include item setup. Once you are satisfied with your item setups, it's also a good idea to set up a saved search of items and with all of their fields. Then export the search results to a **Comma Separated Values (CSV)** file and use this file as the template for importing the rest of your item catalog. You need a file-by-item type and sub-type for imports.

Having a few items in the system helps to focus on a couple of issues that every organization must contend with, when it comes to entering any of the sales transactions, opportunities, estimates, sales order, cash sales, and invoices. If you have a large item catalog, finding the correct items quickly is a challenge. There are a few tricks that might help.

First, notice that in the next screenshot, we have circled the **Add Multiple** button. This is a helpful way, obviously, for when you have multiple items that must be added to an order. When you select the item in the pop-up box, on the right in the following screenshot, the selected items move to the right column.

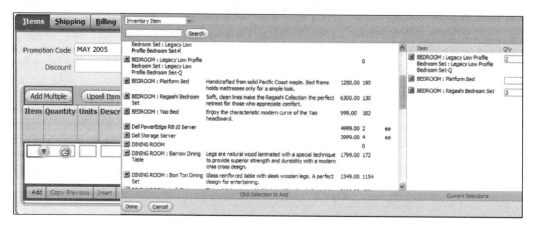

When starting a sales order, or any other transaction in OneWorld, you must select the entity first, in this case, the **Customer**, so that the system knows the subsidiary in which you are working.

In the **Add Multiple** form, you can use the **Search** parameter boxes on the top-left to limit the search in a couple of ways. In the top drop-down, you can select the item type that you want to see. In the free text field, you can enter a keyword, or, as in this case, the parent item name. This is one of the advantages of grouping your items into an item hierarchy with parents and children – it makes it easier to find items in an extensive catalog. (The other main advantage is that OneWorld reflects your hierarchy in reports, such as sales by item.)

Using the **Add Multiple** function, you can line up as many items as you want into the list on the right of the form, and then add your quantities if they are not 1; the default value updates the lines when you click **Done**.

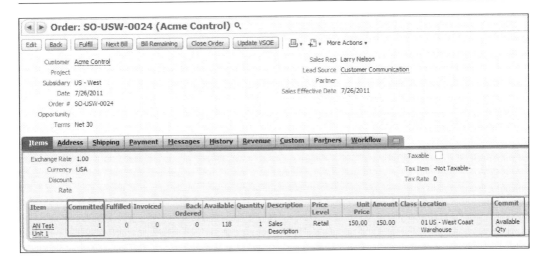

We now have a sales order for the item that we entered previously. In the line, OneWorld tells us that it has **Committed: 1** from our inventory to this order, because our default preference is to **Commit: Available Qty**, (see far right). The sales line also tells us that we have not **Fulfilled** or **Invoiced** this line, and the item is not **Back Ordered**; in fact, we have **Available: 118** at this **Location: 01 US West Coast Warehouse**.

To tie together your understanding of this transaction, consider the following:

- The customer belongs to the US – West subsidiary.
- The sales rep Larry Nelson has the role permission to this subsidiary.
- US - West has a location, 01 US -West Warehouse, where you have received 118 units of the item AN Test Unit 1.
- The US - West subsidiary may transfer inventory to any other location owned by US – West.
- The vendor from whom you purchased the item belongs to the US – West subsidiary.
- You sell AN Test Unit 1 to any customer of US – West.
- You may also transfer the item to a location of another subsidiary where it is sold to the customers of that subsidiary (see *Intercompany Transfer Orders*).
- Another subsidiary may also purchase the item from another vendor belonging to that subsidiary and receive it into one of its own location(s), then sell it to customers of that subsidiary. Each location would keep its own inventory of the item.

Hopefully, this example helps to start laying a foundation of understanding in how you think about your subsidiaries, your item catalog, and your locations.

Inventory item pricing

Note that in the previous screenshot, the customer received the retail price of the item **AN Test Unit 1**. Let's return to the item setup record and look at the **Pricing** tab, as shown in the following screenshot, to understand how pricing works in OneWorld:

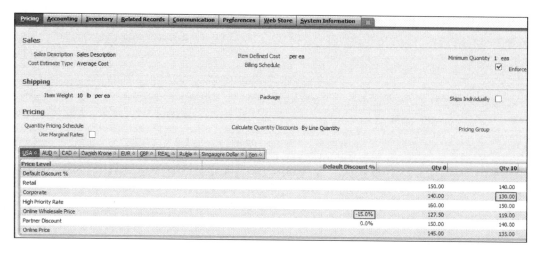

In its simplest form, pricing is set up with a base price, which here we have renamed the **Retail** price. The other row values include **Corporate, High Priority Rate**, and so on, which are additional **Price Levels** that we set up under **Setup | Accounting | Accounting Lists**. In some cases, these are simply a name, and in others, we associate the name with a percentage markup or discount, such as **Online Wholesale Price** (as shown in the screenshot), which has a **15** percent discount.

The columns represent the **Quantity** and their price breaks. You can set up as many columns as you require, by setting the **Accounting Preference** for Maximum number of Quantity Based Price Levels. With quantities and price levels established, you now have a pricing matrix for this item.

The next step is to make sure that each customer receives the correct price. We accomplish this by designating the **Price Level** on the customer record, under the **Financial** tab. When the customer orders a quantity of this item, the system marries the customer's price level to the item's price matrix and finds the correct price. In the previous example, if the customer has the **Corporate** price level and orders at least **10**, the price is **130.00** dollars.

Setting up the pricing matrix for a large item catalog can be very time consuming, so OneWorld offers the **Quantity Pricing Schedule**. In this setup, the schedule establishes the pricing matrix for you. In the following screenshot, we have set up a schedule for our furniture line to use:

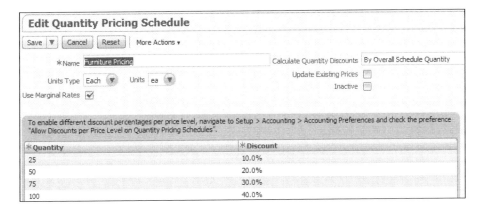

Now when we apply this schedule to the **AN Test Unit 1** item, we see the following matrix immediately:

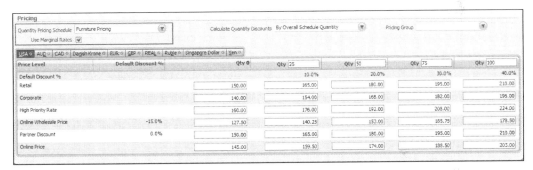

This screenshot also shows us the decisions that we made when we linked the schedule to the item, such as enabling the **Use Marginal Rates** field, for example, which applies the quantity price break to only the quantity above the break, not to the entire quantity.

Any item may have a single schedule. You may also set up pricing schedules for vendors that enable quantity discounts on purchases. See *Vendor Pricing*.

For additional customer pricing flexibility, there is the **Pricing Group**. Set up pricing groups at **Setup | Accounting | Accounting Lists | Pricing Group**. Placing items into a **Pricing Group** allows you to set multiple **Price Levels** per customer, one price level per **Pricing Group**, on the customer's **Financial** tab.

For item pricing in currencies outside of your organization's base currency, you have a couple of options. You can set up pricing at the item level; notice that in the previous screenshot, there is a sub-tab for every currency enabled in our OneWorld account; or you can use the currency exchange rate table to calculate the sales and purchase amounts, per transaction.

Fulfilling inventory

OneWorld sets up all of the inventory item types automatically for fulfillment and receiving. You have the option of fulfilling/receiving the non-inventory items and service items. Fulfillment and receipt are the process steps that occur between sales or purchasing and finance; these are the steps often taken by the operation's staff to ship goods or check them into the plant.

To use **Fulfill Orders**, you must first enable the **Advanced Shipping** feature at **Setup | Company | Enable Features | Transactions**. This is the feature that provides the separate fulfillment step in the sales order management process.

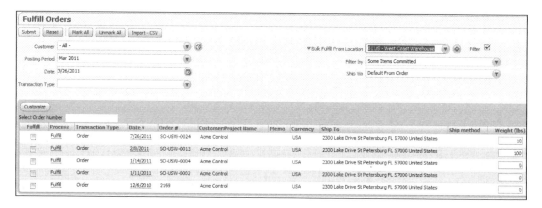

For inventory items, the fulfillment process is where OneWorld debits cost of goods sold and credits the inventory asset account.

You fulfill sales orders by starting at an individual order and clicking the **Fulfill** button, or by fulfilling in bulk using the **Fulfill Orders** form, shown in the previous screenshot. Again, fulfillments always take place from a specific location, so **Bulk Fulfill from Location** is always a required field.

Pick, pack, and ship

Fulfillment can also be done in concert with shipping, if you are using OneWorld's **Integrated Shipping** feature. And for many organizations that fulfill a huge number of orders every day, it's wise to enable the **Pick, Pack and Ship** feature, which breaks down fulfillment into a three-step process. The **Pick, Pack and Ship** and **Integrated Shipping** features can both be enabled at **Setup | Company | Enable Features**.

In short, **Pick, Pack and Ship** requires that you print a picking ticket to use in finding the items in the warehouse bins. Then you print the packing slip and package the goods and get it set for shipping. Finally, you can print the shipping label, place it on the package, and the order is ready for pickup, by your carrier.

Most OneWorld users print picking tickets in bulk, then they package and print packing slips order by order, and finally they print the shipping labels in bulk and apply them to the packages. You can reprint a picking ticket from the sales order, and reprint the packing slip from the fulfillment form. To print in bulk, navigate to **Transactions | Management | Print Checks and Forms**.

Lastly, under **Setup | Accounting | Customize Fulfillment Email**, customize the e-mail that customers receive upon fulfillment of their orders. Use this navigation if you have the **Web Store** feature disabled, meaning you are not going to sell from a OneWorld web store, or if you have the **Web Store** enabled and you want different fulfillment e-mails for web store orders and manually entered sales orders. In the latter case, you must also disable the **Accounting Preference | Use Web Site Template for Fulfillment Emails** at **Setup | Accounting | Accounting Preferences**.

For OneWorld e-commerce users, there are other e-mails that you can use for order acknowledgement, and so on. The *E-commerce* section of this chapter has the details.

Integrated shipping

Organizations that fulfill orders normally also use the **Integrated Shipping** feature. When you enable this feature, you have the ability to set up your Fedex, UPS, or USPS, for US customers, accounts in OneWorld, and also the shipping items and packages that you will use. Shipping accounts are set up at **Setup | Accounting | Shipping**. You need to have each shipper's account number to complete this task.

On this form, you can register your carriers for integrated shipping, and also set up your packages and holiday or non-shipping calendar.

After you complete the **Setup Shipping** form, navigate to **Lists | Accounting | Shipping Items**, to set up a shipping item, as shown in the following screenshot:

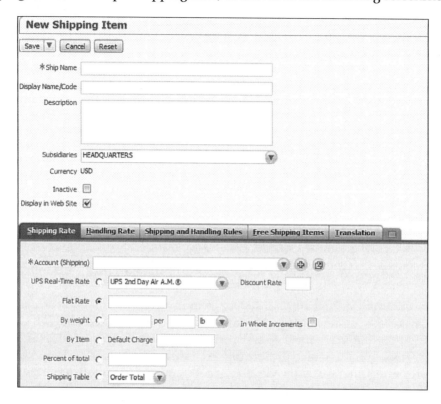

Now that we have **Shipping** set up, we can drive shipping costs into the account of our choice. We can also use real-time rates with our carriers, and if need be, we can increase these to cover costs by using the **Discount Rate**; 1.1, for example, increases the rate by 10 percent. There are also several other methods to determine the shipping rates and handling rates, and other rules to adjust the amount of shipping, based on the details of each order, such as total amount or specific items purchased.

Once you have set up all of your shipping items, return to the **Shipping Setup** form and select a default shipping method if you want. You can also set up a default e-commerce method on the **Web Site Setup** form, under the **Shopping** tab.

Re-ordering inventory

Managing inventory receipt and fulfillment is itself a full-time job in most organizations, so when do you have time for physical inventory counts and adjustments? Weekends seem to be popular, but there are some OneWorld functions, while not eliminating the need for an annual physical count, that can be very helpful.

In the following screenshot of the inventory item's **Inventory** tab, you can see that we have set up our OneWorld account for **Advanced Inventory Management**, meaning that we are going to **Auto-Calculate** the **Lead Time**, **Reorder Point**, and **Preferred Stock Level**, based on a system algorithm and actual transaction history.

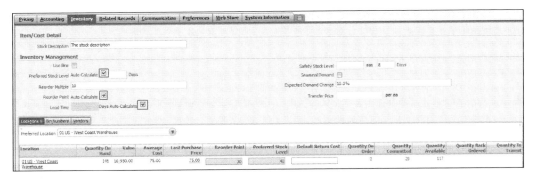

Now there are three options for **Inventory Management**. You can manually set up the **Reorder Point** and **Preferred Stock Level Auto-Calculate** quantities for each item. This is the most basic option, but might work well if your inventory item catalog turns over frequently.

Or you can enable the **Advanced Inventory Management** feature and let the system run its algorithm, based on your selections on the **Inventory Management Preferences** form. After you set up your preferences, you have the option of changing them on any individual item, of course, but as you add items to the system, the default preferences are applied. Over time, as you purchase, receive, sell, and fulfill inventory, OneWorld calculates the quantity to re-order.

Inventory Management Preferences

Save ▼ Cancel Reset

In order to calculate inventory levels for existing items, you need to set the auto calculate flags on these items. You can do that in bulk using mass update.

∗Default Lead Time	14	Days
∗Default Safety Stock	7	Days
∗Default Preferred Stock Level	30	Days
∗Order Analysis Interval	6	Months
∗Seasonal Analysis Interval	1	Months
∗Estimated Demand Change	0%	

Transactions to Consider

Orders ⦿
Actual Sales ○

Day of Week To Perform Calculation Sunday ▼

Save ▼ Cancel Reset

The third option is to purchase the new **Demand Planning** module that NetSuite recently introduced. This module adds a new level of sophistication to your **Inventory Management**, allowing you to forecast demand in a variety of ways, including from your CRM sales pipeline, and then set up your supply plan accordingly. **Demand Planning** turns the forecast into action, through purchase orders, work orders, or both.

You can reorder inventory on the **Order Inventory** form. The items appear here, based on your filters in the top of the form, and because OneWorld has identified them through either your setup of reorder points and preferred stock levels, or through the advanced inventory algorithm, as items that require reordering.

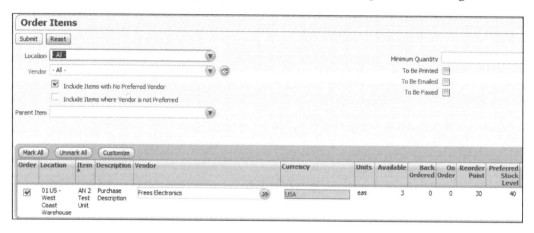

The main point of this form is that it allows you to filter your search for items that require reordering. Once you have the list you want, the lines tell you everything you need to know about an item's current inventory status:

- **Order**: This checkbox means that when you click on **Submit**, the system generates a PO for this item to the **Vendor** chosen.

- **Available**: We originally had 20 in stock; we sold one and have another sales order, on which we committed 18, leaving one available.

- **Back Ordered**: If we enter another sales order for two units, we commit the last unit and then have one unit back ordered.

- OneWorld calculated our quantity using the advanced inventory algorithm and the fact that in the item setup, we entered 10 as the **Reorder Multiple**.

- Upon clicking **Submit**, OneWorld generates a PO.

Purchasing inventory

Purchase orders, as we have seen, generate automatically for drop ships and reorders. You can also set them up manually, or import batches of them through web services or the CSV import tool. We have covered PO setup, but there are a few other things to know about purchasing to round up our discussion.

Landed costs

Landed costs are the costs associated with getting a product to your door. These might include freight, duties, insurance, and so on. OneWorld enables you to land these costs into the cost of the inventory, and therefore include them in the cost of goods sold when you sell inventory. The following setup steps are necessary:

1. Enable the **Landed Cost** feature.
2. Set up **Landed Cost Categories** under **Setup | Accounting | Accounting Lists**, and link to the same expense account as your **Other Charge** items.
3. Set up the **Other Charge** type items for the landed costs and use the same account as the **Landed Cost Categories.**
4. Set up **Inventory Items** with **Track Landed Costs** clicked on.

You can land costs in two ways, depending on the vendor charging you for freight, and so on. If the charges are from the same vendor as the inventory, then you can add the landed cost items to the PO, making them flow through the receipt and the bill. On the **Receipt**, add your cost on the **Landed Cost** tab and it will credit your landed cost expense account; then when you bill the PO, there is an offsetting debit to the same account, leaving a zero net result and landing the cost of the freight, for example, into the inventory asset account.

Alternatively, if you have different vendors for the inventory items and the associated landed costs, then you can set up bills for the costs, designate the landed cost category, and associate the bill with the **Receipt** for the inventory items. Either way, by landing the costs of freight, and so on, you add these costs to the value of the inventory. (Again, all of the vendors must belong to the same subsidiary.)

There are a couple of caveats. When receipts and bills cross periods, and accounting closes the prior period, you may have to estimate landed costs on receipts, since you will not be able to amend the receipt once the period is closed.

Also, you will be able to select only one method of allocating landed costs per receipt, by **Weight**, by **Quantity**, or by **Value**. If you have a lot of goods being received, you will want to find the whitepaper on "Using Landed Costs to Reflect True COGS" on the NetSuite SuiteAnswers site for further information on landed costs.

Vendor pricing

If you have negotiated contracts with your vendors, then you can set up quantity pricing schedules for the items you purchase, by vendor. To set up pricing schedules for a vendor, first navigate to the **Vendor** record and then the **Financial** tab. In **Edit** mode, you can click on the **New Pricing Schedule** button at the bottom of the form. OneWorld allows you to set up different **Discounts by Quantity**. Once you save the schedule, you can add it to the item record for this vendor on one of the vendor lines. (You must have **Multiple Vendors** enabled, even if you have only one. This enables you to enter the schedule on the item record.)

Receiving

Finally, OneWorld allows you to receive partial orders, or even overages, and should you decide not to wait for the rest of the order, you can always close a PO, by closing individual lines that are not completely received. As long as you have open lines on a PO, you will continue to see the PO on the **Receive Orders** list.

Having a separate receiving step in the purchasing process is not absolutely necessary, but in most organizations using OneWorld, it is the norm; enable the **Advanced Receiving** feature at **Setup | Company | Enable Features | Transactions | Advanced Receiving**. Using receiving also alters the accounting of the transactions. When you receive inventory, the **Amount** value debits your **Inventory Asset** account and credits **Inventory Received Not Billed**. When you bill purchase orders, you debit **Inventory Received Not Billed** and credit A/P, of course. Without **Advanced Receiving** turned on, the vendor bill debits the inventory asset account, and credits accounts payable.

Bins

We have not discussed **Bins** yet, so a few lines here are in order. If you want to track inventory at a more discrete level than location, you can use bins. Start by enabling the **Bin Management** feature, and then under **Accounting | Bins**, set up your bins, each of which must be linked to a single location.

Then under the **Item** setup, click on the **Use Bins** field, and designate the bins you want to use for this item. As you adjust, receive, or fulfill inventory, you not only designate the location, but also the bin. An item may be linked to more than one bin and location.

Using bins adds extra work to every inventory transaction. When you receive, you have to designate the bin, and likewise when you fulfill. After receiving items, you must then use the **Bin Put-away Worksheet** form, under **Transactions | Inventory** to transact the items in the correct bin.

Bins can be very helpful when you have a large warehouse or when you have inventory in multiple buildings in a small 'campus'-like setting. If you set up each building as a separate location, then an order for items from multiple locations means multiple fulfillments. Bins help you avoid this situation, by letting you describe the whole campus as one location, and then each building as a bin.

If you are going to use bins, then be committed and do not treat them lightly. Make bins mandatory on every inventory transaction for every user role. If your location inventory and bin inventory get out of sync, then it's a time-consuming problem to fix. It's also not trivial to turn bins on and off.

If, on the other hand, bins are just a nice-to-have feature that helps you find products in the warehouse, then you may want to consider a custom solution. In general, this requires a custom transaction column field sourced from a custom item field.

If you enable the Advanced Bin/Numbered Inventory Management feature, then you will have greater flexibility with bin usage, including the ability to put away inventory, including lot and serialized inventory, into any bin.

Transferring inventory between locations

Once you have inventory through the door, the next step is often to transfer it to another location. Many companies fulfill orders from several locations, but keep some inventory in just one or a few. In other cases, an organization might kit or assemble items and then ship them to another location or to a third-party logistics company for order fulfillment. Whatever the scenario, it's often necessary to transfer inventory between locations.

Transferring inventory is the process of simply moving the inventory from one location to another in OneWorld. There is no change to the absolute value of the inventory asset account, but the value and count of what you transfer does show up under the new location. To perform this transfer, navigate to **Transactions | Inventory | Transfer Inventory**, and select the **From Location** and **To Location**. Most importantly, note that on the **New Inventory Transfer** form, you must select a single **Subsidiary**, and therefore, the transfer must be between two locations owned by that subsidiary. (Remember that each location is owned by one **Subsidiary**.)

One note about locations and transfers; when you set up OneWorld, remember that if you fulfill a sales order from two locations, it produces two invoices (or cash sales, as the case may be). Each fulfillment is from a specific location, so two locations means two fulfillments and two fulfillments means two invoices. We advise that you only set up separate locations for geographically dispersed locations, but not two floors of the same building, for example. In the former case, use Bins, described previously, to designate where the inventory is in the building.

If you need to capture shipping or some other costs for the inventory transfer, then you can use a **Transfer Order** at **Transactions | Inventory | Enter Transfer Orders**. The **Transfer Order** differs from a simple inventory transfer in three important ways:

1. You must fulfill the order from the shipping location, much like a sales order, possibly adding shipping costs, and so on, and then you must receive the order into the receiving location, much like a purchase order, landing the shipping costs into the item's inventory value.

2. The transfer price may differ from the purchase price of the item, meaning that you are marking up the item for the new location, or simply showing a different price for the transfer than for the value of the inventory.

3. Between the time you ship the item and the time you receive it, OneWorld records its value to the **Inventory in Transit** account. This is another **Other Current Asset** type account that works as a place holder until you receive the inventory into the new location.

The following screenshot below shows the details of a **Transfer Order**:

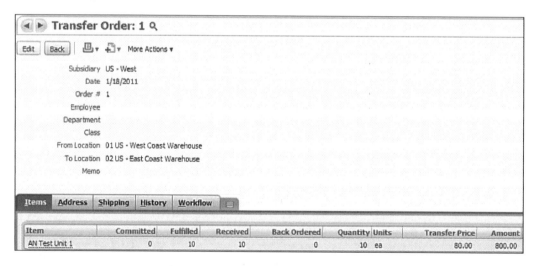

How the system treats the item value for the transfer is determined by the **Use Item Cost** as a **Transfer Cost** accounting preference, and by the **Transfer Price** on the individual item setup.

Transferring inventory between subsidiaries

When you need to move inventory between two locations that are not owned by the same subsidiary, you need to use the **Enter Intercompany Transfer Order**. This essentially does the same job as the **Enter Transfer Order** form, with the important difference that when you receive the goods at the **To Location**, OneWorld does a 4-sided general ledger entry. Intercompany transfer orders only work if you have **Use Item Cost as Transfer Cost** disabled, meaning that the system expects you to enter a transfer cost on the order. In the following screenshot, the GL impact of the fulfillment entry is above the 4-sided GL impact of the receipt entry:

In this transaction, we transferred the item at cost, resulting in no net gain or loss to either subsidiary.

History

We started to delve into transactions quite a bit in this section, so it's a good time to mention that OneWorld has a tab on most forms, where you can see and link to related transactions.

On the transaction forms, such as sales and purchase orders, you have a **Related Records** tab, under which you can see the transactions related to the sale, for example, such as the fulfillments and the invoices. Likewise, there is a **Related Records** tab on the PO, showing receipts and bills.

On entity records, you can view the transactions on a specific vendor or customer under the **Transactions** sub-tab, or list. Even on specific items, you can view all the transactions that included the item under its **History** tab. These are good navigation paths to follow, when you are trying to troubleshoot an issue or a specific transaction.

Assembly, kitting, and grouping

It never ceases to surprise us how OneWorld customers use assembly, kitting, and grouping to formulate quick, clear, and efficient sales lines, or to make a very complex sale simpler for both the sales person and the customer. It's important to understand the differences between assemblies, kits, and groups, so let's start with the basic definitions:

- **Assemblies** are items built through the assembly process with inventory, non-inventory, service, and other charge items, known as the members of the assembly. An assembly posts to its own general ledger accounts for asset, cost of goods sold, and revenue. The building of the assembly relieves inventory from the assembly members. Assemblies are built at a location, so all members of the assembly must be from the same location. Once built, assemblies have a physical count in inventory. An assembly may also be purchased already built from a third party. An assembly may not contain a kit or a group, but it may contain another assembly.

- **Kits** are a defined group of one or more items. The kit never has a quantity or value in inventory. The only general ledger account the kit itself posts to is revenue. When you fulfill a kit, the members of the kit post to their cost of goods sold and inventory accounts. You cannot purchase a kit. The kit sells as you have defined it; you may not alter the kit at the sales order by adding or subtracting members. Kits may contain assemblies, but not groups.

- **Groups** have no accounting whatsoever. Sales transactions for groups simply follow the asset, cost of goods sold, and revenue accounts of the members. A group may not be purchased. Groups, however, unlike assemblies and kits, can be altered at the sales order to include or exclude any item, or change the quantity or price of member items. The value of the group is simply the sum of its members on the sales order. Groups may include any of the normal item types that you sell, as well as assemblies and kits.

The assembly process

An assembly is not only an item, but also a process that decrements member inventory and increments assembly inventory. When you build an assembly, OneWorld removes the value and quantity of the member items from the **Raw Material Asset** account, for example, and places them in the **Finished Goods Asset** account. In the assembly depicted next, OneWorld decrements the counts of **Raw Material A** and **Raw Material B** by **6** and **12** respectively, and increments the inventory count of **AN Test Assembly** by **6**. In the G/L, OneWorld credits the Raw Material Asset account and debits the Finished Goods Asset account. (You can see this under a complete assembly transaction: **More Actions | GL Impact**.)

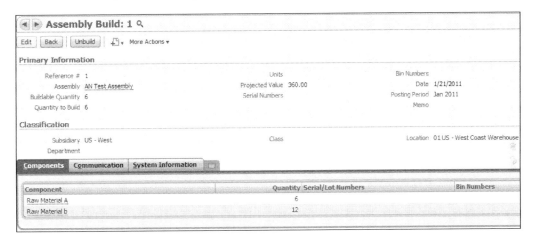

Also notice that the assembly was done for a specific subsidiary and location. This means the assembly and all its member items must be set up under this subsidiary, the location must belong to this subsidiary, and member items must have inventory at this location. The finished **AN Test Assembly** is therefore located at the same location and must either be sold or transferred from this location.

Depending on your business model, OneWorld can tell you how to build assemblies that are based on your manual entries of what you think you need to have in stock at the assembly item setup; or by a system algorithm that determines build points, based on sales and member purchasing lead time; or by sales order if you build to order.

You can also build assemblies in conjunction with work orders in one of two ways. A **Special Order Work Orders** allows a user to create the **Work Order** for an assembly, directly from an approved sales order. The Special Order Work Order ties the assembly to the customer sales order. On your sales order line, there is a column for **Create WO**, or work order, which, when clicked, sets up a new work, as shown in the following screenshot:

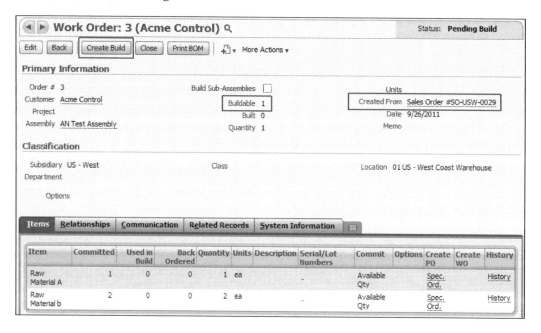

Notice that our work order is buildable, meaning that we have the raw material to build this assembly. Also notice that this work order was created from a specific sales order. We build the assembly by clicking on the **Create Build** button. After we build this order, we can see the Assembly transactions on the **Related Records** tab. Work Orders do not post to the G/L, but assembly builds do.

Alternatively, you can set up Production Work Orders to build a set number of assemblies to increase the assembly stock. In either case, the work order allows you to print a **Bill of Materials (BOM)** to pick the items you require for assembly, from inventory stock. Work orders also tell you how many assemblies you can build, based on member inventory levels. The **Demand Planning** module enables the generation of Work Orders from the demand plan.

Once assemblies are built, you can move them to other locations through an **Inventory Transfer** or an **Inventory Transfer Order**. An assembly, unless it is a serialized assembly, may also be a member of another assembly, and when you build a parent assembly, OneWorld can also build the child assemblies automatically.

There is also the **Bill of Materials Inquiry** form, which allows you to view the inventory levels of assembly members at a selected location under **Transactions | Inventory**.

Kitting and grouping

Kitting simply allows you to take a group of member items, package, and sell them together at a price that you determine at the kit item setup. Unlike assemblies, you will not know until fulfillment if you have the member inventory required to sell the kit. Also, you cannot alter the kit 'on the fly' as they say, meaning at the time of generating the sales order, other than changing its price. The member and member quantities that you defined when setting up the kit item may not be updated on the sales order. The advantage of using kits is that it's easy to sell and set up a single line item. If you pick the members of the kit for each fulfillment, there is an **Accounting Preference** to **Always Print Kit Items on Picking Tickets** to help the staff pick kits.

Item groups offer a lot of flexibility, not only at the time of sale, but also in the item group setup. When you set up the group, you must identify at least one member, but you can add, change, and delete members 'on the fly' in the sales document, as the case requires. Also, when setting up the group, you determine whether or not the customer sees the items that make up the group or simply the group item and its price, again the sum of the members. This can be a valuable tactic when you are selling a product bundle, but do not want to haggle with customers over the price of individual items.

Selling items with deferred revenue

Selling maintenance contracts of any kind, whether it's a software support contract or a product warranty, requires **Revenue Recognition**. When you make the sale, the support or warranty item appears on the invoice, but unlike a product sale, you do not post the sale amount to a revenue account, but to a deferred revenue account because you cannot recognize all of the revenue immediately. If the support contract covers 12 months, then by generally accepted accounting principles, you recognize one-twelfth of the contract value each month. We added revenue recognition to this chapter, because it most often takes place on the sales order. We will also discuss recognizing deferred revenue in the next chapter on ERP financial processes.

To manage this process, the OneWorld customer requires the **Revenue Recognition** module. Rev rec, for short, applies to any item that is sold over a time period, essentially. This includes not only software maintenance contracts, but also product warranties, and even software itself when it's sold as a service, such as OneWorld in fact. Sometimes professional services are sold for a six-month implementation, for example, and invoiced immediately. In this case, the professional service item also requires deferral, so that you can recognize the revenue in the month the work was performed. To get started with rev rec, you need to set up your rev rec items, as the non-inventory item for the following sale:

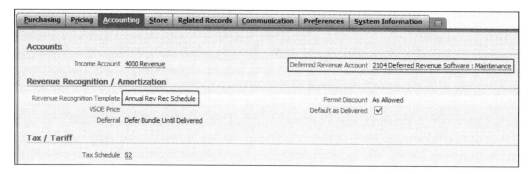

We chose a **Revenue Recognition Template**, but this is not required. You can select the template you need during the sale, or use the default one, as we have done here.

OneWorld revenue recognition allows you to set up templates that define the timing of revenue recognition, as seen in the following screenshot:

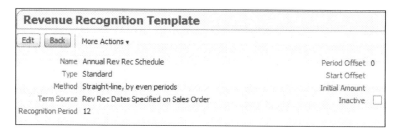

Set up **Revenue Recognition Template** at **Lists | Accounting | Revenue Recognition Templates | New**. This template is about as simple as a rev rec template can get. It's going to recognize the revenue evenly over the period of time entered on the sales order rev rec **Start Date** and **End Date**. When we process this item with our template, OneWorld generates the **Revenue Recognition Schedule**, as shown in the following screenshot:

As you can see, OneWorld generated this schedule for a specific invoice and rev rec template. In this case, the schedule tells us that we are going to recognize the same amount every month for 12 months. Notice, however, that we can also edit the schedule and alter the amounts in the line, or even add a line, if need be. Sometimes rev rec for an order is delayed due to unforeseen circumstances.

It also tells us that we have only recognized one month so far (see the **Total Recognized** field and the **Journal** column). So the next step is to navigate to **Transactions | Financial** and run the **Create Revenue Recognition Journal** Entries process. This process posts the scheduled recognition to the general ledger through a journal entry that debits the item's rev rec account and credits its revenue account. After posting, the invoice's **Revenue** tab and the Rev Rec Schedule display the fact that we have recognized one month's worth of revenue. We also see this under the customer's record on the **Sales | Transaction** tab where the **Journals** are listed; see the **Lists | Customer | Sales Transaction** tab, and change filter to **Journals**.

We have kept the rev rec example fairly simple, but OneWorld handles much more complexity. One important note is that it is possible to put the rev rec fields in the sales lines of the sales order and invoice forms, as opposed to the main line or header. This enables schedules specific to the line items. If you put the rev rec schedule field in the line, then you must also put the rev rec date fields in the lines.

VSOE

Organizations often bundle software and software maintenance and, like anyone, they offer discounts. This makes software sales more interesting, because it introduces the concept of the **Vendor Specific Objective Evidence (VSOE)**. In practice, VSOE spreads out a discount among the several members of a bundle, as seen in the next screenshot of an invoice for a VSOE bundle. Notice that we checked **Transaction Is VSOE Bundle**. When we make changes to the order, we can also click the **Update VSOE** button to auto-calculate the VSOE amounts:

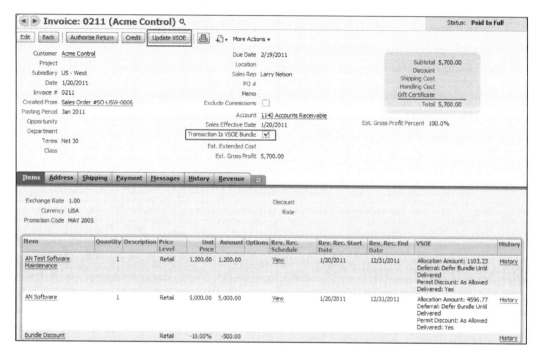

To the software and software maintenance items, we have added a discount of **500.00** dollars. The **VSOE** function calculates the amount of discount to apply to both items, based on their total percent; so for the software maintenance item, the calculation is $1200 - ((1200/6200) * 500) = \$1103.23$. The rev rec schedule then spreads this amount evenly across the 12 periods. One thing you cannot use with VSOE is a posting discount.

Whether you need to use VSOE or not is a question for your accountant, but OneWorld includes the functionality to manage what can be an audit nightmare for software companies.

Selling and managing services

Organizations that offer service contracts to their customers have several options for billing. Some of the most common setups that we have seen are as follows:

- **Contract services,** where you sell a one-or two-year contract to service your products. This is often tied to the **Customer Service** module.

- **Per use services,** where you sell services by the hour per customer's request. It is often tied to the Customer Service module.

- **Fixed price,** where you sell a professional service project at a fixed price and bill it at regular intervals, often using **Advanced Billing**.

- **Milestone project,** where you sell a project and bill, based on completed project milestones, again using Advanced Billing.

- **Time and Materials (T&M)** billing, where you bill based on approved time and expense entries, with or without a project.

These again are just the most common service-based configurations. Let's go through the list, providing guidance on setting these up in OneWorld with the objective of giving you enough information to help set up your prototype.

Contract services

There are many types of contract services, of course. The most basic service simply requires a service item set up in OneWorld and sold on the sales order. You invoice the SO and recognize revenue over the term of the service. You collect time to measure the profitability of the service and to manage your resources. You run a **Time by Client** report and filter it by the service item to get a sense of the gross profitability. Very often, this type of service contract works in conjunction with the Customer Service module. The customer opens a case under their contract, you assign a support rep, and then they enter their time against the customer and case, as seen in the next screenshot. They can even enter their time right from the case form.

Notice that in this case, the time is not billable. Running the Time by Customer report, you see the total number of hours by customer, and by **Service Item**. This time entry has not been approved, but the support rep's supervisor sees that she has time to approve in her reminders or in an e-mail notification.

In the next case, the customer purchases support on an as-needed **Per Use** basis. In this case, again, the customer opens a service case and you assign a rep. The rep works the case and then enters his billable time and any billable expenses, and his supervisor approves it. On a regular basis, accounting navigates to **Transactions | Customers | Invoice Billable Customers**, runs this process to pick up all of the billable time and expenses, and produces an invoice. This makes billing quick, easy, and accurate.

The key point with billable services is the rate at which you bill the service. To make sure that the service rep's time bills correctly, follow this setup list:

- Service rep has a **Billing Class** set up on their **Employee** record
- Service Item has prices set up for each **Billing Class** and each **Price Level**
- Customer has the correct **Price Level** on their **Customer** record

You need to make sure that you have **Billing Class** and **Price Level** set up in **Setup | Accounting | Accounting Lists**.

In the following screenshot, we set up a service item, the lynchpin in OneWorld for billing services:

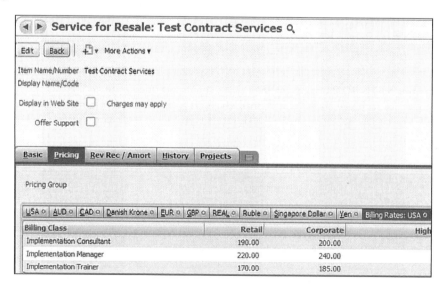

In this example, we have one service item with two different price levels set up for three different billing classes. When you run the **Invoice Billable Customers** process, OneWorld marries the customer's **Price Level**, **Retail**, or **Corporate**, for example, with the service rep's **Billing Class Price Level** for this service item, resulting in billing accuracy.

If the service requires local travel or other out-of-pocket expenses, your reps may also enter an Expense Report. The support rep enters their **Expenses** with an expense **Category** for accounting and, for billable expenses, to a **Customer**. If an expense line does not have a Customer selected, then the expense is simply a payable to the employee. With a Customer selected the expense is billable. Once the rep's supervisor and accounting approve it, the expense is a payable to the employee and ready for billing to the customer, as in the following screenshot:

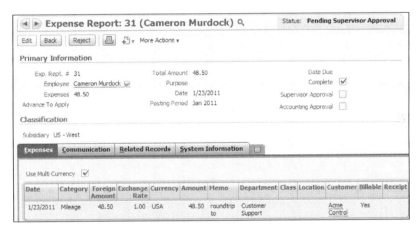

After approval, both expenses and time entries become eligible for billing through the **Invoice Billable Customers** process.

Professional Services

We use the term **Professional Services** to differentiate these services from the support-or warranty-type contract services that you might offer. Professional services, in this respect, are generally consulting-type engagements, where you sell a project and assign human resources to complete it. This section assumes that you purchased the **Advanced Projects** module.

Projects come in various flavors, but there are some useful categories, based on how you bill the project. OneWorld supports the following: Fixed Bid, Interval; Fixed Bid, Milestone; and Time and Materials. Each of these project types has associated billing methods. For proper billing of fixed-bid projects, you must purchase the **Advanced Billing** module.

There are two ways of selling professional services in OneWorld. In this discussion, we focus on the method in which we create a sales order and a project separately, and then link them together. Later, we will discuss the other option of generating projects, directly from sales orders.

At this juncture, we need to discuss the **Accounting Preference | Consolidate Projects** on **Sales Transactions**. This preference changes how projects and sales transactions interact in OneWorld. When the preference is turned off, the **Project** field appears in the main line of the **Sales Order**. After selecting the **Customer**, you select the **Project**, and OneWorld generates a line item, based on the **Billing Item** that you selected on the **Project** form, and the total amount of the project, based on the **Project-Task** set up on the **Project** form. In the following screenshot, we select the **Customer** and the **Project** field, and OneWorld generates the line item:

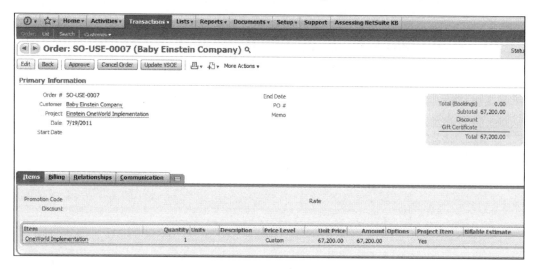

Notice that in the line item, the **Project Item** field is set to **Yes**. This tells you that the project generated this line item. After saving the order and then opening again in **Edit** mode, there is a new button labeled **Refresh Items from Project**, which is used to update the order, if you have changed your project totals. The order also picked up the billing schedule for this project, as we noted previously.

One thing to keep in mind here is that the order picks up a single line item from the project, using the **Billing Item** set up on the project, and not the **Service Items** that you may have linked to the **Project Tasks**. Also, the list of **Billing Items**, from which you make your selection is limited to **Service** type items that have **Can be Fulfilled/ Received** unchecked. (Alternatively, it is possible to sell 'fulfillable' services and use a **Progress Billing** sales order to fulfill and bill, but this is a manual process and not noticeably popular.)

Now, let's turn on the **Consolidate Projects on Sales Order** preference. This changes the location of the **Project** field from the main line of the form to the line items, and allows us to add multiple projects into the line items, as seen in the following screenshot:

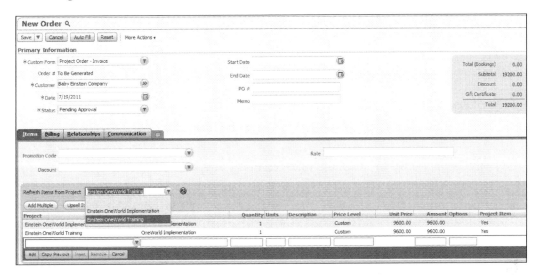

Again, notice that we add a single item for each project, and they both have **Project Item** set to **Yes**.

The last point is that when you turn on **Consolidate Projects on Sales Orders**, and you want to add the projects to the sales order with their respective billing schedules, you must move the billing schedule from the main line of the form to the line items. This way, you will have a unique billing schedule for each project line.

Fixed-bid projects

There are two types of fixed-bid projects, based on whether we bill at intervals or on completion of milestones. In a **Fixed Bid Interval** project, you normally select a pre-defined billing schedule that your organization uses regularly, based on your business practices. For example, you might have a service offering that requires a 6-month project. In this case, you require 25 percent of the total upon signing, and then the remaining amount split equally over the subsequent months of the project. See the following screenshot for the advanced billing schedule that meets this requirement:

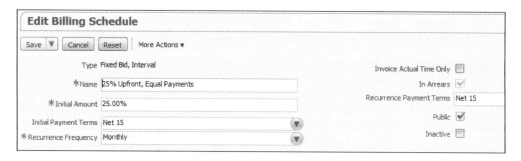

Now that we have a billing schedule, the next step is to sell a project, following this process:

1. Sales person works with a lead and as the discussion deepens, they open an **Opportunity** for the lead; management pipeline now includes this opportunity.

2. As negotiations move forward, a project manager gets involved and sets up a project, status: **Not Awarded**. Service management now has this potential sale on their radar, in their resource metrics, and so on.

3. Prospect asks for a **Quote** for services, and the sales person generates a quote from their opportunity. The quote links to the project, pulling in the service item, amount, and the billing schedule.

4. Customer signs the quote.

5. Service management continues with project setup, including resourcing and a timeline schedule.

6. Sales person generates the sales order and OneWorld generates the actual billing schedule, based on the project per this sales order.

This is just an example of how a professional service organization uses OneWorld to sell and bill a professional service project. The next screenshot shows how OneWorld interpreted the project timeline and project amount, to set up the billing schedule per sales order:

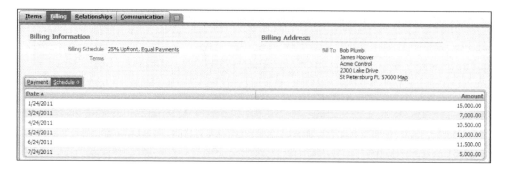

The project total is 60,000 dollars, and from the project resource schedule, the project extends from **1/24/2011** to **7/24/2011**. OneWorld used this information to set up this schedule.

To produce the invoice for this sales order, you can, of course, navigate to this order and click the **Next Bill** button, or alternatively, you can navigate to **Transactions | Sales | Bill Orders** and bill several sales orders in batch mode.

In a **Fixed Bid**, **Milestone** billing type project, you must set up an individual billing schedule for each project of this type. The billing schedule uses your project's task as the basis for billing. In the next screenshot, we have four project tasks, and as they are marked **Complete**, their percentage of the project is ready to bill:

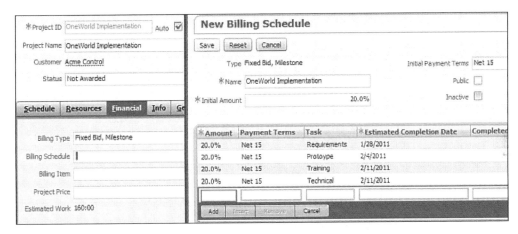

When you set up your milestone project, you need to resource it and add the project tasks. Once your tasks are set up, you can then click the + icon next to **Billing Schedule** and set up the New - milestone billing schedule.

Once we save this billing schedule, we select it into the **Billing Schedule** field on the project setup form and we're ready to bill. The project, at this point, has resources and they have been assigned to project tasks, with estimated completion dates, and so on. Again, the project must ultimately be linked to a sales order, and then as the work progresses and the tasks are marked **Complete**, the sales order comes up for billing in the **Bill Orders** queue.

It is the responsibility of the project manager, in collaboration with the project resources, to mark tasks as **Complete**, and in doing so, set up the sales order for billing. There is a **Project Task** portlet that project managers can put on their dashboard that enables inline editing of tasks. Or, you can have project resources update the project task status from the **Employee Center**.

Using project preferences and templates

When you have to set up several projects a day or week, it may make sense to set up a template. Most organizations run the same type of project over and over again. In this case, set up a project and DO NOT tie it to a customer. Use the project name as the template name. Set up the **Preferences** and **Financial** tab fields and all of the other fields that are important to you. Then when you need a new project record, find the correct template, change the project name, add a customer, and do a **Save As**. Half your effort is now complete and you just need to set up the resources and the dates.

Time and materials projects

Time and Materials means the billing of time and expenses, based on time and expense entries of the project resources. These projects have a time and materials billing schedule that you can set up ahead of time or on the fly, as shown:

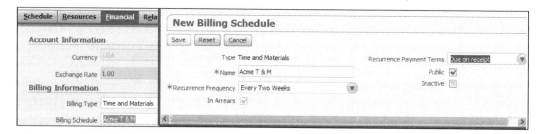

When you link the **Time and Materials** project to the sales order or the quote, the **Billable Estimate** column is set to **Yes**, meaning that the project line item will not be billed from the sales order. This is helpful when you sell several items on an order and you want to generate an invoice for all of the line items except the **Time and Materials** project. We'll cover **Time and Materials** billing using the *Invoice Billable Customers* form in *Chapter 7, Nuts and Bolts of OneWorld ERP—Financial Management*.

Generating projects from sales orders

As we mentioned previously, there is a second way of linking sales orders and projects, by generating projects directly from sales orders. In this scenario, we set up a service item and click on the **Create Project** box on the item's **Project** tab. We also add tasks to the service item. When we sell this item on an order, and approve the order, the order appears on the **Create Projects from Orders** form, under **Transactions | Customers**.

On this form, you select the project you want to create, designate a parent project if there is one, select a project manager, and enter a project name. Click on **Submit**, and OneWorld generates the project and its tasks. After that, the rest of the process is much the same as what we described previously in the *Fixed-bid project* section. The value here is that if you have a lot of projects to set up, and they are very similar in their requirements, then this function could save some valuable time.

Per-employee billing rates

When setting up your project task, you can select a **Service Item**. If you have set up **Billing Rates** on the item, using **Billing Classes**, from **Setup | Accounting | Accounting Lists**, and entered a **Billing Class** on the employee record, OneWorld will marry the item and employee class when sorting out bill rates for T&M projects. This is useful if you have service items that bill at different rates, based on the resource assigned.

Once projects are sold, set up, and resourced, the next step is to manage them as they get underway, including time and expense entry for employees. Make sure to enable the **Bill Costs to Customers** feature.

Time entry and approval

There are a number of setups that impact time and expense entry. First, check the **Accounting Preferences | Time and Expense** tab, and test your choices in the system. If you choose **Default Time to Billable**, for example, then what happens when you have a **Fixed Bid Interval** billing type project?

Also, under **Setup | Accounting | Invoicing Preferences**, there are several preferences for how you want the system to treat your time and expense entries on the customer invoice. For example, the employee's department, class, and location default into the time entry form, if you have these fields enabled of course. When you bill the time, these fields carry over to the invoice, if the preference **Combine Time Items on Invoice** is off. Turn the preference on, and the department, class, and location default from the main line of the transaction to the line items.

In the project preferences, you can limit time entry to resources, and also set up planned time entries for your resources, which they only need to edit each week to transact their time card. When setting up project tasks, select the **Service Item**, and this item defaults into the time entry form.

Time entry is possible from any of the role centers, such as the **Accounting Center**. However, most organizations use the **Employee Center** for time and expense entry. The employee licenses are less expensive and the user interface is simpler. The employee signs in from `http://www.netsuite.com`, as any user, and then has the option to **Track Time**, a single entry at a time, or use the **Weekly Time Sheet** to enter or edit several lines of time. Time entries serve reporting, billing, and payroll for some customers.

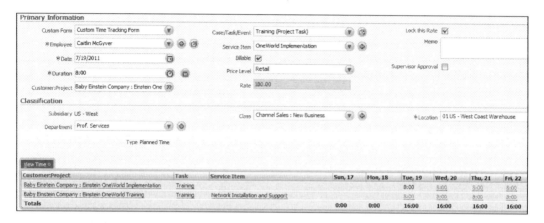

In this screenshot, the employee has planned time entries from two projects that she works on. To edit, simply click on the underlined hours in the bottom right for the date and project to edit, bringing that record into the top of this form.

Time approval is also an option. There is a **Time Approver** field on the employee record. Approvers can be notified by e-mail that they have time to approve, or they can simply use their dashboard reminders to navigate to the **Approve Time** form. The same form is also available under **Transactions | Employees | Approve Time**. Once approved, billable time falls automatically in the queue of the **Invoice Billable Customers** form. Similar to inventory management, it's important to manage the handoffs of time and expenses from employees to approvers to finance.

Expense entry and approval

Expense entry also has several important setup steps, including the **Accounting** and **Invoicing Preferences** mentioned previously. In addition, there are the **Expense Categories** found under **Setup | Accounting**. These categories simply map one to one to an expense account, so that when entering their report, the employee simply selects a category for each charge and OneWorld manages the accounting.

Expense reports that are billable, in whole or in part, to a customer have two G/L entries. On the expense side, there is a payable to the employee and a debit to an expense account. When billed to the customer, the expense report is a receivable from the customer and a credit to an income account. To accomplish this, navigate to the account(s) that you used to map your **Expense Categories**, from **Lists | Accounting | Accounts**, find your expense account, and **Edit**. For accounts of type **Expense** or **Cost of Goods Sold**, there is an additional field called **Track Billable Expenses In**. Select your income account into this field.

Alternatively, you may view these expenses as a loan to the customer and map the **Expense Categories** to a **Current Asset** type account, which is charged in both the payable and receivable entries; the expense report debits the account and the invoice to the customer credits the account. This method, which keeps both entries on the balance sheet, is preferred when the organization does not want to overstate gross income. Either method works fine for tax purposes.

In the next screenshot, the employee had a sales expense, which is not billable to the client. Under US law, part of the amount is taxable and should be steered to an expense account set up specifically for reporting taxable expenses. Client reimbursable meals should have a different expense category.

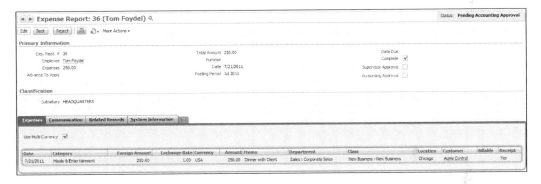

Expense reports have two approval levels, namely, the employee's **Expense Approver** and **Accounting Approval**. Once the report is marked **Complete**, as shown in this screenshot, it falls into the approval queue. Again, these two groups can receive e-mail notifications, use their Reminders, or both. Click on the **Reminder for Expense Reports to Approve**, and you land on the **Approve Expense Reports** form.

In a typical business case, expense approvers are often line managers with first-hand knowledge of the projects and expenses under review. For them, it's normally necessary to open each report and view the detail, before giving **Supervisor Approval**. Managers approach the approval task from **Transactions | Employees | Expense Reports | List**, where they can see the list of the reports waiting for their approval. There is a **Status** field in the footer of the **List** that they can use to alter the list results. From here, they can navigate to each individual report and make their judgment.

If they choose to reject the report, there is an e-mail notification box, to the employee, that pops up, where they explain what they need in order to approve the report. The employee makes their changes, again marks the report **Complete**, and it re-enters the approval queue.

Accounting approval, in this scenario, is normally just making sure that the receipts add up to the report. Accounting approvers are more inclined to use the **Approve Expense Reports** form from the **Reminder**.

Before gaining **Accounting Approval**, expense reports do not impact G/L, so they are charged to the non-posting **Unapproved Expense Reports** account. You navigate to this account's register, by opening a new expense report and clicking on the **Approve Expense Reports** link in the header. Alternatively, you can navigate to this register from the **List | Accounting | Accounts**, and clicking on **Unapproved Expense Reports** account, if you have this permission. From the register, you can navigate to any unapproved report. Once approved by accounting, the report posts to the ledger.

Materials and other expenses are also billable to the customer, directly from a **Purchase Order**. On the PO, enter your line items, a **Customer**, and click on **Billable**. We transact expenses payable to the business, not to an individual, like this.

E-commerce in OneWorld

There are two main phases of the e-commerce implementation in our experience. There is the artistic design of the frontend site and there is the setup of the backend system, so that you can turn on the new site and start transacting business immediately.

We want to focus our discussion of e-commerce on the basic functional requirements that you need to complete in order to transact e-commerce business. Much of the system configuration has already been covered in previous discussions of item and account setup. Setting up the basic accounting of your items and understanding the process of purchasing, managing, selling, fulfilling, and billing products is no different for an e-commerce firm than a brick and mortar. There are some additional tasks that an e-commerce firm needs to be aware of, and many of these fall in the overlap of frontend site and the backend system.

For OneWorld customers, there is the added question of whether you want to sell online from more than one subsidiary. If you want to enable a subsidiary other than your primary or root subsidiary, navigate to **Setup | Web Site | Setup Web Site** and on the bottom of the **Setup** tab, there is a list of all of your subsidiaries. You select the ones that you want to appear online. Now, when visitors come to your website, they will see the option to **Select a Region**, enabling them to view the site with the language, taxes, payment processing, and other attributes of the subsidiary that they select.

Preparing e-commerce content for search engines

Before starting to work in the system, we suggest you hold a brainstorming session, where you come up with the top keywords list for your site. This is important for the **Search Engine Optimization (SEO)** of your site. Very few organizations, in our experience, bother with this task, but it's really important. You might have an item catalog of several hundred or even thousands of items, but what do you really sell? Modern high-end lighting? Architectural lighting? Art objects? A useful SEO Keywords list is very challenging to produce, but it's also a very useful exercise because it forces the organization first to understand where they stand in the market, and second how consumers are going to find them.

When your site lacks a cohesive message, it not only fails to inspire but also does not impress the search engines. When you go to write the site content in the Tabs, Categories, and Items Descriptions, it's a very good idea to include these keywords.

The other important step is to take a conceptual inventory of what you sell and how you organize it into a site navigation map. How many different paths do you have to get to a single item? Or another way of asking the same question is how many menus do you need? OneWorld offers a hierarchical menu structure, as every customer requires at least the basic primary menu of tabs and categories, but you can place an item into several categories, and display several menus on your site, with some help from a developer.

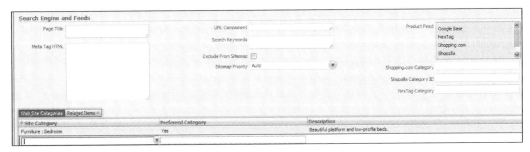

This screenshot displays several other fields that are very important for search engine optimization. Each tab, category, and item has a **Page Title**. This is the verbiage that you see in the **Browser** tab. Page titles should not be generic except for the **Home** page.

The **Meta Tag HTML** field does not appear to the shopper, but behind the scenes; some search engine crawlers still read these lines. These need to be written in the following form:

```
<head>
<META name="description" content="Kitchen Cutlery for the home" />
<META name="keywords" content="knives,cutlery,kitchen accessories" />
<META name="author" content="John Doe" />
<META http-equiv="Content-Type" content="text/html;
  charset=ISO-8859-1" />
</head>
```

URL Component is another important SEO field. Enable the **Descriptive URL** feature to get started. OneWorld takes the URL component of the tab, category, and item to generate a URL string in plain language, not 'computerized', replacing `mysite.com/it.C/id.255/.f` with `mysite.com/home-kitchen/knives/3-in-paring-knife`.

When you import your items, include the URL component. Complete the `tab/category/item` hierarchy and then from **Lists | Web Site | Bulk Set URL Components**, you set up the combinations that become the URLs of your site.

Search keywords are the words that your shoppers might type into the site's search box. These should include the obvious, such as parry knife in our example, and also some common but not obvious searches, such as pary knife, perry knife, or vegetable knife.

Sitemaps

There are two purposes to the sitemap. The XML version is kept in your file cabinet after generation. You then submit this file to the search engines and /or give the URL address. The HTML file can be used on your site to display a sitemap to visitors as a series of links. Both files are **Available without Login,** by default, making them accessible to the search engines that know where to look.

When you set up your tabs, categories, and items, you can **Exclude From Sitemap** if for some reason you do not want them indexed. Otherwise, OneWorld sets every tab, category, and item with an **Auto priority**, which you can change, if you like. The priority for tabs is 1.0, for categories is .5, and for items is .3. You can alter these values if you think it makes sense to raise or lower the priority of some objects, based on your business model; the higher the priority, the greater the likelihood that the search engines will index the page.

Once your site navigation and item setup are complete, you can generate your sitemap from **Setup | Web Site | Sitemap Generator**.

Product feeds

If you want to display items from your catalog in Yahoo! Shopping, Google Base, or other shopping sites, OneWorld offers several searches already designed for the job. When you set up your items, you include them in the product feed searches, by selecting one or more **Product Feeds**. Also, some of the sites require a special ID, which you must set up per item, and some also require data, such as the name of the manufacturer, and the stock description.

When you set up your test items, put them into all of the feeds you are going to use and then run the searches from **Setup | Web Site | Product Feeds**, and make sure that you have all of the fields needed to populate the files. You can run and submit these files to the shopping networks on a regular schedule.

If you have multiple sites and/or multiple subsidiaries selling on the web, you can filter your product feed results by one or by both of these fields.

The main point to understand about product feeds is that to minimize your workload, understand what you need to set up for each item and for each feed, before you import your item catalog.

Customization

Advanced filters are often a requirement for e-tailers with large item catalogs. Again, know what these are and how you plan on displaying these on the site to your visitors, before you get started in the configuration, because they may require additional custom fields on the item setup. For example, if you have products in brass, silver, and brushed nickel, then you might want to offer visitors a way to narrow a search by these characteristics, so a custom field on the item setup with a list of values makes sense, and it would be ideal if you set up this field prior to item import. Custom filters also require JavaScript on the site, so work this into your project plan.

Images

Images are obviously a very important component of an e-commerce site. Make sure that you start editing the images for your site, before you need them set up. It takes time to edit images. OneWorld offers an auto image resizer that you can set up at **Setup | Web Site | Image Resizing**, but we suggest that you do some of this yourself, since large, high-resolution images slow down your site. If you call for a category image thumbnail size of 250px X 100px, and a drilldown, or item page, image of 400px X 200px, then having the system perform this task from a high-resolution image that's 2350px X 1600px is going to make visitors wait for images to populate.

To save time, images can be uploaded in ZIP files, which the system can unzip for you. It's also important to organize your image files, so that after uploading, you can find them in the list of values and add them to your items.

Setting up your site for selling

After doing some of this preparatory work, you are ready to start system setups, with the view of having a prototype test system in short order.

First, you need to visit **Setup | Web Site | Setup Web Site**, and make some of the basic decisions about how you want the site to look, and more importantly, how you want it to operate.

Basic setup

On the **Setup** tab, make your site viewable from within your OneWorld account only by leaving the **Primary Web Site URL** field blank, and appending the name of your temporary site address into the http://shopping.netsuite.com/ field, for example, http://shopping.netsuite.com/mywebstore. When you navigate to **Setup | Web Site | Preview Web Site**, you view your site as it will look when it goes live, but until then, it is private to you and your staff.

Also on the **Setup** tab is the **Price Level** field. The online price level is used when you want to offer an item at a different price in the Webstore. When you set up your **Price Level** under **Accounting Lists**, you designate the **Online Price Level(s)** for one or more of your price levels. You must also enter a price for this price level for every item you sell on the Web. If you only sell online, then you can make the base price the online price level and save yourself the trouble of multiple prices per item. If you sell through multiple channels, then you probably need a price level for online shoppers, one for retail, and one for partners, for example.

Shopping options

On the **Shopping** tab, select your **Web Store Out of Stock Items** function. Your selection becomes the default **Out of Stock Behavior** for your Webstore items. You can change the default by item, and also add an **Out of Stock Message** by item.

You can use **Pass URL Promotion Code To Checkout** in order to discount items, based on the shopper clicking an ad that has a promotion code appended to the URL. For example, if you want to do a promotion on back-to-school backpacks, you could place an advertisement on a website and append a promotion code that you set up in OneWorld with a discount to your URL, such as `http://www.backtoschool.com/backpacks&promocode`. When the shopper clicks the advertisement, they are redirected right to the backpack page, and when they check out, the promotion codes pass the discount to them.

In **Sales Order Type**, select **Per Customer Basis** if you have both credit card and 'on term' sales, meaning you have customers with terms who shop and receive an invoice, then select your preferred form for both in the next two fields. However, if you only do credit card sales, simply select your preferred sales order – cash sale form in this field.

There are several other fields on this tab that impact the shopping experience. Most of them are fairly self-explanatory, but a few go to the heart of the type of site you want and your relationship with the shopper. Is the site for B2C only? For B2B only? Both? Do you expect repeat business? If you have a strong handle on your business requirements, your selections should be clear and easy.

Customizing e-mails and site text

On the **Email** tab, select the actions that initiate e-mails to the shopper. If you want to customize the e-mails, navigate to **Setup | Web Site | Customize Text**. Copy the **Default Text**, make your changes in a text editor, such as Notepad – do NOT use a word-processing program, such as MS Word —and paste the new text into the **Customization** box. If you would like to add legal verbiage to all of your e-mails, configure the **Global Footer** field at **Setup | Company | Printing, Fax & Email Preferences**.

While you are on the **Customize Text** form, you can also make many other required changes to standard website boilerplate text.

Upsell and related items

For e-commerce customers, the **Upsell** feature allows you to show items to online customers, based on your sales algorithm. On the **Upsell** tab, you decide if you want **Upsell Items** chosen by OneWorld, based on its algorithm and actual sales, with your parameters. Alternatively, you can sell only **Related Items**, manually selected by you and linked to each item on the **Item Setup** form. You can also sell both Upsell and related items, or neither.

OneWorld's Upsell manager looks for correlations between what the current shopper selects and what others, who have selected the same item, have purchased, and then makes recommendations. Upsell has the additional benefit of finding surprises among your customer's buying habits, making connections that are not obvious.

Related Items are simply the items that you know make sense to purchase together, such as sport socks with tennis shoes. You can manually add individual related items to an item's setup at **Lists | Accounting | Items** under the **Webstore** tab and sublist **Related Items**. To save time, you can also set up groups of **Related Items** by navigating to **Setup | Web Site | Related Item Categories**. Then add these categories to an item in the same way you would add a single related item.

Launching your site

As you can see, setting up a new website in conjunction with the normal ERP operations work, makes for a challenging project, and it adds another layer of complexity. After you understand how OneWorld handles e-commerce items through the sales and operations processes, it's time to start getting ready for the next steps: *Processing credit cards* and *Shipping*.

Credit card processing takes three entities to accomplish. NetSuite OneWorld, of course, has the checkout process including the input of the credit card information by the shopper. The next step in the process is the *Gateway*. OneWorld offers several choices of gateways at **Setup | Accounting | Credit Card Processing**. Each of the vendors listed has their own advantages, and so on. Finally, you require a merchant bank to process your credit cards. Once you decide on your choices, you can start the setup of the credit card processing in **Test Mode**.

Shipping also requires some setup, from **Setup | Accounting | Shipping**. You will need your unique customer code for each service you want to set up.

Your goal here is to process the e-commerce sales order through the entire process, from order to shipping and credit card processing. With credit card processing in test mode, you will be able to run transactions and then log in to your gateway and learn how to navigate your transactions, check statuses, run reports, and so on. A good rule of thumb is to have your credit card processing set up in test mode at least a month before you go live, so that you can take some time to learn the system and view results. Also, don't be concerned with test shipping transactions. Unless the shipping carrier actually picks up the package and delivers it, they will not charge you. Later, when you clean up your test transaction, you will delete all these transactions.

As you wrap up the implementation, you should have a clear idea of the go-live date. Often we use Sunday as a go-live for e-commerce companies, since it is often the slowest day of the week for sales. On Saturday morning, we call the registrar of your domain. This company has the setup for your domain. We ask them to direct your domain(s) to `http://www.shopping.netsuite.com` through a CNAME redirect. And in OneWorld, we make sure all of your domains are set up under **Setup | Web Site | Domains** and that the **Primary Web Site** is now listed on the **Setup | Web Site | Setup Web Site** form. It will take some time for the Internet's computers to all pick up the changes, but as soon as they do, your new site will be live.

Summary

Hopefully, this chapter gives your implementation/operations team enough information to get started in setting up their first OneWorld prototype and understanding how transactions start the handoff to operations, the fulfillment of sales, billing, and revenue recognition. We cannot state the level of importance of prototypes. We understand that prototypes are sometimes difficult politically, since business managers and project sponsors are often unhappy when viewing anything but a completely finished product, but we have also received the occasional call from a stressed organization that has spent huge effort to load items into the system only to find out that they are the wrong type.

The early work that you do to set up a prototype also lays a foundation of knowledge that makes it a lot easier to start building the larger structure. Without a foundation, you will hit a lot of big bumps later on, trying to sort out why things are not working, and these are often huge time sinks. It makes a lot more sense to spend some time upfront to understand the important basics of the system, then as you add more functions and solve more detailed problems, you have a good place to start.

In the next chapter, we take the next big step and start talking about the financial transactions. *Chapter 7, Nuts and Bolts of OneWorld ERP—Financial Management,* is another important foundation-building step; only this time, the accounting team is the primary focus group, though I would suggest that you also involve the operations group as well. It's important for everyone to know that what they do in OneWorld has a direct impact on the organization's financial standing.

7
Nuts and Bolts of OneWorld ERP – Financial Management

Chapter 6, Nuts and Bolts of OneWorld ERP, was largely devoted to operations management in OneWorld and the handoff from sales or purchasing to operations. This chapter now takes the next logical step, the handoff from operations to accounting and finance. Here, we match vendor invoices to OneWorld bills on the A/P side, and we generate invoicing on the A/R side; we perform check runs and collect payments from customers; and we allocate expenses and amortize liabilities.

These are just the major tasks of this chapter. As the implementation moves forward, we now invite the accounting/finance team to join in. We need to know the details of cash management, business policies of A/P and A/R, and project management.

For the implementation team, the key to success is to understand the purpose of what you do everyday. You were directed to do x, y, and z, and you have done them diligently. Why do you do them? We ask because brute experience has taught us that OneWorld processes differ from your current processes, and the solution to most process 'gaps' is either one of the following:

- Adopt a slightly different process that serves the same purpose as your current process does
- Customize the OneWorld process to meet your requirement

Well, then why not customize every process to meet your requirement? Sometimes, customization, which we will cover in depth in *Chapter 9, OneWorld Data Migration*, is the simple addition of a field, but sometimes it means writing code, and writing code means adding expense. Every implementation has a budget as well, so it's not a good idea to lob all unmet requirements into the proverbial *Phase 3 OneWorld Customization* bucket. In many cases, a little creativity and flexibility combine to produce OneWorld processes that achieve the right purpose.

Just like *Chapter 6, Nuts and Bolts of OneWorld ERP,* by the end of this chapter, we want a working prototype of the accounting/finance process. The prototype provides enough data and system configuration to work transactions through the system successfully. Use the *80/20* rule: Let the first prototype cover the most common 80 percent of your processes. Participants ought to see and confirm that the test transactions meet their requirements. Also, it's important to keep a list of all of the uncommon requirements that make up 20 percent of the organization's transactions. Take these requirements as far as you can in the first prototype, and then finish them in the second prototype.

In this chapter, we cover the following in depth:

- Accounts payable processing
- Accounts receivable processing
- Cash management
- Month-end close
- Financial reporting

Accounts payable processing

There are several transactions that culminate in the payment of cash to vendors. Depending on your organization's business model, you may use all or just a few of these, including purchase orders, straight bills, expense reports, sales and payroll taxes, and commissions. Since we started the last chapter with the drop ship/special order process, let's pick up there again and complete the process. From there, we move on to the rest of the A/P transactions.

Purchase order processing

In the drop ship/special order process that we saw in *Chapter 6, Nuts and Bolts of OneWorld ERP,* OneWorld generates the PO automatically. There are other ways of generating a PO, such as the Order Items form that tells us the items we need to bring up to stock par. There are also purchase requests, entered by employees in need of supplies or equipment. When approved, these also become a PO.

Of course, we can also simply enter a PO manually, as purchase managers often do. In all of these cases, we now have a PO that starts in **Status: Pending Receipt**. Once the operations staff receives the order, the PO status changes to **Pending Billing,** and it falls into the **Reminder Purchase Orders to Bill**. When you click on the **Purchase Orders to Bill** link, the **Bill Purchase Orders** batch form comes up. You can also navigate to the same form from **Transactions | Purchases/Vendors | Bill Purchase Orders** to bill orders in batch.

Of course, you can always bill a single PO simply by navigating to the PO you want to set up as a payable and clicking on the **Bill** button. If you do not see the **Bill** button, there are two explanations: You do not have permission to **Bill Purchase Orders** on your role, or you have turned on the accounting preference **Enable Custom Purchase Order Approval Process**, in which case OneWorld makes the button available as part of a custom workflow.

Advanced receiving

If you enable **Advanced Receiving**, your process is PO, receipt, bill, and payment. **Advanced Receiving** enables a separate step for operations to receive goods into the warehouse. Likewise, **Advanced Shipping** enables the fulfillment step from the warehouse. For **Drop Ship** orders, the process is PO, mark shipped, and bill.

Advanced Receiving goes hand in hand with the **Multi-Location** inventory, a feature we suggest any company with inventory should enable. With multiple locations, both **Advanced Shipping** and **Advanced Receiving** are required.

Whether processing individually or in batch, the end result is a bill. Your OneWorld bill ought to match the vendor's invoice. In the following screenshot, notice that we entered data in several fields that are important later, when we make payments, such as the **Reference No.** field and the **Memo** field:

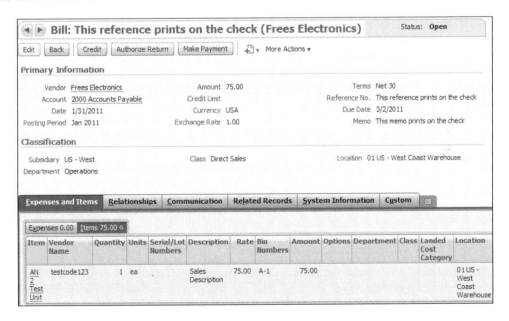

The **Memo** field prints in the bottom-left corner of the check and the **Reference No.** field, normally the vendor's invoice number, prints in the voucher column **Description**. Notice that the **Account** field also displays on this bill, because we have more than one **Accounts Payable** account in this OneWorld instance.

Let's review the processing of bills in the context of multiple subsidiaries. First, the vendor on this bill belongs to the **Subsidiary US – West**, which was set up on the vendor record. We enabled **Account 2000 Accounts Payable** for the parent and all child subsidiaries of **US – West**. Of course, we also enabled the items purchased for the **US – West** sub. Now, when we go to pay this bill, we must use a bank account enabled for this subsidiary, and all of the accounts must be in one of the currencies that we enabled for the subsidiary.

There are several business cases common to organizations that use purchase orders extensively. The PO – receipt – bill – payment process rarely happens so neatly. Let's take a look at some of the common process bumps.

First, you may receive less than the quantity ordered. You may pay for only what you received, then wait to receive the rest and make a second payment. Or you can pay for what you received and close the PO to further receipt; or wait to receive the rest of the order before billing at all.

Purchasing, receiving, and billing are often done by three different departments, so it's important to manage the handoffs correctly to make sure that you only pay for what you receive. In some organizations, Receiving hands the paperwork that comes with the goods over to Purchasing with their notes. Purchasing then makes the decision depending on the status of the PO. Accounting is instructed to bill only those orders on which all lines are closed, meaning that the full amount of the goods has been received or Purchasing decided to close a line that was not received or partially received. As you can see, handling purchase orders depends on your business practices as well as the system. In some cases, you may need additional fields and a custom workflow in order to convey the correct next step.

In some instances, you may have to pay upfront before receiving the goods. How OneWorld behaves in these cases depends on the accounting preference **Bill in Advance of Receipt**. If you turn this on, you will able to generate a bill directly from a PO, without any receipt at all. When the goods arrive, you receive against the PO as normal.

Second, for large or blanket POs, you may have several receipts over time. Again, generate a bill for only the amount that you have received, if you have **Bill in Advance of Receipt** turned off.

Third, POs generated using drop ship items behave slightly differently, as we covered in *Chapter 6, Nuts and Bolts of OneWorld ERP*. A drop ship PO must only be **Mark Shipped** to generate a vendor bill, and after a fulfillment, an invoice to the customer. There is no receipt, and the fulfillment does not post to the GL.

Processing vendor bill variances

When processing inventory through OneWorld, your receipt credits **Inventory Received Not Billed**, and debits your **Inventory Asset** account. The bill debits **Inventory Received Not Billed**, and credits **Accounts Payable**. Variances in the PO, the receipt, and the bill for an item's cost, quantity, or exchange rate often generate a balance in **Inventory Received Not Billed**.

At regular intervals during the period, OneWorld enables you to generate journal entries that relieve the balance in **Inventory Received Not Billed**, by using the **Post Vendor Bill Variances** form. How you process variances depends on how you have set up the **Match Bill To Receipt** field on your items and/or your transaction forms. The accounts that the system uses to post variances are also part of your item setup.

OneWorld generates variances in one of two ways: Enable **Match Bill To Receipt** and the system generates the variance between the receipt and the bill; turn it off and the system generates the variance between the PO and the bill. In order to generate the variance between the PO and the bill, all lines on the PO must be closed, either because they have been completely received and billed, or because you have manually closed them. Again, as with the bill in **Advance of Receipt**, how you decide to manage the vendor bill variances depends on the business rules you follow in your purchasing department.

Processing bills

You may have many bills generated from purchase orders, but there are many others that are not part of the PO process. These include bills from utilities, legal counsel, other various services, and so on. These are simply entered into the system as they arrive. In most cases, you enter these with expense lines, but you could also use items if you want to display quantity.

There are just a couple of simple things to mention here. First, when you import your vendors, take the time to set up **Terms** and a **Default Expense Account**. This makes entering bills a lot easier.

Second, your bills form ought to reflect the setup decisions that you made for **Department, Class and Location,** and your organization's reporting needs. Take the simple bill in the following screenshot for the **December Cell Phone** use:

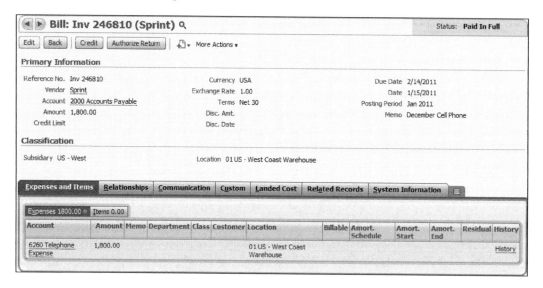

In this bill, we select the location on both the main line of the bill and on the inline. As a result, we have the following general ledger impact, which you can see from **More Actions | GL Impact:**

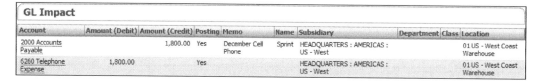

As a result of the form setup and the setup of the locations, we can view both balance sheet and income statement accounts, by location. We could, of course, do the same for departments and classes, and for other transaction forms. This is not to say that you must set up OneWorld in this way, only that it is possible and you must determine what is right for your organization, based on how you want to report results. Also, recall that the locations available to select on the form are determined by the subsidiary of the entity, the vendor in this case. Each location is owned by a single subsidiary.

Amortizing expenses

When entering a bill, we can also select an amortization template. The template, as the one below, details how we want OneWorld to treat the amount of the expense over time.

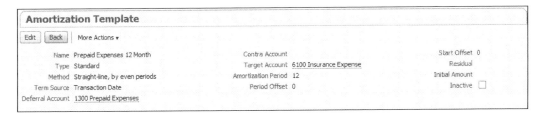

In this template, we designate the account in which we hold the expense: the **Deferral Account**, and the number of periods over which to amortize the expense: **12** periods, and how to amortize the expense: **Straight-line, by even periods**.

When we set up the bill, we select the amortization template on the expense line, along with the start and end dates of the amortization period, as we did in the following screenshot:

After saving the bill, OneWorld sets up the amortization schedule. For our example, the schedule amortizes the same amount over the **12** periods evenly, and by clicking on **View** on the expense line; we view the schedule in the following screenshot:

Amortization Schedule

Edit   Back

Name Prepaid Expenses 12 Month	Term Source Transaction Date	Start Offset 0
Created From Bill #Invoice #987654321	Amortization Period 12	Residual 0.00
Project	Start Date 1/1/2011	Initial Amount 0.00
Template Prepaid Expenses 12 Month	End Date 12/31/2011	Remaining Deferred Balance 11,000.00
Type Standard	Status In Progress	Total Amortized 1,000.00
Method Straight-line, by even periods	Period Offset 0	Amount 12,000.00

Account	Posting Period	Is Recognized	Date Executed	Journal	Amount	Total Amortized
6100 Insurance Expense	Jan 2011		1/31/2011	74	1,000.00	1,000.00
6100 Insurance Expense	Feb 2011			- None -	1,000.00	
6100 Insurance Expense	Mar 2011			- None -	1,000.00	
6100 Insurance Expense	Apr 2011			- None -	1,000.00	
6100 Insurance Expense	May 2011			- None -	1,000.00	
6100 Insurance Expense	Jun 2011			- None -	1,000.00	
6100 Insurance Expense	Jul 2011			- None -	1,000.00	
6100 Insurance Expense	Aug 2011			- None -	1,000.00	
6100 Insurance Expense	Sep 2011			- None -	1,000.00	
6100 Insurance Expense	Oct 2011			- None -	1,000.00	
6100 Insurance Expense	Nov 2011			- None -	1,000.00	
6100 Insurance Expense	Dec 2011			- None -	1,000.00	

This is only the schedule. So every month, Finance, as part of the period-end process, navigates to **Transactions | Financial | Create Amortization Journal Entries**, selects the period, the subsidiary, and the schedules to submit. OneWorld automatically generates the journal entries for that period.

Amortization can also be used for depreciating assets, though it is by no means a full-on fixed assets module. But if you have the occasional need for depreciation, then set up your amortization template with a **Contra Account,** in which you capture the amount depreciated over time. (NetSuite recently purchased a Fixed Assets module built as a SuiteApp. OneWorld customers can add this to their account today.)

Processing expense reports

Employees enter expense reports either through a normal user login, or through the employee center. In either case, the user interface is the same and so is the processing. Depending on your setups, the expense report goes through one or more approvals. The first is the **Supervisor Approval** and the second is **Accounting Approval**. There is an **Expense Approver** field on the employee's record. When Accounting approves the expense report, it becomes a payable bill and shows up on the **Pay Bills** form.

There are just a couple of things to remember about expense reports. You must set up the expense approvers on the employee record, and the approvers must be in the system as employees. An employee is one of several types, including contractor. There is a **System Email Template** that notifies the approver of time and expense entries needing their attention. In the absence of the approver, Accounting can perform both approvals. Finally, if you have **Multiple Currencies** enabled, you can enter expense lines in both your own and a foreign currency, if you incurred expenses outside of your home country.

Intercompany time and expense

There is the option of having an employee from one subsidiary work on a project for a customer in another subsidiary. This results in intercompany time and expense. When the employee enters their expense report, as shown in the next screenshot, they can enter it in the currency they paid, and be reimbursed in their own currency. After the employee's expense approver and the accountant both approve the report, it is payable to the employee, and billable to the customer – identified in the line item.

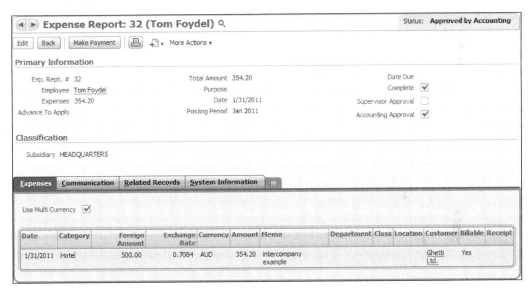

The employee works in the **HEADQUARTERS** Subsidiary, but his expense is being billed to a customer in the **Australia** subsidiary. At regular intervals (normally, part of your period-end checklist), the accountant navigates to **Transactions | Financial | Create Intercompany Adjustments**, bringing up the following form:

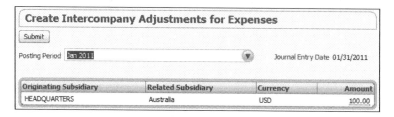

After selecting your posting period, OneWorld finds the adjustments to be done in this period. After you submit, OneWorld generates the following journal entry:

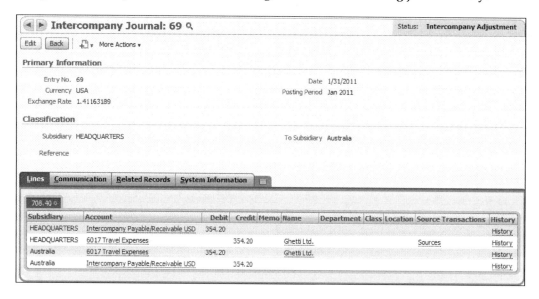

The effect of this journal entry is that the expense is backed out of the **HEADQUARTERS** subsidiary and charged instead to the **Australia** subsidiary. When viewing a report that consolidates the subsidiaries, the expense is not doubled up.

Processing commissions

Employee and partner commissions, similar to expense reports, have a two-tier approval process. In the first step, sales managers and sales people can both view estimated commission reports and the dashboard commission portlet. Then, when the commission period comes to an end, commissions are authorized from **Transactions | Commissions | Authorize Employee Commissions**. (Follow the same process described here for *partner commissions*.) Depending on your organization, sales management or Finance authorizes commission payments. The **Authorize Commissions** screenshot pictured next allows you to authorize several commissions at once. Alternatively, by clicking on the **Authorize** link in the lines, you can view and authorize each commission individually.

If you do not use OneWorld commission schedules, you can still import your commissions from a spreadsheet and use the authorization and approval process.

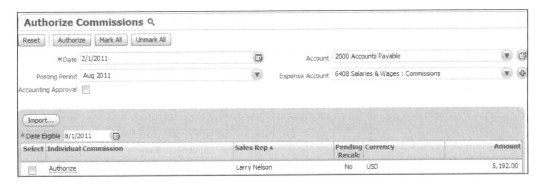

When you click on the **Authorize** link, the **New Commission** form opens, as in the following screenshot. Here you can see all of the individual transactions that impacted commission, if you have **By Transaction** schedules, or the total **By Period**. When you **Save**, you **Authorize** the new commission, and as you can see, it is now **Pending Accounting Approval**.

For accounting, there is both an **Approve** and a **Reject** button. If you reject the commission, there is a reminder for the authorizer's dashboard letting them know that you rejected a commission and they need to follow up and make changes, if necessary.

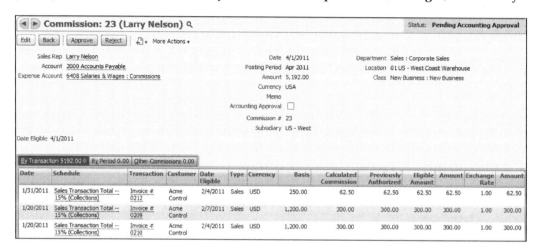

If you click on **GL Impact** under **More Actions**, you see how the commission charges to the ledger. However, if you run the financial statements for this period, the commission does not impact GL until it has **Accounting Approval**, as shown here:

Account	Amount (Debit)	Amount (Credit)	Posting	Memo Name	Subsidiary	Department	Class	Location
2000 Accounts Payable		5,192.00	Yes	Larry Nelson	HEADQUARTERS : AMERICAS : US - West	Sales : Corporate Sales	New Business : New Business	01 US - West Coast Warehouse
6408 Salaries & Wages : Commissions	62.50		Yes		HEADQUARTERS : AMERICAS : US - West	Sales : Corporate Sales	New Business : New Business	01 US - West Coast Warehouse
6408 Salaries & Wages : Commissions	300.00		Yes		HEADQUARTERS : AMERICAS : US - West	Sales : Corporate Sales	New Business : New Business	01 US - West Coast Warehouse
6408 Salaries & Wages : Commissions	300.00		Yes		HEADQUARTERS : AMERICAS : US - West	Sales : Corporate Sales	New Business : New Business	01 US - West Coast Warehouse

After accounting approval, the **Posting** column displays **Yes**.

An approved commission not only impacts the ledger, but also puts the commission into a payment queue. If you have purchased OneWorld payroll, then payment can take place in the next payroll run. This is a fairly straightforward process.

However, if you use a third-party payroll service, we suggest that you create a **Commission Clearing** bank account and a **Commission Payable** accounts payable. Charge all approved commissions to **Commission Payable**, and your commission expense account. You must pay all approved commissions to remove them from your **Pay Bills** queue; therefore, pay them from the **Commission Clearing** account. This relieves the balance in **Commission Payable**. Then, journal out the balance of **Commission Clearing** and your commission expense – the amounts ought to be equal.

Finally, after your third-party payroll run, import your journal for the payroll run to update the balance of the commission expense and your bank account. The journal's credit to your bank account shows up on your bank reconciliation.

Setting up a prototype for commissions can often be frustrating, since you must configure the system in several areas before commissions calculate. Here's a list of setups to check if you are having issues:

- There is a **Setup Commission** feature at **Setup | Sales | Commissions**. Make sure during testing that you set the **Commission Eligibility Period** to **0**, so you can see the results of today's test today. You can change and test this again before you go live.

- You can only assign employees who are marked as **Sales Reps** on their employee record to commission plans.

- **Sales Reps** and **Partners** must also be **Eligible for Commission** – enable this on the employee or partner record.

- A sales rep or partner may belong to only one plan at a time, but a plan may have multiple schedules.

- Configure the **Commission Schedule**, add it to a plan, and then assign your sales rep or partner to the plan. Remember that each commission schedule links to a subsidiary. In order to calculate commissions, the customer must belong to the subsidiary of the schedule, or one of its children. The sales rep or partner should also have access to the customer's record through their role.

- **Employee Commission Transaction** is the role permission that allows a user to authorize commissions. Partner commissions also have a role permission for authorization.

- **Employee Commission Transaction Approval** is the role permission for approving commissions. Again, partner commission approvals also have a role permission for approvals.

Processing corporate credit card use

There are several methods of tracking the use of the corporate credit card for corporate purchases, and the method you decide to use, depends on how you use the card.

When you use the corporate card for significant purchases and you want to track both the card and the vendor, you can use the **Credit Card Transaction** form at **Transactions | Banking | Use Credit Card**. This option lets you enter each of the charges, or credits, individually and track the vendor of each. The downside is that these transactions do not show up in the normal payable lists, searches, and reports, because the liability account is a credit card account. You must generate custom transaction searches that include both bills and credit card type transactions. The upside is that you have the details of your credit card charges. You then pay down the credit card account, by writing a check to the credit card company from **Transactions | Bank | Write Checks**.

The other option is simply to **Enter a Bill**, as we have done in *Processing Bills* previously, for the CC vendor, and list all of the charges as separate expense lines or line items. This method works well when the expenses are trivial, or when you want to limit your data input, or also when the vendor on the purchases is not important to your organization.

To save each vendor from individual charges, navigate to **Transactions | Banking | Use Credit Card**. Select the credit card account for the card you used, the vendor, and then list all the expenditures to this vendor. After using this form, you can also reconcile the credit card statement.

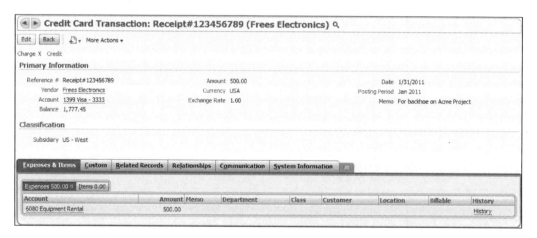

Note that credit card accounts, such as bank accounts, are assigned to a single subsidiary. So, in this case, the vendor and the credit card must belong to the same subsidiary. Also, using the corporate credit card means that the company receives and pays the bill. This process is not for individual credit cards issued under the company name, used, and paid by individual employees. Use the expense report process for those case.

Many companies today use their corporate credit card to make important payments, and this is where logging individual charges against a card is useful. Obviously, if the card is used primarily for lunch, it probably doesn't make sense to bother.

Paying sales and payroll taxes

The discussion of the taxability of what you sell is probably something that you have already discussed with your accountant. We just want to make sure that you understand how taxes are calculated on transactions and then how you pay these taxes and relieve your liability.

Payroll taxes are also fairly well known, so it is not our intention here to spend any time on taxability. Payroll taxes are simply the result of the payroll items that you set up and the payroll run calculations. We do not spend any time here on how these taxes calculate, but only how to pay them.

Sales taxes are calculated on the sales order and are charged to the ledger once you bill the sales order and generate an invoice. In the following screenshot, we have a sales order on which we have a taxable customer buying a taxable item in a taxable jurisdiction; therefore, we have sales taxes:

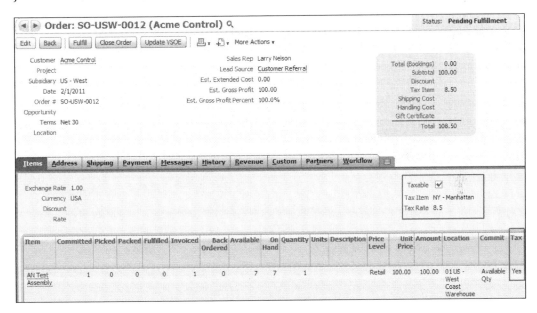

Order taxability derives either from the customer's record—the **Taxable** checkbox is on the **Financial** tab—or by checking the **Taxable** field on the order itself. The defaults for how OneWorld treats taxability are part of the base setup of taxation at **Setup | Accounting | Setup Taxes**. OneWorld determines the **Tax Item** to use on an order from the customer's **Ship To** address. Of course, it is possible that a single order contains both taxable and non-taxable items; therefore, we have the **Tax** flag in the line columns. You can set up item taxability on the item record.

When the sales order processes into an invoice, OneWorld charges the sales taxes to the correct sales tax payable account, as shown in the following screenshot:

Account	Amount (Debit)	Amount (Credit)	Posting	Memo	Name	Subsidiary	Department	Class	Location
Accounts Receivable	108.50		Yes		Acme Control	HEADQUARTERS : AMERICAS : US - West	Sales : Channel Sales	New Business : New Business	01 US - West Coast Warehouse
4006 Revenue : Accessories		100.00	Yes		Acme Control	HEADQUARTERS : AMERICAS : US - West	Sales : Channel Sales	New Business : New Business	01 US - West Coast Warehouse
2050 Sales Taxes Payable		0.50	Yes	NY City Tax	New York City	HEADQUARTERS : AMERICAS : US - West	Sales : Channel Sales	New Business : New Business	01 US - West Coast Warehouse
2050 Sales Taxes Payable		6.50	Yes	NY State Tax	New York State	HEADQUARTERS : AMERICAS : US - West	Sales : Channel Sales	New Business : New Business	01 US - West Coast Warehouse
2050 Sales Taxes Payable		1.50	Yes	NY County Tax	New York County	HEADQUARTERS : AMERICAS : US - West	Sales : Channel Sales	New Business : New Business	01 US - West Coast Warehouse

The various tax authorities are broken out, while in this case the charges all post to the same liability account. When we process these into payments, OneWorld produces three checks. If you want to pay the liability to a single tax agency, the individual tax codes must all be set up with the same agency.

For OneWorld customers in the US and Canada, generating the invoice also lands the sales taxes in the **Pay Sales Tax** queue under **Transactions | Bank | Pay Sales Tax**. Use this form to prepare tax liabilities for a check run. Like the other batch processing forms that we have seen in this chapter, the pay sales tax form allows you to pay batches of sales taxes.

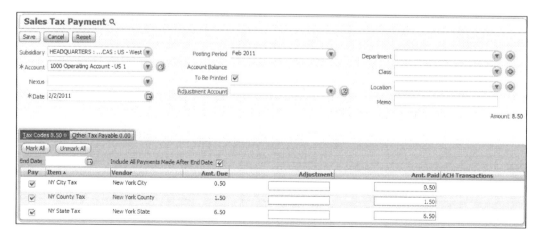

Remember to check the **To be Printed** box, so that you can print these checks after you **Save**. Use the **Adjustment Account** and **Adjustment** column to record discounts that you receive for prompt payments.

Like sales taxes calculate in the sales process, payroll taxes calculate in the payroll process, and are paid similarly at **Transactions | Bank | Pay Payroll Liabilities**.

Let's take just a moment to review the many processes that generate payables in OneWorld:

- Processing purchase orders into bills
- Entering a bill
- Approving an expense report
- Approving commissions
- Using the corporate credit card (not a payable, but it does create a balance in the CC account)
- Processing a sales order with sales tax into an invoice or a cash sale
- Processing payroll

Of course, if we want to pay an expense without first entering a payable, we can always **Pay a Single Vendor**, or **Write Checks**.

Paying payables

When managing your payables, we suggest that in most instances you want to save the record as **To Be Printed**. You can make this your default, by setting the accounting preference as **Default Vendor Payments to be Printed**. The exception, of course, is when you have made an online payment, as happens more often these days. In this case, you can process the payables in batch with **To Be Printed** checked, and then navigate to the bill payments at **Transactions | Purchases/Vendors | Pay Bills | List**. By editing the payment and entering the online transaction ID, you remove the item from the check-printing queue. We suggest that you also use a short alpha prefix, such as ONL, to identify the payment, and also to prevent OneWorld from assuming that this was a check number that you entered.

If you do not pay the bill online, and you mark the payment **To Be Printed**, it falls into the check-printing queue. To print checks, navigate to **Transactions | Management | Print Checks and Forms**. This form is a portal for many different printable forms, from mailing labels to invoices to checks.

Printing checks is fairly straightforward, if all goes well. The payments that display to be printed depend on the bank account you select. You simply need to tell the system what check number you want to start with, and if it is different from the number the system has in the **First Check Number** field. (Why it is different is something you probably need to track down.) OneWorld tracks check numbers for each bank account.

Also, as most OneWorld customers have checks with pre-printed numbers, you must tell the system to **Print from Back to Front**, if your checks stack moves through the printer from higher to lower. If you have checks with pre-printed numbers, then you must also customize the check form at **Setup | Customization | Transaction Forms PDF Layouts** to prevent OneWorld from printing a number on the check. We cover form customization in detail in *Chapter 8, OneWorld Customization and Advanced Configuration.*

Most OneWorld customers also use a three-part voucher check. Set your default check type at **Setup | Company | Print/Fax/Email Preferences**. The three-part voucher has the check, a voucher for the vendor, and a voucher for you.

This **Print Checks** setup printed eight checks starting with number **127**. Here's an example, with the check and the first voucher:

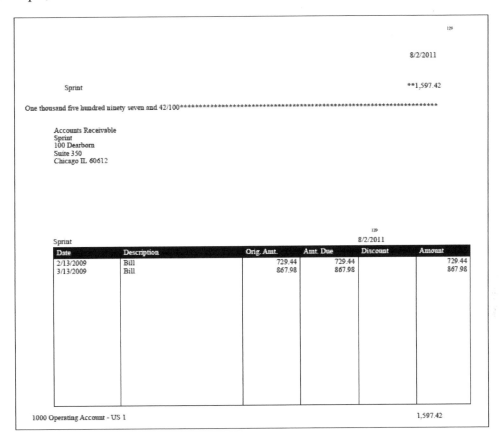

The questions about check printing normally come up when there are problems, such as the checks loaded into the printer incorrectly, or not loaded at all, or somehow ruined in a printer jam, and so on. There are basically two things you can do to rectify printing issues. First, you can void the payments, by navigating to each payment and clicking the **Void** button. This normally generates a reversing journal, based on the **Accounting Preference Void Transactions Using Reversing Journal**, and sets up the bill to be paid again. Second, you can also set each payment up to be reprinted, by editing and checking the **To Be Printed** box. The solution you select depends on the circumstances of your unique problem. This also brings up the question of role permissions, since it is not wise to allow the clerk who prints checks to also set up reprints.

In either case, to find the payments, you can navigate to **Transactions | Purchases/Vendors | Pay Bills and List**. The **Number** column is the check number that OneWorld generates for each payment. If you have a lot of reprints to do because you forgot to put checks into the printer, for example, then you can customize the view, add the field **To Be Printed**, and then turn on **Inline Editor**. Now you can set up reprinting for a number of checks.

ACH payment method

When not paying online by credit card or wire transfer, or by printed corporate check, you have another option. You can pay electronically, by enabling the **ACH Vendor Payments** feature. This enables you to store information about your vendor's bank account, on the **Vendor record | Financial | ACH** tab. Then when you to pay the vendor the **Check #** field states 'To ACH.' After you set up your ACH bill payments, an accounting supervisor approves them at **Transactions | Purchases/Vendors | Approve Vendor Payment Transfers**.

ACH payments require a third party and there is a small fee. When you enable the feature, a document pops up and explains what you need to do in order to use this function. The same applies to **Online Bill Pay** and **Electronic Funds Transfer** (EFT).

Processing vendor returns

We have not discussed returns yet, but there is a process for returning products to vendors and setting up a **Bill Credit**. If you have done returns for your customers, you will see that this process is the mirror image. Normally, the trigger for the process is some issue with the product, resulting in communications with the vendor. When the vendor accepts the return, he/she usually gives a return authorization number. You can enter this number into the **Reference** field, as shown in the next screenshot, when you set up the vendor return at **Transactions | Purchases/Vendors | Enter Vendor Return Authorizations**:

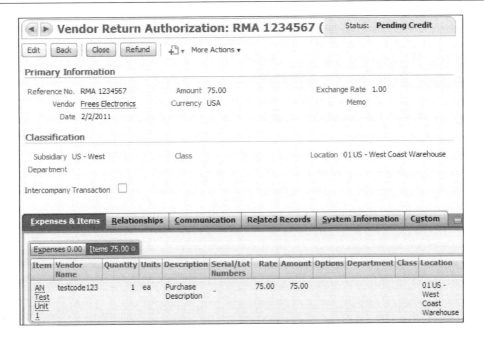

When you approve the return authorization, it displays a **Return** button. Clicking on **Return** brings you to the **Item Fulfillment** form where you set up the normal fulfillment information, such as shipping, and so on. The fulfillment posts to **Inventory Returned Not Credited**. This is another account that must be reconciled monthly to make sure that the amounts credited to you by the vendor equal what you expected to be returned; otherwise, you will carry a balance in this account.

Once the operations staff ships the product, Finance refunds the vendor authorization, generating a bill credit, and you apply the credit to the next due bill for the vendor. Of course, if the vendor doesn't want the product back but agrees to a refund, you simply start at **Transactions | Purchases/Vendor | Enter Vendor Credits**.

If you have no further business with the vendor, set up the vendor credit, and when the check comes from the vendor make a deposit into your bank account at **Transactions | Bank | Make Deposits**. On the **Other Deposits** tab, be sure to enter the vendor in the **Name** field. Then navigate back to the vendor credit, edit, and apply the deposit to the credit. This closes the credit, and your business, with the vendor.

There are reminders that you can set up for all steps in the vendor return process.

Accounts receivable processing

An old piece of received wisdom claims that the closer you are to the corporate revenue stream, the more money you make. This may or may not be true, but there is no question that the closer you get to accounts receivable processing, the closer you are to the heart of the organization. How your organization bills customers and collects accounts receivables is second only to what you sell when it comes to potential competitive advantage in the market place. For this reason, organizations take A/R very seriously.

Your first order of business is to understand what documents your organization uses when it charges customers: invoices, cash sales, or a combination? Do your cash sales come in over the Web by credit card? Or in person with a mix of cash and credit? If you sell online, are all sales cash? Invoice? Or a combination? When a customer makes a purchase, how are they billed? All at once? Over time? Based on your delivery?

The hybrid billing solutions that we meet in the marketplace always surprise us. Organizations are really creative when it comes to making the sale simple, easy, and profitable. Obviously, much depends on your sales item catalog and how you configure your items. There ought to be a direct connection between your item configuration and your billing methods, since these normally walk hand in hand.

Billing sales orders

We spent a fair amount of time in *Chapter 6, Nuts and Bolts of OneWorld ERP*, discussing sales of all the various item types OneWorld offers, from assemblies to the services, and the process of fulfilling those sales. Now we want to take the sale to next step – a cash sale or an invoice. Setting up your sales orders correctly is the important first step to billing customers correctly. Correct fulfillment and billing of product inventory, billing of services, and revenue recognition all depend on the sales order setup.

It's important to select the right transaction form for your process:

- **Standard Order — Cash Sale** form: B2C e-commerce normally uses this form. After you fulfill an order with this form, you bill it and it generates a cash sale, and charges the customer's credit card. The form assumes a fulfillment step in the sales process.

- B2B sales online or in person normally use the **Standard Order – Invoice** form, offering payment terms to the customer. This form also assumes a fulfillment step in the sales process. It is also the norm for drop ship and special order transactions.

- What if you have a mix of B2C and B2B on your sales, some online, some in person? If this is the case, you should use the **Standard Sales Order**. This form has logic such that when a customer has a credit card record and does not have terms, it processes to a cash sale; however, when the customer has terms, it processes as an invoice.

- If you are selling to customers at a retail counter, you use the **Standard Cash Sale** form, probably in concert with a **Point of Sale (POS)** system. The single cash transaction handles cost of goods sold and cash charges.

- In the wholesale distribution business model, it's possible to sell from a counter to a customer with terms using the **Standard Product Invoice**. We assume you have no fulfillment process, so using this form enables you to decrement inventory and charge cost of goods sold and accounts receivable in a single transaction.

These forms describe a direct to customer sale, either through e-commerce or in person, without the use of opportunities and/or estimates.

If your organization depends on signed estimates (you might call them quotes or proposals) as a contract, then the sales order is simply a short, but absolutely necessary, stage between estimate and invoice.

- The **Standard Order – Invoice** is the normal choice if you have advanced billing schedules or revenue recognition, as the sales order is where you stage the invoice processing. Of course, this form also works if the sale includes any item that requires fulfillment.

- The **Standard Order – Progress Billing** is useful if you manually decide what percentage of the sales order to invoice, and therefore expect several invoices from one sales order.

If you do not have one of these scenarios, then it is possible to process an invoice directly from an estimate, a process we have seen some organizations follow.

Of course, we mention the delivered standard forms here, but we realize that you will customize them. It's important to understand the functionality of each form, however, so you know which one you want to customize and make the preferred sales order form. We cover form customization in *Chapter 9, OneWorld Data Migration*. We also realize that you may need more than one sales process and we cover that as well in *Chapter 9*.

Hybrid billing scenarios proliferate among OneWorld customers. Can you use an advanced billing schedule, for example 12 equal monthly payments, with the standard sales order – cash sale and the batch **Bill Orders** form? Yes, you can. In this scenario, you have the customer's credit card on file, and each time you bill the sales order, OneWorld generates a cash sale on their card.

Can you bill a software sale, generate an invoice, and add approved time, expenses, and materials, putting them together on one invoice? Yes, you can; just keep in mind that you have to first approve the time and expense reports, and secondly generate the invoice from the **Bill Orders** form, or from the specific sales order. Then you add the billable time, expenses, and materials to the individual invoice, as shown in the following screenshot:

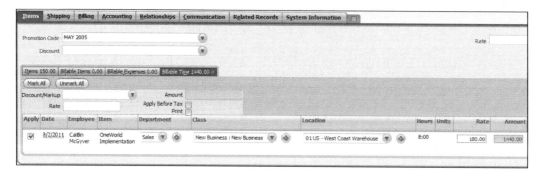

In this screenshot, notice that we have items worth **150.00** dollars plus the billable time we applied, worth **1440.00** dollars.

Billing sales orders is the process of generating cash sales or invoices from sales orders. You can do this from individual sales orders, by clicking on the **Bill** button, or in batch mode at **Transactions | Sales | Bill Orders**. In batch mode, the **Bill Orders** queue includes all of the sales orders that have been processed by Operations and await billing. These might include sales orders that have been completely or partially fulfilled, or sales orders containing items that do not require fulfillment, non-inventory items, for example; or sales orders with an advanced billing schedule that's ready for billing. If you turned on the **Invoice in Advance of Fulfillment** accounting preference, all sales orders, regardless of fulfillment status, fall into the **Bill Orders** queue.

There is no question that our discussion of customer billing does not cover every business case. But hopefully you have enough information to understand what's available to you and you can begin to configure the system.

Invoicing billable clients

For OneWorld users who invoice customers for time, expenses, and material used on a project or job, there is an alternative process at **Transactions | Customers | Invoice Billable Customers**. The queue on this form includes any customer for whom you approved billable time and/or expense, or customers who have billable items on a vendor bill.

Of course, billable time and expenses normally undergo two levels of approval, first from project managers or supervisors, then from Accounting. The assumption is that once Accounting approves time and expenses, they are ready for invoicing. If you sell software or a product from an inventory and want to include it on the same invoice as time and expenses, then start by billing the sales order. Then add the billable time and expenses on the individual invoice.

If you are a project-driven organization, and you use the **Advanced Project Management** module, you have a couple of options depending on the project types that you sell. For fixed-bid projects, the normal process is a signed estimate, which serves as the contract, and a sales order generated from the estimate. The sales order stages invoicing, either at regular intervals, based on a billing schedule, or at project milestones, based on a milestone billing schedule. In both cases, project resources may enter non-billable time against the project, so you can estimate profitability. But time does not queue for billing.

For time and materials projects, you can still generate the sales order from the estimate. Having a sales order is useful if you calculate commissions on sales orders, or if you manage sales activity, based on orders. All of your billing, however, generates from approved time and expenses. If you use **Billing Schedules**, you can apply a **Time and Materials** billing schedule to the sales order, preventing it from ever falling into the **Bill Orders** queue.

The **Invoice Customers** form displays all of the customers with approved time and expenses:

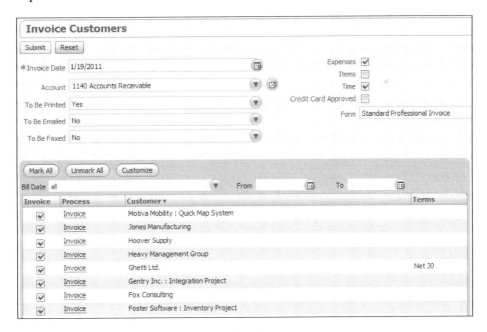

Setting the **Invoice Date** sets the posting period of the transaction, in this case February 2011. With **To Be Printed** set to **Yes**, the invoices can all be printed together at **Print Checks and Forms**, along with mailing labels.

Keep in mind that there are **Accounting Preferences** that affect how the invoices present time and expenses, including how they tag time and expense lines with department, class, and location fields.

Refunds, credit memos, and customer returns

If you have problems with the products shipped or services performed, and the customer demands remedy, OneWorld has processes to assist you. Let's start with product issues.

The first question here is do you want the product back? OneWorld customers differ on this question.

- If you want the products returned, do a customer return material authorization, or RMA. Navigate to **Transactions | Customer | Issue Return Authorization**. This opens the preferred RMA form; make sure it is the correct one for this transaction:
    - ° If you billed the customer by cash sale, then use the **Standard Return Authorization – Cash**, as this form's process ends with a cash refund (in most cases a credit card refund).
    - ° If you billed the customer by invoice then use the **Standard Return Authorization – Invoice**. This form's process ends with a credit memo.
    - ° It's a good idea to have a special location set up, into which you can receive returned goods; keep the goods separate and you can easily view everything returned in both quantity and value.

- If you don't want the product returned, or if the refund is for a non-product item, then jump forward to the refund. If the customer paid cash, then navigate to **Transactions | Customers | Refund a Cash Sale**. If the customer received an invoice that is as yet unpaid, then navigate to **Transactions | Customers | Issue a Credit Memo** against the invoice. If the invoice has been paid, and you don't intend to do more business with the customer, then you must write them a check and apply it to the credit memo from the **Issue Customer Refund** form. In the next screenshot, we have a customer who paid an invoice, and subsequently asked for a refund. We set up a credit memo, and now we generate a refund against the credit memo:

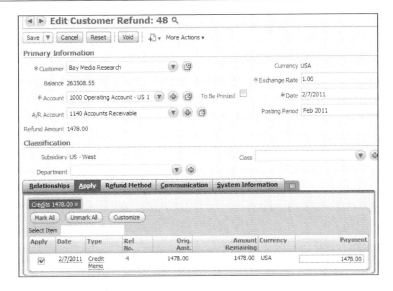

We print the check from the normal check-printing queue.

Payments, deposits, finance charges, and bad debt

After setting up your invoices, printing, and mailing or e-mailing them, the next step, of course, is collections. Payments are taken against invoices from **Transactions | Customer | Accept Customer Payments**. From the following screenshot, notice that a single payment can be taken against multiple invoices:

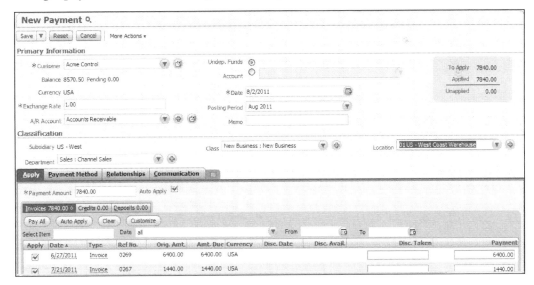

In this example, we used **Auto Apply** to apply the payment to multiple invoices. We also used **Undep Funds** to hold the check until we make a bank deposit. On the **Payment Method** tab, we enter the customer's check or wire information.

When taking payments through a bank-to-bank wire, there is often a charge incurred, which the bank subtracts from the payment. To manage this, you can take payment for the entire amount, including the wire transfer fee, against the invoice(s). This clears the receivable. Then, when doing your bank deposit, at **Transactions | Bank | Make Deposit**, enter the fee on the **Cash Back** tab, as shown in the following screenshot:

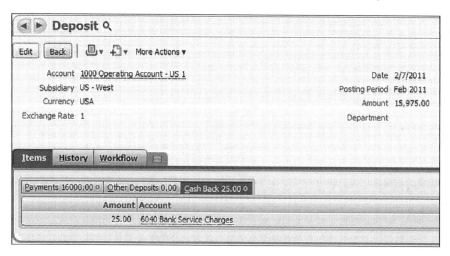

In this example, we took a payment of **16,000.00** dollars against a number of invoices, and we are depositing **15,975.00** dollars into the bank, after taking **25.00** dollars charge for the wire transfer. The payment relieved accounts receivable, and with this deposit, the bank now reflects the correct cash balance.

OneWorld also provides the ability to create a hierarchy of customers and to accept consolidated payments. For example, you might sell products to several customers who are all sub-customers of a parent. By enabling the **Consolidated Payments** feature, OneWorld allows you to invoice and take payment at any level of the hierarchy, depending on business practices. This is helpful because you may invoice the child but receive payment from the parent. Without this feature enabled, you invoice and take payment from the sub-customer.

For some OneWorld users, the sale requires a customer deposit prior to fulfillment of goods and/or services. For this requirement, navigate to **Transactions | Customer | Record Customer Deposit**.

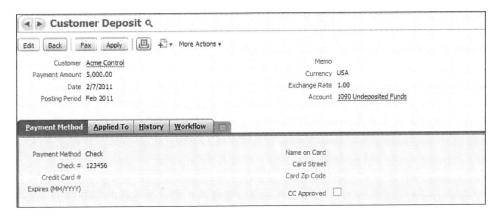

You can take a deposit in any of the methods in which you take payments: credit card, check, wire transfer, and so on. After you log the deposit into the system, you must still make the bank deposit, as shown in the previous screenshot, and also apply the deposit to an invoice once you generate the invoice. In most cases, OneWorld users who take deposits also enable the **Invoice in Advance of Fulfillment** accounting preference.

Finance charges are often assessed when selling on terms. To start, we must first do the base setup at **Setup | Accounting | Finance Charge Preferences**. In the following screenshot, we have set up our **Finance Charge Preferences**:

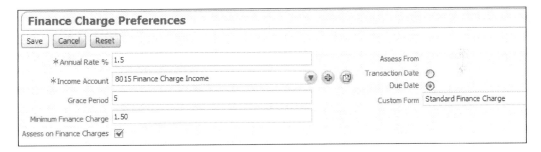

Navigate to **Transactions | Customers | Assess Finance Charges**, to open the following batch form:

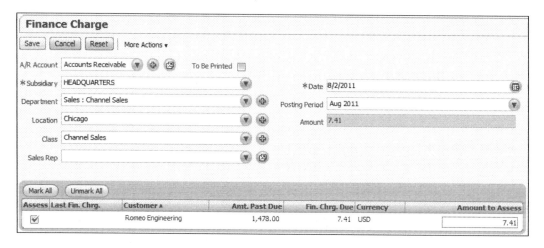

When you **Save** your selections on this form, OneWorld generates invoices, which serve to charge the finance charges to the correct GL accounts.

The next step is to **Generate Statements**. These will include any finance charges you transacted. You can do this from the customer record, under **More Actions**, or you can navigate to **Transactions | Customers | Generate Statements** for multiple customers at one time. This process creates a PDF file with one page per customer, as shown in the following screenshot:

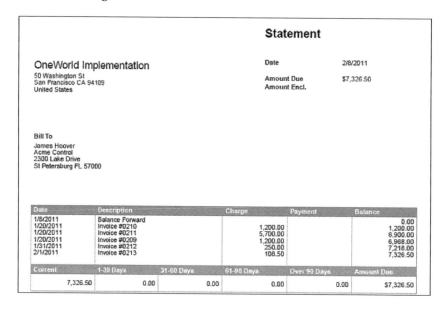

Dunning letters, in which you remind a customer to remit their balance, can be done in either MS Word or in Adobe PDF. Any information from the customer record or from the main line of a customer transaction can be integrated into a document. The process, for MS Word, is to build a template that incorporates OneWorld's tags and loads it into OneWorld under **Documents | Templates | Letter Templates | New**. Then from the customer or transaction record, you simply hover on the **Create New** icon, as shown in the following screenshot, and select **Letter**:

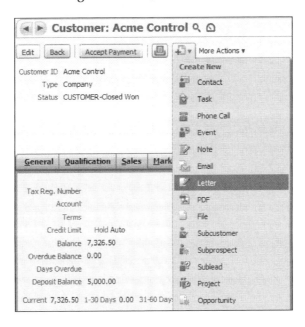

Then you enter the letter you want and OneWorld generates it with information from the customer's record, including, in this case, their balance due under the **Financial** tab.

Processing a bad debt when you have an accounts receivable that you cannot collect on is a two-step process. First, generate a journal entry at **Transactions | Financial | Journal Entry**. Credit A/R and debit your bad debt expense account. On the A/R line, select the customer. Then navigate to the **Accept Customer Payment** form, and select the invoice(s) that are uncollectable on the **Invoice** tab, and select the journal you just generated on the **Other Credits** tab. The two should cancel each other out, making the payment net to zero.

If you want to stop doing business with a customer with bad debts, you can place them on a **Credit Hold** on the customer record. Opening a sales order or invoice throws either a warning or a hard hold, depending on how you set up the **Accounting Preference | Customer Credit Limit Handling**.

Cash management

We separated cash management from payment processing, because many OneWorld customers divide these functions among the accounting staff for internal control purposes. After checks, credit card charges, and wires are logged as payments against either an invoice or a cash sale by one staff member, another staff member prepares the bank deposit. Likewise, after vendor bills are generated in the system by one staff person, another staff person prints the checks and sends them to vendors.

Bank deposits

In the most common case, we use the bank deposit for a group of checks that come in the door through the postal service. In B2B sales, this is still the most common method of payment.

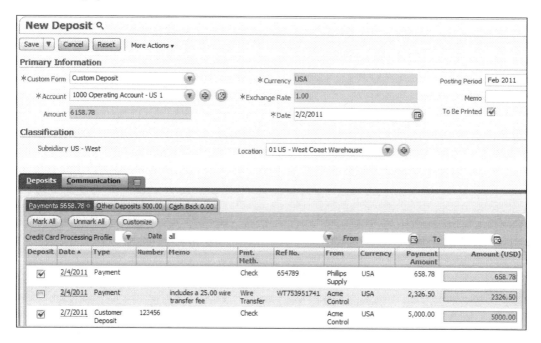

In this example, we want to print a deposit ticket for the bank with three checks, two from customers selected on the **Payment** tab, and another one from a vendor for a rebate, which we entered on the **Other Deposits** tab. After we save and print this deposit ticket, we can then do another deposit that updates our checking account with the amount of the wire transfer minus the **25.00** dollar fee. Since the cash from the wire transfer is already in the bank, we don't need a printed deposit ticket for that payment.

CC payments processing

When you take credit card payments for goods and services, whether through your online Webstore, through manual entries into OneWorld, or through batch processes, such as bill orders, the first order of business is to make sure all of your credit card sales in OneWorld match the credit card sales in your gateway. The best way to do this is a daily reconciliation between OneWorld and the gateway using a report, such as **Sales by Customer**, and customizing it to include only sales by through credit cards.

There is often a lag between the credit card charges and the funds deposited into your bank account. To manage this lag, one option starts by setting up your credit card payment methods, at **Setup | Accounting | Accounting Lists | New | Payment Method**, to **Group with Undeposited Funds**. This charges your credit card payments to the undeposited funds account and then you use the **Make Deposits** form, as shown in the previous screenshot, to deposit the payments into your bank account per credit card vendor, using a report from your gateway. Notice on the screenshot of this **Deposits** form, there are filters for the **Credit Card Processing Profile**, such as **VISA**, **MasterCard**, and **American Express**, and the dates to deposit.

Doing cash sale credit card deposits is a bit more work, but it helps to reconcile the actual cash deposits to your bank account from the credit card companies to the credit card charges you processed in OneWorld, in the process making visible any disputed charges, and so on. Also, when you make the cash sale deposit, use the **Cash Back** tab to enter the credit card and gateway fees for the batch. Finally, the deposit allows you to reconcile easily to the bank account statement, since your statement tells the total deposit everyday from the credit card companies.

Gift certificate income

Companies that sell B2C, whether online, in person, or through telesales, often sell gift certificates. This is the process for using gift certificates in OneWorld:

1. Enable the **Gift Certificate** feature.

2. Set up a **Gift Certificate** item. You must give it a specific **Price** in every currency in which you intend to sell it. Also, make the item available to any subsidiary that may sell it.

3. For an online sale, set up the item's **Store** tab and place it in the desired store category.

4. When purchased, the buyer supplies their name, the recipient's name, the recipient's e-mail address, and a short message.

5. The recipient receives an e-mail with the gift certificate code and they subsequently make a purchase and apply the gift certificate as payment.

6. Each gift certificate sale generates not only the sales record, but also a record of the certificate, as shown in the following screenshot:

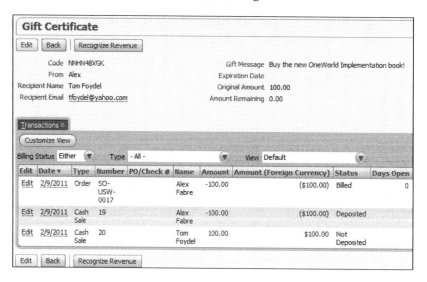

Navigate to the gift certificate record, by clicking on **View** in the line of the sales order in which you sold the certificate, or by navigating to **Lists | Accounting | Gift Certificates**.

It's a good idea to include a **Days to Expiration** value on the **Gift Certificate Item** setup. Gift certificates are treated as a liability until they have been redeemed or until they expire. To recognize gift certificate sales or expired gift certificates as revenue, navigate to each certificate or go to **Transactions | Financial | Recognize Gift Certificate Income** at period end.

Period-close processing

At this point, we have covered the basic OneWorld transaction processing with customers, employees, and vendors. This is the activity that happens all the time at your organization. But at the beginning of each month, there are several other processes performed by the accounting department to bring the books into order and close the prior accounting period. Each organization has or should have its own period-close checklist. It's important for the implementation that you get a checklist together as soon as possible, as the task exposes a lot of work that is often forgotten until it needs to be done. The spreadsheets and other supporting documents that you use for the month end are also an important source of information for the implementation team. Do not wait until you close your first month in OneWorld to go over the period-close processes carefully.

We discuss some of the processes done at period end here. These are just the common OneWorld tasks; you must add your own list to complete period end. Also take into account the period-end checklist, as shown in the following screenshot. Find this under **Setup | Accounting | Manage Accounting Periods**, and then click on the icon in the **Checklist** column.

Go To Task	Task	Status	Modified By
	Lock A/R	✓	
	Lock A/P	✓	
	Lock All	✓	
	Resolve Date/Period Mismatches	✓	Tom Foydel
	Review Negative Inventory	✓	Tom Foydel
	Review Inventory Cost Accounting	✓	Tom Foydel
	Create Intercompany Adjustments	✓	Tom Foydel
	Revalue Open Foreign Currency Balances	✓	Tom Foydel
	Calculate Consolidated Exchange Rates	✓	Tom Foydel
	Eliminate Intercompany Transactions	✓	Tom Foydel
	Close	✓	Tom Foydel

Period Close Checklist: Jan 2011

Period Name FY 2011 : Q1 2011 : Jan 2011   Start Date 1/1/2011
Status Open   End Date 1/31/2011
Notes

Notice that period ends must be done sequentially, and though it is less obvious, the tasks must also be done sequentially. The period-close checklist should be the last task on your own checklist. There are some important tasks here, but before you get here, you want to make sure that you completed all of your transaction processing.

- **Lock A/R** and **Lock A/P** prevent you from entering new invoices and vendor bills in the period. If both A/R and A/P are ready to be closed, you can also click on **Lock All**. You lock Periods by Subsidiary so that your individual controllers can lock their own periods without locking out one of their colleagues. After these are locked for the period, you can still edit non-posting transactions, such as sales orders. It is also possible to grant a role **Permission to Override Period Restrictions**, allowing them to post transactions in closed periods. Obviously, you need to handle this carefully.

- **Resolve Date/Period Mismatches** opens a form with a list of transactions, in which the transaction date is outside of the period. If this is an error, then correct the transaction(s) and come back to this task. If it is not an error, as this is not an uncommon business practice, then simply click on **Mark Task Complete**, and move on.

- **Review Negative Inventory** checks for inventory items with negative counts, sometimes called underwater inventory. If you sell products out of inventory, then you obviously want to avoid this situation, but if for some reason you have negative inventory, now is the time to investigate and correct the situation(s). When done, you again click on **Mark Task Complete** to move on. (There is a good **Help** text on avoiding underwater inventory.)

- **Review Inventory Cost Accounting** runs a process that corrects the cost of goods sold numbers after negative inventory items have been corrected. When the process has finished, click on **Mark Task Complete**, to move forward.

- **Create Intercompany Adjustments** is for OneWorld accounts that use intercompany time and expense. You can also access this function from **Transactions | Financial**. The form opens with all of the intercompany adjustments for the period selected. By submitting these, you create the intercompany journals, which correct the expenses of an employee of one subsidiary who worked for a customer of another subsidiary.

- **Revalue Open Foreign Currency Balances** is the process by which you revalue open transactions, such as invoices, for example, at the end of the period when the invoice is a currency other than your base currency. OneWorld uses the period-end exchange rate to revalue, in our example, the balance of A/R.

- **Calculate Consolidated Exchange Rates** is the process that sets the period-end exchange rates for companies with subsidiaries with different base currencies. These are used for consolidated financial reporting. When you open this option, the form presents all of the exchange rates between related subsidiaries. There is a **Calculate** button on the bottom of the form for auto-calculation.

- **Eliminate Intercompany Transactions**: Best practice process to auto eliminate intercompany transactions. This process may require some additional setup of elimination subsidiaries and elimination vendors and customers, but it forces a balanced intercompany journal entry.

- **Close Period** brings the OneWorld period-close process to completion. Notice on this page that there is a **Notes** field, in which you can see the entire history of how you closed the period.

Again, before you get to the **Checklist**, make sure that some of the following processes are complete, based on your business model.

Allocating expenses

Many organizations allocate expenses across departments, and some even allocate across subsidiaries. In either case, if you want OneWorld to help you perform this chore, then you must have the **Advanced Financials** module. If you don't have advanced financials, you can always set up memorized journals to manage the allocation. The option you select probably depends on the volume of allocations you manage.

The allocation process starts with the setup at **Transactions | Financial | Create Allocation Schedules** or **Create Intercompany Allocation Schedules**. In either case, you tell OneWorld what expense account you want to allocate, from where, and to where. For simple department, class, and location allocation within a subsidiary, use the allocation schedules.

But when you need to allocate between subsidiaries, use the intercompany allocation schedule. When you pay the rent for two subsidiaries from a bank account belonging to subsidiary A, you can allocate it by percentage to subsidiary A and subsidiary B. The allocation to subsidiary A generates a simple two-sided allocation journal. The allocation to subsidiary B generates a four-sided intercompany journal. If you need to allocate amortized expenses, do the amortization journal first, then the allocation.

In each period, you must navigate to your allocation schedules and **Create Journal Entries**.

Amortizing liabilities

We now need to amortize expenses to generate journal entries.

To review, we set up up the **Amortization Template** under **Lists | Accounting**. The template, as in the following screenshot, requires that you select a **Method**, a **Deferral Account**, and a **Target Account**. The **Contra Account** serves to accumulate depreciation. You'll need to set up templates for every amortization scenario.

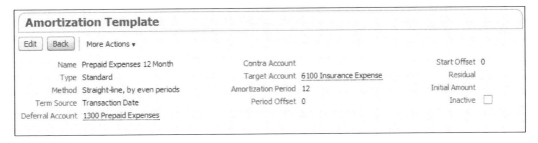

When you enter vendor bills into OneWorld, select the amortization template and the start and end dates on the expense or item line. Then, as part of your period end, navigate to **Transactions | Financial | Create Amortization Journals**, bringing up a batch processing form that allows you to select which schedules you want to process. OneWorld generates the journal entries.

The amortization journal always processes in the **Subsidiary**, in which you entered the vendor bill, as shown in the following screenshot:

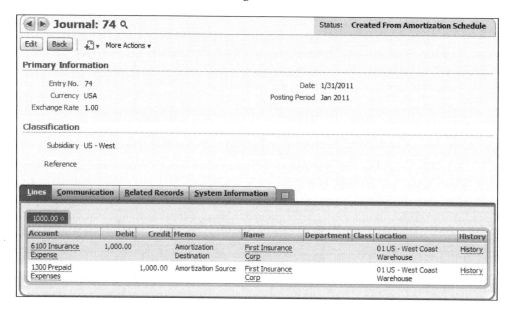

Revenue recognition

The last step in revenue recognition is to navigate to **Transactions | Financial | Create Revenue Recognition Journal Entries**. Again, this is a batch process form that allows you to filter the rev rec items in many different ways, but you must select at least a subsidiary, as shown in the following screenshot:

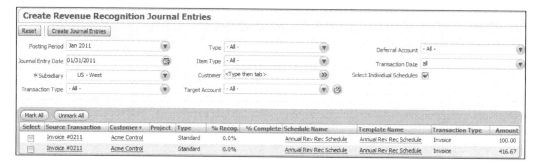

Journals and intercompany journals

It seems that every company requires a few journal entries at the end of the period, in order to reflect business outside of OneWorld, such as the payroll run, or activities outside of the normal transaction processes that affect the company's balance sheet. In some cases, you might need to transfer money between the bank accounts of two subsidiaries. When the journals are required within a subsidiary, use **Create Journal Entries**, and when you require journals between subsidiaries, use **Create Intercompany Journal Entries**.

Bank reconciliation

Part of any month-end close is the bank reconciliation. There are a couple of important things to mention here. First, you can clear bank account items on a more regular schedule if you want. Since most of us have access to our accounts online, it is common to clear items weekly, making the month-end process much less time consuming. To clear items, navigate to your chart of accounts, from **Reports | Financial | Chart of Accounts**, or from **Lists | Accounting | Accounts**. Select the account you want and you will land on the account register page. Here, you can clear the items that were transacted on this account. Then, when you go to do your bank rec, you can easily see any items that were not yet cleared, investigate, and complete the reconciliation.

The second note concerns importing your bank statement from your bank. OneWorld accepts imports in OFX, QFX, or QIF files. First, you need to download the file from your bank and store it on an accessible hard drive. Then start the process from **Transactions | Bank | Import Online Banking Data**. After you select your file and bank account and click on **Submit**, the following form presents OneWorld's matches to your imported records:

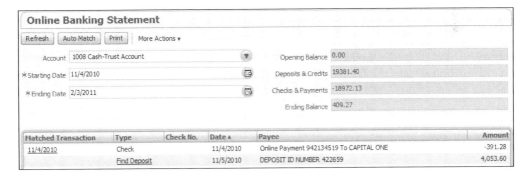

If a record fails to match, then you have to **Find** a transaction to match it to, or possibly enter a transaction. All matched transactions show up on the **Bank Reconciliation** form as **Cleared**.

Financial reporting

At this point, we have run our transactions, reconciled them, and closed the period. Now it's time to look at financial reporting.

The purpose here is simply to bring some important information about OneWorld's financial reporting engine to the discussion, as this can often be an important guide to how you finally choose to configure the system.

If you take a look at the cash flow statement, the balance sheet, and the income statement, you will notice in the footer of the report that you can select the subsidiary context. Run any of these reports, by a single subsidiary or by one of your parent subsidiaries. In the next screenshot, you can see the list of subsidiaries available for the report. You can view any parent by itself or in a consolidated view – the parent and all its children.

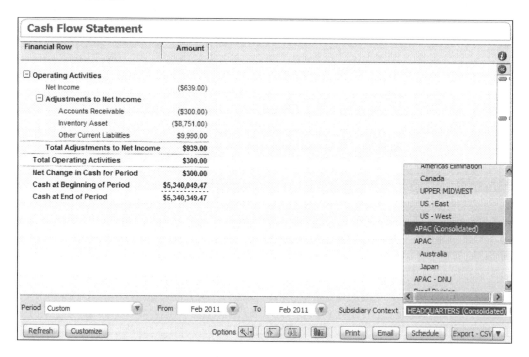

The point here is that it's important to understand the consolidated views available to you before you complete your subsidiary hierarchy. Also, take a moment and think about future growth and how this might reflect in the hierarchy.

Also notice that there is a **Column** list of values in the footer. Here, you can select the departments, classes, locations, or subsidiaries, with or without their hierarchies, to compare across the columns of the report. Now that you have some data in your account, it's time to run reports and see if your setups have added value to your reporting.

Financial report generator

While all of the delivered reports are customizable in OneWorld's report generator, financial reports have the added capability of the financial report generator. We suggest that before you try to generate new reports with the financial report generator, first spend some time working with one of the delivered financial reports. Open the income statement, for example, and click on **Customize** in the footer. You have opened the financial report generator. There are five separate pages to this form: **Edit Layout**, **Edit Columns**, **Filter**, **Sorting** (Optional), and **More Options**. Make yourself familiar with each one of these pages. From the **Columns** page, you can add additional columns of data from the left side panel **Add Items**. Likewise, on the **Filter** page you can also add additional filters from **Add Items**.

It's important to understand what's available for slicing and dicing your data. You may come away more confident in your first prototype, or you may feel the need to reassess your configuration decisions. Either way, now is the time to take stock of your first prototype and make changes to your base configurations, if need be. It's still early on, and changes are quite easy at this point. Our test transactions can be deleted, giving us the opportunity to start over. That's what the first prototype is all about.

Summary

Chapters 2 through 7 have hopefully enabled you to build a first prototype in OneWorld and assess the soundness of your assumptions and configuration decisions. You have reached the first major milestone of the OneWorld implementation. The passage to this point is difficult and, at times, slow. It can take a lot of time to translate current business practices into a new system.

But with your first system prototype complete, you should have gained a lot of experience both with OneWorld and your business process team. For certain, confidence in your OneWorld skills and business acumen increases throughout the process of building the prototype. Going forward, the implementation becomes more challenging, because the pace picks up from here. But you have a solid foundation now to build on.

We have not talked a lot about documentation to this point, because it's time consuming and everyone has their own take on what's important, and how to document it. But we did mention, and reiterate here, that's it's important to document major decisions and have all of the stakeholders agree. Now might be a good time to revisit your decisions. Have you learned anything new through the first prototype that causes a new take on your past decisions? If the answer is yes, then you have probably done a worthwhile prototype.

From here, we start building the rest of our OneWorld structure in preparation for our second prototype and conference room pilot. We start to customize OneWorld, learn how to administer it more finely, and take a deep dive into data analysis and presentation. In *Chapter 8, OneWorld Customization and Advanced Configuration*, we add fields, records, formulas, and customize our forms and roles. *Chapter 9, OneWorld Data Migration*, takes us into data analysis, and in *Chapter 10, Data Analysis*, we start to migrate our data.

8

OneWorld Customization and Advanced Configuration

This chapter gives an in-depth review of OneWorld's customization features and functions; the aim is to provide implementation team members, business leaders, and IT pros with the knowledge of what's possible in OneWorld and how to get started setting it up.

Using the first prototype to walk through the system with your experienced business experts is the important first step to customization. It is only when you and the business expert both understand the delivered forms, functions, and processes in a specific business domain that you can successfully expand OneWorld's functionality to adapt to your organization's business goals. The first prototype should also help you to hone your business goals; just keep asking *"What are we trying to achieve?"*

All too often, we have been asked to offer our advice to a business that has spent a great deal of time customizing the system only to fall short somewhere along the way. When we ask *"What is the purpose?"* when considering some customization, we often hear silence. Knowing ahead of time precisely what you want to achieve is really important. Starting to customize the system before understanding either OneWorld or the business goal thoroughly leads to dead ends in most cases. Often, we see customizations that actually mimic delivered functionality that the users did not understand.

OneWorld is incredibly customizable, but don't chase customization as an end in and of itself. The wise system analyst does not ask, *"What other fields do you need?"*. Rather, while working through the business process in OneWorld, they note the need for a customization, along with its purpose, and try to understand it within the wider context of the organization's goals.

To illustrate the point, take the case of the customer record after sales management was asked, *"What other fields do you need?"*. The result is several additional sub-tabs filled with over 40 different custom fields. Looking through the fields one by one, it was found that each had some small significance, but after almost a year of using the system, it was obvious that no one was willing to update and maintain all of these fields. When we drilled down on each field, it was also obvious that management had never really stated and discussed the objective. What was more revealing is that no one had ever written the reports that would yield useful information from all the data, even if they had taken the time to enter it. In the end, 37 fields went away and management was able to look at a report that included the remaining three fields and see some useful information.

While we introduce the customization of OneWorld in this chapter, we hope that you keep the need for simplicity in front of you. The biggest problem with most systems is that they grow large over time and, together with customization, overwhelm users. Keep in mind then that customization is not only addition, but addition by subtraction in many cases. If you are not using fields and functions on the forms, then remove them to the degree possible. In the end, we want to offer the users a simple, straightforward, and purposeful interface that they learn easily and see the benefit of, over time.

In this chapter, we cover the following main customization features of OneWorld that can be achieved without custom code:

- Adding custom fields
- Adding new records
- Adding records to forms
- Configuring custom forms
- Configuring custom roles
- Developing custom centers
- Designing custom workflows

Adding custom fields

It's possible to add custom fields to almost any entry or transaction form in OneWorld. Entry forms include the forms for customers, vendors, partners, employees, and items. Transaction forms include any of the forms that you use as part of the purchasing or sales processes. It is also possible to pass along a custom field value from an entry form to a transaction form.

Setting up custom fields varies slightly, depending on their purpose and on the form to which you add them, but is largely the same in most cases. Let's take a look at some different custom fields, their purpose, how we set them up, and how they work.

Item fields

If the items in your catalog have attributes that you would like to sort by, adding a custom item field often fits the bill. For example, if you sell lighting products and you want to allow customers to easily sort through your catalog for bathroom lights, then you may add a field for **Room**. A custom **Room** field gives visitors the opportunity to sort through lights on your website, and it also gives you the ability to look at sales or profitability by the same criteria.

Set up the custom item field at **Setup | Customization | Item Field**. In the following screenshot, we set up a custom **List/Record** and **Type** field, and below, a custom list of **Values**, at the same time:

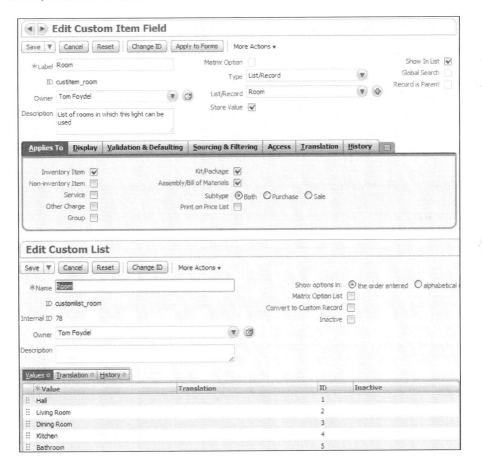

Notice that, on the new custom field, we select the items on which we want this new field to appear. Also, make sure to set up the tab on which you want the field to **Display**. For the system ID, on both records, we entered **_room (customlist_room** in this example). This is a good rule of thumb to follow, since OneWorld adds its own prefix to all customizations and, should you need to use the field in a script, it will be easier to have them all set up similarly.

For security, use the **Access** tab to limit the view and edit permissions on this field to roles that have access to items.

Transaction column fields

In the previous example, we set up a **List/Record** type field for **Room**. Now, when we purchase or sell a light, we want the **Room** field to default to the line item on the transaction, giving us the ability to report on purchases and sales of lights, by **Room**. To accomplish this, we set up a new custom **Edit Transaction Column Field** and source it from our custom item field. In the following screenshot, you see how we use the **Sourcing & Filtering** tab:

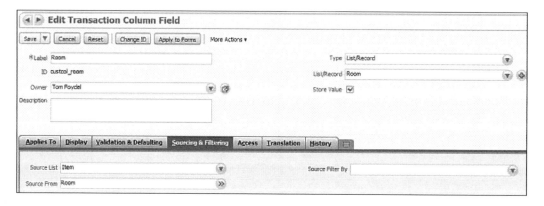

On the **Applies To** tab, you set up the transaction(s) on which you want this field to appear. When you select an item on a purchase or sale transaction line, and the item has the **Room** field entered, the the transaction column field fills in automatically, just as the item's department, class, and location fields fill in on transaction lines, as shown in the following screenshot:

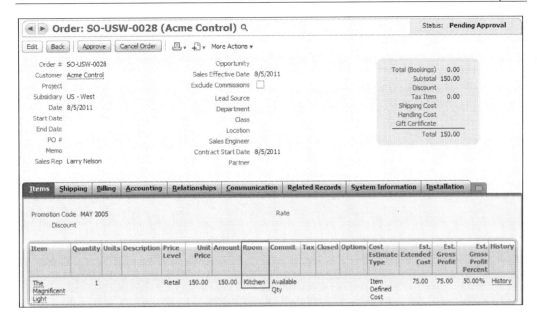

With the item's room on the transaction line, you now have the necessary setups to run a sales by room report for your lighting products.

Of course, you can have custom transaction column fields that are not tied to items or other entities.

Entity fields

When we enter vendors, partners, contacts, or customers into OneWorld, they often require additional fields to complete our understanding of who these entities are and how we expect to do business with them.

If you sell software, then you might want a custom field to note the prospect's operating system. If you pay vendors online, from your bank account, a custom field on the vendor record to note payment method helps the accounts payable clerk to decide which bills to pay by check and which to pay online. Let's look at this last example more closely.

We start by adding a custom entity field for vendors from **Setup | Customization | Entity Field**, as shown in the following screenshot:

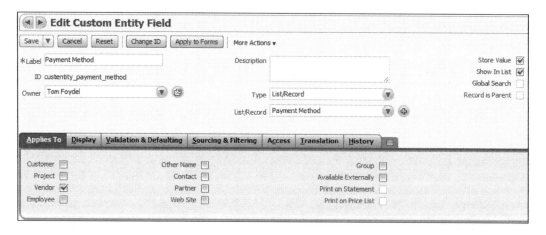

For this custom field, we check **Vendor** on the **Applies To** tab and we add it to the **Financial** tab, on the **Display** tab. Notice that we made the field a **List/Record** type and that we use the delivered **Payment Method** list. If you want to add to the **Payment Method** list, navigate to **Setup | Accounting | Accounting Lists**. Finally, on the **Validation** tab, we select **Check** as our default, since the vast majority of vendors are paid this way. In the next step, we add this field to transactions.

Transaction body fields

We use these fields to add data to the main line or header of a transaction record. In this case, we are going to add the vendor's preferred payment method to the purchase order and vendor bill, on the **Applies To** tab, so that we can easily sort bills by payment method. In the following screenshot, we source our new field from the vendor payment method:

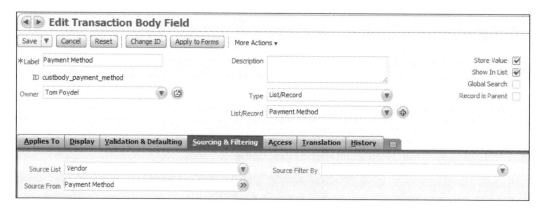

Now, when we open a bill or PO for a vendor, the payment method defaults from the vendor's record to the transaction.

When we go to **Pay Bills**, we can add the **Payment Method** field to the form and also use it as a filter, if we desire, as shown in the following screenshot:

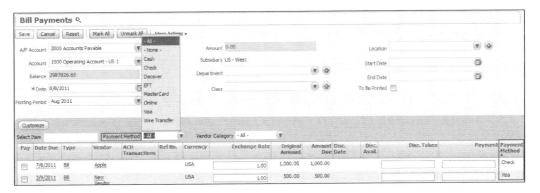

We can now pay these vendor bills offline with our credit card and record them correctly in OneWorld, before we do our regular check run.

Adding new records

There are times when a custom field or even several custom fields do not suffice. If you ask the question, *"Are there multiple instances of the same group of custom fields?"* and the answer is, *"Yes,"* you need to add a custom record. The custom record has multiple fields and it allows you to enter and save multiple instances of the record, keeping a history of all instances.

Take the example of computing assets that your organization purchases and that come with product warranties. Any employee might have several assets, and each asset could have several warranty renewals. You could have several custom fields to hold the details of each asset and its warranty but, each year, when you enter the new data, you lose the current data. If this history is important, then a custom record is a better fit.

To start a custom record, navigate to **Setup | Customization | Record Types** and click on **New**.

In our next example, we have a professional services organization that purchases phones and computer equipment for all of its employees and needs an easy way to track the purchases by employee, giving them a guide for warranty renewals and asset returns upon employee termination. The process starts when an employee enters a purchase requisition.

To set up the new record, we give it a name and configure some of its basic details:

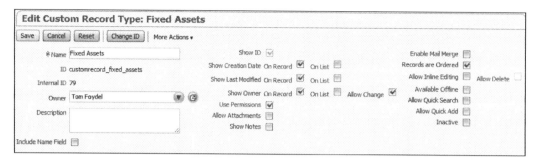

If you check **Include Name Field**, then OneWorld expects you to give each individual record its own name. **Show Owner** puts the name of the user entering the data on the record. The rest of the fields are fairly self-explanatory and you can always return to your configuration and make changes after you become more comfortable with what you want.

Once you save the definition of the new record, OneWorld refreshes the form and you now see several new tabs along the bottom, including **Fields**. Click on **New Field** to start setting up the fields for this record.

First, enter the fields that you want to track on the new record, such as **Date of Purchase, Vendor,** and so on. For this example, we set up the **Vendor** field to source from a list of all vendors, where the **Vendor Category** is **Hardware**, as depicted in the following screenshot:

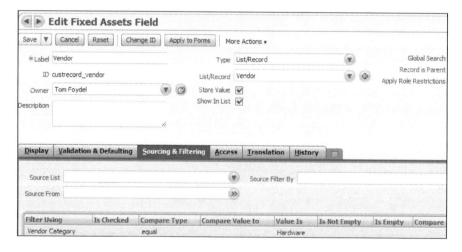

We added the **Vendor Category** as **Hardware** under **Setup | Accounting | Accounting Lists**.

When you have all of the fields that you need for the record, the next step is to add the fields that join your new record to the delivered or built-in records. In this case, we want to join the **Fixed Asset** record to the **Purchase Order** and the **Employee** records. Again, click on **New Field**, and add a field to enter the employee on the record. For this field, make **Type** equal to **List/Record** and then select **Employee** in the **List/Record** field; finally, check the box next to **Record is Parent** and add this record to the employee **General** tab, as in following screenshot:

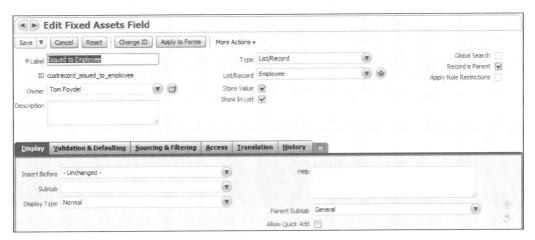

What we have done here is to make our new record a child record of the **Employee** record. This provides us with the ability to enter, view, or edit asset records from the **Employee** form.

Finally, we want to link our custom record to the **Purchase Order**. Again, click on **New Field**, and add a **List/Record** sourced from **Transactions | Purchase Orders** and, again, check **Record is Parent**, as shown in the following screenshot:

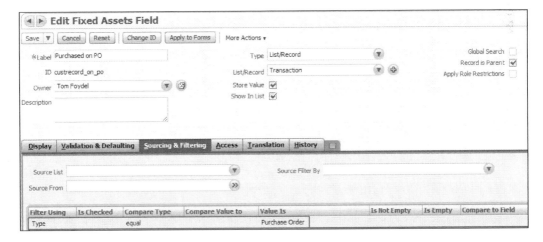

Now let's see how our custom record works in 'real life.' An employee enters a purchase requisition for a new notebook; when **Approved**, this becomes a PO. When the new machine arrives from the vendor, the IT department logs it into the system right from the PO, as the next screenshot of the PO, overlaid with the asset record, depicts:

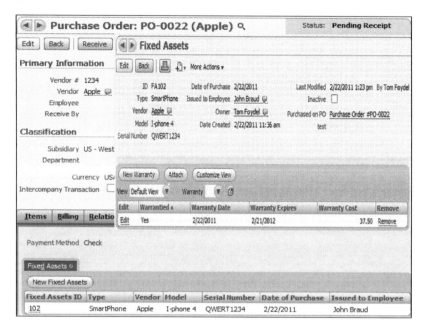

When we click on **New Fixed Assets** from the PO, the system automatically knows the value of the **Purchased on PO** field. After saving this record, we are able to view this fixed asset record in three places: The PO record, as shown in this screenshot; from the **Employee** record; and from the **Fixed Asset** records, which you can place in any center and under any center category, when you set up the **Links** tab on the **Fixed Asset** custom record. We placed ours in the **Classic Center** under **Lists | Accounting | Fixed Assets**, as an example.

Custom records are very useful, as you can see, especially when joined to the built-in records of OneWorld. Of course, with this information in the system, it's easy to run a report or search to see the assets given to any employee and the warranty dates, should you want to renew.

Custom records use permissions like any other record, so it's easy to set up **View**, **Create**, **Edit**, or **Full** permissions for various roles. You can even limit access to certain fields, if need be.

Custom records can also be linked to other custom records. So, returning to our warranty record example, if we wanted the warranty information to be entered as a new record every year, we would set up a new record for the warranty information and link it to our asset record, just as we linked the asset record to the employee and PO records. The result is that we can now enter multiple warranty records for each asset record, as in the next screenshot. Notice that we also enabled **Inline Editing** on the custom **Warranty** record, allowing us to type directly into the record's fields, without opening it up in a separate window:

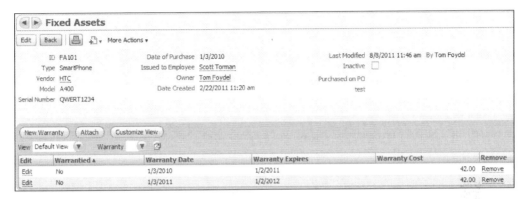

We now have a warranty record attached to the asset record. Over time, we can add further warranty records and, again, we can view/update both the asset and warranty records from the purchase order, the employee record, the list of assets, or the list of warranties. We can also write reports on our new records, as well as searches and alerts.

Adding records to other records and forms

We saw how we can add a custom record to one or more of OneWorld's delivered or built-in records. Now, let's take a look at adding one built-in record to another built-in record. For example, let's say that our business case requires that every time we sell certain products, we also set up an installation for the product. For this requirement, we decide to use the OneWorld customer service module. To meet our requirement, we need to add a new case function to the sales order. When the sales manager approves the sales order, it falls into operation's fulfillment queue and they open a new case to schedule the customer service visit from the sales order, making sure that the product is at the customer location before the installation service rep.

To implement this requirement, we start by adding a new custom **CRM Field** to OneWorld sales orders, as seen in the following screenshot from **Setup | Customization | CRM Field**:

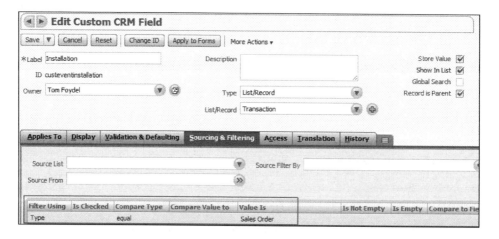

On the **Applies To** tab, we selected **Case**. We also selected **List/Record** for the **Type** field, and **Transaction** for the **List/Record** field. Finally, under the **Sourcing & Filtering** tab, we selected **Type, equal and Sales Order**. So, what we have is a new field on the case form that allows us to select from a list of transactions where **Type** equals **Order**. Because we also select **Record is Parent**, we now have the ability to generate a new case from the sales order, as shown in the following screenshot:

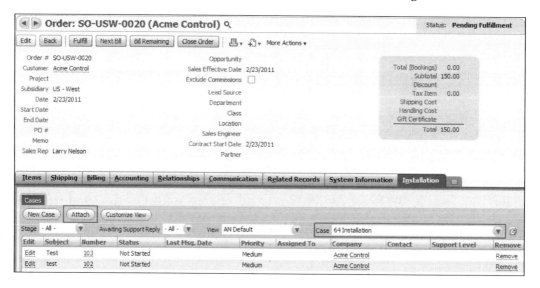

By clicking on **New Case**, we open the case form and automatically save the SO number to our custom CRM field when we save the new case. The case is then linked to this SO.

If we have another case pertaining to this SO, but not started from the SO, we can select the case in the **Case** field and **Attach** it, as depicted in the previous screenshot.

We have now linked the delivered case record to the delivered sales order record, in support of an important business requirement. If we want the new case to inherit some of the main line fields from the SO in this case, we configure a workflow. We describe this process in the *Custom Workflow* discussion, later in this chapter.

Configuring custom forms

Before you finish the implementation, you almost certainly will customize all of your forms. You may need to add fields, remove fields, rearrange fields, add new functions, deploy scripts, and so on. The reasons for customizing forms are many and, for this reason, we often start the process ahead of time. After we get a good understanding of the business processes, we navigate to **Setup | Customization | Entry Forms** (or **Transaction Forms**) and we rename all of the standard forms that are pertinent to the implementation at hand. When we add new custom fields, and so on, we **Save** and **Apply** to **Forms** and they are automatically added to the custom forms.

To customize your forms, open up the list of forms, either transaction or entry, and simply click on **Customize** for each form you expect to use. Normally, we simply add the client's name or an abbreviation to the name of the form in place of the word **Custom**. We try to keep the rest of the form's name, so that the form functionality is easily-identifiable. For example, if you want to customize the **Standard Sales Order – Invoice** form, open it up and replace **Custom** in the form name with XYZ for your organization, leaving XYZ **Order – Invoice**. This allows you to understand the functionality to expect from the form; in this case, a billed sales order becomes an invoice.

When you have the details of your implementation more or less set, you can take the time to set up your forms for production use. It was always possible to include or exclude tabs and fields, and to move fields between tabs; but, with the 2010 release, you can also add your own regions in the form of **Field Groups**. **Field Groups** allow you to place related fields together with a label, to make forms with a large number of fields easier to read. For example, if your main line of a transaction form includes department, class, location, and subsidiary, you may want to put all of the fields into a group called **Classification**, so that they stand out from the rest of the main line fields.

In the following screenshot, we have a custom **Customer** form. We decide what **Fields** we want, what tab they are on, and what **Field Group** they belong to:

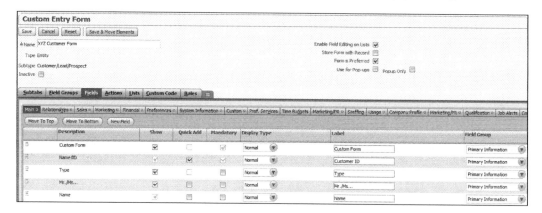

Of course, if you don't want some of these fields in the main line of the transaction, you can simply remove them by unchecking these fields on the **Main** tab. In many cases, for example, **Class** might be a field set in a transaction column, based on a specific item, and not necessarily in the main line.

After you decide which fields you would like to include on the form, by checking or unchecking the **Show** column, you can also decide if you want them to be **Mandatory**. Also, if you want the users of a form to see a field but not change it, you can set it to **Inline Text** from **Normal** in the **Display** column.

To change the location of a field on the form, you have two options:

- You can move the field on its current tab by highlighting the field with a click and then dragging it up or down the page with the right mouse button depressed

- You can click on the **Save** and **Move Elements** button to place the field on a new tab altogether

These are some of the attributes that entry and transactions forms share, but there is also functionality specific to each form type.

Entry forms

While entry form customization is similar to transaction forms, there are a couple of small tricks to remember for custom entry forms.

First, if you want to have separate forms for leads, prospects, customers, and sub-customers, you can set these by the role, as we detail in our discussion of *Custom Roles*. There are obviously a lot of details about a lead/prospect/customer that are interesting to operations but not to sales, and vice versa. Setting your **Entity** form preferences by role is a nice way of managing the needs of different users. Keeping forms as simple and streamlined as possible is often a key point for sales managers, as they try to make using the system as easy as possible for their direct reports.

You can also set the lead, prospect, and sub-customer form preferences for the entire account, if you expect all of your users to use the same forms. Set the preferred **Lead and Prospect** forms at **Setup | Sales | Sales Preferences**. Set the preferred **Subcustomer** form at **Setup | Company | General Preferences**.

As we mentioned before, it's a good idea to remove as many fields and tabs as possible, by role. Keeping forms simple and easy to read makes the system, as a whole, much easier to adopt.

Transaction forms

If your organization supports more than one sales or purchase process, you may want to use **Linked Forms**. This allows you to link a transaction form to downstream transaction forms: quote to sales order, to item fulfillment, to invoice, for example, as seen in the following screenshot:

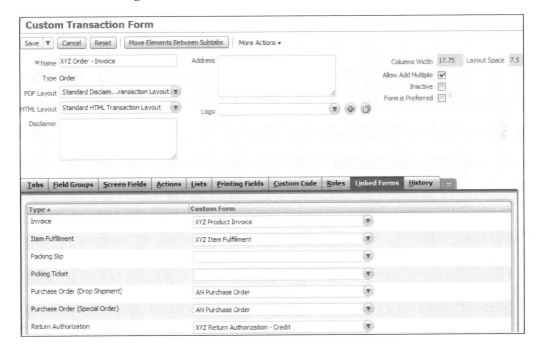

The system now knows what forms to bring up as your users click through transactions. You can tighten this up a bit more for your users by navigating to the **Roles** tab and making a particular form **Preferred** for some users.

Some companies have very large product catalogs and have different sales forces for different lines within their catalog. Other companies who assemble or kit may only want sales persons to see the finished products (not individual members), when they enter items on a sales form. To limit the catalog for any user, you can navigate to the transaction form, normally a quote or sales order form; under **Screen Fields | Columns**, there is a field called **Item Filter**. Set up a **Saved Search** on **Items** and it will appear in the list of values for this field, allowing you to limit the items a user of the form sees, for example, **Finished Assemblies**:

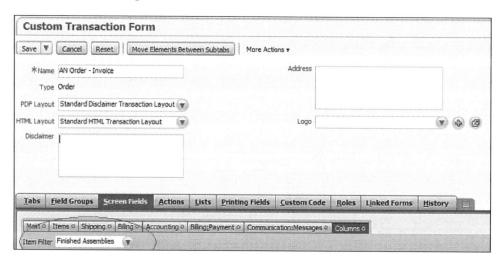

Forms and layouts for printing

So far, we have only discussed the forms in terms of online use. But, of course, the transaction forms also serve as the foundation of your printed documents that you send to partners, customers, vendors, and employees.

The transaction forms, as the one in this screenshot, have a tab called **Printing Fields**. Here, they organize the fields you want to print in four sub-tabs: header, footer, body, and columns. The header is the top-left of the page, including your logo, name, address and contact information, and the customer's address. The body is the top-right of the page and includes the document name and number, and any other information you deem appropriate from the transaction, such as the **Sales Rep** name. The columns include the items that were purchased or sold. The footer includes a customer message, discount, taxes, shipping, and so on. Below the footer is any disclaimer that you might need for the document.

Regarding the disclaimer, you need to first write it in an application such as notepad, in order to see how it will look on a printed page. Only then can you cut-and-paste it into the disclaimer field, at the top of the transaction form on which you want it to appear. Disclaimers take some careful tweaking to get them just right. If you need to include underlines for a signature and date, for example, then these usually require a few tries to perfect.

The important point here is that the transaction form is where you decide what fields you want on the document. The next step is to decide which of the PDF and HTML layouts you want to use, and then customize these until the printed document looks just as you want it.

We suggest that you start by configuring the transaction form printing fields first, and see how they display using one of the basic **Standard** or **Classic** layouts. Then navigate to **Setup | Customize | Transaction Form PDF Layouts**, to set the form layouts for printed or e-mailed documents. If you prefer HTML layouts, navigate to **Setup | Customization | Transaction Form HTML Layouts**, to customize your forms. In the following screenshot, we see the top-half of the delivered **Standard Disclaimer Transaction Layout** form just as we begin the customization:

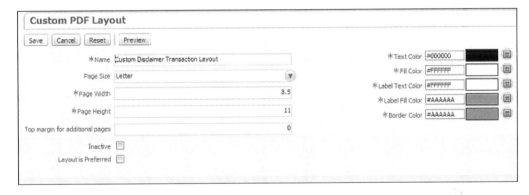

In these fields, we can set a lot of the basic information about the form, such as size and colors. The fields are self-explanatory.

The more challenging fields on the form are on the bottom half, as seen in the next screenshot. As your cursor rolls over the form elements on the right, it changes to four arrows and gives you the ability to move the elements about the page. Also notice that, when you click on an element, OneWorld outlines it and places a small gray box at the lower-right corner.

You can use this box to change the size of the element. Once you click on an element, you can also alter it by changing any of the fields in the editor on the left side of the form, as shown next:

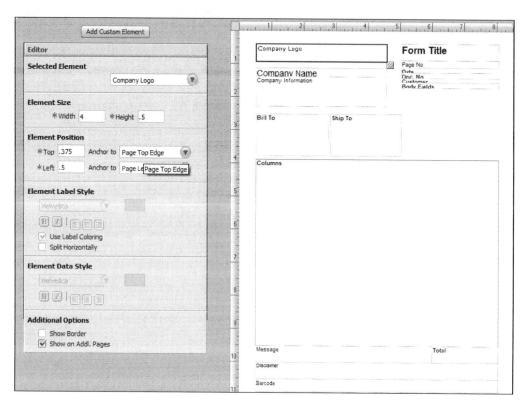

One note we'll mention is that while the drag-and-drop functionality is great, when you want to get your layout exact, it's sometimes easier to use the **Element Position** fields to line up your elements. Also, if you want to remove an element completely from your form, for example the barcode, you can drag-and-drop to move it to an unused area of the form and then make it into a single point using the element sizing function.

When you have custom information that you want to place on the form, you can **Add Custom Element**. This feature allows you to generate a new and configurable element for any field that was not available for adding to your **Printing Fields** on the transaction form setup. Custom elements are often added under the **Body Fields**.

Configuring custom roles

After custom fields, records, and forms are 80 percent complete, you can start to configure your custom roles. Invariably, it will take custom roles to help you manage your business processes, based on how you divide your business functions today. You manage all of your OneWorld security with custom roles, meaning that you allow or disallow access to records, based on role permissions. The best way to get a handle on the current division of labor is to set up a matrix, as shown in the following sample:

Purchasing	VP Operation	Purchasing Manager	Customer Service	Warehouse Manager
Enter Vendors				
Enter Items				
Manage BOMs, Kits, Groups				
Generate PO				
Receive Physical Inventory				
Receive Inventory in Systenm				
Check Quality				
Stock Inventory				
Return Material to Vendor				
Package Returns				
Enter Vendor Credit				
Apply Vendor credit				
Bill Purchase Orders				
Enter Bills				
Pay Bills				
Take Physical Inventory				
Enter Inventory Adjustments				
Close Purchase Orders				
Customer Service				
Receive Service Requests				
Assign Cases to Service Reps				
Schedule Installation				
Schedule Service Calls				
Manage Case Closure or Escalation				

Obviously, this is only an example of a much larger spreadsheet, but the point is that before you start designing roles, you really need an 'inventory' of who does what in the organization. After you sort things out here, moving into OneWorld and customizing roles becomes a lot easier. This exercise might also help to accelerate some of the change management that any organization undergoes when it installs a new ERP system. Also, both the rows and columns will change for your business and organizational model; add the current titles/roles in your organization into the column header row to get started.

In many cases, you will see a crossover in some areas. For example, Operations and customer service often both have the need to manage cases. Once you have an idea of what functions a role needs, you'll be able to make a judgment call on what delivered role to begin with, as you start to customize roles. In most cases, your custom roles start with a standard role.

Once you have a general idea of what role each user needs, the second step that we recommend, before you start the detailed work of customizing roles, is to give access to the standard roles to your primary users during your first prototype testing and let them use the standard roles as they are defined. This will bring up some interesting requirements. Use these requirements to hone the roles until users find that have just what they need and nothing more.

To get started on the process of customizing roles, let's take a look at the commonly-used **Sales Person** role as an example.

Security for sales persons differs markedly by organization. Sales ownership of customer and transaction records, and what sales persons can view, update, or initiate from a customer's records are just a few of the options that must be taken into account. For sales roles based on the Sales Center, there are also a couple of important security features at **Setup | Sales | Sales Preferences**.

First, the preference **Standard Sales Roles** offers us three options for managing how the delivered standard roles behave. Since most organizations using OneWorld opt for custom roles, we'll just mention that if you want to stay with the delivered sales center roles, these options work fine. If you need to change anything in the delivered roles, such as limit them to specific subsidiaries, then this preference is not going to help you.

Second, the preference **Restrict by Transaction Sales Rep Only** is useful if you want to allow a sales rep to see only the sales transactions they initiated on their customer's record, not transactions initiated by another sales rep. If your sales team has access to customer records on which they are not listed as the sales rep, and they can initiate new sales transactions with the customer, then this preference makes sense for your organization. If, on the other hand, a sales person only sees their own customers and handles all of the transactions for their customers, then this preference does not help you.

The next step is to customize the role itself. The following is a screenshot of the delivered sales person role, which serves as a foundation for our custom role:

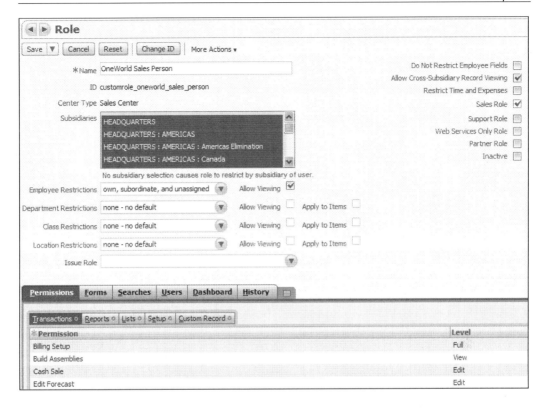

Give the role a name but make sure that, between the name and the ID, you note the standard role with which you started the customization process. As with the forms, it becomes important over time to know how you started your customizations as you move to make new forms and roles for your ever-changing organization.

The **Center Type** is not changeable for roles built from a standard role. If the center of a standard role does not work for your organization, you must either select a different standard role with a different center or go to the next section on custom centers.

Select the **Subsidiaries** to which this role has access. This is a multiple-select field, so you can select more than one. You must select each individual subsidiary to which you want the user of the role to have access, meaning access to the customers and vendors of the subsidiary and their transactions. If you also want to provide view-only access to the records of other **Subsidiaries**, check the **Allow Cross-Subsidiary Record Viewing** checkbox, on the right-hand side of the form.

There are then several ways of restricting the role further: employee, department, class, and location. Each of these restricts access to some entity records, transactions, and possibly item records, based on records that have these fields. The **Employee Restrictions**, for example, also restricts access to customer records, when the customer record has an employee sales rep link.

There are four options for each of these restrictions, from the default and least restrictive **none – no default** to the most restrictive **own and subordinates only**, so you have a good deal of leeway here.

Take a normal sales team of a products company, with geographic representation across Australia and roughly 20 members, including managers. They assign new leads, by territory and industry category, with some members selling to 'for profit' companies and others selling to universities and hospitals. They all have the same subsidiary. They all have large sales funnels, so, to keep the reps focused on their own sales, they limit the customer and transaction records that they view and edit to their own.

The setup for this sales role is fairly straightforward. We customize the standard sales person role and create an Australia Sales Person role. We restrict the role to the Australian subsidiary and, on the **Employee Restriction**, we select **own and subordinates only**. With no further setup, this role allows the user to view and edit their own and any subordinate's customers and transactions. When we add **Allow Viewing**, we can now view (but not edit) the other sales person's customers and their transactions; and when we add **Allow Cross-Subsidiary Record Viewing**, we can also view the customers of other subsidiaries and their transactions.

Sales line managers of the Australian subsidiary have similar role security, with a small change to the **Employee Restriction** of **own, subordinate, and unassigned**, in case a new lead comes into the system and does not get routed to a sales rep automatically.

A new position opens for a **National Sales Manager** (NSR), who oversees a product line that is sold to both 'for profit' companies, hospitals, and universities. The organization uses a matrix model to accommodate the national sales manager, allowing reps to roll up to their sales manager supervisor, but in some sales to the NSR. In order to manage their product line across the country, the NSR needs access to all employees, partners, and transactions that are tagged with the **Class** of this product line, even though the employees are not his subordinates. To manage this model, we set up a sales role with the **Employee Restriction** set to **none – no default**, while setting the **Class Restrictions** to **own and subordinate only**. Now, the NSR views and edits only the records of employees who share their class, for example, only the sales transactions tagged, by the sales rep with the correct class.

After setting the role view and edit restriction, we turn to the **Permissions** tab in the lower half of the form, under which are five lists, where we further define the role's security in great detail.

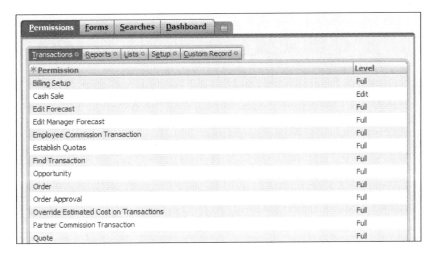

The first list is **Transactions**. When you start with a standard role, and (again) each standard role links to a **Center Type**, you have a starting point for the **Transactions** normally associated with the role. Each transaction allows you to select the **Level** of security: **View**, **Create**, **Edit**, or **Full**. **View** is simply view-only, while **Create** gives the role the ability to create a transaction, but not edit. With **Edit**, they can both create and update, and with **Full** they can create, update, and delete. Obviously, you need to be very careful about handing out the ability to delete to your employees.

Setting up transaction permissions is often of interest to the CFO, who needs to make sure that there are some auditable controls set up in the system. Providing the correct transaction permission at the right level can prevent the same user from entering, altering, paying, and deleting a vendor bill, for example.

The permissions themselves are fairly self-explanatory, but we should mention that if you do not find what you are looking for on the **Transactions** tab, then you should take a look under **Lists**, where many of the data objects and other functionalities of OneWorld are exposed. For example, if you want to allow a role to see a customer's or vendor's financial transactions from the entity's record, you need to add **Financial History** to the role.

After making changes to a role, it is sometimes necessary to log out of OneWorld, clear your browser's cache and then log back in to see the changes.

If, after working on the **Permission** lists, you still cannot find the functionality that you want for a role, then there is another angle to take. Under **Setup | Users/Roles | Show Role Differences**, you can compare two roles, one of which, of course, has the functionality you want to add to the other.

After you complete the **Permissions**, you must also visit the **Forms** tab to make sure the role has access to the correct forms. Giving access to a transaction also gives the role access to the forms required for that transaction; however, if you have custom forms and you want to enable them for this role, you can do that on the **Forms** tab. A form that has been **Enabled** can then be made **Preferred**, and a role can then be **Restricted** to a **Preferred** form. Again, there would be three levels of security. A note of caution on **Forms** restrictions and custom forms: make sure that if you have linked your custom forms together (for example, a custom quote to custom sales order to custom invoice), you have enabled all of the forms in the chain for roles that require them.

The **Searches**, **Users**, and **Dashboard** tabs mainly tell you what access to searches and dashboards you have provided to this role, or which users have this role. Providing access to searches and dashboards is normally done at publication, a function that we discuss in *Chapter 10, Data Analysis*.

Developing custom centers

If the delivered center types, such as the accounting center or sales center, do not meet your needs, you can develop your own centers or simply customize the delivered centers. In the next screenshot, we set up a new center, added it to a new role, and the following:

- A custom tab: **Fulfillment and Service**
- Three new categories: **Orders**, **Fulfillment**, and **Installation**
- A custom link: **Fulfill Orders**

All of these options are available at **Setup | Customization**. As is normal, if you want to start from scratch, you first start with the lowest level of development, in this case **Center Links**. This allows you to add links to custom forms, for example. Truth be told, the **Fulfill Orders** link did not have to be custom; all of the links used in delivered center types are available to be added to custom categories. The delivered categories are also available to be added to your custom tabs, and delivered tabs are available to be added to your custom center. Your takeaway here is that custom centers can actually be built by using a lot of the pieces OneWorld delivers. Your options here are many:

- Customize a delivered center that simply adds an additional tab with several delivered categories. For example, you can add a custom tab, such as **Assemblies,** to the **Sales Center**, with a custom **Assembly** category, based on the delivered **Build Assemblies** link.

- Add a new category to a delivered center and tab. For example, if sales persons need to track the progress of their customer's assembly, you can add an **Assembly** category to the delivered **Sales Center | Customer** tab, using the delivered **Build Assembly** link. (In this case you must also add the **Build Assembly** transaction permission to the sales role, with **Level - View**.)

- Create a new center type, for example, a combination warehouse and customer-service role: a custom **Center** of custom **Center Tabs**, with custom **Center Categories**, based on delivered and custom **Center Links**.

There are, obviously, a lot of possibilities to build a custom user interface, and you can use a lot of the delivered system to make the job easier and quicker. Keep in mind that, before you begin, you must have a detailed layout of exactly what you want the end result to look like (each tab, category, and link, as well as the dashboard portlets you want on every tab), or else the job becomes confusing very quickly. Also, you must synchronize the permissions of the role, using the new center, with the links you set up on the center.

Designing new workflows

We have already seen several workflows throughout the previous chapters. For example, we have seen that a sales order with a drop ship item, once approved, generates a purchase order. This process can be generally described as a workflow as it kicks off actions, generates records, and makes decisions, all based on the approval of a sales order.

In 2010, NetSuite introduced in its products, including OneWorld, a new customization tool called Workflow or SuiteFlow, allowing users to initiate their own automatic workflows in the system, based on business needs. We take a closer look at the functionality of workflow in a couple of simple examples. The goal at this point is to introduce you to the workflow functionality and some of the thinking that will help you to design your own workflows.

The first example is a simple-action workflow, adding a new record to OneWorld each time we add a new lead to the system, or when a lead completes an online lead capture form. The business case here is that marketing wants to know when a new lead has been added to the system, but has not been contacted promptly by sales. It is sometimes difficult, in OneWorld, to report on what has not happened; so, when we add a new lead record to the system, the workflow generates a phone call record for the lead. Over time, we can look at a report of phone calls that have not been completed, or that do not have notes added by sales, and get a good idea of whether or not new leads are being handled efficiently and effectively by sales.

The following screenshot shows the basic setup of our workflow:

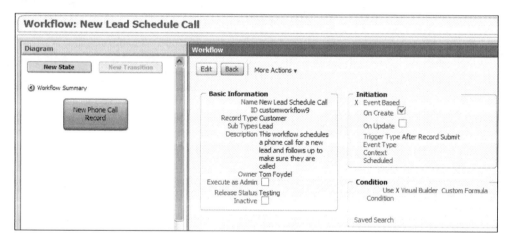

We set up the basic information first, telling the system that we want this workflow to run on **Record Type: Customer**, specifically **Sub Type: Lead**. We initiate the workflow **On Create** of the new lead record, and it triggers **After Record Submit**; we initiate for all new leads, without any conditions.

We click on **New State** to generate our single state and set it up as follows:

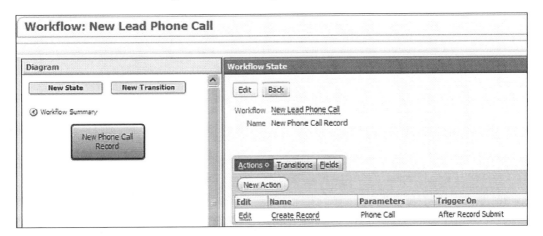

When we click on **Edit**, on our state, we see the details of what we set up and how it's going to work:

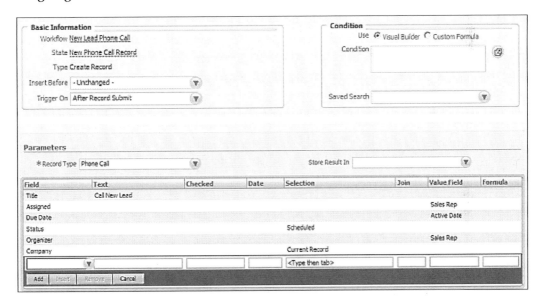

You can see that we are going to create a new phone call record after we submit the lead record. We are defining some of the fields for our new phone call record, including to whom it is assigned – the sales rep from the lead record – and the status of the phone call record. The sales person who uses their activities dashboard can now see this newly-scheduled phone call and respond.

We assume that we have lead routing to sales persons through territories set up already, in order to make this workflow successful. We also assume that we are going to write an activity search or report that tells us when a lead record was created and the status of the phone call record.

Key takeaways here are that workflows require a very specific business case. You need to ask the following questions before you start to set up the workflow:

- What initiates the workflow?
- What changes when the workflow runs?
- At what point do the changes take place?
- What decisions are made during the workflow?
- What is the output of the workflow?
- What business value does the workflow provide?

In order to work properly, workflows must be part of a larger solution that often requires setups in other modules that are complete and working properly, such as lead routing and sales territories, in this example.

Using workflow with other customizations

In the next workflow, which is slightly more complex, we combine workflow with our previous customization—adding the ability to generate a case directly from a sales order. The business case here is that, when we sell a product unit, we need to arrange installation with the customer after delivery. Then operations wants to survey the customer on the efficiency and quality of the installation. In this workflow, the new case record inherits data from the sales order. Then we monitor the case record and, when it closes (when we complete installation), we send a survey to the customer asking them to rate the installation. We only want the workflow to run on new cases generated directly from the sales order. Summarized, our requirements, as follows:

- Initiate the workflow for new cases generated from the sales order
- Have the new case inherit data from the sales order where possible
- Make the **Contact** and **Email** fields on the case mandatory
- Email the customer on the need to schedule installation, with a link to update the case with a date convenient to them
- Follow up installation with an e-mail and link to an installation customer survey

In the first step, we set up the workflow definition, as shown:

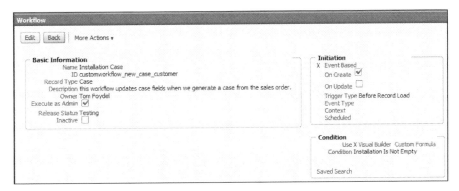

We identify the **Record Type** that we want to run the workflow on—**Case**. We initiate the workflow **On Create, Before Record Load**, and it triggers the **Before Record Load**.

Also, keep new workflows in **Release Status**: **Testing** during initial setup. This allows you to see a log of what's happening on the workflow when it fires on the target records.

Our addition of the custom CRM field **Installation** to **Case** added the sales order number to the case, but only when we generated the case from the sales order. Our **Condition** tells the workflow that we only want the workflow to run when the case field **Installation** is not empty. This prevents the initiation of the workflow from a case generated in the normal customer service process.

This workflow, again, has several states, as seen in the left-hand panel, in the following screenshot:

Also, notice that we customize the workflow field to hold the value of a campaign response.

Let's walk through how these states and transitions work:

1. The first state, **Update Case Fields,** saves the user time by populating the case with data from the sales order. We also send an e-mail to the customer contact to arrange a time for the installation. The last action of this state is **Subscribe to Record – Case Status**. When the **Status** of the case changes to **Closed,** we **Transition** to the second state.

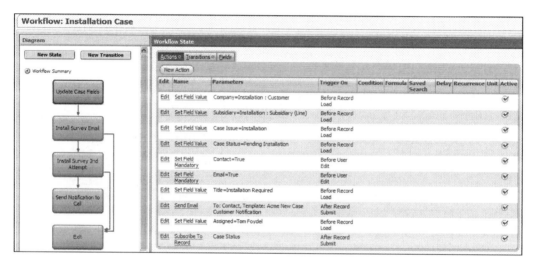

2. In the second state, we send an e-mail, part of a marketing campaign, to the customer, asking them to fill out our online customer survey about the installation and providing a link. We store the response in our custom workflow field, so we know when the customer clicks on the link.

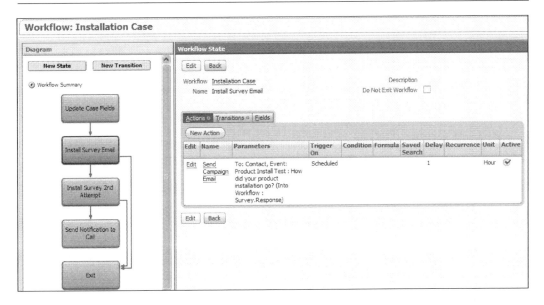

3. If there is no response after seven days, we transition to the next state and send the e-mail request again. Once the customer responds to the e-mail, we exit the workflow. If the system finds no response after another seven days, we send a notification to the assigned customer service rep to call and take the survey over the phone.

In this workflow, we brought together several customizations and native built-in records and functions to shape a single workflow. This is why we often wait until the last weeks of the project to set up our final workflows. However, if we know, at the outset, that we need a workflow in order to achieve an important business objective, then it's a good idea to capture the business case early on, so that we keep in mind the data and functions that we need to set up the workflow later.

In the same vein, we often recommend to clients that they hold off on workflow configuration until a second phase of the project. In this scenario, we complete the configuration and the absolutely required customizations of OneWorld that take us through: a second prototype, a testing phase with users, data migration, training, and then go-live. Once we settle the system and the business down, after a couple of weeks, we launch a second phase, which focuses on reporting and workflow enhancements. When users and managers have a better understanding of daily life with the new system, their needs often change markedly and they are more apt to make good choices when it comes to where the organization will focus resources for OneWorld enhancements.

Summary

This chapter was an introduction to the many ways that OneWorld allows users to customize their account through advanced configuration. When you think about all that we covered in this chapter, you should be surprised that we still have not had to write any code at all. Everything that we did was all custom configuration: no JavaScript required! For those of you who have worked with other systems, some just a few years older than OneWorld, this will be astonishing news.

With the new workflow builder, the need for code has lessened even more. Now, you can construct some very interesting workflows for your organization in very little time and without computer language skills.

One important note that we must add here is that the advanced configuration we presented in this chapter has one often-overlooked advantage over custom code—it is much more resilient than code and, therefore, causes far fewer problems over time. Business users often don't understand how much effort custom code requires, not only in the initial writing and testing, but in the constant upkeep and maintenance. Every time you replace custom code with configuration, you make a true contribution to the long-term mental and financial health of your organization.

Now that we have the discussion of system configuration behind us, we can turn to **Data Migration**. We often start the process of gathering information about the data migration very early in the implementation, because some of this information guides us as we move forward. But the actual loading of data into OneWorld normally waits until after the configuration is nearly complete, since we want to include as many of the data fields as possible for every record that we load.

9
OneWorld Data Migration

Data migration, defined as the task of moving data from its current home into OneWorld, can be a very time-intensive project task and one that requires some specialized knowledge to perform adequately. In some (or even most) cases, depending on your business model, data migration is also a one-time event. The data objects you might move include customers, vendors, the chart of accounts, the Item catalog, and transactions.

Migration is just one flavor of data integration. We import data as part of data migration, though we also import data for many other reasons. This brings us to a decision point quite early in our discussion: If you are not going to import data into OneWorld on a regular basis, does it make sense to learn data import tools and technical details? Only you can make this decision, but here are listed some of the ways that OneWorld customers often use data migration in ongoing data import efforts, well after they complete the implementation:

- Importing lists of trade show attendees
- Importing transactions from another system
- Updating transactions that are in OneWorld, but completed in another system, for example, sales orders that are invoiced from a third-party system
- Importing financial results from a third-party general ledger
- Importing vendor price lists
- Importing budgets

If you see that you are going to use the data import functions of OneWorld after the implementation, then it probably makes sense for your organization to learn these skills. Otherwise, if data migration is the only reason to understand data import, then you might seriously consider using a third-party application for your migration needs.

For the purposes of this chapter, we focus our discussion primarily on OneWorld's **Comma Separated Value (CSV)** file import tool. There are other ways of migrating data using NetSuite's web services API, or application programming interface, as you would for a OneWorld integration with another system. But, for most OneWorld customers, at least some of the data that they migrate during the implementation comes through the data import tool.

There are several considerations to the data migration task, listed as follows:

- What records and fields we need to import
- When we need to import the records in the context of the project plan
- Where the source data comes from and in what shape we'll find it
- Why we need to import each record type
- How we need to prepare records and files for import
- How much volume we expect to import for each record type

Basic information about the legacy data is very important to understand, in order to manage the migration process successfully. In this chapter, we want to cover not only the physical migration of the data but also how it fits into the overall implementation, and the business analysis skills required to manage the process successfully. We cover the following topics in detail:

- Data migration in the implementation
- The data migration spreadsheet
- Data scrubbing
- Using internal and external IDs
- The import tools
- Importing transaction records

Data migration in the implementation

The OneWorld implementation is obviously the first time you import data into OneWorld. Let's take a look at how the imports happen in relation to other implementation tasks.

First, there is a normal progression for data migration, based on data and implementation dependencies. The main tasks look like the following:

- Confirm and configure your subsidiary's structure.

- **Taxes**: If you sell taxable items, then set up your taxes now.

- **Chart of Accounts**: This is the first import to complete and brings to a head your discussions of how the organization wants to operate financially. A new OneWorld account has several of the basic accounts. Your easiest way forward is to set up the delivered accounts manually and then import your other accounts as an **Add** or **Update**. Also, the tax setup generates accounts which you must complete with the correct name, rollups, and so on.

- **Vendors**: After you import the COA, you can add a default expense account to your vendor file and import it.

- **Items**: Some items depend on vendors being set up; all items for sale, resale, or purchase depend on the COA.

- **Employees**: Other imports require sales reps, project managers, and so on.

- **Partners**: Same as *Employees*.

- Leads and Contacts.

- Prospects and Contacts.

- Customers and Contacts.

- **Inventory**: If you need to add inventory items to a transaction, then you must add enough inventory to the system to cover your transactions.

- **Transaction History**: Some companies have requirements to load the history of certain transactions, in the form of invoices, for example. This is a complex and time-consuming undertaking, but it might prove worth the effort, in some circumstances.

- **Open Payables and Open Receivables**: At some point in the implementation, you mark a date on the calendar as the go-live date, meaning that, after this date, you enter all new transactions in OneWorld. To prepare for this date, you enter all of your open payables and receivables as of that date. You can enter open items into the system before or after the go-live date, of course.

- There may also be some closed items that need input. For example, paid invoices with revenue recognition, or paid bills with amortization, need to be input with their current, unrecognized balance to establish their schedules for ongoing recognition or amortization.

- After you enter all the transactions that you require, you clear the books by running a **Trial Balance** report for each period and entering a journal that backs out the effects of all of the transactions for the period.

- At this point, you can enter your beginning balances at a point in time, for example, last period of the prior fiscal year. Then, enter net activity for each month, until the go-live month. Your books are up to date now and if you run a balance sheet, an income statement, or other financial reports the numbers should match your legacy system.

This is just a general outline of the data migration path and how and where it intersects with the overall OneWorld implementation project.

The data migration spreadsheet

After the initial discussion of how your organization wants to use OneWorld, the next step is to put together a data migration spreadsheet. The basic outline of the spreadsheet we have in mind is shown in the following screenshot. The columns answer specific questions about the data you migrate, while the rows represent specific records that you need to migrate. The details of your spreadsheet probably differ from the one shown next, but hopefully this is a start:

Data Record	From System	Volume	% Valid	Projected Import Date	Export Date	Add Data
Lead						
Prospect						
Customer						
Contact						
Non-Inventory Items						
Service Items						
Inventory Items						
Matrix Items						
Assembly Items						
Opportunities						
Estimates						
Sales Orders						
Fuflments						
Invoices						
Vendors						
Purchase Orders						
Receipts						

A few of the columns, here, deserve additional explanation. **From System** refers to the system in which the data currently resides. There are cases of some records where the answer might be NA (or not applicable), such as in the example of an organization using a OneWorld record that they have not used in the past. Also, a spreadsheet is not a system in itself; but, if the data does reside in a spreadsheet, get a copy of it and put it into a shared directory for the project with the address, here, as a marker. Migrating data from spreadsheets is not uncommon.

Volume is an important factor, since setting up the migration files is time consuming and it doesn't make sense to spend a lot of time doing the necessary setup for low-volume records that are easier to key in manually.

The next column, % **Valid**, asks what percentage of the records is good, meaning useful, without a lot of extraordinary effort. If you have 10,000 lead records, you need to think about whether you want all of them in the new OneWorld database, especially if some are several years old and are probably out of date. The key understanding you should take away from this column is how much effort in data scrubbing is required to get to some useful data.

The next two columns concern the project plan. When you determine the import date, based on business needs and contingencies, you then determine the export date. There are several approaches here. If you have a record type that grows quickly, you may need to take the export as close to the OneWorld go-live as possible. However, if you need to scrub the data hard, to put it into a presentable shape, then you might take a first export early in the project with a time stamp, scrub the data, and then take a second export later of only the new records.

In other cases, you might have a record type that's very stable, in which case you could plan to get this out of the way before the time crunch at the end of the project. Employee records are a good example here.

Other records simply have to go in early, as a matter of system configuration. The first file is always the **Chart of Accounts** (COA), followed closely by vendors and the Item catalog. Item catalogs depend on the COA, and your second prototype depends on the Item catalog.

Finally, **Add Data** refers to the need to add additional columns of data to your records. This happens when you decide to add functions in OneWorld that you have not used in the past. For example, you might decide to use customer category as one of the lead routing rules, so that OneWorld routes leads to different sales people working in manufacturing companies and hospitals. If you need to add the customer category to every lead record in the system, then make a note here, since this will take time and a broad understanding of your system decisions to execute.

Finally, our screenshot does not include a column for 'Why,' but it's useful to answer this question even when it seems academic, as the more rocks you turn over, the more useful information you'll recover from your discussion.

Data scrubbing

The most important step in data scrubbing is having business users hand over the data in some format to you, as early as possible. There are several things to keep in mind here. First, the same record type might exist in more than one source. Make sure that data owners understand that you want to see all of the leads, not just the ones in the sales spreadsheet, but the ones in the marketing system, and others in the website's database. Second, keep track of who owns the legacy data. Data ownership indicates power, so owners eventually play an important role in the implementation. Data owners are often the people who have the most input on how the organization operates in OneWorld. They can help the implementation succeed. A good business analyst recognizes the organization's key operators and works to draw their input. Data owners are demanding, but they rarely lead you astray.

Each implementation sees wide variances in the quality of the data. In most cases, you can find fairly good data in regards to financial transactions. However, the further away from the financial transactions you go, the more data scrubbing you need to do. Lists of leads, for example, are often in poor shape and require real effort to massage into useful records. It's not uncommon even for the COA to have many defunct accounts, such as old bank accounts, loan payable accounts that have been paid off, and so on, or for the financial team to see an opportunity in the implementation to clean up and redefine some accounts. Make sure that users understand that data migration is time consuming and that you expect there to be real effort in making the data files clean.

Also, when you ask for the data files, a discussion breaks out. The act of handing over the data tends to focus the mind, so you obviously can't wait until the day you expect to receive the import files to start the discussion about the data. The sooner you ask for the data files, the sooner the discussion begins, and concludes.

Item files are always an area of concern. Most organizations generate items, based not only on what they buy and sell, but also on how they want to do business. As a result, OneWorld might offer different opportunities for efficient business processes and, consequently, the legacy Item catalog becomes outmoded.

When making changes to either the COA or the Item catalog, be clear about the consequences for other data migration files. If you end up loading a year's worth of monthly financial results in order to see year-over-year financial analysis, then you are going to need a mapping from a defunct account, if it had a balance, to some other account. Likewise, changes in the Item catalog are going to impact the import of sales orders, as an example, or open invoices. By the end of this chapter, you should have a very good idea where the dependencies in data migration exist and how to manage them.

The area that often requires the most time and effort for data migration is that of the lead/prospect and customer files. Many organizations have these records in multiple systems. The most complete customer records are normally in the financial system for B2B sales through invoices. For e-commerce business to consumer sales, the customer records are often housed in the shopping cart system. However, the organization likely has other systems that also house records for customers, as well as leads and prospects. Users need to make choices here to prevent a lot of duplicate records. Duplicate detection and merge after the import is a possibility, but we think that you will find the process very time consuming.

So, how does one scrub a data file? At the very least, data files need to have a header row that defines the content of each column. Obviously, all of the data in a column must be of the same type. Also, there are some fields in OneWorld that require the data in specific formats:

- Web Address: `http://www.sightlinesconsulting.com`; OneWorld requires the entire address, no shortcuts.

- Email address: `tfoydel@sightlinesconsulting.com`; the @ cannot be replaced with 'at' or anything else.

- **Currencies**: Look up your currency under **Lists | Accounting | Currencies**, and use the **Symbol** column.

- **Countries**: Look up your countries under **Setup | Company | Countries**, for example, **United Kingdom (GB)**.

- **States**: Lookup and/or set up your states under **Setup | Company | States/Provinces/Counties**, and use the **Short Name**.

- **Phone numbers**: All of the phone number fields are limited to 21 characters.

- **Addresses**: Every address needs to be broken into fields, such as **Addressee, Address Line 1, Address Line 2, City, State/Province/County, Country**, and **Postal Code**. If your address is a single line of text, then you have some work to do to set them up correctly.

- **Accounting and CRM Lists of Values**: For the values that you use in Accounting Lists and CRM Lists, you must have the exact matching values in your files. This is also the case for fields such as **Lead Source**, where your values must match the names of your marketing campaigns.

This is, of course, not an extensive list of every field in OneWorld but rather a collection of some of the common issues that we see on a regular basis.

Getting your data setup in spreadsheet CSV files can also be tricky in some cases. For example, if your phone numbers are simple long integers, then the CSV file might express `18775259280` as `1.88E+10`. Make sure that when you open the CSV, it has not actually changed the number. Also, if you must import a data field that has a number with a leading `0`, then you must change the column type to **Text**, to prevent the CSV file from dropping the `0`. Keep this in mind when opening and closing the file. Since CSV drops formatting on closing the file, it makes sense to work with the data in a true spreadsheet file and then, in the end, **Save As** a CSV file.

In other cases, legacy systems often save an employee, individual, or contact name as a single field. It's best when you import these to have first name and last name also. You have to use the functions in your spreadsheet program to accomplish some of this.

Once you think you have a file that can import, we recommend that you start with three to five records. Map the import and test. It's a lot easier to fix errors that you find in your test, than in the main file. After you have a small file that clears all hurdles and imports, go into OneWorld and look at the imported data. Sometimes, seeing the data in its imported form brings up some good questions. If your data passes this test, move on to a file of 50 records and try the import again. When you have an import created and saved, you can easily send through multiple files with little effort.

Once you have your import set and you are confident in your data, it's also a good idea to break down large files into smaller units, for ease of use. For large conversions, we always try to work on files of about 500 records. You are almost sure to throw some errors and it's a lot easier to fix three or four records than it is to fix, say, 175 or so. Plus, the system runs through smaller file sizes quickly, so you don't need to wait for long stretches for the import process to conclude.

It is not rare for OneWorld customers to require new columns of data added to extracts from the legacy system. Legacy systems come in all shapes and sizes and, as a result, the data from them often requires additional fields in the records. There are several ways to accomplish this.

If you need to marry records in order to update OneWorld correctly, it might be wise to use an external ID. This would allow you to easily update a record already in OneWorld by referencing its external ID, which you passed with the record's original load. Also, keep in mind that you can update records, once they are in OneWorld, by using the **Mass Update** tool, though there are constraints with the records and fields available for update.

Using internal and external IDs

We thought it might save you some real time, effort, and frustration to mention that you can use two types of IDs to handle some data import situations.

For example, we were once asked to load a client's employees into OneWorld. As a norm, we always include a value in the external ID field, since the cost of adding the field is zero and the benefits are often many. In this case, we took the primary key from the legacy system, and mapped it both into the employee number field and into the external ID. Later, the client asked if we could import the emergency contacts of the employees, a file that she had forgotten about. Since we loaded the employee's primary key from the legacy system into the external ID field of the system, we were easily able to marry the emergency contacts to our OneWorld records, through the external ID.

Legacy primary key and external ID

Our recommendation is that you load the legacy system's primary key into the OneWorld external ID for each record type you load. Should you need to update the loaded records later, you have a way to marry the legacy records to the records loaded into OneWorld.

The internal ID is an ID that OneWorld assigns to every record that you import, and to every record generated through the normal business processes. If you want to see the internal IDs that the system generates, then you need to navigate to **Home | Set Preferences** and click on **Show Internal IDs** under **General | Defaults**.

The value of the internal ID for the import process is that it allows you to make changes to OneWorld records that you have previously uploaded or generated in the system. We have seen instances where a client starts with CRM and then rolls out ERP some months later. As a result of this phased approach, they have many hundreds of transactions in the system without the proper department, class, and location. The most efficient solution is to query the records out of the system (based on some criteria) with the record's internal ID, then make changes in the file to add the necessary fields and, finally, to load the updated records back into the system, using the internal ID as the primary key.

We have also used the internal ID to correct errors in imports. For one client who inadvertently imported customer records with the wrong address, we used a custom search to extract the customer records, including the internal ID, and then load them back into the system with the **Advanced Option | Overwrite Checklists**, an option on the **Import Assistant** that was clicked so that our updated addresses were the only ones in the system after the update.

The import tools

The most common tool is the **Import Assistant**, found under **Setup | Import/Export | Import CSV Records**. The assistant walks you through a 5-step process to identify your import record, load your file, map the file to OneWorld, and then save and start the import.

In this first form, you select the record you want to update and then load your CSV file to OneWorld:

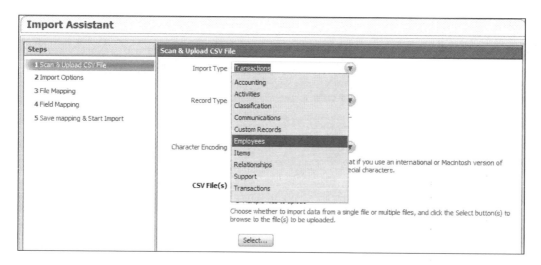

The **Import Assistant** supports several **Import Types** and, within some, there are several **Record Types**. For example, **Transactions** cover all of the transactions in the following screenshot:

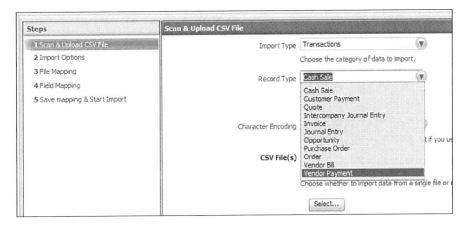

After selecting the import and record type, you can change the character encoding, if you are using a non-Windows machine and, more importantly, you can choose to either import a single file or multiple files.

It is possible, in many instances, to include all of the data in a single file, but, for those situations where you have two files of related data, you can import them together. This happens when you have a many-to-one relationship, as in, many contacts to one customer record. The best way to import multiple contacts for one customer is to split up the records into two files—one for customers and one for contacts—then set up your import, as shown in the following screenshot:

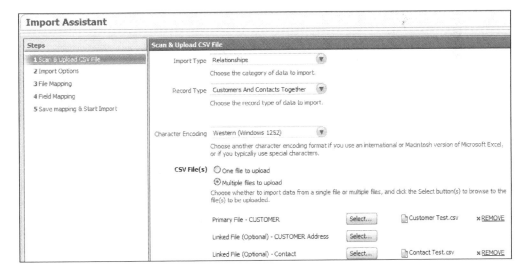

Here we are going to import **Customers** and **Contacts** together with **Multiple files to upload**. Our primary file is the customer file, as you would expect.

In the next step, we set up our import options and, under **Advanced Options**, we select the **Standard Customer Form**. At this point in the implementation, we may have started to customize our entity forms; however, it's often easier to import against the standard forms. If you have made fields for which you do not have data in the legacy system, your import will throw an error. This is just one example of the issues that can arise with custom forms.

Also, notice that as none of these records exist in the system, we select **Add**. If you need to alter an earlier import, select **Add or Update**; if you want to extract your current records from OneWorld (or take a past extract from legacy), make changes to the file, and re-import it, select **Update**.

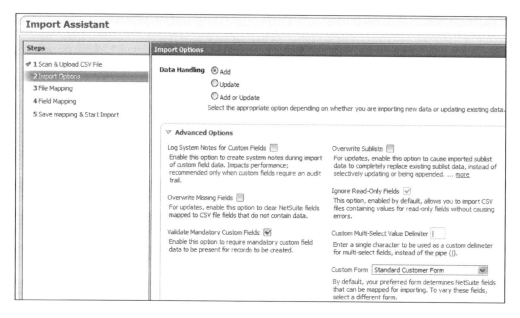

However, the two files must share a common ID so that the system knows how to relate the data. In our example, the import of **Customers** and **Contacts** as two separate files, OneWorld requires that you set up the following additional form, where you tell the system how the two files relate:

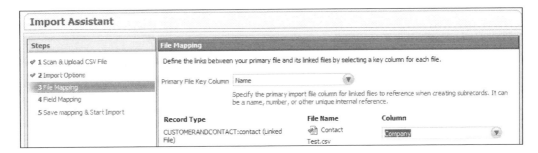

In the previous screenshot, we link the **Name** column in the customer CSV file to the **Company** field in the contact file. Keep this in mind because it affects the next form, where we map the columns in our two files to the OneWorld fields, as in the following screenshot:

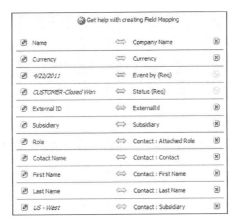

First, notice that we mapped our customer file **Name** column to the OneWorld **Company Name**. Since we do not have auto-numbering set up for our customer record, the **Customer ID** field is simply copied from the name, allowing us to map to the company name field.

Data imports and auto-generated numbers

In general, it's smart to turn off auto-numbering for entities, until after your imports are complete. This is so that, should you need to make changes to the imported data, it is now known in OneWorld by its number and not the entity name. Once you complete the import, you turn on auto-numbering and update the records. If, however, you would like to pass to OneWorld the customer's legacy **Name ID**, you must **Allow Override** on the auto-numbering form for the entity in question and probably make some changes to your import file, so that the **Name ID** matches what OneWorld generates on the entity form.

Second, we did not map the customer file **Name** field to the contact file **Company** field. We already did this in the previous screenshot, when we mapped the relationship between the two files. If you try to re-map this relationship here, the system throws an error.

Third, we mapped the subsidiary in two different ways. For the customer subsidiary, we simply mapped the values in our file column. To express these values correctly, look at a list of customers with the subsidiaries in OneWorld. In our case, the subsidiary value in the list is **HEADQUARTERS : AMERICAS : US – West**. This is how you must express the value in your file column, observing all of the spaces, colons, and so on. Alternatively, you can also select a default subsidiary, as we did for the **Contact Subsidiary**.

The legacy system also had a primary key for the customer record, so we mapped this into our **External Id**. It's really an insurance policy; in case you need to take a second legacy extract and update your OneWorld customers, this **External Id** helps you to marry files from legacy to OneWorld.

When you create custom fields and attach them to your form, even the standard form, the rules you used in the field's setup also apply to the import. As a result, the **Event By** field that we set up, for an earlier Suiteflow example, is now required.

The last step is simply to name and save your import. It's not a bad idea to save your imports even if you need to make small mapping changes later, for other files of like type. It can save valuable time.

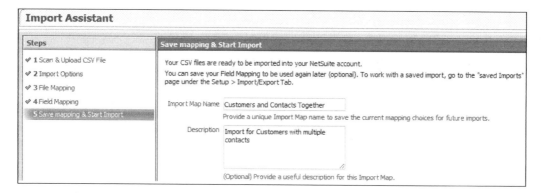

Other imports

There are several other ways of getting data into OneWorld. We don't need to go into great detail here, as the mechanics of these imports are fairly straightforward. But it would be a good idea if you knew that they are available:

- **Beginning Balances**: There is a special form under **Setup | Accounting | Enter Opening Balances** that allows you to enter debit or credit amounts by period or by subsidiary. It's not strictly an import, but a useful form for entering balances manually; we thought it should be mentioned.

- **Journal Entries**: Under **Transactions | Financial | Make Journal Entries | Import**, you can import a journal. There is a sample file to download that helps.

- **Project Tasks**: If you use Advanced Projects and Microsoft Project, you can upload your .mpp file to a project record. Find directions under **Activities | Scheduling | Project Tasks | Import**.

- **Commissions**: If you calculate some commissions outside of OneWorld but wish to import them to the commission module, click on the **Import** button on the **Commission Authorization** form, found at **Transactions | Commissions | Authorize Employee (or Partner) Commissions**.

- **Budgets**: This is especially helpful for companies with multiple budgets. Navigate to **Transactions | Financial | Setup Budgets | Import**.

- **Vendor Prices**: If you want to change the price of goods you purchase from a specific vendor, navigate to **Lists | Relationships | Vendors | Item | Import Price List**.

- **Update Prices**: If you need to update your sales prices, you can do it under **Lists | Mass Update | Update Prices**. Alternatively, you can export the items you would like to change, including the internal ID, make your changes and import items, using the internal ID as the primary key.

- **Order Fulfillment**: If you have a third-party logistics provider who fulfils your orders, you can receive a fulfillment CSV file from them and import it into OneWorld at **Transactions | Sales | Fulfill Orders | CSV Import** (it's a button on the top of the form).

- One feature, often overlooked in data migration, is the ability in OneWorld to **Direct List Edit**. There are times when you discover a small requirement late in the game and, in order to meet it, you must add something to your data. For many records, or if this is a small addition to a handful of records, the easiest way is to create a search for the records you need to change, and edit them right in the list. Certain conditions do apply, as they say—for example, some records may not be available for direct list editing—but, it's always worth a look.

Importing transaction records

We have primarily discussed entity record imports to this point, but, in recent releases, NetSuite added transaction record import capabilities to OneWorld.

The opportunity here is to bring over some important transactions from your legacy system. However, we would suggest that you think hard before you commit to importing historical transactions. There certainly are organizations that can make an excellent case for importing thousands of sales transactions. There's history in those transactions, which the organization really needs to see, in order to transact new business. But, bringing over historical transactions invites major problems when no need exists. When pressed on this point by clients, we often forestall a decision until we have a better grasp of the implementation project. Normally, the experience with simply configuring and customizing OneWorld is enough to help senior managers see that historical transactions have little value when compared to the really important tasks that the project demands.

At any rate, there will be some transactions to import, in all likelihood. Pending sales orders or sales quotes are good examples, as are purchase orders, unpaid vendor bills, and open invoices. Preparing to import any of these records really requires that you first understand all of the dependencies of the imported transaction.

In our example, we are going to import open invoices. We always start with a **Transaction** search of OneWorld; filters include **Type = Invoice**, and **Status = Invoice : Open**, **Main Line = Yes**. We assume here that you have done enough initial testing for you to have several open invoice transactions in the system. If not, you can always add a few transactions. Make sure that the transactions have a complete dataset, based on your implementation requirements. Of course, you can start with a file of legacy transactions, but our idea is to use something we know will work, then compare to the legacy records, and finally manipulate the legacy records to meet the import requirements.

Once you have a test list of transactions, export it to a spreadsheet and compare it to your current legacy system. Do the fields that you require match up? Do any fields require manipulation in order to match each other? For example, in the following search, notice how OneWorld expresses the **Period**. Your file needs to match this.

Subsidiary	Date ▲	Period	Tax Period	Number	Name	Amount	Billing Address 1	Billing Address 2	Billing Addressee	Billing City	Billing State/Province	Billing Country	Billing Zip
HEADQUARTERS : AMERICAS : US - West	2/12/2009	Feb 2009	Feb 2009	0106	Apeture : Nelson Software	21,565.00	123 Main Street		Nelson Software	San Mateo	CA	United States	94403
HEADQUARTERS : AMERICAS : US - West	2/12/2009	Feb 2009	Feb 2009	0107	Kendra Consulting	215,000.00	4500 Smith Avenue		Kendra Consulting	Tampa	FL	United States	50010

Invoice List for Import: Results Inline Editing **ON**

The next step is to take a second export that includes the line items and the column fields that we want to include on the real import later. Once we have these two test files, we're ready to try a transaction import in OneWorld using the **Import Assistant**, with a few small changes to make the records appear to be new records, for example, changing the invoice number.

We identify the two files; one, the main line of the invoice, and the other, the line items. We then link the two files using the invoice number field.

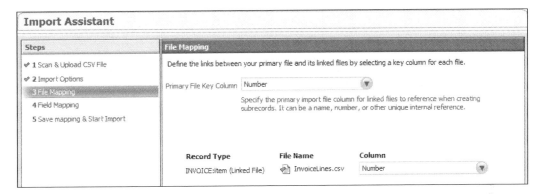

In the next step, we map the fields from both files to fields in OneWorld. Notice that we map a column in our file, labeled **External ID**, to the **ExternalId** field in OneWorld. The **External ID** can be a number from the legacy system, or it can be a number that you add to the spreadsheet as you ready it for import. In the next step, we are going to import **Customer Payments**, so we will need to identify the **Invoice** that we are making the payments against; this is done through the **ExternalId**.

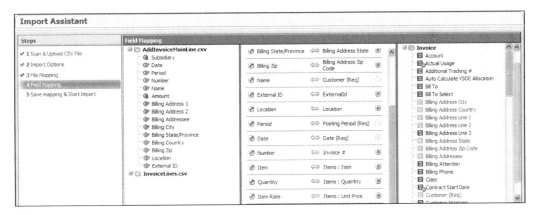

Also notice that there were a couple of fields that we did not need for the invoice import. OneWorld derives the **Subsidiary** field from **Customer**, so we do not need to include it in the file. Also, the **Amount** for **Invoice**, and the **Amount** for any line item are not necessary, as OneWorld does the math for us, using the **Quantity** and **Rate** from each line item.

After importing our invoice, we can also import customer payments. In the next screenshot, you can see how we have linked the payment to the correct invoice by using the invoice's **ExternalId** from the previous screenshot. (We also imported the **Payment ID** from the legacy system to the **ExternalId** of **Payment**. Don't confuse the two!)

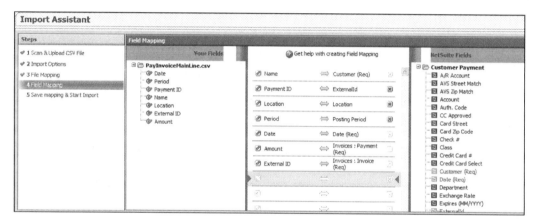

There are other prerequisites to take into account before you start the wholesale import of transactions. For example, if you import open invoices with inventory items, you must first enter an **Inventory Adjustment** to bring the inventory up to the levels you need. When OneWorld sees a transaction, such as an invoice without the **Created From** field populated, it assumes that there was no fulfillment, decrements inventory, and charges **Cost of Goods Sold** (COGS) on the invoice. So, the first thing you need to do is to manually generate a test of the transaction that you want to import in OneWorld, in order to understand what the dependencies are.

Finally, understand the final state of your transactions. For example, if you import a lot of sales orders, at some point, you must close the orders that never were fulfilled. This is itself another time-consuming task, whether you do it manually or import another file to do it.

Summary

The data migration portion of the OneWorld implementation stretches in the first few weeks of the implementation, when accounts are loaded, gets more involved in the middle of the implementation, and becomes of flurry of activity as you close in on your go-live. Along the way, have your data migration spreadsheet handy and keep a concise journal of where you are and the anomalies and challenges that you met. If you need to backtrack in time to understand what you imported and when, a well-maintained record is very important.

Above all else, test your data and your processes after you import. Make sure, first with small datasets and then with larger ones, that your records look correct and behave as you expect. Start a transaction for an imported customer and contact, and see if it works as you expect. Have you forgotten a custom field that you need for a workflow? Test an imported transaction to make sure that you can take it to the next step in its process. Can your sales order enter the fulfillment stage or become an invoice?

That you will meet with some frustration in the data migration work is a given. There is probably nothing that causes more gray hair among implementers than migration! We often remind ourselves that, at the end of the day, data is one of the simplest things ever created — just a collection of 1s and 0s. So, normally, the solution to data migration problems is just as simple, and often very difficult to see, as a result.

Hopefully, this chapter has also strengthened our case for an iterative and agile implementation. Most likely, not every record that you import will be perfect. Sometimes, you have to take more than one pass to get the data to the state you require. At the very least, the data migration spans the entire project and builds on itself.

Now that we have data in the system, we will discuss how to get data out in the form of reports, searches, dashboard **Key Performance Indicators (KPIs)**, and KPI Scorecards, in the next chapter.

10
Data Analysis

We present **Data Analysis** at this point in the book for the simple reason that you write the majority of the reports, the key performance indicators, and other data analysis queries towards the end of the project. Also, at this point, we have a good idea of what our data looks like in OneWorld, which is half the solution to any data analysis question. We also have enough data from testing the system that we can begin to look at data analysis in depth.

But while we do most of the work on new reports, **Key Performance Indicators (KPI)**, and so on, late in the project, we must consider reporting throughout the project, especially in the business requirement discussions around departments, classes, locations, and subsidiaries, as well as other key business differentiators. If we want certain data out of the system, then we need to make sure that we configure OneWorld with our requirements in mind.

There are several main tools for data analysis in OneWorld that we'll cover in this chapter. We can create custom queries that can be used in a variety of ways (on dashboards, on forms, for custom KPIs, and for data extracts to a spreadsheet). There is also a more traditional reporting tool for generating formatted reports. There is a financial reporting tool specifically designed for configuring financial reports for your organization. Finally, there is the KPI scorecard, where we compare KPIs, which has its own form, and we cover this as well.

Both the custom queries and the reporting tool come with a group of data objects (let's call it the metadata level) already defined for you, meaning you do not need to worry about making joins between tables, as these links have already been configured. The upside is that this saves you a great deal of time learning the database schema and, over time, OneWorld's metadata level has become fairly comprehensive. Most records and most fields are exposed to the analytical tools through this metadata level.

But if you discover that fields, records, or links that you want to report on are not exposed, then it's also worth mentioning that there is the **Open Database Connectivity (ODBC)** driver . The ODBC driver is a separate line item on your OneWorld invoice, but it allows you to define your own metadata level and generate your own reports, using a third party tool, such as Business Objects, for example.

After completing this chapter, you will have a good idea of what tool to use for each analysis requirement, as well as how to use each tool. We cover the following topics in detail:

- Lists, views, and custom searches
- Customizing standard reports
- Configuring new reports
- Custom financial reports
- Key performance indicators
- KPI scorecards
- Dashboard management

Lists, views, and custom searches

If you navigate to **Lists | Customers**, and click on **Customers**, then you will see a form similar to the following screenshot, showing a list of data, based on the values selected in the footer:

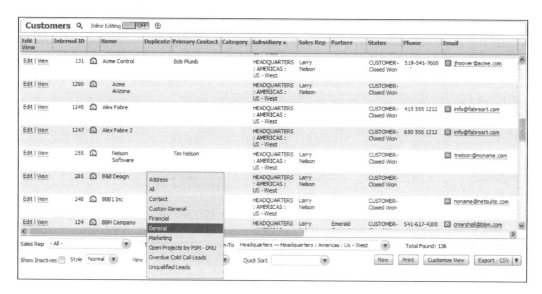

Notice that the list we are viewing is of a certain data type: **Customers**, and that there are several views of this data type.

We could also open up the **Search** form for customers and see something like the following form, where we are able to enter several search criteria in order to pull up a specific list of customers:

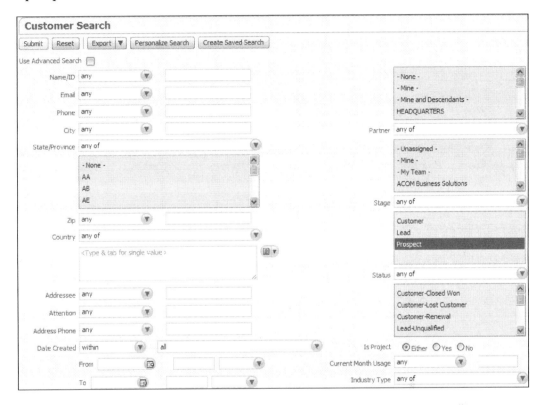

Notice the **Use Advanced Search** checkbox at the top-left of the form. When you click on this option, the form changes to the one shown in the following screenshot, allowing you to set up not only the search **Criteria**, but also the list **Results**:

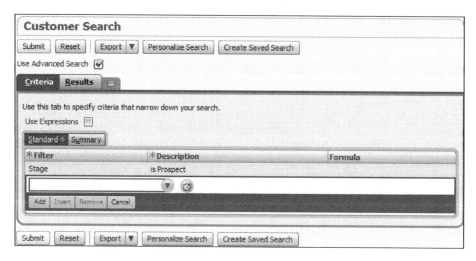

From this form, you can click on the **Create Saved Search** button, which brings up the full **Saved Customer Search** form, as shown in the following screenshot:

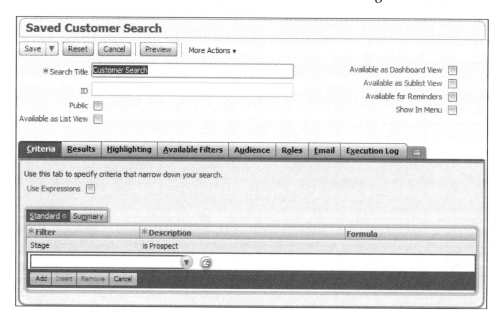

This is a roundabout navigation to create a new saved search. You can also do this from **Lists | Search | Saved Searches | New**. But our point here is simply to help you understand how the lists, views, and saved searches of OneWorld are related to each other.

To summarize, the **List** is the results of a search, and each **Saved Search** is for a specific data type, and each saved search represents a **View** of that data type.

In the previous screenshot, when we click on **Available as List View**, this saved search can be selected in the footer **View** drop-down whenever you are looking at a list of customers, for example. If we click on **Available as Sublist View**, we can select this search when looking at a list of customers on a form, for example, from the **Partner** form. We can also make the search **Available as Dashboard View**, if we want to see a **Custom Search List** on one of our dashboards, or to use it in our dashboard **Reminders**, we can make it **Available for Reminders**.

Every search is of a **Type**. When you start by navigating to **Lists | Search | Saved Search | New** to create a new saved search, your first choice is to select the type from a list, as shown in the following screenshot:

Search Type includes all of the records you are using in your OneWorld account, including **Custom Records**.

Customizing searches

The best way to get started with custom searches is to open up a search in the system and understand how it was configured. To do this, navigate to any list under either **Transactions** or **Lists**, and open it up. In the following example, we navigated to **Transactions | Purchases/Vendors | Enter Bills | List** to view a list of all of the vendor bills in the system:

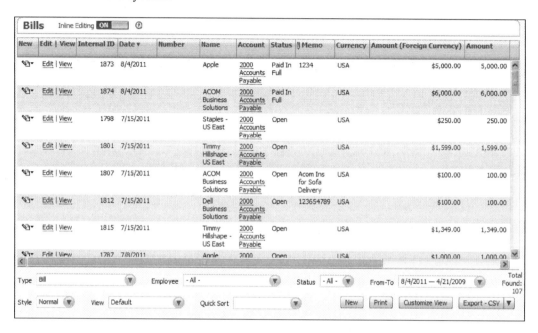

Now, to take a closer look, click on the **Customize View** button, which will open up the following form:

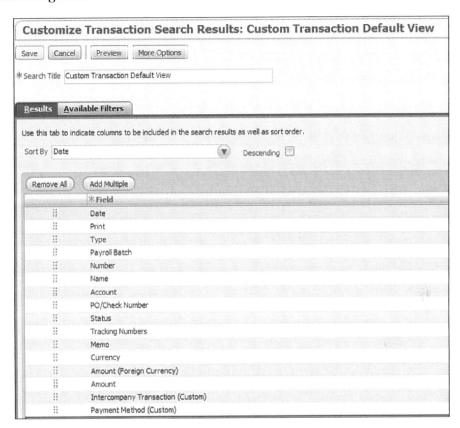

Here you can add additional search results or add additional filters to the footer of the search, in addition to **Employee**, **Status**, and **Type**, for example. Make your changes and click on **Preview** to check the result in the list. Then click on the **Return to Criteria** button from the list, and when you are happy, change the **Search Title** and click on the **Save** button.

If you want to add more criteria or change other aspects of the search, then you can click on **More Options**. This opens up the complete custom search form, with several additional tabs, as shown in the following screenshot:

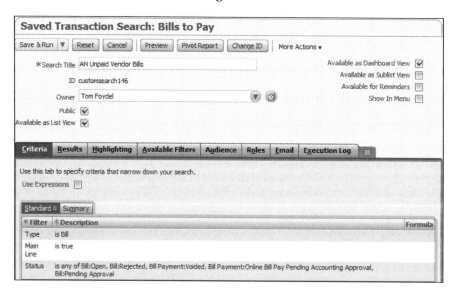

Let's note some basics about this form.

- **Preview Button**: Click the Preview button at any time during the configuration of a search to see the results your search returns. This button saves a lot of time and prevents you from going to far down a dead end.

  When you view the results you easily any issues with the search and then have the option to Edit the search and return to the setup page.

- **Pivot Report Button**: Press this button to see your criteria and results fields in the new pivot report tool. Using the drag-and-drop pivot report tool, you can then look at the data in various cuts and format it much like a custom report. (Currently in beta but definitely worth a long look.)

- **Header**: The system supplies a unique ID to each saved search, if you do not. **Public** is a quick way of making the search available to all users, whose role has permission to this data.

- **Criteria**: These are conditions of the search. In our example, you might select **Status = Open**, if you only want open vendor bills in your results. You cannot change criteria in the footer of the search on the fly, as you can for **Available Filters**.

- **Highlighting**: This tab gives the ability to highlight lines of your search, based on their meeting certain criteria, such as vendor bills over 1,000.00 dollars.

- **Available Filters**: These are the criteria that you add to the footer of your search and change on the fly.

- **Audience**: Allow a user or group of users to view the results or the search.

- **Roles**: Use this tab to enable or make the search preferred for your system roles—another reason why it's a good idea to configure custom searches and reports, after the bulk of the system has been set up.

- **Email**: On this tab, you configure the recipients of the results of the search and how they are notified through their e-mail. This is useful for setting up alerts on key events in the system.

- **Execution Log**: This is a useful tab, if you are trying to troubleshoot auto-e-mailing results or if you want to see who exported data from the system.

The **Criteria** of the search can be simple or complex, depending on your requirements. If you list more than one criterion, OneWorld simply assumes an '**And**' between them, so if you have three criteria, then X must be true, Y must be true, and Z must be true. If you want to construct a set of conditions that include an '**Or**,' click on the **Use Expressions** box. This adds additional columns to the criteria lines, so that you can place conditions into parentheses and use an 'Or' or an 'And' between them. You can also set up formulas to narrow your results, by selecting a **Formula** field in the **Filter** column. **Formula** combines SQL expressions, or functions, with OneWorld fields. In the following example, we want to find sales orders with a line item discount greater than or equal to 40 percent:

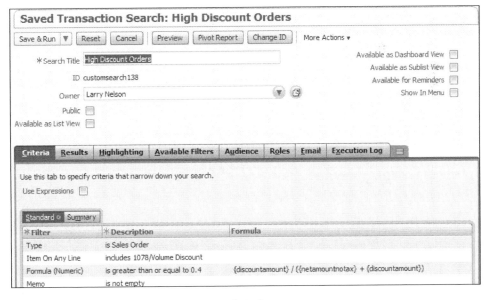

For more help on using formulas, there is a good help guide and also a list of available SQL expressions.

Main Line = Yes

If you are doing transaction searches, and you want to see only the totals for the transactions, and not every line item, then add **Main Line = Yes** to your criteria. The main line is the header of the transaction, and its inclusion in your criteria yields a search with one line per transaction.

The **Results** themselves are simply the columns of data that you see when you run the search. The available results for any search are the fields and related records that NetSuite has defined for this data type. The selection is not unlimited. After you scroll through the fields associated with the record type you are searching, you come to a list of associated data objects. These are more complex groups of fields that NetSuite has already linked to your record type, allowing you to broaden your search results. For example, if you are searching the vendor bills, you could use the **Applied To** record to add the purchase order the bill was applied to, and then add any fields from the PO, as shown in the following screenshot:

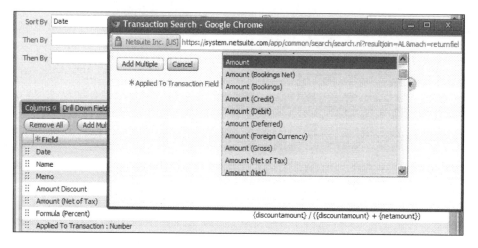

The data object we selected is the **Applied to Transaction Fields…**, where the three dots signify that this is not a single field, but a group of fields. Then you select a field from within this object, such as **Number** or **Amount (Debit).** You can set the conditions that the field must meet for the record to be added to the search. If you use a data object, such as **Applied to Transaction Fields,** for a **Criteria,** you can also set conditions as you would for any other field.

Time out

When building custom searches or reports, it's really a good idea to start by giving the new search or report a name and save it. If you get a phone call in the middle of your task, you then run the risk of having the system time-out your work. In which case, you must start over again.

There is some formatting available in the custom search tool. You can decide how to sort the records and you can **Show Totals**. But if you need the data formatted in more conventional ways, you really have two options: use the reporting tool or export your search to a spreadsheet and do the rest of the formatting there. In many cases, a custom search is used to aggregate raw data from the system, and further analysis is done in a spreadsheet.

Customizing standard reports

Like the custom search tool, the best way to learn the reporting tool is to start by customizing the delivered reports. This will shorten your learning curve dramatically. We use the **AN Sales by Sales Rep and Customer Summary** report to illustrate this idea.

First, notice that in the footer of the report, we have several options already available to us, should we need to see the report for other time periods, subsidiaries, or under the **Column** field, for any of our departments, classes, and location:

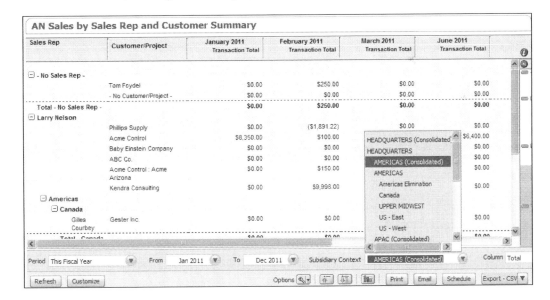

Summary reports are often matrix or columns within column reports, and they include an additional footer option called **Column**, as shown in the following screenshot:

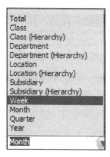

The point is that before you start customizing reports, it's worth your while to understand what's already available as a separate view of the same data. There are also some other choices under **Options**, and the green arrows allow us to collapse or expand the report on our groupings.

We want to add the customer name to our sales summary report, so we click on the **Customize** button and open up the **Report Builder** form, as shown in the following screenshot:

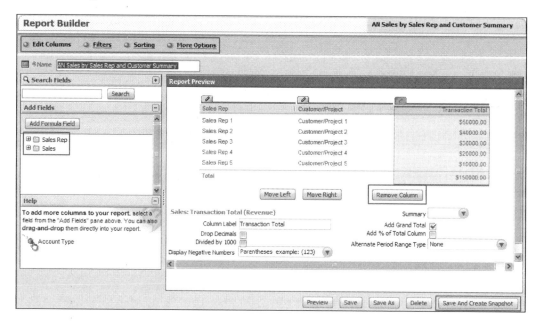

This form has a lot of functions, so let's go through them in detail:

- The report name is in the top-right corner, but can easily be changed in the left header region.

- There are four pages to this form: **Edit Columns**, **Filters**, **Sorting**, and **More Options**. (We are looking at the **Edit Columns** page; notice the term is not underlined.)

- In the left panel are the **Search Fields** and **Add Fields** regions. If you have an idea of the field you want, you can type a general search term, such as Amount and see a list of results. To return to **Add Fields**, you will need to open it up again by clicking the **+**. In either case, when you select a field by clicking on it, you see a **Help** definition appear below.

- Each report has a metadata layer defined for it. In this case, we have two main data objects: **Sales Rep** and **Sales**. Each of these contains many fields and many sub objects, which also contain many fields. For example, under the **Sales** object is a sub object called **Customer** (or **Customer/Project**, depending on your account). Within the **Customer** object are many fields relating to the customer record. Likewise, under the **Sales Rep** object, there are fields and sub objects.

- As we click on fields under **Add Fields**, new columns appear in the **Report Preview** to the right. We can remove columns or move columns simply by highlighting the columns and clicking on the **Move Left**, **Move Right**, or **Remove Column** button in the middle of the **Report Preview** form. Also, notice that currency fields present a number of other options for totals, and so on.

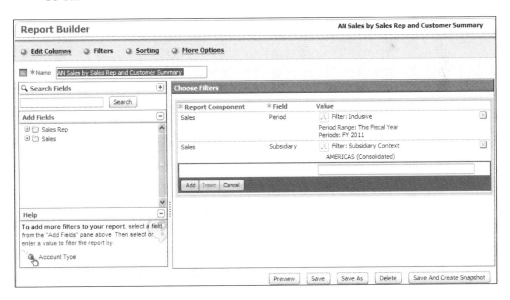

Save and create snapshot

If you see this button on your custom report, then it means that you can save your report and simultaneously generate a snapshot for dashboard use. Be ready to set up the x-axis and y-axis.

Adding filters is much like adding columns. Find the field you want to add to the filters, click on it, and it moves to the **Choose Filters** lines. To delete a filter, click on the little box with the **x** on the right-hand side of **Choose Filters**.

If the **x** is gray, this means that you cannot delete the filter, though in some cases, you can replace the filter. In this example, the original first line of the filters had the **Field** as **Date**. We highlighted this line by clicking on it, and then we clicked the **Insert** button. We were able to replace the **Date** field with **Date Shipped**, and then we clicked on **Done**. Now, when we select our dates in the report footer, the report is looking for the **Date Shipped**, not the **Date** of the sale.

The **Sorting** page is self-explanatory. The **More Options** page allows us to select the audience for the report. Remember that any custom reports you generate follow the same role-based security as the delivered reports. But if you need to limit access to a subset of the role, you can do that here. Also, in our examples, we created both: a custom summary and custom detail sales-by-sales rep report, and on the **More Options** pages of the summary report, we are able to link it to the detail report in the **Drill Down Report** field. Now, if you click on the totals for any of the sales reps in the custom summary, you can see all of the details that generated this number.

Configuring new reports

In some cases, you may want to create a brand new report. Just as in custom searches, you must first select the type or metric of report that you want to develop. Start by navigating to **Reports | New Report**, select your metric, and the report builder opens up. The first page here is where you designate the basic structure and components of the report, based on the metric you chose. In the next screenshot, we selected the **Open Orders** report metric, which opened the following form. We then configure a report that asks what items are committed to open sales orders:

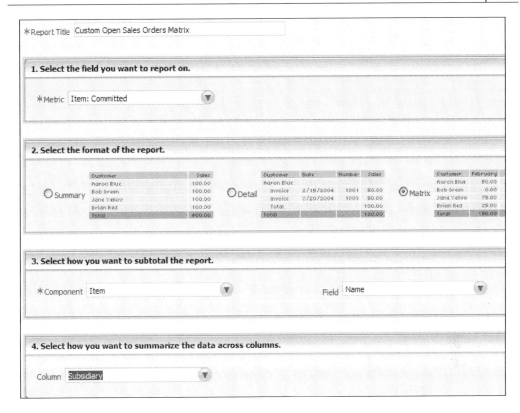

The field we report on, **Item: Committed**, is a sub-object of the **Open Orders** object. We select the **Matrix** format, allowing us to view the **Item** committed to open sales orders by **Subsidiary**.

The result of our configuration is as follows:

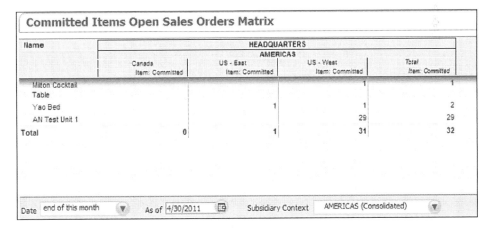

To understand how the choices we made work for this report, consider the next screenshot. Notice that the two objects added to the report are **Item** and **Open Sales Order**, due to the fact that these are the two metrics that we chose:

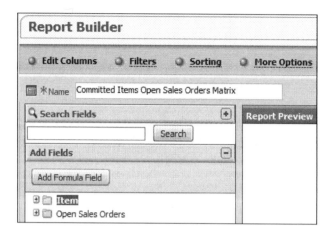

This is a simple example of the reports that you can configure using the custom reports tool. Frankly, you will have to spend significant time understanding custom reports, before it starts to pay dividends. With that in mind, it makes sense to first try to customize the delivered reports, before moving on to configuring custom reports.

Custom reports use the same metadata objects as the built-in, standard reports; see the **Item** and **Open Sales Orders** objects in the previous section. So, while you can put together novel custom reports, you must do so with the delivered metadata objects.

Custom financial reports

There is a separate tool for configuring custom financial reports, which you can find by navigating to **Reports | New Financial Report**. Again, the learning curve here is a bit steeper, and you can leapfrog a lot of questions and head scratching by simply customizing the delivered financial reports.

However, if you want to start from scratch, open up the **New Financial Report**, and select the financial report that you want to create: **Income Statement**, **Balance Sheet**, or **Cash Flow**, by the **Subsidiary Editions** you have set up. (Recall that each **Subsidiary** must operate in a specific **Edition**: US, UK, AUS, and so on.)

One of the advantages here is that there is some additional functionality for the **Report Layout**. For example, if you set up your chart of accounts to match **Income** accounts to **Cost of Goods Sold** accounts, then you can set up a custom income statement that shows income account 4100 and COGS account 5100, and then run the report, by **Class** or **Location**, to get a breakdown of sales and gross profits for a certain item family, by your class or location fields. The need to measure discrete areas of the organization, by line or product manager for example, is the most common requirement that we see for custom financial reports.

Also, you can set your financial reports up as comparative reports, comparing some current period, **This Quarter** for example, with the same quarter of last year. For comparative financial reports, start with the **Comparative Income Statement** or the **Comparative Balance Sheet**, and, again, customize to your organization's specific needs.

You can add the same column to a report several times, and by adjusting the **Period Range**, see different results to compare.

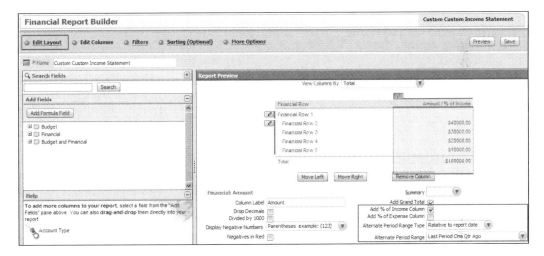

Custom report tab

After you have amassed a fair number of custom reports, it's a good idea to set up a custom tab for each of your OneWorld roles, where you can organize the custom and standard reports in categories. Navigate to **Setup | Customization | Centers and Tabs | New Center Tab** to get started. Then add the reports as **Links** in a new **Center Category**.

Key performance indicators (KPIs)

Among the most popular dashboard features for management users of OneWorld are the key performance indicators. These are simply a quick way to assess the health of the business at a glance, instead of waiting for monthly or quarterly financial statement results, and take action.

There are two types of KPIs. The standard KPIs are a set of completely configured indicators that you simply add to the KPI portlet on your dashboard. The custom KPIs are the results of your custom searches, expressed as either a currency amount or an integer value. For example, you might have a custom search that retrieves the balance of your operating bank account(s) in currency amount(s). This can easily become a KPI. You could also have a custom search that gives the headcount of regular employees in the organization, expressed as an integer value. This also can be a custom KPI.

Before getting started with custom KPIs, we again suggest that you take a close look at the standard KPIs that OneWorld delivers. There are several dozens of these and the odds are that a lot of what you want is here already. One indicator that most managers want to see is **Accounts Receivable** and how it is trending. Add the **Key Performance Indicator** portlet to your dashboard, and on the title bar, click on the little **Setup** arrow. This opens the following selection box:

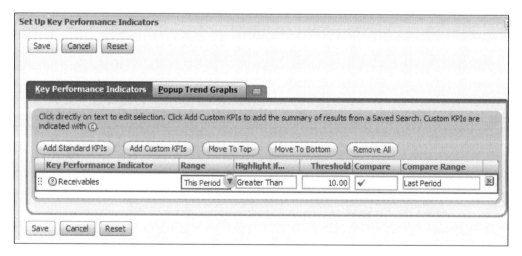

From here, you simply need to click on the **Add Standard KPIs** button, and make your selections. What's interesting is to offer managers the full sweep of the income side of the business, depending on your business model, as shown in the following screenshot:

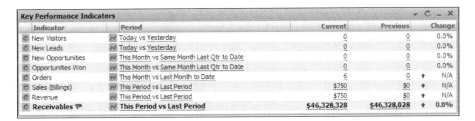

The range of the KPIs can be easily set, by using the **Quick Date Selector** portlet, normally found in the left-side panel of the dashboard. Each of the standard KPIs can also be graphed, just by clicking on the little graph icon between **Indicator** and **Period**. The **Receivables** indicator shows the following graph:

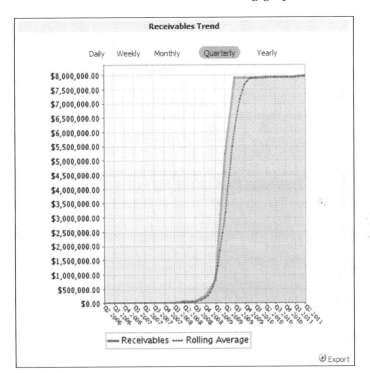

Even these graphs can then be manipulated to display the data in various time ranges.

Custom KPIs

Adding custom KPIs is actually very simple; the difficult part is writing the searches for your KPIs. Almost any search can serve as a KPI, but displaying the results in your KPI portlet can be tricky. In the following example, our **Orders with Discount > 30%** simply displays the current number of these orders. The **High Severity Bug List**, however, is also a custom search KPI, but it displays the results in a range of time, because it follows these rules:

- There are no date fields in the search **Criteria** and no **Summary** criteria.

- There should be a date field in the **Available Filters.**

- The results should have one **Summary Type**. Our search includes a **Count** of the bug IDs.

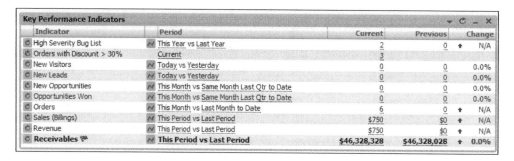

Key performance scorecards

Once you have a strong group of KPIs, and enough data in your OneWorld system so that the KPIs have real meaning, you can then turn to the **KPI Scorecards**. These allow you to compare one KPI with another. For example, the customer service manager might want to compare the number of cases with the number of support reps, the time to close a case with the number of support reps, or the number of escalations with the number of cases opened. The possibilities are nearly endless, but you do have the opportunity to create a scorecard for each role in the system, though you can only place a single scorecard on the home tab dashboard for any particular user. They can have additional scorecards on other center tabs.

Start your scorecard configuration at **Setup | Customization | Centers and Tab | KPI Scorecards**. NetSuite delivers OneWorld with a **Financial Ratios** scorecard that is very helpful to give you a sense of how scorecards work. When you open this up, by clicking on **Customize**, you find the following form:

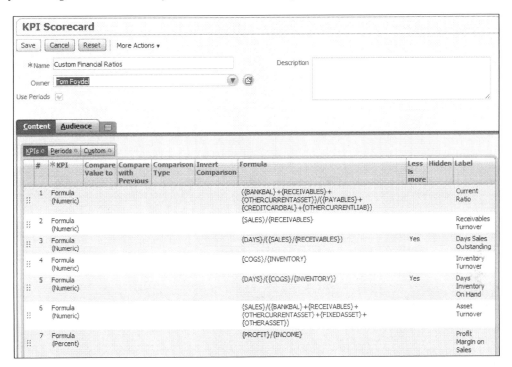

In this example, the KPIs are all derived from formulas to calculate the organization's financial ratios. Notice that the **Use Periods** box is checked. Bear in mind that these financial ratios may not work correctly for users who have selected **Never** under **Set Preferences | Reporting/Search | Report by Period**, especially if your organization has a habit of entering transaction dates outside their normal accounting period.

When generating formula-based KPIs for your scorecard, you open up the **Formula** form and build your formula, by adding standard or custom KPIs with the necessary mathematic functions. The form builds the formula for you as you make your selections. Keep in mind that if you have selected **Use Period** in your scorecard setup, the only custom searches that you can use as custom KPIs are those that have the accounting period setup as one of the available filters. Some searches, such as **Case** or **Employee**, do not offer **Period** as a filter, so you must set up these scorecards with the **Use Period** box unchecked. Following is a screenshot of the **Formula** form:

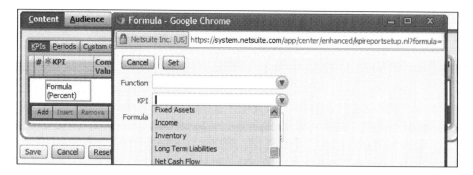

Obviously, financial results are the most common type of scorecard, but as we mentioned, other managers in the organization can also benefit from the scorecards. In the next example, we started a scorecard for the customer service manager. We left the **Use Periods** checkbox unchecked, as we are going to use both standard and custom KPIs that do not include a **Period** filter. In our example, we want to compare the number of escalated cases to the number of bug defects:

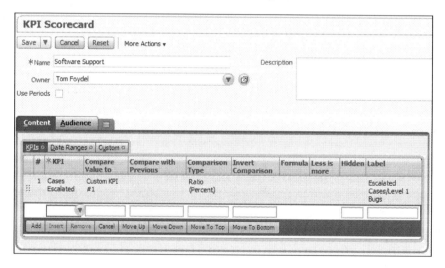

On the **Custom** tab, we select the **High Severity Bug** list, which is a custom search, as our **Custom KPI #1** for this scorecard. On the **Date Range** tab, we selected **This Year**. The result shows on our dashboard as follows:

This means that this year, **50.00%** of our escalated cases were severe bugs, so our support reps appear to be using case escalation as it was intended.

Dashboard management

We have touched on dashboard management in our discussion on *KPIs* and *Scorecards*. There are a lot of other values that you can gain from OneWorld's dashboard functionality. Keep the following in mind:

- You do not have to put everything on one dashboard. Your **Home** dashboard often becomes a single bucket for everything, but the result often minimizes the importance of the content. Each of your **Center** tabs can be used for a dashboard, and it makes good sense to organize the content by the tab, for example, add customer and A/R content to the **Customer** tab.

- Also remember that you can set the tab you log into under **Set Preferences**, if you do not want to open the **Home** tab immediately upon login.

- To start the dashboard customization, click on the **Personalize Dashboard** link on the righthand side of the menu bar, on any tab.

- When you, as the OneWorld administrator, start to generate custom dashboards for your users, keep in mind that you must have the same **Center** as the user's role. For example, if you want to set up a dashboard for the **Accounting Center**, you must have a role that uses the **Accounting Center**, and it must also have the **Setup** function: **Publish Dashboards**. Log into OneWorld using this role, customize the dashboard, and then publish to some or all of the roles, using the **Accounting Center**. You have the option to allow the users to edit the dashboard or not. Publishing dashboards is a good way of helping your users get started with using OneWorld information in their everyday jobs.

- Under **Set Preferences**, there is an option to **Use Classic Interface**. The classic interface should be familiar to you by now, as we have used it almost exclusively in this book, working as the OneWorld Administrator. Sometimes, organizations find it easier to train OneWorld if everyone has the same interface. However, if your users adopt the classic interface, you will not be able to publish dashboards to them.

To start, log in to OneWorld with a role that has the **Publish Dashboard** function. You can add this function to a role by navigating to **Setup | Users/Roles | Manage Roles**, and after selecting the role, look under **Permissions | Setup**. In our next example, we are logging in as the **Sales Administrator**. We are going to customize the dashboards for all of the users who use a role with the **Sales Center**, by customizing our dashboard, and then publishing it to other users.

Some of the obvious things that we do right away as a **Sales Administrator** are set up the reminders and the KPIs for the sales staff. We can also set up **Shortcuts** and configure the **New Bar** icons that we want to present. Then, we add **Custom Lists** or **Custom Searches** to the dashboards, which are helpful ways for sales people to find customers, leads, quotes, and so on, that they need to work on immediately. Then we can add some of the visual elements, such as **Trend Graphs** and **Report Snapshots**.

When we are finished, we go to our leftside panel and click on **Publish Dashboard**, which brings up the following form:

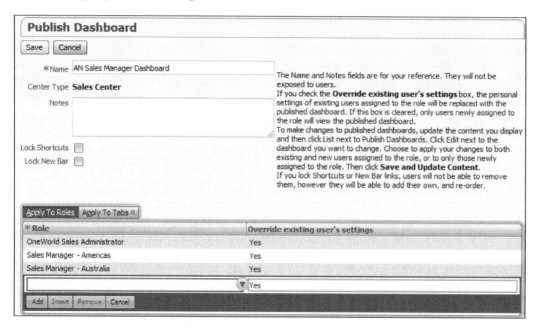

Here we have chosen several of the roles to which we will publish this dashboard. On the **Apply to Tabs** tab, we select how much control we want to give to the users of these roles to edit their dashboards, as shown in the following screenshot:

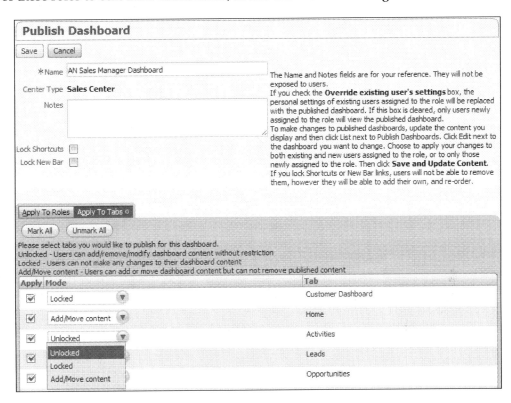

Dashboard publication takes time, but it is not a complex task. We have also found out that the most challenging aspect is helping your organization's managers, as they decide what they want staff to see and work with on the dashboards. This is especially tricky in the early days after initial training, and as they are just becoming more practiced users of the system. Sometimes, it takes several months of using OneWorld before the users and especially managers have a better idea of what they want to see on their dashboards.

Summary

We have now walked through the better part of OneWorld and its implementation process. At this point, you should have a good working prototype with not only a representative data set, but also forms, security roles, and a start on custom searches, reports, and dashboards.

The next step before training is to tighten up any areas that have not been met with approval from the project sponsors. You may also have some custom work that you need to finish.

At the outset of the project, there were probably a couple of important functions that you knew were indispensable to your organization, but for which you would have to develop custom solutions in OneWorld. By this point in the project, these solutions may be nearing completion and testing, or they may be waiting for you to complete the base configuration of OneWorld, so that they can be started. At this point, you hopefully have enough data in OneWorld and setups completed and can now develop and test your custom work units robustly.

You should also be thinking about training at this point. If you have a sandbox account, then you have fewer worries, since you can use the sandbox for training, and all of your test transactions wash away when you copy a clean production account to the sandbox. But if you are using your production account for testing and training, then you have to decide how to perform training. In some cases, there is a session where users train by entering a few sample transactions, which are then removed, and there is another session where they start entering real transactions with the help and guidance of the project team. In either case, project coordination is crucial, since you want to hold these training sessions as close to go-live stage as possible.

In the *Appendix* that follows, we cover the next steps, including training and what to expect as a OneWorld administrator after go-live.

Tools, Training, and the Next Steps

This chapter provides additional coverage of the key aspects of OneWorld implementation that we have not discussed so far. Some of our implementation tools, such as the statement of work, project plan, interview questionnaire, and customization plan deserve more focus, as does the training plan and your next steps with OneWorld post implementation.

Software projects are never as straightforward or as complete as we hope. There are always twists and turns to a project, and there are always loose ends. Training can help to smoothen a bumpy ride and provide some needed closure to the project, but training itself is never complete when software and users continue to change. In this appendix, we provide some of our experience with the basic blocking and tackling of the implementation, in the hope of giving you a head start to complete your project successfully.

Tools

Every implementation uses its own set of tools to ensure that the project succeeds on time and on dime, or budget. We just want to give you some ideas here of how to use the typical project tools to manage your OneWorld project. Almost every consulting firm has its own ideas around its consulting tools, but one concept that must be present is alignment. Your project tools must be aligned with each other and with the goals of your project. Too often, we see tools that look pulled together from many different sources, and as a result, they do not share a common approach or help you to advance to a common goal. The tools that we discuss in this appendix are aligned to a specific project management method. You may not share this method, but you should appreciate how the tools work together.

The statement of work (SOW)

By the time the sales process concludes, you should have a quote for OneWorld licenses, which can serve as a good place to start for the **Statement of Work (SOW)**. The SOW takes the modules you have purchased and explodes them into a document that speaks in detail about the specific functions that are going to be covered in the implementation, what you expect from each function, the parties responsible, the team that participates in testing, and the integration of each function with other functions.

For example, the OneWorld purchase includes the base ERP system for inventory management, purchasing, order management, accounting, and finance. Your SOW might include a table defining the specific functions that you are going to cover in the implementation, as shown in the following table:

Function	Description	Owner
General.01	Set up currencies	CIO
General.02	Set up subsidiaries	CIO
General.03	Set up Chart of Accounts	CIO
General.03	Set up departments, classes, and locations	CIO
Sales.01	Customer record and form setup	VP Sales
Sales.02	Contact record and form setup	VP Sales
Sales.03	Partner record and form setup	VP Sales
Sales.04	Opportunity and form setup	VP Sales
Sales.05	Sales territories	VP Sales
Sales.06	Lead routing	VP Sales
Sales.07	Quota management	VP Sales
Sales.08	Pipeline and forecast	VP Sales
Sales.09	Quote and form setup	VP Sales, Controller
OM.01	Sales order and form setup, approval process	VP Sales, Controller
OM.02	Item order entry: identify item setups, gross sales	VP Sales, Controller, Warehouse Manager
OM.03	Item pricing	VP Sales, Controller
OM.04	Sales discounts	VP Sales, Controller
OM.05	Fulfilling sales orders	VP Sales, Controller, Warehouse Manager
OM.06	Billing sales orders	AR

Order management is the primary business process

Notice in this table that the first process we focus on in implementation is the sales process, as one must expect. Sales are what keep us employed, but more importantly, they also serve as the main focus of the implementation, since so many important business decisions ultimately impact the sales process, for example, the chart of accounts and the item setups. Nothing focuses the organization like sales does. We recommend that you spend the first valuable weeks of the implementation squarely devoted to order management. Even those organizations who decide to do CRM first ought to have detailed discussions about how the full order management process must work when they implement the ERP modules later.

One of the most important discussions that ought to take place at about the time you are sorting out the SOW, is the priority of the functions you must implement. There are several different ways of implementing OneWorld. Some organizations start with CRM, since it is less challenging than ERP. Other organizations want to fix the pain as soon as possible, so they opt for ERP first. Some organizations decide to do multiple phases in order not to stress the workforce. Regardless of how you decide to go, you must prioritize your work units. This brings us to the project plan.

The project plan

After you reach a decision on the order of implementation for the main modules, the next step is to lay out the individual functions, as we did in the SOW. Finally, we prioritize and schedule these functional work units on the project plan. How you schedule the functions differs, of course, for each organization, but as long as you try to follow a logical thread, you can set up a workable plan.

Note of caution: Linear implementation projects

One thing that you must keep in mind is there are dependencies in the software and in your business, which you must address. For example, to test lead routing properly, you must have already decided what constitutes a business sales territory and you must have implemented this in OneWorld. If you use good common sense, most of the main dependencies are obvious.

However, it is not usually possible to have a perfectly linear implementation. You must move forward on many functions before you understand all the dependencies. So, iteration is an important concept. The need to revisit your work in light of new understanding should not be thought of negatively. It just means that you are being fastidious and persistent.

In the following screenshot, we display a typical project plan for a OneWorld CRM/ERP implementation and its major milestones:

	Task Name	Duration	Start	Finish
1	⊟ NetSuite Project Plan	70 days	Fri 4/1/11	Thu 7/7/11
2	Setup Project Plan and SOW with Client Management	1 day	Fri 4/1/11	Fri 4/1/11
3	Complete Contract	5 days	Mon 4/4/11	Fri 4/8/11
4	⊟ Implementation	38 days	Mon 4/11/11	Wed 6/1/11
5	⊟ Configure First Prototype	24 days	Mon 4/11/11	Thu 5/12/11
6	Configure Base Account: Currencies, Countries, Languages, Subsidiaries	1 day	Mon 4/11/11	Mon 4/11/11
7	Configure Company and Enable Features	0.5 days	Tue 4/12/11	Tue 4/12/11
8	Setup General Preferences	0.5 days	Tue 4/12/11	Tue 4/12/11
9	⊞ Accounting Setup	9 days	Wed 4/13/11	Mon 4/25/11
15	⊞ Inventory and Item Catalog	9 days	Tue 4/26/11	Fri 5/6/11
21	⊞ Sales Force Management	4 days	Wed 4/13/11	Mon 4/18/11
31	⊞ Customer Service	3 days	Tue 4/19/11	Thu 4/21/11
37	⊞ Marketing Automation	2 days	Fri 4/22/11	Mon 4/25/11
42	⊞ Order Mangement	8 days	Tue 4/19/11	Thu 4/28/11
51	⊞ Billing, Collections and Revenue Recognition	4 days	Fri 4/29/11	Wed 5/4/11
55	⊞ Purchasing, A/P Supply Chain	6 days	Thu 5/5/11	Thu 5/12/11
62	⊞ Employee Management	2 days	Tue 4/19/11	Wed 4/20/11
68	⊞ 2nd Prototpe Test with Management	3 days	Thu 4/21/11	Mon 4/25/11
70	⊞ Customize the Account	10 days	Tue 4/26/11	Mon 5/9/11
73	⊞ Data Analysis	8 days	Tue 5/10/11	Thu 5/19/11
76	⊞ Data Migration	5 days	Fri 5/20/11	Thu 5/26/11
78	⊞ End User Training	4 days	Fri 5/27/11	Wed 6/1/11
81	⊞ Cutover to NetSuite	24 days	Thu 6/2/11	Tue 7/5/11
87	⊞ Project Wrap Up	2 days	Wed 7/6/11	Thu 7/7/11

Note that the **Cutover to NetSuite** includes 24 days of project support; so the implementation actually takes roughly 50 days or about 10 weeks. This, of course, differs with the number of additional modules or customizations you need. Also note that there are several tasks happening at the same time. For example, we start the **Accounting Setup** and the **Sales Force Management** tasks at the same time. Normally, the client's employees cannot afford to spend whole days on the project. Therefore, we spend time with several different groups on any given day.

The last point to make on the project plan is that it should coincide with the SOW. So, if your SOW says that you are going to implement opportunities, quotes, sales orders, fulfillment, and invoicing, then these tasks need to be on the project plan, under one of the milestones. In our example, you might choose to put opportunities and quotes under **Sales Force Management**, and sales orders, fulfillments, and invoices under **Order Management**. You then need to coordinate the sales and operations group as you move through the prototype configuration and testing. Also, the project plan may have more details than the SOW; for example, fulfillment might breakdown to several tasks, such as, warehouse picking, packing, and integrated shipping.

Some project managers use the project plan exclusively, sort of like the project catch all. We use it simply as a scheduling tool that lets us, and all the implementation team members, know where we are at any given time and what to expect as far as time on the project for meetings, testing, and so on. When the project plan becomes the project's sole tool, it normally means that the project is in trouble.

The results, issues, and decisions list

All of our implementations have a spreadsheet that serves as the central reference point for the implementation. We take the list of functions from our SOW and paste them into a sheet. We write the business managers' narratives on their processes into one sheet. We use another sheet to gather the results of our system configuration and testing. If there are any notes, and so on, then they are all gathered here. We also list any issues that come up through the testing on a separate sheet. Finally, we enter any decisions that we make during the configuration and testing, and why we made them. The project closes when the issues list has no more open items. Some items might be left as phase 2 work or awaiting an answer from NetSuite, but all issues have been addressed to the greatest degree possible. It may sound like a lot, but we keep all entries as concise as possible, and there is none of the normal consulting verbiage.

The SOW, the project plan, and the results, issues, and decisions list are the three main tools that we use for implementation. Again, these may differ for other organizations; we do not have a monopoly on implementing best practices. But what you must expect is that the tools used for your implementation are aligned to maximize their value. In our case, the modules and functions that we describe in the SOW are reproduced in the project plan and the results, issues, decisions list, and the resources working in each module.

The business narrative

We have mentioned the business narrative several times in the course of this and previous chapters. It would probably be helpful to give an example and an explanation as to why we use the narrative.

In explanation, the alternative to the narrative is the what? The process flow diagram? We tried these over several implementations in an earlier career, and they were a time sink. Also, instead of increasing user participation, they had the opposite effect of confusing everyone. Looking for another idea, we noticed that users often told us the 'story' of how they work and how the organization as a whole operates. We started paying close attention and noticed that these narratives were bursting with excellent information that we needed in order to understand the organization's business. Not only did the narrative discuss the process in its logical sequence, but also some important and common exceptions; we also started to understand the organization's business policies and rules.

The following narrative was altered just enough to protect the client's business secrets:

"We install wiring in homes. Most of the time, we install wiring for a contractor who is building new homes in a sub-division. We bid on the business and install, based on a fixed bid per home. The bid includes the wiring, all the outlets, boxes, and so on, and the time. Once the home is built, we then return to the buyer and offer our services to complete the set up of wireless, security system, cable, satellite, and so on. We even install televisions on walls. This is a separate contract for a new customer, but on the same property. We maintain records, by customer and by property.

Each time we wire a home, we have to take materials out of the warehouse inventory and stock one of our service vans. We look at the work orders every morning and stock each van according to the scheduled work. On the sales order, it states that we wired a 2,400 square foot home with three bedrooms, three bathrooms, and so on, but each line must pull inventory through the warehouse.

On some occasions, the home already has a buyer before we do the wiring. These custom homes have a different sales process, since we sell directly to the new homeowner and not to the contractor. It might be a fixed bid, or it might be time and materials. In either case, what we sell to the homeowner is a service; on the backend, we pull inventory and invest employee time."

You can see from just this short first draft of the narrative that the speaker has provided not only interesting information about their business, but also information that invites us to dig deeper, and in an hour or so, we start to see the outlines of the challenge this business model presents to us.

This is why we have come to believe so strongly in the narrative. Trying to model what the speaker has told us in a visual picture is very difficult and what value does that have to him or her? From experience, we can answer that question: none. What people are good at, generally, is verbally describing their reality. It sometimes requires patience to get the discussion started, but eventually, the information you receive is very beneficial. Also, when you have a small group discussing the business, the depth of the conversation increases as they continue to hone in on their many challenges.

It is actually quite difficult to expose business policy in a process flow diagram. The trail of activity, which is what the process flow ultimately depicts, simply does not do a good job of describing a business policy and practice, such as configuring a work van with supplies from a stack of orders. We know that it is done from the process flow, but we do not know how or, more importantly, why.

More on agile

In the earlier chapters of this book, we discussed the idea of the agile implementation and why it is important and better than the waterfall method. Now that you have a clearer understanding of OneWorld and what a OneWorld implementation requires, it makes sense to return to the agile discussion to see how agile works in practice.

First, agile focuses on functional work units, not project phases. In the waterfall project, gathering business requirements, system configuration, and unit testing are three separate activities that happen in separate phases, one after the other. In agile, requirements gathering, configuration, and unit testing all happen at roughly the same time, through the milestone task. Initial discussions during the sales process offer a foundation for the implementation team to work with, when drafting the functional work units. Detailed requirements, configuration, and testing are then done with the implementation and business people working in tandem. The value of this approach is that the OneWorld system offers all parties of the discussion a common focal point, greatly reducing miscommunications.

Secondly, agile requires that you break down the implementation into manageable work units. We identify each work unit in the in the SOW, the project plan and the results, issues, and decisions spreadsheet. Each work unit has an owner and a testing team. Each work unit has an expected outcome and an end date, when all work must be complete. When we plan a project, we look for work units not to exceed four hours, including requirements, configuration, and unit testing. In many cases, they take less than four hours.

Thirdly, each work unit must have a client team member paired with an implementation consultant, and to the greatest degree possible, they should work on the functions together. This does not mean that they have to be sitting right next to each other, but it does mean that they need to share a single screen, when it comes to configuring and testing OneWorld for each function, and this could be an online meeting.

Pairing up the implementation consultant(s) with a client team member is a very important step. Yes, it means that you must schedule some of your key employees away from their 'regular' jobs during the implementation, but the time spent in collaboration throughout the configuration and unit testing phases pays back huge dividends over any possible alternative. You stand to gain untold hours of reconfiguring, fixing, and retesting OneWorld when you discover, as you will, late in the game that miscommunications have led to bad choices. Spend the time you need upfront to get it right.

There are other important points to make about pairing. When two people look together at the same function and the same OneWorld forms, they tend not to waste time, and they tend to communicate in interesting ways. As an implementation consultant, our experience is that the initial configuration of the system brings up a volume of thoughts, ideas, concerns, and questions that otherwise lay below the surface, until the go-live, at which time they often overwhelm the whole implementation team.

When you pair-up one of your team with the implementation team, make sure that they take good notes. Whiteboard notes are useful, but even notebook notes are okay. What you need at the end of the configuration and testing meeting is a list of concerns, questions, and possible issues, even if they have already found answers or solutions. You want to make sure that they 'covered all the bases' and were attentive to detail. Experienced people often try to skip through these meetings quickly. A paper trail prevents carelessness.

When you complete individual work units within a module, it's time to pull in a larger group and test the entire module. This step should not take more than an hour, as the focus is on the main processes.

Training

Software as a Service (SaaS) is a very similar experience for end users as on-premise software that we have all used. We boot the software, in this case the browser, and sign in. Then we go about our business. The training schedule should also align with the other project tools, so that you end up training the same function and modules that you implemented.

There are, however, some subtle differences that we should mention here.

Implementation training

Firstly, there is the training requirement as part of the implementation project. This is a major training event, where you invite all users to a training session, specific to their role in the system. You might also hold a general training session where you introduce OneWorld and some of its vocabulary to the whole user group, including managers. But firstly, we need to ask where the users are located.

As it happens, many organizations that use OneWorld have distributed work forces. Sometimes, it makes sense to bring them together in one room and train together, especially if you dovetail training with the quarterly sales meeting, for example. Other times, you can hold training online and have everyone participate. The only concern about online training is that some users will try to multi-task and lose a lot of the value. If you have multiple operation locations that require training, our recommendation is that you have a key user from the HQ visit the location and be present for the training to introduce OneWorld to the users, answer basic questions about navigation, and so on, and facilitate the whole session.

Another recommendation is that you have an implementation team member from your organization lead the training. This approach is often called train the trainer, meaning that the implementation focuses on making one or more of the end users experts in the system, to the degree that they can teach other users how to use OneWorld, and also administer the system after go-live.

But does OneWorld training differ from other types of system training, or is it roughly the same? Our experience is that OneWorld does train differently from other software systems for two reasons. First, OneWorld's user interface is very different from those of many legacy systems. There is a less hierarchical navigation structure to OneWorld – you have many different options for getting from point A to point B. Younger users will see this as a more intuitive interface and jump right in (and start clicking like mad). This can be a problem because while the UI is more intuitive, the business processes are still the business processes, and you need to exercise discipline to process transactions correctly and achieve correct results. Older workers (of course, we are making broad generalizations here, but this is honestly our experience) often find the UI confusing at first. They tend to ask for specific directions as to how they can approach tasks in OneWorld. You will need to handle both of these situations at most organizations.

The second reason that OneWorld training differs is that OneWorld is integrated, which is not often the case for legacy systems at many organizations. The warehouse often operates in a different system from sales and accounting, so their actions don't necessarily affect the financials in real time. In OneWorld, each action by a sales person, operations staff, or accounting/finance has the potential of directly impacting the other departments in the organization. Hopefully, this chasm has been bridged long before training, but it will always be necessary to remind users that, for example, receiving and fulfilling directly impact key accounting values, such as inventory and cost of goods sold.

In service companies, likewise, portfolio or project managers often operate without a lot of integration with finance. This can be very different in OneWorld, if you are using advanced billing milestones, for example. The time and expense entries also affect AR and AP directly. Any gates that you might have used in the past to screen these transactions are now gone; once approved, these entries 'hit the books.'

With these points in mind, we recommend the following for OneWorld implementation training:

- **Train the trainer**: Yes, it's easier said than done, but this approach tends to focus on key users in your organization, since they know that they must eventually stand up and explain OneWorld. Success, here, also means that you have transferred knowledge from your OneWorld expert to your organization, and this bears a lot of fruit for years to come.

- **Thread your business processes from the beginning to the end of the implementation**: You start the implementation with a list of your main business processes from acquiring a new customer to delivery of goods and services, finance, purchasing, and so on. These processes serve as the foundation of the entire implementation, including training. When introducing tasks to any user/department, make it very clear how their tasks play in the entire process. What causes items to appear for reorder? Who approves time and expenses? And what happens when you do? You are always practicing tasks and teaching processes.

- Take some time for every new user/department and explain the UI in detail. Users who find the UI overwhelming will take a breath and relax; users who find the UI intuitive you must ask to slow down, stay with the class, and concentrate on the processes, for which they are responsible.

- If you need to hold online training sessions for a distributed workforce, do what you can, to have one of your team's reps in the room facilitating. Training is difficult, and not being able to see the student's faces makes it a guessing game as to whether they are processing the info well, or at all. Don't assume that the obvious makes sense to your organization's most proficient users.

- Let trainees collaborate with each other. There are a lot of products on the market today for group collaboration and your organization probably already has one of these. If you have a sizable user group, it makes sense to set up a place for them to learn from each other. In most cases, training is just an introduction to OneWorld; the real learning takes place over time, as users work with each other in the system and answer questions together.

- The training itself normally takes the following form:
  - ° An introduction to the UI and explanation of basic OneWorld vocabulary
  - ° A walkthrough of a test transaction, followed by allowing the users to try a test transaction
  - ° Users try a real transaction
  - ° Questions, explanations, and more real transactions
  - ° Repeat with another transaction type

- We have abandoned the idea that users will on their own take the time to set up their own tools in the system. For example, you can easily set up your own e-mail templates and then e-mail sales documents to customers from OneWorld, giving you a clear history on the customer's record of what was sent and when. Most sales staff will, however, continue to download the sales documents to their computer and use their e-mail client to send an attached sales document to a customer. You must help them set up their own e-mail templates and then have them practice using these. When you consider what we are stating here, you begin to understand the time commitment you need for training. It will take you a minimum of two hours to train the sales staff in setting up and using an e-mail template.

- Make sure that you document, prior to training, your basic processes and keep these 'solutions' in an internal knowledge base. All OneWorld accounts have the opportunity to set up their own knowledge bases, and when you have new hires, these solutions can be invaluable to get them up to speed quickly. Also, knowing that the processes they are learning exist in written form for review after training lets new users breathe easier.

- Training will extend for at least a month, after the actual session. It takes at least this long for users to feel comfortable with the system. Be prepared to have someone ready to answer questions and follow up on issues.

Ongoing training

Secondly, OneWorld currently has two major updates a year. These are not sensational events, but they are important. There are fixes to defects in the software on a nightly basis with OneWorld, but for the introduction of new functionality, OneWorld uses the semi-annual release.

Consider how this differs with on-premise software. We implemented Oracle 11i applications at a large company in 2002 and they are only this year, 2011, upgrading to release 12. It's a major event, taking months and months of preparation. Surely, it will also require extensive user training.

With OneWorld, the upgrades process starts when you receive notifications of an impending upgrade. These come well in advance of the actual upgrade. Then, you also receive an invitation to use your system in a beta version to test the changes in the new release. Finally, you are notified of the actual date of the upgrade. The process requires that you closely monitor the new functionality as it comes out and implement as needed.

You might also require training for some features. In the most recent release, OneWorld added many important features, including Demand Planning and Gross Profit, and some lesser features, such as an improved Manage Accounting Period form. Let's take a look at these in turn, from the perspective of an organization already live on OneWorld, to understand the training requirements for each.

Demand planning almost certainly involves a small implementation project, including user training. There are important decisions to be made and then there are some extensive setups that must be done. If you are like most users, you will also have a lot of questions that can only be answered by testing several transactions. Demand planning, therefore, takes someone a full week or two to implement properly.

Gross profit is a smaller, though still important, addition. It requires a meeting or two to hash out the potential, a few hours to set up the item catalog with the required values, and then a heads-up to the sales staff, to let them know what they are seeing on their sales forms. You may also need to incorporate some of the information into sales reports. Obviously, gross profit may be used in other modules, such as commissions, and in this case, the time investment increases.

Finally, the improvements to the accounting period form do not require a lot more than a heads-up to understand the new functionality.

Both demand planning and gross profit require changes to the items in your item catalog which a strong user needs to manage.

When you look at the total upgrade to 2011 release 1, you should make a decision on which users/departments need a true training session and which can handle a 15-minute online presentation, added to their weekly meeting. This changes from release to release, so the main point is that you have to stay committed to your OneWorld implementation, and be prepared to continue to implement new features and functions as NetSuite releases them.

Next steps

OneWorld is a unique software product, or service really. It offers small and medium enterprises and the divisions of large enterprises the ability to manage an organization over vast geographies and business processes. In a single OneWorld account, users from Japan log in to a system interface in Japanese and Yen, while users from Brazil log in to Portuguese and Real. It is highly functional from a global perspective.

It also carries a lot of responsibility. One of the most difficult hand-offs in business is the handoff of a new system from the implementation team, including all resources internal and external, to the business team. We offer the following advice to managers overseeing this handoff:

- There is a tendency to treat your internal resources, who worked on the implementation, as the informal administrators of the system. Take system administration seriously and make a formal announcement about who is going to handle administrator responsibilities going forward. When you leave it to chance and treat it casually, you create resentment among the troops, who put in extra effort to get the system live; they start to see participation as punishment and wonder what they did wrong. Your new OneWorld system, the implementation of which just chewed up a big piece of your annual IT budget, is only as good as the human capital resources that use it and keep it running smoothly day to day. Treat them well.

- The implementation exposes the organization in ways that management does not expect. By go-live, the organization is normally tired and needs to catch its breath. You purchased OneWorld to smooth out your business and make it more efficient, yet the effort of the implementation does not always seem smooth. Take heart. As the weeks roll by, your best and brightest resolve most issues and the value of the implementation solutions starts to take hold. This doesn't happen automatically; you must encourage it. Make sure that the implementation team knows you appreciate their efforts and continue to work with them through ongoing status meetings to solve problems and make headway. Most of the bumps are human-resource related, as OneWorld challenges old job descriptions. Continue to help your users smooth these out.

- As our discussion of training suggests, the implementation of OneWorld never really has an end point. You must, of course, close the implementation project, but it makes sense to continue to spend a couple of hours a month reviewing the system and managing it. There is a tendency to forget about OneWorld after the implementation, since you do not have to manage the infrastructure, technical upgrades, and bug fixes yourself. This is a mistake. OneWorld, like all systems, requires constant care and feeding to fend off general entropy over time.

Summary

We wrote this book with two audiences in mind: the business manager who needs a new system and wonders if OneWorld meets their needs; and the business manager who must implement OneWorld after the license contract has been signed. To make the book useful to both audiences, we decided to not only discuss what OneWorld is and how it works, but also how to implement it.

Discussing OneWorld functionality alone does not do it justice, since it is only by implementing it that you understand how the pieces fit together and meet business requirements. On the other hand, there are lots of books on the market that describe software implementation. The key, we believe, is to combine the specific functionality of OneWorld with a software implementation guide that any organization can follow successfully. Our goal is the successful marriage of OneWorld functionality to your practical, real-world business experience, and getting you to church on time, as they say. You now have a complete guide that not only explains OneWorld in detail, but also walks you through the implementation process from A to Z, and offers some real-world advice about what works and what does not work in software implementation.

But a book, by itself, does not ensure success. Software projects are difficult, because in the end they are really about people, not software. We hope this book gives you the practical knowledge that you need to succeed with OneWorld, and we hope that we have also encouraged you to try some things that make it easier for you, your implementation team, and your users to implement and use OneWorld successfully. But it will be your brain, courage, and heart that win the day. We wish you all the very best.

Index

ERP modules 181
Estimates 67
Expand Account Lists 73
Expense Allocation 66
expense reports, accounts
        payable processing
  intercompany time and expense 243, 244
  processing 242
expenses, period close processing
  allocating 271

F

file cabinet 65
finance charges, accounts
        receivable processing 261-265
financial reporting
  about 274
  generating 275
financial reports
  customizing 344, 345
First In First Out (FIFO) 78
Fixed Asset record 285
fixed bid projects, professional services
  about 219-221
  per-employee billing rates 223
  projects, generating from sales orders 222,
    223
  time and material projects 222
forms
  and layouts for printing 292-294
  customizing 289, 290
  entry forms 290, 291
  records, adding 287-289
  transaction forms 291, 292

G

general ledger section
  about 73
  Aging Reports Use 73
  Allow Transaction Date Outside of
    Posting Period 73
  Cash Basis Reporting 73
  Enable Accounting Period Window 73
  Expand Account Lists 73
  Minimum Period Window Size 73

Require Approvals on Journal Entries 73
  Use Account Numbers 73
  Void Transactions Using
    Reversing Journals 73
general setup
  about 43
  company information setup 43
  counties 44
  e-mail preferences 46
  fax preferences 46
  features, enabling 43
  general preferences 44
  personal preferences 45
  printing preferences 46
  provinces 44
  records, renaming 44
  states 44
  transactions, renaming 44
Gift Certificate Auth Code Generation 79
gift certificate income, cash management
  267, 268
Gift Certificates 70
Gross Profit 68
groups 48, 132, 208

H

help desk 56

I

IDs
  external 317, 318
  internal 317, 318
implementation, basics
  about 95
  business, changing 97, 98
  historical data 95, 96
  software, changing 97, 98
  starting 97
Implementation Master (IM) spreadsheet 97
implementation training 362-365
import tools
  about 318-322
  other imports 322
Include Reimbursements in Sales and Forecast Reports 77

Thank you for buying
NetSuite OneWorld Implementation 2011 R2

About Packt Publishing

Packt, pronounced 'packed', published its first book "Mastering phpMyAdmin for Effective MySQL Management" in April 2004 and subsequently continued to specialize in publishing highly focused books on specific technologies and solutions.

Our books and publications share the experiences of your fellow IT professionals in adapting and customizing today's systems, applications, and frameworks. Our solution based books give you the knowledge and power to customize the software and technologies you're using to get the job done. Packt books are more specific and less general than the IT books you have seen in the past. Our unique business model allows us to bring you more focused information, giving you more of what you need to know, and less of what you don't.

Packt is a modern, yet unique publishing company, which focuses on producing quality, cutting-edge books for communities of developers, administrators, and newbies alike. For more information, please visit our website: www.packtpub.com.

About Packt Enterprise

In 2010, Packt launched two new brands, Packt Enterprise and Packt Open Source, in order to continue its focus on specialization. This book is part of the Packt Enterprise brand, home to books published on enterprise software – software created by major vendors, including (but not limited to) IBM, Microsoft and Oracle, often for use in other corporations. Its titles will offer information relevant to a range of users of this software, including administrators, developers, architects, and end users.

Writing for Packt

We welcome all inquiries from people who are interested in authoring. Book proposals should be sent to author@packtpub.com. If your book idea is still at an early stage and you would like to discuss it first before writing a formal book proposal, contact us; one of our commissioning editors will get in touch with you.

We're not just looking for published authors; if you have strong technical skills but no writing experience, our experienced editors can help you develop a writing career, or simply get some additional reward for your expertise.

Oracle Database 11g – Underground Advice for Database Administrators

ISBN: 978-1-849680-00-4   Paperback: 348 pages

A real-world DBA survival guide for Oracle 11g database implementations

1. A comprehensive handbook aimed at reducing the day-to-day struggle of Oracle 11g Database newcomers

2. Real-world reflections from an experienced DBA — what novice DBAs should really know

3. Implement Oracle's Maximum Availability Architecture with expert guidance

Oracle E-Business Suite R12 Supply Chain Management

ISBN: 978-1-84968-064-6   Paperback: 292 pages

Drive your supply chain processes with Oracle E-Business R12 Supply Chain Management to achieve measurable business gains

1. Put supply chain management principles to practice with Oracle EBS SCM

2. Develop insight into the process and business flow of supply chain management

3. Set up all of the Oracle EBS SCM modules to automate your supply chain processes

Please check **www.PacktPub.com** for information on our titles

Made in the USA
Lexington, KY
25 March 2017